EARLY MODERN TRAUMA

Early Modern Cultural Studies

Early Modern Trauma

Europe and the Atlantic World

EDITED BY ERIN PETERS
AND CYNTHIA RICHARDS

University of Nebraska Press
LINCOLN

All illustrations courtesy of the
National Cryptologic Museum

Library of Congress Cataloging-in-Publication Data
Names: Peters, Erin, editor. | Richards, Cynthia, editor.
Title: Early modern trauma: Europe and the Atlantic
World / edited by Erin Peters and Cynthia Richards.
Description: Lincoln: University of Nebraska
Press, [2021] | Series: Early modern cultural studies |
Includes bibliographical references and index.
Identifiers: LCCN 2020041081
ISBN 9781496208910 (hardback)
ISBN 9781496227492 (epub)
ISBN 9781496227508 (mobi)
ISBN 9781496227515 (pdf)
Subjects: LCSH: Psychic trauma in literature. |
Collective memory in literature. | European
literature—History and criticism. | Psychic trauma—
Europe—History. | Collective memory—Europe.
Classification: LCC PN56.P914 E17
2021 | DDC 809/.9335825—dc23
LC record available at https://lccn.loc.gov/2020041081

Set in Garamond Premier by Mikala R. Kolander.
Designed by N. Putens.

A Klee painting named *Angelus Novus* shows an angel looking as though he is about to move away from something he is fixedly contemplating. His eyes are staring, his mouth is open, his wings are spread. This is how one pictures the angel of history. His face is turned toward the past. Where we perceive a chain of events, he sees one single catastrophe which keeps piling wreckage upon wreckage and hurls it in front of his feet. The angel would like to stay, awaken the dead, and make whole what has been smashed. But a storm is blowing from Paradise; it has got caught in his wings with such violence that the angel can no longer close them. The storm irresistibly propels him into the future to which his back is turned, while the pile of debris before him grows skyward. This storm is what we call progress.

—Walter Benjamin, *Illuminations*

CONTENTS

ILLUSTRATIONS

ACKNOWLEDGMENTS

The origins of the idea for an interdisciplinary volume that considers trauma in an early modern context took place in 2015 at the annual meeting of the American Society for Eighteenth Century Studies. Since then it has taken half a decade to work through the manifold ways in which scholars from the twenty-first century can begin to approach and observe this phenomenon from the distant past, and we are delighted to have this opportunity to gratefully acknowledge those who made this volume possible.

First and foremost we wish to thank our contributors. Collectively their individual expertise spans the early modern era in Europe and the Atlantic world, and their contributions to this volume have served to underscore how past subjects are products of their historical moment yet have core experiences that link them across time. We also wish to thank the readers of the manuscript for immensely helpful suggestions and support, and Matthew Bokovoy and Heather Stauffer at the University of Nebraska Press for their support throughout this project.

Erin Peters wishes to extend thanks to the University of Gloucestershire for a period of sabbatical leave to work on this project. She also extends her thanks to History team colleagues at Gloucestershire for their continued support and friendship. Finally, for inspiring conversations, practical assistance, and much-needed lightness, she is grateful to Nicola Rivers, Christian O'Connell, Cynthia Richards, and Janet and John Peters. For important lessons in rebellious optimism, she couldn't wish for better examples than Thomas and Ava.

Cynthia Richards wishes to extend thanks to her students at Wittenberg University and the University of Dayton who helped her think through the concepts in this work. She also thanks the University of Dayton for awarding her the Ruff Chair in Eighteenth-Century Studies in 2016 and for helping to jump-start this collection. For their generosity in providing thoughtful feedback, she is grateful to Mary Ann O'Donnell, Robin Inboden, and Karen Gevirtz, and for their deep and loving support, to her family, Adam, Lily, and Samuel. Finally, for her model of resilience, professionalism, and collegiality, she thanks her coeditor, Erin Peters.

A final note is, we feel, necessary to frame this volume in its own historical moment. The final phase of this project took place in 2020. As such, contributors and editors of this collection on early modern trauma were concentrating on this topic while simultaneously experiencing a moment of collective trauma themselves as the COVID-19 pandemic gripped the world and forced us all into global lockdown. In addition, the Black Lives Matter movement, which began in the United States and quickly spread across Europe, served to highlight deeply ingrained and enduring transgenerational and cultural traumas that continue to influence the modern world and which were primarily drawn from the early modern era. We wish to acknowledge this, and to express our sincere hope that this volume will offer a way forward even as it offers a new way to look backward at the many experiences of being human and what it means to feel pain. We very much hope that the work included in this volume can serve to reinforce the connection between past and present, and to offer a starting point to consider how we can identify core human experiences and understand them in their own context as well as in relation to our own time and place.

EARLY MODERN TRAUMA

Reading Historical Trauma

Moving Backward to Move Forward

ERIN PETERS AND CYNTHIA RICHARDS

Trauma studies is a rich, well-developed, and multifaceted field of inquiry that, from a humanities perspective, has engaged historians, cultural theorists, sociologists, and those who study gender, race, literature, language, and narrative forms. As Monica J. Casper and Eric Wertheimer have recently outlined in *Critical Trauma Studies*, deciphering the various meanings and manifestations of trauma has led to a robust body of work covering areas such as history and memory (e.g., Caruth 1995; LaCapra 2001; Cubitt 2007; Rothberg 2009; Hirsch 2012; Assmann 2016), narrative forms and expressions (e.g., Scarry 1985; Hartman 1995; Caruth 1996; Balaev 2014), memorialization and commemoration (e.g., Sturken 1997, 2007; LaCapra 1998), cultural trauma and notions of collective identity (e.g., Cvetkovich 2003; Alexander, Eyerman, Giesen, Smelser, and Sztompka 2004; Kaplan 2005; Alexander 2012; Eyerman 2019), testimony and witnessing (e.g., Felman and Laub 1991; Goodman and Meyers 2012; Kramer and Weigel 2017), postcolonial trauma (e.g., Ifowodo 2013; Ward 2015; Visser 2015; Craps 2015), and genealogies of trauma (e.g., Leys 2000; Orr 2006; Luckhurst 2008; Buelens, Durrant, and Eagleston 2014; Bond and Craps 2015).[1] These important studies have been shaped by and comprise predominantly western, twentieth- and twenty-first-century catastrophes (including war, genocide, terrorism, revolution, and natural disasters alongside more commonplace experiences of violence, loss, injury, accident, and disease). These theorists have been influential in setting up discussions around everyday and exceptional instances of trauma, individual and collective trauma, historical and present trauma, and how those instances take shape in narrative and discursive forms. Furthermore these contributions have helped to shift the study of trauma from the biomedical, psychological sphere into a domain that is also distinctly cultural. They have "brought the study of trauma firmly within the purview of the humanities and social sciences."[2]

Yet, although trauma is ubiquitous and trauma studies has grown exponentially as an academic field of study over several decades, no study to date has broadly explored the possibilities of its expressions and appearances in the context of the early modern European and the Atlantic worlds. Almost all studies of trauma take as their focus our modern age, and scholars of trauma are quick to point to the phenomenon as uniquely modern. Contemporary trauma theory originated with the psychiatric approaches of nineteenth-century physicians and theorists such as Jean Martin Charcot, Pierre Janet, Sigmund Freud, and Josef Breuer. It was further developed by scholars of the First World War, the Holocaust, and the Vietnam War, and led to the diagnosis of trauma and post-traumatic stress disorder (PTSD) in the DSM-III (*Diagnostic and Statistical Manual of Mental Disorders*) in 1980. More recently, trauma theory has been used to interpret experiences of physical, psychological, or sexual abuse and violence. While the DSM-III diagnosis and the subsequent widening applications of trauma theory marked a turning point in ideas of the causes, impacts, effects, and treatments of trauma, it also served to reinforce the notion of trauma as a thoroughly modern experience. The very term "trauma," derived from the Greek word meaning wound, has modern-day connotations, most commonly associated with the impact of industrialization and horrific events since the turn of the twentieth century. Originally used in the seventeenth century to refer to physical injuries, Luckhurst explains that "the predominant popular connotations of trauma now circle around metaphors of psychic scars and mental wounds."[3] While from a biomedical perspective the historical and contemporary use of the term still refers to a physical wound, the "unbounded movement of trauma from its original wound is dramatically demonstrated by the very reach the term has now attained."[4] The result of the present-day widening of the boundaries of the concept of trauma is that trauma theory—both individual and collective—has been heavily shaped by responses to modern catastrophes, which has served to prevent or problematize its application to earlier periods.

To illustrate these points, take, for example, some recent characterizations: Nancy K. Miller and Jason Tougaw suggest that "consciously or unconsciously, we live in the wake of the atrocities brought by war and genocide, in the long shadow cast by their prolonged aftermath. If every age has its symptoms, ours appears to be the age of trauma."[5] Paul Lerner and Mark S. Micale write that "in light of the catastrophes and cataclysms that have marked twentieth-century history, it is scarcely surprising that trauma has emerged as a highly visible and widely invoked concept . . . trauma has become a metaphor for the struggles and challenges of late twentieth-century life."[6] Roger Luckhurst, in *The Trauma Question*, traces the genealogy of the concept and points to areas commonly associated with modernity (industrialization, urbanization, the break with traditional ways of life and living, and technological innovation) to place the phenomenon of trauma, and interest in it, firmly within the realm of modernity.[7] As such, the criteria for claiming trauma to be strictly a late modern phenomenon appears to rest on the development of the concept in the nineteenth century, and subsequent claims that modern experiences and considerations of atrocities, catastrophes, ruptures, and changes are somehow unique.

While the concept of trauma is often seen as inherently linked to modernity (Luckhurst 2008), the phenomenon of trauma's appearances, we argue, is not. Psychological trauma as a result of distressing or disturbing experiences is a human response, and evidence of this phenomenon can be found across times and cultures that predate our modern world. Given that, for example, the long seventeenth century (1598–1715) has been described as a period of almost continuous warfare (Konnert 2008) and as such has been termed a "General Crisis" (Hobsbawm 1954), and given that, besides warfare, the sixteenth to eighteenth centuries in Europe and North America saw the development of slavery, colonialism, and nationalism, as well as the persistence of natural catastrophes such as plagues, floods, and the "little ice age" (Parker 2013), and significant sociopolitical, -economic, and -religious transformation, the claim that trauma is strictly a modern phenomenon is highly surprising.[8] Furthermore early modern chroniclers were eager to record these devastating experiences, and accounts exist from a variety of times and places, although the culturally produced frames of reference available in an early modern context differ from those of our present day. The paradox between trauma's supposed modernity and the evidence of traumatic encounters in the early modern world leads us to consider: What counts as trauma, for whom, and under what circumstances? How was the reaction to extreme events and circumstances articulated in the early modern period, how can these reactions be identified and conceptualized today, and what can we learn from this?

Thus, the first aim of this volume is to explore the applicability of trauma theories beyond and before the contemporary experience. There are a number of methodological and disciplinary questions that arise in applying theories of trauma, both collective and individual, that were developed in the twentieth century to evidence left behind of the experiences of people and cultures that predate it. How universal is the experience of trauma and can it transcend various centuries and contexts to remain intact as a marker we can apply to an experience that today might generally be considered traumatic? How may we measure the difference between a "normal" event and a "traumatic" event in the early modern world? In addressing these points, we take as a central premise that the experience of trauma is not necessarily universal, as the causes and conceptualizations differ. In other words, the recognition that an event or experience is traumatic is predicated on the historically specific requirements of the individual or culture in question. For example, scholars have argued that the coherent, autonomous self purportedly fractured by a traumatizing event is itself a modern concept, and that what we take as a sign of instability today would have been perceived as normative during the early modern period.[9] Or that the representation of loss in art did not accommodate the traumatic during the early modern period as the prevalent notion of an afterlife foreclosed the possibility of irrecoverable or unassimilable loss. As Gregg Horowitz argues, the function of early modern art was to "transmit the past," and "narratives of redemption" prevailed.[10] In addition, then, to historicizing "trauma," discussions of traumatic wounding in the early modern period must also address changing definitions of the functional self and the shifting role of literature and the historical archive in giving voice to such experiences.

That said, the phenomenon of psychological trauma, while triggered by contextually specific events and manifesting in various ways, transcends time and circumstance and is capable of being felt by individuals and cultures who have been exposed to, have endured, or have witnessed extreme events. These experiences of change, violence, and crisis, which fragment the notion of identity and community, are typically irrevocable and irreversible. While a rupture of this sort is important for the maintenance of trauma theory, psychological reactions to extreme situations manifest through a complex interaction between an individual or collective and his or her environment and culture. Thus, trauma and its residual evidence is historically and contextually specific and may take different names and occasion a variety of complex effects, but to divorce our modern-day understanding of psychological suffering from a historical past is to de-historicize our modern understanding.

As an example of this specificity, in his work on combat trauma in classical antiquity, Jason Crowley has warned against the universality of combat trauma and instead points to the very different and historically specific circumstances that disallow for modern notions of trauma to be retrospectively applied to ancient Greek soldiers.[11] While we accept the difference of experience between the ancient and modern worlds that makes Crowley's argument convincing, we also acknowledge the significant difference that exists between the origins of trauma theory in the nineteenth century and its manifestation in the twenty-first. Indeed, understanding that difference has greatly enriched the field. Theorists such as Ann Cvetkovich and Michelle Balaev, for example, have reminded us of how trauma manifests differently in different communities, but rather than rejecting trauma theory as a construct as a result of this difference, they have instead worked to make trauma more context specific. Balaev explains that doing so "locates meaning through a greater consideration of the social and cultural context of traumatic experience."[12] As a result, as theorists we can be more cognizant respectively of how trauma presents in queer communities or in postcolonial contexts while discussing this experience in a framework that gives political and ideological weight to this pain.

With this context-specific requirement in mind, it is worthwhile to consider the similarities of experience in the early centuries of the modern world that specifically allow us to mark it as "(early) modern." Developments in areas such as print and mass literacy, modern warfare and weaponry, and advances in technological, medical, and scientific knowledge. Events that caused significant cultural shifts and divisions, such as the Reformation and the subsequent religious crises it produced, several large-scale sociopolitical revolutions and revolts, and experiments with various forms and types of governments. And finally the origins of modern colonialism and slavery, the rise of nationalism, and modern ideas of economics and industry all occurred within and influenced the early centuries of the modern period, even while they predated the development of the concept of trauma. While experiencing these changes, early modern contemporaries did not have a widely accepted definition of trauma, much less a diagnostic manual or conceptual theories to turn to. Furthermore, the language available to them to explore their distressing experiences was marked and preconditioned by their historically specific circumstances. That said, the chapters in this volume work to demonstrate that the similarities of the early modern experience to the period that saw the development of the concept of trauma allow for its application. In making this claim the chapters in this collection do not seek to engage in retrospective diagnosis, but rather to explore what the application of trauma, as an analytical lens, can reveal about the early modern experience. In doing so, chapters have adapted contemporary trauma theory to adjust its applicability to the period in question.

This brings us to the second aim of the present collection: the work included here is intended to build upon existing studies of trauma in the period and to develop a foundation for further research in this area. The intention is to expand both the history of human response to suffering and that of early modern studies more broadly, or as Melinda Rabb describes it in the afterword, to create "a general momentum for additional scholarship." While *Early Modern Trauma: Europe and the Atlantic World* is not the first study to explicitly address trauma in this period, the present volume works to extend the types of textual sources and evidentiary bases used in these analyses while also increasing the interdisciplinary nature of the subfield of early modern trauma studies. In this regard, chapters in this volume supplement earlier studies, the majority of which take stage-based and/or fictional representations of early modern trauma as their focus to examine the cultures that produced them, and none of which extends these analyses into the eighteenth century. These works have been influential in shaping the current volume and establishing how trauma can be responsibly and productively discussed in an early modern context.

Thomas P. Anderson's *Performing Early Modern Trauma from Shakespeare to Milton* (2006), for example, locates in the work of William Shakespeare and John Milton patterns that reflect the tropes of trauma, evidence that "cultural loss alters normative modes of expression and representation," and complicates Horowitz's thesis that "nontranscendence" in literature functions exclusively as a marker of modern literature.[13] In the work of both writers, the past cannot be overcome—he argues—and "the afterlife of the Reformation, the impact of royal death, and the violence of regicide" haunt their works in forms recognizable as traumatic return. In *Unto the Breach: Martial Formations, Historical Trauma, and the Early Modern Stage* (2008), Patricia A. Cahill shifts the focus to the early modern audience, and explores "what it means that theater audiences were forced to reckon with the deeply unsettling sights and sounds of early modern warfare." Also attuned to the "traumatic specters" of Elizabethan drama, she goes one step further than Anderson, however, in naming the effects of war as producing "breaches in understanding—specifically, the 'shattering breaks' in experience that, in the realm of psychoanalytic discourse, signal psychic trauma."[14] Cahill's work is buttressed by Catherine Silverstone's *Shakespeare, Trauma and Contemporary Performance* (2011), a work that looks at how Shakespearean drama continues to perform a cathartic, restorative function with contemporary audiences and on global stages, a case study approach that points to the "ongoing negotiation" between early modern understandings of traumatic disruption, and current ones.[15] Lisa Starks-Estes historicizes this form of transhistorical reading, arguing that "Shakespeare creatively transforms Ovidian subjects to grapple with them, foregrounding the trauma inherent in subjectivity and shifting conceptions of the self." More specifically, confronted with the representation of traumatic loss in Ovid's work, Shakespeare reworks it to reframe classical notions of masculinity and to examine the "tragic effects of violence."[16] All of these works steer clear of diagnosing specific characters or writers as having experienced trauma, but instead pay attention to patterns of repetition that suggest an active, conscious engagement with the effects of violence on the part of early modern writers, and in terms akin to a modern understanding of traumatic loss.[17] Each asserts, as does this volume, the value of looking at both differences and "continuities" in how extreme loss is imagined in the Renaissance and how it is addressed today.[18]

The chapters in James Allard and Mathew Martin's collection *Staging Pain, 1580–1800: Violence and Trauma in British Theatre* (2009) also focus on the efforts of early modern theater to represent pain.[19] More specifically, two chapters in the collection, by Mathew Martin and Zachariah C. Long, directly draw upon trauma theory (Žižek's and Freud's) to analyze the working through of representations of suffering in dramatic performance, and Long, in particular, creates space for acknowledging the experience and not simply the representation of trauma during this period. Martin's own study, *Tragedy and Trauma in the Plays of Christopher Marlow* (2016), directly engages with psychoanalytical trauma theory to argue that Marlow's plays result in a "trauma aesthetic" as they initially conform to the conventions of the genre of tragedy and then shatter them, thereby subverting narrative closure and catharsis.[20] Finally Cynthia Marshall's *The Shattering of the Self: Violence, Subjectivity, and Early Modern Texts* (2002) examines the function of violence in Renaissance texts. While not directly addressing trauma, Marshall argues that the profound shift toward individuality that occurred during the Renaissance was addressed in the literature of the period through texts that provided an opportunity to disperse, rather than stabilize, a sense of selfhood. Her pioneering work foregrounds profound, historical differences in the conceptualization of the self, but also focuses on how our contemporary understanding of a psychological self emerges from those historical contexts. As she explains, psychoanalysis "evolved from traditional discourses emphasizing the complexity and instability of the subject."[21]

While trauma studies has been slow to gain traction in early modern literary and historical studies, recent growth in interdisciplinary areas such as the history of emotions, affect studies, disability studies, and memory studies have contributed to a growing interest in this area. For example, the collection of essays edited by Erika Kuijpers, Judith Pollmann, Johannes Müller, and Jasper van der Steen, *Memory Before Modernity: Practices of Memory in Early Modern Europe* (2013), examines evidence of memory practices from early modern Europe. Chapters consider the emotional, physical, and spiritual response to violence, loss, and disaster in the period and how these shaped individual and collective memories of the events. The introduction chapter discusses these experiences as episodes of "traumatic loss" and posits a context of early modern Christianity, "which put so much emphasis on the benefits of suffering and sacrifice and on a providential God," and that

> offered a framework in which many people apparently managed to make sense of experiences and thus to cope with them in ways that helped them to move on. Modern psychologists say there are people who are capable of turning traumatic memories into what they term "personal growth." Although no early modern person would have described the process in that way, the notion that spiritual growth was to be had from a terrible experience was widely available as a cultural model.[22]

Similarly, Allie Terry-Fritsch and Erin Felicia Labbie's collection of essays, *Beholding Violence in Medieval and Early Modern Europe* (2012), explores the cultural representation of violence in this period and the ways in which early modern individuals and communities have acted as participants, observers, and interpreters of violence events.[23] While the focus of the essays is not explicitly on the topic of trauma, the analytical concentration is placed on how episodes of violence were understood in the period. This approach is also evident in Domenico Cecere, Chiara De Caprio, Lorenza Gianfrancesco, and Pasquale Palmieri's collection, *Disaster Narratives in Early Modern Naples: Politics, Communication and Culture* (2018), which explores natural disasters to investigate the relationship between catastrophic events and narrative strategies.[24] In both these collections, then, the focus is placed on how experiences of violence and disaster were conceptualized and communicated in the early modern period. Jennifer Spinks and Charles Zika's collection of essays, *Disaster, Death and the Emotions in the Shadow of the Apocalypse, 1400–1700* (2016), while also not engaging directly with the concept of trauma, takes the historical and social nature of disasters and the emotional response they incur as its focus to demonstrate the intense emotions generated through the religious, providential, and apocalyptic frameworks that provided these events with meaning.[25]

More recently we are indebted to Judith Pollmann's work on early modern memory and her consideration of the applicability of contemporary theories and concepts to that period. Her excellent study, *Memory in Early Modern Europe, 1500–1800* (2017), contains a chapter that takes as its focus memories of violence and explicitly discusses these in the context of trauma. Offering examples drawn from episodes of violent disruption across Europe in the period, Pollmann explains that "scholars have traced PTSD among people in many different cultures, and there is every reason to believe it was also present in pre-modern societies." She goes on to caution, however, that "we should expect early modern ways of coping with such memories to have been different from what they are today."[26]

Addressing some examples of early modern coping mechanisms, Cynthia Richards's article, "Wit at War: The Poetry of John Wilmot and the Trauma of War" (2014), analyses the poetry of John Wilmot after his experience in the Second Anglo Dutch War.[27] Richards discusses his poetry, famous for its candor and obscenities, as both classic examples of war trauma narratives and innovative period-specific works that reframe traumatic dissociation as restorative poetic wit. Following this, her chapter "History without Trauma: Recovering Bodily Loss in the Eighteenth Century" (2017) argues for the need for a new direction in eighteenth-century literary scholarship that applies historicized readings of trauma to literary texts of the long eighteenth century and that links this new approach with the materialist focus of disability studies.[28] In "Living Memory, Embodied Experience, and What Gets Lost in Alexander Pope's *The Rape of the Lock*," (2019) she uses this dual framework to read this poem as an example of active remembering and traumatic return; its meaning is processed and shaped by current events just as it was shaped by the politics of its time.[29]

Also taking early modern responses to trauma as her central focus, Erin Peters's work focuses on the aftereffects of combat trauma on those who experienced or witnessed the English Civil Wars. Her article, "Trauma Narratives of the English Civil War" (2016), explores how these experiences were conceptualized in relation to seventeenth-century understandings of the damaged mind, and how investigating this topic can further contribute to our understanding of the conflict's wider impact.[30] Her subsequent study, *Commemoration and Oblivion in Royalist Print Culture, 1658–1667* (2017) includes a chapter that considers the ways in which the collective trauma of the civil wars was addressed by the Restoration regime.[31] A further chapter, "'The Deep Staines These Wars Will Leave Behind': Psychological Wounds and Curative Methods in the English Civil Wars" (2018), investigates the public narration of psychological disability brought on by the lingering effects of combat trauma and memories of fear among soldiers and civilians. This chapter argues that the conflict allowed for a popular understanding of the disabling nature of psychological damage caused by exposure to external experiences to develop.[32]

As demonstrated by these studies, this shift in focus among early modern scholars reflects a growing awareness that there is potentially more to be gained from exploring and experimenting with the application of these theories than from avoiding them through concerns of accusations of anachronism or retrospective diagnosis. Maurice E. Stevens makes this point,

> History (and the practice of "taking histories") is haunted by stories that have gone unincluded in the realm of the historiography "trauma narratives" require. History grows gaunt and distracted in its confrontation with events that test its ability to represent, and in its encounter with affect that won't stay still and is difficult to inscribe with any accuracy, if at all. Hunched over, squinting, and losing its flexibility, these taken histories worry at the frayed edges of incomplete narrative, hidden transcripts, dream images, and unruly sensations . . . trauma interventions can begin the work of putting narratives together.[33]

While discerning and deciphering narratives and experiences of trauma from the early modern period is a potentially contentious task, which requires expanding and altering our understanding of the phenomenon and its appearances and recognizing distinctive early modern frames of referencing and manner of representing trauma, doing so can also be illuminating. Dominick LaCapra explains,

> It is astonishing how little historians recognize the significance of individual and collective trauma even when they write of events and processes in which it is prevalent, such as genocides, wars, rape, and various forms of victimization and abuse both of humans and of other animals. It is more difficult to document psychic trauma or post-traumatic effects than it is

to count numbers dead or wounded. But there is evidence on the basis of which one may infer traumatic experiences, and some writers may even address those experiences in explicit fashion.[34]

While attentive to accusations of anachronism, each chapter in the volume endeavors to explain and justify its application and adaption of trauma theory as a lens to explore these experiences, and in so doing we find, in line with arguments recently put forth by Pollmann, that accusations of anachronism serve more to hinder what might be discovered rather than to help preserve historical context. Writing of the study of memory broadly, but relevant to the topic of trauma, Pollmann argues that defining early modern people by their lack of modernity "does little for making sense of them in their own right."[35] Pollmann argues for the virtues of anachronism, that there is something important to be gained from recognizing the similarities of the past, rather than the differences and its separation from the present. The chapters in this collection uphold that principle also.

Studying experiences of trauma in the past is, of course, studying the memory of an event as it is attempted to be recounted by those who experienced it. In this sense a central question of trauma studies becomes a reconsideration of "how a memory becomes a charismatic wound, an injury that attracts everything to it."[36] The traumatic event itself often defies representation but is often too important a part of the story to be left out of the narrative completely. For example, Pollmann has considered early modern accounts of traumatic experiences and notes the lack of emotive response in the recounting of the events. In exploring survivor accounts from events such as the French Wars of Religion or the Thirty Years' War, she notes that accounts tend to detailed description rather than reflection on impact. That said, early modern individuals and communities recorded their experiences in ways that "we may not immediately recognize as emotive." These include such things as detailed inventories of material losses endured, damages inflicted, and the enumeration of dead and injured.[37] From this perspective, looking for expressions of trauma that are, themselves, early modern, it is possible to trace the culturally produced frames of reference available in an early modern context to recount and attempt to mediate trauma.

Highlighting these in the chapters that follow brings us to the third aim of the current volume: to present examples of the ways in which early modern contemporaries understood and narrated what today would be termed psychological or cultural trauma. How did evidence of this manifest and what were the strategies employed for narrating, conceptualizing, and coping with these distressing memories? How might trauma compound the manner in which early modern writers recount their experiences and how can we read trauma in the accounts of witnesses of the past, shaped as they are by their historically prescribed context?

All the chapters in this volume pay attention to the variations of representation available to early modern contemporaries to depict, decipher, and delineate extreme events, both collectively and individually. Studying the accounts left by those who experienced extreme events increases our understanding of the contexts in which traumatic events have been constructed and interpreted over time. Understanding why and how harm was done in the past, and how it was conceptualized, gives us invaluable insights into some of the most pressing issues of today. As Pollmann suggests, while the early modern world did not have "a psychological theory to account for the lasting damage such experiences can produce or to explain the reemergence of painful memories later in life," it would be overly simplistic to claim that early modern contemporaries did not feel such pain.[38] Rather they articulated and interpreted it within a framework that took on its own characteristics. The chapters in this volume uncover elements of that framework and work to shed light on early modern interpretations of trauma.

They do so, in part, by practicing "*synchronic* or *analogical*" reading, what Pollmann associates with a "much older and pre-modern way of thinking about the past . . . because it privileges the similarities rather than the differences between past and present, which it treats as one and the same thing."[39] To be clear, none of these chapters propose an absolute correspondence between the past and present. Rather, as noted earlier, each attend to the local, contextual differences that inflect representations of overwhelming or unexpected pain and do so with precision and thoughtfulness. Yet significantly they also refuse to treat the past as "non-repeatable," what can be read as symptomatic of modernity if, as others have argued, "[m]odernity" functions as "a form of self-awareness that makes people think of themselves or others as modern and as different from people in the past."[40] If we understand the provisional nature of this difference, then, remaining open, as Long describes it, "to the uncanny similarities between [the early modern] descriptions of the effects of sudden and overwhelming fear, sadness, and those detailed in modern trauma studies" becomes not only less problematic but also ethically necessary.[41] The result is a series of chapters that point to the usefulness of analogical attentiveness, both to deciphering early modern texts and to exposing the limits of dominant modern modes of understanding trauma.

In both cases, new strategies of resilience—historical forms of survival—become rhetorically and culturally available. This focus on the "*plurality* of possible responses to traumatic events" represents, according to Luckhurst, the future of the field. That future fittingly requires—as these chapters demonstrate—a return to "the traumatic past," as Luckhurst likewise urges; they elucidate how we must move backward to move forward.[42] They also help us see a "traumatic past" that extends beyond the elusive origins of the "modern"—and arguably the even more elusive moment when the modern became "traumatic"—and beyond a model of a singular event that largely privileges the experience of the white European male, and literary and historical constructs that focus primarily on militarized political loss and restoration. In doing so they also help us rethink what Cathy Caruth identifies as the "bearable" or what Luckhurst references as "breach[ing] the defenses of 'ordinary fortitude,'" the contemporary legal standard that makes suffering actionable or deserving of legal redress.[43] Thus, these chapters engage the framework of trauma in the early modern period not only to denaturalize the suffering of the past but also to complicate what are considered "normal emotions of pain and grief," and to reexamine whose pain matters.

Significantly, none of these chapters argue for a new origin story for trauma nor make the case that trauma begins in the early modern period. Rather the collection draws attention to how fluid that narrative is, and how many of the markers we use to place trauma prove unstable. For example, if modern technology produces the conditions for trauma, then these stories point to the ever-present reality of emerging technologies, and how those lead to extreme circumstances. Either war or industrialization, including industrialization's dehumanizing manifestation in plantation economies, underlies nearly all these early modern narratives of suffering and loss. As such, these chapters push us to rethink the politics of framing modern trauma as unique, or as Michael Rothberg argues in *Multidirectional Memory*, "those who understand memory as a form of competition see only winners and losers in the struggle for collective articulation and recognition." Rather these chapters participate in a "form of comparative thinking, that like memory itself, is not afraid to transverse sacrosanct borders of ethnicity and era," and in doing so make possible "the articulation of other histories of victimization."[44] Together these chapters point to how productive, even necessary, transhistorical readings can be in understanding psychological pain and identifying strategies for surviving that loss.

Thus, the organization of the volume draws attention both to what early modern texts can teach us about the concept of modern trauma and what the modern concept of trauma can teach us about early modern texts. In part 1, "Reframing Modern Trauma," each chapter uses trauma theory as an interpretive framework, and in doing so reveals not only the usefulness of this framework but also the limits of the modern conceptualization of overwhelming pain and unforeseen suffering. As a group, the chronologically organized chapters in this section reframe how experiences recognizable as trauma in modern terms were represented and managed in early modern contexts. The chapters in part 2, "Recognizing Early Modern Trauma," also use trauma theory as an interpretive framework for understanding early modern pain and its representation, but in this case demonstrate how recognizing trauma in these early modern texts can help decipher traditionally difficult and misunderstood texts or historical events. They illustrate how "trauma interventions," as Stevens describes it, "can begin the work of putting narratives together enough for them to be legible to the archives of history taking, and History making."[45]

In demonstrating the limits of modern conceptions of trauma, the first set of chapters in "Reframing Modern Trauma" also historicize extreme emotions, and what mechanisms facilitated their management in the wake of catastrophic events or personal crises. For example, Susan Broomhall's lead chapter in this first section draws our attention to early modern representations of "nature in crises," and in one example, how technological change in sixteenth-century France contributed to the perception of catastrophic change, the polluted waterway of the "Beivre river" occasioning court poetry that equated those "doleful consequences" with the sexual trauma of rape. Radically this chapter argues "the suffering caused by these destructive [environmental] events was neither contained to human bodies alone nor expressed only as forms of pain." Focusing on a range of sixteenth-century French texts, including first-person journals and essays and the more mediated poetry of the French court, Susan Broomhall identifies various spiritual, philosophical, and theological "templates" that guided responses to environmental devastation. Although far from uniform, these varied responses point to how significant the "supernatural" was in framing environmental disaster, resulting in "ambiguous, sometimes even affirmative, sentiments about such destructive events." If read as a manifestation of "God's mercy," for example, environmental disaster could even promote "feelings of belonging in the performance of communal affective and spiritual practices of prayer and procession." These culturally specific readings of eco-trauma point to the necessity of understanding historical difference in interpreting responses to natural disaster while at the same time acknowledging a continuity between a newly coined term such as *solastalgia* and an early modern sense of nature in distress, one that extended victimhood to nature itself.

Likewise Amelia Zurcher identifies continuities between the "structure" of the early modern Christian conversion narrative and the modern trauma narrative: "At the moment of conversion there is a subjective rupture . . . and then in the light of that rupture the self casts its newly reflective eye backward over the past self to give it meaning as a type (or antitype) of the present." Looking specifically at Hannah Allen's *A Narrative of God's Gracious Dealings with that Choice Christian* (1683), Zurcher identifies both similarities and differences in that structure and its effect. "For the subject who could trust in experience," she explains, "the writing and rewriting of promises and meditations was not traumatic repetition but the approach to God." This was especially true for the female subject for whom the "threat of trauma" was a daily event, early modern women imagined as naturally "susceptible to madness." Repetitive "spiritual writing" becomes in this context a means of "tending to the spiritual split in self." Still, she argues, the framework of the trauma narrative encourages us to "paus[e] the story" and in this case achieve both a better understanding of how loss shaped female experience and how allegorical religious reading practices promote both uplifting spiritual identification and a lingering recognition of an ever-present gap or excess in understanding.

Katherine Ellison also looks at an early modern form of communication that made deliberate repetition the norm: "cryptography"—the practice of which "flourished and was popular" at the time of the Wars of Three Kingdoms. As she notes, "ciphering and deciphering are . . . controlled repetitions" and "rely upon analogic representation" that "occupies the mind with a series of steps." Designed primarily as a mechanism for safely communicating distress during combat, they accrued—she argues—in the seventeenth century a secondary function as a teaching tool for "processing trauma and circumventing and conventionalizing the communication and reading of suffering." Cryptography, through employing analogical representation, assumed the therapeutic virtues of poetic ambiguity and revelation, while at the same time it offered a computational transparency akin "to the pure global language gifted to Adam and Eve before the Fall." As such, it offered new modalities for communicating authentic emotion and new strategies for both understanding and removing oneself from a sense of immediate danger, strategies not dissimilar from current innovations in "affective computing." Thus, all three of these chapters point to how recognizing differences in how trauma manifested in the early modern period allows for new connections to ongoing struggles in communicating emotion and in understanding suffering. They point to the varied ways in which early modern subjects "worked through" trauma in a period that offered up different structures of restoration, and one that spoke to the everyday experience of ordinary citizens and marginalized others.

Chapters by Zachariah Long, Ismini Pells, Peter Walmsley, and Melissa Antonucci in "Reframing Modern Trauma" likewise focus on key differences in how psychic pain was recognized in the early modern period but also point to the significance of rhetorical frameworks that foregrounded emotional distress and rendered "trauma" actionable. Long, for example, puts Sándor Ferenczi's modern concept of "identification with the aggressor" in conversation with early modern humoral theory and uses this framework to demonstrate the progressiveness of William Shakespeare's sixteenth-century poem, *The Rape of Lucrece* (1594). What might otherwise be taken as unclear referents, or even a lack of accountability, become in this framework a "poetics of distraction," one that makes present Lucrece's overwhelming fear through rendering suspicious her invasion by another's feelings.

Pells, like Ellison, examines the time period following the seventeenth-century civil wars in England and a form of communication connected to combat experience: "petitions submitted by, and on behalf of, maimed soldiers to English quarter sessions in order to claim financial relief from the state." These petitions functioned as performance, often drafted by others and playing upon calculated sympathies or employing scripted language known to be effective. However, their very scriptedness—she argues—points to how seriously emotional distress was addressed during the early modern period, and how a "sad condition" was operationally viewed as having an external not internal cause. Moreover, the public nature of these petitions provided cathartic release and aided in both personal and political restoration, with individual psychological distress proving "reminiscent of the disrupted state of the country during the Wars" and the soldiers' petitions representing "'the bodily trace' of those events."

Peter Walmsley's chapter examining an entry in a medical journal included in Hans Sloane's *Voyage to Jamaica* (1702, 1725) and his treatment of the house slave, Rose, further reflects on what makes trauma actionable, or more pointedly how "the early modern melancholic and the late modern trauma survivor bear powerful, if sometimes unwelcome, messages about what cannot be accepted, assimilated, and forgotten." Sloane's "clear obsession with the traumatic experience of the Jamaican slave, and his just as obsessive evasions of this trauma" point to the tension between acknowledging a recognizable medical condition and refusing to grant its sufferer humane treatment, particularly when the ability to work was at issue. As he argues, it is important to recognize that Sloane's general diagnosis of Rose's taciturn behavior clearly relies on an early modern understanding of melancholia—a humoral imbalance resulting from an excess of black bile—and operates within "the politics of early modern melancholy," one that granted this disease the status of social critique. However, trauma, particularly as understood within a postcolonial context and a form of mundane, persistent, and communal trauma makes recognizable this "melancholic stance as resistant, even subversive": it "violates the script by which master/slave relations are managed," and creates a telling gap or aporia in Sloane's understanding of Rose's condition as well as his own complicity in returning her to work. It exposes "Caribbean chattel slavery [as] a trauma engine, extraordinary in its violence, and the more so because it is equally inexplicable to both perpetrator and survivor."

Melissa Antonucci's chapter on Unca Eliza Winkfield's *The Female American* (1767) also addresses "the limitations of psychoanalytic constructions of trauma" by focusing on this novel's "protracted trauma" of colonialization, "specifically, first contact among Europeans and Indigenous communities of North America" and how that "alters the structures and symbols individuals rely upon to make sense of themselves and their environment." In her reading, *The Female American*'s biracial female protagonist—half English, half Indigenous—becomes prototypical of both the "chronic loss" experienced through first contact and the "modes of rehabilitation" that persistent cultural exile require. Stranded on an island and in a permanent state of exile, Unca Eliza relies on "her prosthetic memories of the past" to confront the intergenerational trauma that is her own legacy and that of the Indigenous people she encounters there. The novel frames that recovery in the familiar early modern terms of Christian conversion, but as with the soldiers' petitions and Sloane's medical diagnosis, this rhetorical framework draws attention to the power of emotional distress to trigger cultural recognition of irrecoverable and unassimilable loss. These three chapters further act to denaturalize the suffering of the past—early modern soldiers, for example, were not immune to the psychological impact of combat, and the state recognized that—and the last two act to decolonize it, pointing to the everyday trauma of coerced labor and exile and how evidence of that suffering challenged western history's official narratives.

In the volume's second section, chapters in "Recognizing Early Modern Trauma" continue to outline the specific historical, cultural, and literary contexts that frame early modern discussions of catastrophic loss but emphasize instead how modern trauma can help decipher previously indecipherable, and often misread, texts. This approach is most pronounced in the chapters by Adam Beach, Cynthia Richards, and Andreas Mueller. In fact Beach begins his chapter by identifying William Okeley's "description of his loving relationship with his last slave master in Algiers" in *Ebenezar* (1675) as one of "the most troubling and misunderstood in the canon of British literature about slavery in the long eighteenth century." Drawing attention to the current "upsurge in slaveries around the world" and the new research emerging from mental health practitioners studying its effects, Beach links the current "confusion" over the effects of psychological coercion on victims of captivity with scholarly misreadings of Okeley's ethical dilemma over escaping his master. In both cases victims can be blamed for not resisting more actively, and the "horrors of slavery" are potentially underplayed; in the case of Okeley, scholars can even unwittingly participate in "powerful ideologies that forward the idea that benevolence is not mutually exclusive with its practice of slavery," thus reading Okeley's debate over the ethics of escape as a "sign of the master's kindness, goodness, and generosity." By contrast, the work of psychologist Judith Herman elucidates how psychological coercion in captivity robs victims of individual autonomy and can productively reframe readings of Okeley and other eighteenth-century slave narratives.

Cynthia Richards takes issue with a standard reading of Aphra Behn's entry into the imperfect enjoyment genre, "The Disappointment" (1682), as promoting a more utopian, reciprocal vision of heterosexual desire than its male-authored counterparts. Rather she argues for the value of viewing both its female protagonist, Cloris, and its female author, Behn, as psychologically "acting out." The poem ends abruptly and never names Cloris's loss; rather the poem testifies to the significance of Cloris's wounding in this sexual encounter and departs from Ovidian depictions of the female as emblematic of male trauma. Moreover, Behn's decision to dramatically truncate the French poem she is translating suggests that this depiction of male bodily dissolution may have triggered her own memories. The chapter concludes by noting parallels between this poem and a key scene in Behn's penultimate work, *Oroonoko* (1688), and how these parallels suggest that Behn herself may have been "working through" in that novella an experience of traumatic loss. If so, then it "can help account for 'the vicarious suffering' that distinguishes this 'melanchol[ic]' text," and "how *Oroonoko* renders its readers witnesses to a loss that is visceral rather than abstract."

Andreas Mueller addresses the "exceptional status" of Daniel Defoe's *Journal of a Plague Year* (1720), but rather than attributing its unusual insightfulness regarding the plague to "historical verisimilitude," makes the case that "Defoe's exceptionally vivid depictions of plague trauma were intended to have a psycho-prophylactic purpose." Drawing upon Marianne Hirsch's framework of "postmemory," he compares Defoe's use of *tableau vivant* to Hirsch's description of the photographic image in transmitting intergenerational trauma. Like the photograph, Defoe's vivid descriptions imaginatively transmit the "mental experience" of trauma, in this case, the "horrors of a plague visitation" while in Defoe's case, have additionally the practical effect of preparing Londoners for its arrival, thus promoting "resilience and ideal conduct in the face of severe trauma and emotional distress." As Mueller demonstratives, the framework of intergenerational trauma exposes the "dynamism" of a text that verisimilitude alone cannot explain.

Just as these literary readings use the framework of modern trauma to rethink standard readings of canonical texts, Eamon Darcy and Erin Peters use trauma narrative, and its distinguishing features, to complicate typical historical accounts. For Darcy, this means exploring the "stories of trauma" in early modern Ireland and how these reflect on English colonization. Acknowledging the challenge of examining a culture split by language, religion, and national identity, he unearths how resistance to cultural genocide took the form of Irish language anthologies, the testimonies of "ordinary people" telegraphing the pain of dispossession through extraordinary tales of ghostly apparitions, and the absent voice of Irish literati in the political poetry in the decades following the civil wars of the seventeenth century. Paying attention to the language of ordinary citizens and the submerged resistance of its elite, Darcy's chapter pieces together a language of grief and mourning as it was dispersed across an Irish diaspora. Recognizing trauma in these historical narratives, or acknowledging them as "stories of trauma," can make the vague apprehensions recorded in oral narratives and the deliberate silence of Irish poets' testimonies to loss.

Erin Peters's chapter reframes the Glorious Revolution within the "discourse of trauma" and counteracts a history of reading this event as "suggest[ing] an absence of collective suffering." Applying sociologist Piotr Sztompka's taxonomy, she recasts the origins of Jacobitism as a response to "traumatogenic" social change, and points out how exile, both external and internal, operates as form of resistance and left undecided in England for years to come the shape and meaning of both the mid-seventeenth-century civil wars and British national identity. History may have reframed this event as bloodless, but early Jacobite writings "can be read as evidence that the significant levels of wide-reaching change were culturally traumatic, tinged as they were with recourse to memories of past episodes of cultural trauma." These two chapters draw explicit attention to the mid-seventeenth-century conflicts in the British Isles and Ireland, and to their continuing effect on British and Irish cultural identity into the eighteenth century. Remarkably, however, nearly all the chapters in the "Recognizing Early Modern Trauma" section, and many in the "Reframing Modern Trauma" section, point directly or indirectly to how incomplete political restoration after the Interregnum proved, and how deeply the scars of division and conflict continued to run in the aftermath of the 1640s and 1650s. Thus, the wars, upheaval, and violence of mid-seventeenth-century Britain and Ireland serve as a political and ideological aporia that haunts many of the texts included in this volume and helps explain why so many of these chapters discuss works produced between 1640 and 1720.

Chapters by Tamar LeRoy and Joseph Harris return the discussions of early modern trauma to the more familiar terrain of theater, a genre that has inspired much of the early work on trauma during this period. LeRoy's and Harris's chapters argue, as others have, that theater provided a collective space in which trauma could be reenacted and audiences were required to confront its ongoing effects. LeRoy, however, extends this scholarship by pointing to how comic theater allowed for "trauma negotiation" and not solely confrontation. Focusing on a popular patriotic play of the eighteenth century, *The Recruiting Officer* (1706), LeRoy shows how "lack of sustained consideration of the soldier's vulnerability in the play has left unexamined its management of the traumatic effects of prolonged military engagement." Like others in this section, LeRoy deciphers this play and "the unpredictable ways [it] was taken up in performance" by foregrounding the "traumatic, ritual effect [of] humor" and the intersection of the play's army plot and marriage plot. That intersection draws attention to the vulnerability of the soldier's body in combat by comparing it to "more familiar" and "culturally legible" vulnerability of the female body, as portrayed by the cross-dressing Sylvia who "serves as a ghostly but more vibrant echo" of the male protagonist Plume. LeRoy's work points to how theater can reframe narratives of bodily wounding to address unspoken, even forbidden, realities of temporal life, and further links that discussion to important work in disability studies.

Joseph Harris takes as a transhistorical example to reframe narrative of bodily wounding the story of matricide committed by the Greek mythological hero Orestes and his subsequent pursuit by the Furies, and one that "has proved a compelling yet troubling one for dramatists across the ages." His focus, however, is "the ways in which the myth was understood, adapted, and developed in the late seventeenth and early eighteenth centuries," and specifically two *Electre* plays by Longespierre (1702) and Crebillon (1708). Both these plays emphasize the psychological state of remorse over the physical one of vengeance, a reframing that creates intriguing parallels to the modern understanding of perpetrator trauma with Orestes pursued by the equivalent of Cathy Caruth's "unclaimed experience," the hallucinatory Furies. Harris's reading remains unresolved as to whether the character Orestes experiences trauma in these plays but makes clear that early modern French audiences found his repetitive actions more sympathetic when presented as following from an unconscious gap in understanding. As with others in the "Recognizing Early Modern Trauma" section, LeRoy's and Harris's chapters demonstrate how knowledge of the structures of modern trauma can help decode problematic early modern literary and dramatic texts, and the usefulness of being open to multidirectionality in reading. This approach both explains how loss manifests differently across time yet how consistently that loss takes the representational form of traumatic wounding or a structural gap or aporia. As Amelia Zurcher, one of our contributors, aptly describes it, "traumatic narrative might be more useful than other kinds for pausing the story and letting us dwell on its constituent parts."

Finally, Melinda Rabb, in an afterword that fittingly reads also as an introduction, argues not only for the trauma narrative's capacity to "paus[e] the story" but also for how it can move us forward. "The effect" of the approach is to make us "see in new ways," she argues, citing Raymond Williams's famous phrase, and asks: "What might be a next step that carries this volume's insights forward?"[46] For one, it allows us to rethink standard "modes of expression," and to uncover in "the distancing and mitigating effects of irony" a wounded "urgency." She writes, "Trauma's infliction of pain should factor into assumptions about satire's vitriolic militancy and into rationales for its status as a distinguishing achievement of the eighteenth century," and then shows us how Jonathan Swift's satire speaks to a "restoration" never fully achieved.

This moving backward to move forward reflects the tenor of the volume. Even as the chapters in this volume congregate around two broad categories ("Reframing Modern Trauma" and "Recognizing Early Modern Trauma"), they are in conversation with one another in multiple ways and engage trauma theory through varied but overlapping lenses. Both Beach's and Walmsley's chapters, for example, speak to a resistance to acknowledging the trauma of slavery and the value of this contemporary reframing. Long's chapter addresses this same psychological phenomenon for sexual trauma. Both Pells's and LeRoy's chapters acknowledge the psychological effects of war on early modern soldiers and the rhetorical strategies needed to make them assimilable to an early modern audience. Both Zurcher's and Richards's chapters locate in first-person narration disguised evidence of visceral, disruptive, and continuing personal pain. Similarly, Ellison's, Darcy's, and Peters's chapters address the coded language of loss and change when direct communication is militarily, culturally, and politically imprudent. Both Antonucci's and Mueller's chapters draw attention to intergenerational trauma and how it shapes eighteenth-century prose narratives. Broomhall's and Harris's chapters contribute significantly to a history of emotions as enacted in the French court and on the French stage. In addition these chapters represent a broad range of approaches, their authors incorporating disability studies, feminism, eco-criticism, aesthetics, affect studies, memory studies, linguistics, sociological and psychological studies, among others. They take as their subject matter both historical events and literary texts. They examine both first-person "real-life" accounts—written, oral, and coded—and third-person fictional representations, and include poetry, memoir, journals, and novels in addition to drama. They document both European wars and their imperial effects in Ireland, North America, and the West Indies. They focus on natural catastrophes, including disease and plague, as well as the man-made environmental changes of exile and agricultural denudation. The breadth of the approaches and evidentiary bases enables an extensive examination of what counts as trauma, for whom, and under what circumstances. In recognizing that the experience of trauma predates its definition, and that modern definitions of trauma require adaptation and remolding to fit early modern contexts, the chapters that follow uncover what we can learn from this approach about the early modern experience more broadly, but also what we can learn about the malleability and flexibility of the concept of trauma and the history of human responses to, and narration of, extreme events.

NOTES

1. Monica J. Casper and Eric Wertheimer, eds., *Critical Trauma Studies: Understanding Violence, Conflict, and Memory in Everyday Life* (New York: New York University Press, 2016), 3. Also see: Cathy Caruth, ed., *Trauma: Explorations in Memory* (Baltimore: Johns Hopkins University Press, 1995); Dominick LaCapra, *Writing History, Writing Trauma* (Baltimore: Johns Hopkins University Press, 2001); Geoffrey Cubitt, *History and Memory* (Manchester: Manchester University Press, 2007); Michael Rothberg, *Multidirectional Memory: Remembering the Holocaust in the Age of Decolonization* (Palo Alto CA: Stanford University Press, 2009); Marianne Hirsch, *The Generation of Postmemory: Writing and Visual Culture after the Holocaust* (New York: Columbia University Press, 2012); Aleida Assmann, *Shadows of Trauma: Memory and the Politics of Postwar Identity* (New York: Fordham University Press, 2016); Elaine Scarry, *The Body in Pain: The Making and Unmaking of the World* (Oxford: Oxford University Press, 1985); Geoffrey Hartman, "On Traumatic Knowledge and Literary Studies," *New Literary History* 26, no. 3 (1995): 537–63; Cathy Caruth, *Unclaimed Experience: Trauma, Narrative, and History* (Baltimore: Johns Hopkins University Press, 1996); Michelle Balaev, ed., *Contemporary Approaches in Literary Trauma Theory* (New York: Palgrave Macmillan, 2014); Marita Sturken, *Tangled Memories: The Vietnam War, the AIDS Epidemic, and the Politics of Remembering* (Berkeley: University of California Press, 1997); Marita Sturken, *Tourists of History: Memory, Kitsch, and Consumerism from Oklahoma City to Ground Zero* (Durham NC: Duke University Press, 2007); Dominick LaCapra, *History and Memory After Auschwitz* (New York: Cornell University Press, 1998); Ann Cvetkovich, *An Archive of Feelings: Trauma, Sexuality, and Lesbian Public Cultures* (Durham NC: Duke University Press, 2003); Jeffrey C. Alexander et al., *Cultural Trauma and Collective Identity* (Berkeley: University of California Press), 2004; Jeffrey C. Alexander, *Trauma: A Social Theory* (Cambridge:

Polity Press, 2012); Ron Eyerman, *Memory, Trauma, and Identity* (Palgrave Macmillan, 2019); E. Ann Kaplan, *Trauma Culture: The Politics of Terror and Loss in Media and Literature* (New Brunswick NJ: Rutgers University Press, 2005); Shoshana Felman and Dori Laub, *Testimony: Crises of Witnessing in Literature, Psychoanalysis and History* (New York: Routledge, 1991); Nancy R. Goodman and Marilyn B. Meyers, eds., *The Power of Witnessing: Reflections, Reverberations, and Traces of the Holocaust: Trauma, Psychoanalysis, and the Living Mind* (New York: Routledge, 2012); Sybille Kramer and Sigrid Weigel, eds., *Testimony/Bearing Witness: Epistemology, Ethics, History, and Culture* (New York: Rowman & Littlefield, 2017); Stef Craps, *Postcolonial Witnessing: Trauma Out of Bounds* (Hampshire, UK: Palgrave Macmillan, 2015); Ogaga Ifowodo, *History, Trauma, and Healing in Postcolonial Narratives: Reconstructing Identities* (New York: Palgrave Macmillan, 2013); Abigail Ward, ed., *Postcolonial Traumas: Memory, Narrative, Resistance* (Hampshire: Palgrave Macmillan, 2015); Irene Visser, "Decolonizing Trauma Theory: Retrospect and Prosepcts," *Humanities* 4 (2015): 250–65; Ruth Leys, *Trauma: A Genealogy* (Chicago: University of Chicago Press, 2000); Jackie Orr, *Panic Diaries: A Genealogy of Panic Disorders* (Durham NC: Duke University Press, 2006); Roger Luckhurst, *The Trauma Question* (Oxford: Routledge, 2008); Gert Buelens, Sam Durrant and Robert Eaglestone, ed., *The Future of Trauma Theory: Contemporary Literary and Cultural Criticism* (New York: Routledge, 2014); Lucy Bond and Stef Craps, *Trauma* (Oxford, UK: Routledge, 2015).

2. Casper and Wertheimer, *Critical Trauma Studies*, 3.
3. Luckhurst, *The Trauma Question*, 3.
4. Luckhurst, 4.
5. Nancy K. Miller and Jason Tougaw, *Extremities: Trauma, Testimony, and Community* (Champaign: University of Illinois Press, 2002), 1.
6. Paul Lerner and Mark S. Micale, eds., *Traumatic Pasts: History, Psychiatry, and Trauma in the Modern Age, 1870–1930* (Cambridge: Cambridge University Press, 2001), 1.
7. Luckhurst, *The Trauma Question*, 20–21.
8. Mark Konnert, *Early Modern Europe: The Age of Religious War, 1559–1715* (Toronto: University of Toronto Press, 2008); Eric Hobsbawm, "The General Crisis of the European Economy in the 17th Century," *Past & Present* 5, no. 1 (1954): 33–53; Geoffrey Parker, *Global Crisis: War, Climate Change and Catastrophe in the Seventeenth Century* (New Haven CT: Yale University Press, 2013).
9. See Cynthia Marshall, *The Shattering of the Self: Violence, Subjectivity, and Early Modern Texts* (Baltimore: Johns Hopkins University Press, 2002), for a detailed and particularly cogent articulation of this position. In her opening chapter Marshall states this position thusly: "An emergent sense of the autonomous self, individually operative as never before in the spheres of politics, religion, and commerce, existed in tension with an established popular sense of the self as fluid, unstable, and volatile."

However, in her first chapter she just as cogently argues for the limits of a critical approach that would not allow for psychoanalytical framing as it "neglects the question of why sadistic spectacles of this sort appeal to audiences, and this is its real poverty as critical method" (30). Also see Zackariah C. Long, "'Uncollected Man': Trauma and the Early Modern Mind-Body in *The Maid's Tragedy*," in *Staging Pain, 1580–1800*, eds. James Robert Allard and Mathew R. Martin, 31–46 (Surrey: Ashgate, 2009), for a discussion of this "familiar historicist warning" (31).

10. Gregg Horowitz, *Sustaining Loss: Art and the Mournful Life* (Palo Alto CA: Stanford University Press, 2001), 4, 23.
11. Jason Crowley, "Beyond the Universal Soldier: Combat Trauma in Classical Antiquity," in *Combat Trauma and the Ancient Greeks*, eds. P. Meineck and D. Konstan, 105–30 (Hampshire: Palgrave Macmillan, 2014).
12. Michelle Balaev, "Literary Trauma Theory Reconsidered," in *Contemporary Approaches in Literary Trauma Theory*, ed. Michelle Balaev, 1–14 (New York: Palgrave Macmillan, 2014), 3.
13. Thomas P. Anderson, *Performing Early Modern Trauma from Shakespeare to Milton* (New York: Routledge, 2006), 4; Horowitz, *Sustaining Loss*, 4.
14. Patricia A. Cahill, *Unto the Breach: Martial Formation, Historical Trauma, and the Early Modern Stage* (Oxford: Oxford University Press, 2008), 3, 6.
15. Catherine Silverstone, *Shakespeare, Trauma, and Contemporary Performance* (New York: Routledge, 2011), 17.
16. Lisa Starks-Estes, *Violence, Trauma, and Virtus in Shakespeare's Roman Poems and Plays: Transforming Ovid* (Hampshire: Palgrave Macmillan, 2014), 2–3.
17. For another pioneering critical analysis applying the "logic" of trauma to an early modern text, see Heather Hirschfield, "Hamlet's 'First Corse': Repetition, Trauma, and the Displacement of Redemptive Typology," *Shakespeare Quarterly* 54, no. 4 (2003): 424–48, esp. 425.
18. Starks-Estes, *Violence, Trauma, and Virtus*, 35.
19. James Robert Allard and Mathew R. Martin, eds., *Staging Pain, 1580–1800: Violence and Trauma in British Theatre* (Farnham: Ashgate, 2009).
20. Mathew R. Martin, *Tragedy and Trauma in the Plays of Christopher Marlow* (Oxford: Routledge, 2016).
21. Marshall, *The Shattering of the Self*, 8.
22. Erika Kuijpers et al., *Memory Before Modernity: Practices of Memory in Early Modern Europe* (Leiden: Brill, 2013), 19.
23. Allie Terry-Fritsch and Erin Felicia Labbie, *Beholding Violence in Medieval and Early Modern Europe* (Farnham: Ashgate, 2012).
24. Domenico Cecere et al., *Disaster Narratives in Early Modern Naples: Politics, Communication and Culture* (Rome: Viella Editrice, 2018).

25. Jennifer Spinks and Charles Zika, eds., *Disaster, Death and the Emotions in the Shadow of the Apocalypse, 1400–1700* (Hampshire: Palgrave Macmillan, 2016).
26. Judith Pollmann, *Memory in Early Modern Europe, 1500–1800* (Oxford: Oxford University Press, 2017), 161.
27. Cynthia Richards, "Wit at War: The Poetry of John Wilmot and the Trauma of War," *Eighteenth-Century Fiction* 27, no. 1 (2014): 25–54.
28. Cynthia Richards, "History without Trauma: Recovering Bodily Loss in the Eighteenth Century," in *The Future of Feminist Eighteenth-Century Scholarship*, ed. Robin Runia, 13–30 (New York: Routledge, 2017).
29. Cynthia Richards, "Living Memory, Embodied Experience, and What Gets Lost in Alexander Pope's *The Rape of the Lock*," *English Language Notes* 57, no. 2 (2019): 133–42.
30. Erin Peters, "Trauma Narratives of the English Civil War," *Journal for Early Modern Cultural Studies* 16, no. 1 (2016): 78–94.
31. Erin Peters, *Commemoration and Oblivion in Royalist Print Culture, 1658–1667* (Hampshire: Palgrave Macmillan, 2017).
32. Erin Peters, "'The Deep Staines These Wars Will Leave Behind': Psychological Wounds and Curative Methods in the English Civil Wars," in *Battle-Scarred: Mortality, Medical Care and Military Welfare in the British Civil Wars*, ed. David J. Appleby and Andrew Hopper, 156–73 (Manchester: Manchester University Press, 2018).
33. Maurice E. Stevens, "Trauma Is as Trauma Does," in *Critical Trauma Studies: Understanding Violence, Conflict, and Memory in Everyday Life*, ed. Monica J. Casper and Eric Wertheimer (New York: New York University Press, 2016), 34.
34. LaCapra, *Writing History, Writing Trauma*, x.
35. Pollmann, *Memory in Early Modern Europe*, 20.
36. Michael S. Roth, *Memory, Trauma, and History* (New York: Columbia University Press, 2012), xviii.
37. Pollmann, *Memory in Early Modern Europe*, 165.
38. Pollmann, 185.
39. Pollmann, 48.
40. Pollmann, 47.
41. Long, "Uncollected Man," 31.
42. Luckhurst, *The Trauma Question*, 211, 213.
43. Caruth, *Unclaimed Experience*, 7; Luckhurst, *The Trauma Question*, 29.
44. Rothberg, *Multidirectional Memory*, 5, 17.
45. Stevens, "Trauma Is as Trauma Does," 34.
46. Raymond Williams, *The Long Revolution* (London: Chatto & Windus, 1961), 18.

Part I

Reframing Modern Trauma

I

Devastated Nature

The Emotions of Natural World Catastrophe in Sixteenth-Century France

SUSAN BROOMHALL

This chapter explores how early modern individuals managed perceptions of environmental destruction, including such natural events as floods, storms, and fires, and such human interventions as logging and agricultural practices. It focuses on a variety of sixteenth-century genres, among them, journals, essays, and poetry. These texts narrate exceptional occurrences of destruction as their authors bore witness to them; some even conceptualized the possibility of pain and trauma experienced by nature itself. Contemporaries described, visualized, and materialized their observations of unusual, extreme, and damaging events in the natural world in both pragmatic and creative works through early modern conceptual frameworks—spiritual, philosophical, and theological among them—that created templates not only for what could be perceived as catastrophic destruction but also appropriate responses to such events.

A growing body of scholarship examines how early modern populations expressed changes that they observed in the natural world around them.[1] These offer additional attention to a period before the Romantic period, the ideas of which some such as Timothy Morton have argued have become foundational to present-centered ecocriticism and its ideas of "nature."[2] Indeed, early modern English literary critics have played an important role in our own contemporary discussions of environmental futures.[3] Broad historical studies have begun to assess the consequences of climate change in the early modern period.[4] There is, however, room for more and deeper studies of specific times and places, which draw upon a larger range of early modern source types understood in their context.[5] There are, for example, few studies of early modern French texts to match the rich corpus of early modern English literary studies emerging on this topic.[6]

Similarly, in recent years the burgeoning multidisciplinary research on trauma has begun to consider natural disasters such as hurricanes, tsunamis, superstorms, earthquakes, and landslides.[7] This scholarship has highlighted that destructive environmental events of both natural and human making can result in debilitating distress for victims, some of whom find pathways to recovery in narrative and other therapeutic activities. Recently, scholars of film studies have begun to employ the term "eco-trauma" to identify the particular nature of modern traumatic responses to environmental crises as articulated on film.[8] A range of scholars have also been attracted to the possibility of *solastalgia*, a term coined by philosopher Glenn Albrecht to express the distress caused by environmental trauma of another kind: that caused by human interactions with the natural world. This term hearkens back to its shared classical linguistic roots with nostalgia as well as its aural and conceptual similarity.[9] In this chapter I explore the possibilities for analyzing early modern perceptions of destruction of the natural world and its catastrophic consequences through the responses of its victims, its witnesses, and those who experienced it in the mediatized forms of the period.

This context, however, requires careful investigation of the key terms that the scholarship employs. Among them is the very word "trauma" that is central to this literature. As historians Ruth Leys and Wulf Kansteiner observe, scholars pursuing this field stem from a wide range of disciplines and analyze with widely divergent aims and methodologies as a result. Both Leys and Kansteiner argue that a consequence of these interventions has been a broadening of the meaning and application of trauma to multiple populations and events, and a conflation between the distinctive experiences of victims, bystanders, and perpetrators as forms of trauma.[10] As a result, in their view the analytical power of trauma, where it is used broadly as what Kansteiner terms the metaphor of cultural trauma, has been markedly reduced.[11] This requires us to be attentive to the referents and variations when trauma is used as a concept in the literature. A body of scholarship aims to distinguish between the nature and longevity of mediatized experiences of trauma for bystanders from what might be termed its more immediate victims.[12]

Significantly, Kansteiner emphasizes that this broad usage has tended to "obliterate the very historical precision and moral specificity that the concept had originally helped to establish" and produces "little insight into the social and cultural repercussions of historical traumata."[13] Following work by anthropologist Allan Young, which locates post-traumatic stress syndrome (PTSD) as a diagnosis specific to a particular historical moment and its ideologies and practices, Kansteiner argues that trauma is made in and for, and experienced in, our contemporary context.[14] For historians of the early modern period, then, the term "trauma" poses an intellectual challenge. We must not only be alert to the language, discourses, genres, and other contexts in which early moderns could articulate the catastrophic, but we must also develop a vocabulary that attends to the specificity of its historical moment. At the same time, such a vocabulary should aim to avoid isolating historical moments in silos of specialized language and conceptualizations, from which experiences can be recovered for comparative study only with great difficulty. In examining a range of catastrophic articulations within sixteenth-century genres from France, it is quickly apparent that there are key conceptualizations of the relationships between the supernatural, the natural, and the human that must be recognized to understand these expressions. While the notion of "ecology" in eco-trauma conveys the inter-relatedness of human-natural dynamics, it does not satisfactorily articulate the significant supernatural, primarily divine but also potentially diabolical, dynamic at the heart of early modern conceptualizations of nature.[15] Clearly, "nature" was, as it remains, a human construct, but few, if any, early modern authors expressed ideas about the natural world in which the supernatural was not a potential, if not a fundamental and active, shaping force. Under the influence of God, or occasionally Mother Nature, nature was no passive context for human activities; it communicated the divine and diabolical, challenged human endeavor, and frequently resisted human attempts to control it. I prefer "nature," then, over "ecology" as a term that enables modern comprehension yet encapsulates a worldview where nature was an active, responsive, and challenging companion of human existence.

Other modern terms such as *solastalgia* and the trauma of eco-trauma present further challenges for the early modernist. In addition to the concerns expressed by Leys and Kansteiner about the breadth of application of the cultural trauma concept, both *solastalgia* and trauma assume a devastated response of victims and bystanders to the perceived natural disaster or environmental damage. In two ways this does not aid analysis of the early modern context—namely, the suffering caused by these destructive events was neither contained to human bodies alone nor expressed only as forms of pain. In the following material, as we will see, authors perceived nature in crises; they saw profound alteration to the natural world and saw those alterations as having catastrophic consequences. However, they did not perceive the victims and survivors of these events as solely human, but also included nonhuman entities, such as flora and fauna; that is, nature itself.

Moreover some authors, as both human victims and bystanders, held ambiguous, sometimes even affirmative, sentiments about such destructive events. These emotional articulations, as the scholarship of the history of emotions reminds us, must themselves be interpreted in the context of early modern social, rhetorical, and generic conventions for feeling expression.[16] A nuanced interpretive framework of historical emotions is fundamental to analysis of what may constitute catastrophic destruction in the past. The analysis of early modern destructive events can fruitfully draw upon complementary bodies of scholarship on emotions. These consider how violence was more broadly perceived in deeply emotional terms in the early modern period.[17] Erin Felicia Labbie and Allie Terry-Fritsch adopt the term "beholding" to convey the active, phenomenological nature of perceiving violence, which entails a high degree of attentiveness and participation from the individual beholder and "synaesthetically transfers affect and cognition through the visual encounter."[18] Studies on early modern recognition of psychic forms of violence and harm also extend the definition of what constituted violent behavior in that society, including mediatized access to violence through viewing, reading, and hearing information perceived as fearsome and threatening.[19] Alongside these studies, Erika Kuijpers and Judith Pollmann, among others, have explored how culturally specific memory templates for acts and texts could strengthen or dissipate feelings of traumatic events at individual and collective levels.[20] Kuijpers emphasizes how the expression of emotions by early modern victims of terrible and challenging events operated within narrative schemes that were appropriate and logical to their social and cultural framework.[21] Responses to natural world catastrophe by early modern authors were likewise embedded in their communities of interpretation. They were also shaped by the genres that determined how such events and the feelings attached to them could be articulated. Responses to nature in crises were thus particular to both the local contexts of authors and to the genres used.

Given these contexts, early modern sources present challenges for those seeking the traumatic in times past through modern conceptualizations. Discussing modern trauma narratives, literary scholar Cathy Caruth identifies an "oscillation [. . .] between the story of the unbearable nature of an event and the story of the unbearable nature of its survival."[22] Identifying the "unbearable" in past accounts is more difficult, since these textual sources of early modern victims of catastrophic events necessarily render these experiences at least expressible in their cultural terms. They may be selective in meaningful ways that point to challenges and difficulties in the narration of their experiences, but in writing, they are, in some form and in their own ways, mechanisms for expressing these experiences. These sources are direct or indirect attestations of survival by Christians who had to bear God's will, for to despair was a sin.

Analyzing the complex relationships between emotions and natural world perceptions within historical moments is still in its infancy.[23] However, understanding the nature of emotional communication and behavior in its historical, social, rhetorical, and generic contexts is crucial to their interpretation and their capacity to contribute to analysis of early modern expression surrounding disastrous events. The consideration of emotions in a robust analytical framework enables understanding of historical responses to destructive events because their expression and the nature of that expression are key interpretive elements of what constitutes the psychological elements of the modern trauma experience. Given that the consequences of such ruinous events were not perceived to only relate to human experiences, or only to be expressed in terms of suffering in the short- or long-term, the wholly deleterious and human-centered disposition of the modern concept of trauma does not appear to represent the diversity of early modern responses to what were understood to be watershed moments in nature's destruction. To be clear, I argue that the events reported by early modern authors were perceived as damage that held significant psychic and moral consequences, but that these dramatic consequences were neither solely limited to human populations nor necessarily destructive.

We can draw usefully here upon an early modern word that seems to encapsulate some of the ambiguities of these responses to perceived natural disaster or environmental damage, the term "catastrophe." This word is first documented in French in the 1552 Épigraphe to the *Quart Livre* of the adventures of Gargantua and Pantagruel by the author François Rabelais. Here catastrophe implied a turning point, but one which could be either beneficial or deleterious.[24] Over the next one hundred years or so, this term shifted meaning to define more exclusively a terrible end point, but for our purposes it captures the ambiguities of these sixteenth-century articulations of nature undergoing decisive change. The use of the word "catastrophe" and of "catastrophic" in this chapter should be understood in the context of its sixteenth-century sense.

Religious Engagements with Disasters in Nature

A range of diary accounts recorded events perceived to be disastrous in nature, the vast majority of which were written by men who were largely part of an educated elite of secular and religious professionals. Diaries recorded a wide range of contemporary events understood to be profoundly destructive, even catastrophic, including floods, frost, rain, hail, and overflowing rivers. Importantly, these were accounts produced as the experiences were lived and they reflected the immediate feelings of their victims and the bystanders who read and heard of these ruinous events.

A religious framework governed the interpretation of many diarists to disaster in nature and informed their responses to it. Contemporaries, both Catholic and Protestant, read divine feelings with catastrophic consequences into natural world destruction. Pepin, a little-known musical canon in the Sainte-Chapelle of Dijon, was clear in his attribution of destruction in the natural world to supernatural intervention. In February 1572 he described how "on the 20th, it froze, snowed and was as cold as Christmas, which showed that God was very angry; the vines were just beginning to appear and all the goods and fruit of the earth were at their most tender which made everyone worry that all would be lost."[25] However, through such events and disasters, communities renewed their compact with God, as Pepin's account demonstrated. In the same month,

> On 13 February, it was very cold in the morning with great wind all night, and the day was very snowy, so much so that all the granaries of Saint-Fiacre had four thick fingers' worth of snow on top of the piles of wheat and oats. [. . .] On the day of Purification, the frost and cold began again without ceasing until 3 March and each day froze so violently [. . .] but the good Lord protected the goods of the earth, which were not spoiled, and on the 2 March, a lovely general procession was conducted.[26]

Thus, events perceived to be catastrophic in the natural world could also be affirmative since they could potentially demonstrate God's mercy. Pepin's diary entries and the community actions that they recorded demonstrated how people could define a sense of agency and empowerment—feelings of belonging in the performance of communal affective and spiritual practices of prayer and procession—as part of recovery from the impact of natural world destruction and its catastrophic consequences.

Those who read and heard of such destructive events were isolated from the communities that responded through collective spiritual mechanisms, yet they were no less affected by the wider messages that many understood these events to convey. As a result immediate responses as reflected in diaries often displayed heightened emotional tone but fewer expressions of resilience or reconciliation after such events. Pierre Driart, a canon at the Augustinian Abbey of Saint Victor near Paris, reported a series of notable, terrible events in and around Paris in the 1520s and 1530s that had certain, unequivocal meaning, and that he wrote about in dramatic terms. In January 1524 Driart recorded: "It was never in living memory seen or heard nor found in written sources of such a loss of grain sown in the earth as it was in this year, for in all the kingdom, fortune completely stunned people."[27] Later, in May 1527, "The disposition of the present month was more remarkable than any living had seen before, for it rained every day, apart from the second last day, and in great abundance."[28] More than three thousand had been killed by rivers bursting their banks as a result, he noted, adding that "it would be long to recount all the damage in many places."[29] In almost every year, Driart reported disasters for which "there was no man living who said he had seen it before."[30] His work emphasized the shocked reactions of contemporaries (perhaps also his own) to these extraordinary events rather than any consolidated, communal response. As a result these events were attested to for posterity but remained rhetorically unresolved within his work's narrative. The enumeration of such events seems to have served here as part of an eschatological framework pointing to end-times. From this perspective a productive narratological pathway to personal psychic recovery within the journal was difficult, and a tone of desolation both to the natural world and to human populations predominated in these entries.

Other diarists recorded similar feelings of shock and devastation as responses to destruction in nature but appeared to use their written accounts to ameliorate the potential consequences of these events. Gabriel Breunot, a Catholic counsellor at the *Parlement* of Dijon, who created a journal of "the most remarkable things at the Parlement of Dijon from 25 June 1575," nonetheless found room in his account for destructive environmental events he became aware of via pamphlet literature and letters.[31] In June of 1593 he noted that "near Soissons and the town of Reims there was hail of such excessive size that there were found stones of a weight of 35 pounds, monstrous and prodigious things, with this, there was lightning that burned many houses, fruit entirely lost, and more than 1,200 people killed."[32] As did many others of his faith, these were interpreted as signs of God's anger wrought on the natural world. Breunot did not number among the local populace who were this disaster's immediate victims. Thus, he did not record the words and deeds of local survivors as responses to the event. However, he too felt the impact of the devastating implications of this event, and responded personally, writing a supplication for divine assistance explicitly into his diary. He concluded this entry with an impassioned plea: "May God take pity upon us!"[33] Breunot's textual response aimed to engage actively with what he perceived as the meaning of such destructive events. It was a resolution independent of that of the local victims, but reflected his own identification as a victim, numbering among the human populations subject to God's anger.

How different authors chose to narrate their immediate responses to catastrophic natural events of which they were victims, auditors, and readers, reflected their different spiritual and intellectual communities. Their texts functioned variously as survivor and reader records of shock, resilience, and attestation, and as affirmative accounts of community and faith. These diaries were actively managing disaster observed in nature and explaining its meaning for their own lives and the world around them.

Philosophical Reflections on Natural World Destruction

The philosophical essays of Michel de Montaigne offer a striking counterpoint to the responses of diarists in the immediate aftermath of catastrophic events in the natural world. Across a range of essays that reflected his attraction to Stoic philosophy, Montaigne articulated a relationship between humanity and the natural world that involved a critique of contemporary explanations for the meaning of devastating events frequently found in contemporary journals.

Observing the extraordinarily destructive movements of the Dordogne River over his lifetime, Montaigne reflected

> that in twenty years it has gained so much, and undermined the foundations of so many houses, I perceive it to be an extraordinary agitation. [. . .] In Medoc, by the seashore, the Sieur d'Arsac, my brother, sees an estate he had there, buried under the sands which the sea vomits before it: where the tops of some houses are yet to be seen, and where his rents and domains are converted into pitiful barren pasturage. The inhabitants of this place affirm, that of late years the sea has driven so vehemently upon them, that they have lost above four leagues of land.[34]

Montaigne recognized that these movements of river and ocean courses were profoundly economically and socially destructive to the human communities who inhabited the region. Montaigne's compelling language of a violent natural world in "agitation," "driven so vehemently" to "vomit" sand and to create "pitiful" wastelands unfit to support human life implicitly highlights how these events were devastating, life-changing experiences for these populations.

In contrast to the responses of many contemporaries, Montaigne claimed no special relationship between ruinous damage in the natural world and its meanings and consequences for humans. Indeed, Montaigne explicitly critiqued the possibility of divine emotional responses expressed in adverse weather phenomena:

> When the vines of my village are nipped with the frost, my parish priest presently concludes, that the indignation of God has gone out against all the human race, and that the cannibals have already got the pip. Who is it that, seeing the havoc of these civil wars of ours, does not cry out, that the machine of the world is near dissolution, and that the day of judgment is at hand; without considering, that many worse things have been seen, and that in the meantime, people are very merry in a thousand other parts of the earth for all this? [. . .] To him who feels the hailstones patter about his ears, the whole hemisphere appears to be in storm and tempest.[35]

Montaigne argued that humility alone should cause humans not to assume such importance or interpretive capacity. He maintained a powerful and detailed interrogation of the relationship between humans and nonhuman entities, in which he again emphasized humanity's relative insignificance: "Reason has instructed me, that thus resolutely to condemn anything for false and impossible, is arrogantly and impiously to circumscribe and limit the will of God, and the power of our mother nature, within the bounds of my own capacity."[36] To argue thus was a position of humility, one that read catastrophic acts as signs simply of nature's superfluity and diversity.[37] This was not the modern concept of disavowal as a response to eco-trauma.[38] For Montaigne, practiced emotional control, such as humility and detachment, was an active intellectual process, one that his essays helped to perform. Through his works Montaigne developed a complex philosophical response to natural world destruction and its human consequences. For Montaigne, recognition of humans' subordinate place in the hierarchy of their environment, a neo-stoic philosophical stance, and faith in nature's capacity for renewal appeared to provide him a measure of detachment that enabled him to persist and to resist more debilitating feelings.

Poetic Voicing of Devastated Nature

For another contemporary, though, it was precisely human action that was the causative agent disturbing God's plan for the natural world and bringing catastrophe to it. The court poet Jean-Antoine de Baïf produced a rhetorically powerful lament on waterway pollution in the Bièvre River that flowed in and through Paris during the sixteenth century. His work voiced the desolation and devastation of a river in crisis, as well as its hopes and desires, in a deliberately emotionally charged performance of rhetorical and classical conventions.[39]

"La Ninfe Bievre" (The Nymph Bièvre), first published in Baïf's collected works of 1573, addressed the doleful consequences for the river, a tributary to the Seine, as a result of industrial pollutants from nearby tapestry workshops. In this work, Baïf spoke as the voice of the water nymph, Bièvre. Baïf articulated the pollution as a form of rape, expressing the nymph's emotional devastation, shame, and dishonor at this catastrophic violation. Adopting contemporary assumptions of feminine modesty, Baïf's nymph lamented:

> Today I flow wretched,
> For the inhuman dyers
> Who make from the water of my bank
> A wash in their tubs
> Of woads and pastels mixed together,
> That afterwards vomit into my breast
> And shame me with their chemicals.[40]

Modern research identifies how sexual violence, as well as other forms of trauma, can result in shame as a multifaceted and debilitating experience with humiliation, loss of self-worth, and isolation.[41] Baïf's Bièvre reflects many of the same destructive emotional consequences from her catastrophic interaction with human industry. The nymph dolefully voices her desire for isolation in fears of rejection from the (male) Seine, into which the Bièvre River flowed as it made its way through Paris: "I fear offending you, ashamed / To mix my water in your course [. . .] / Wretched as I am."[42] Baïf articulates how the nymph perceives these ruinous human acts as catastrophic; indeed, this destruction has resulted in her effective death. He speaks to the destruction of her sense of self in the loss of her name, her identity, and her purpose as a water resource:

I no longer carry my name
That these Gobelins took from me
My shame I hide poverty
And my name, I no longer regret
For they have stolen my beauty.[43]

Baïf voices the devastating, incapacitating consequences of female shame wrought through destruction perceived as a form of sexual violence.

Noticeably, Baïf identifies the cause of this profound damage as entirely of human origin, in contemporary social and economic changes that were reconstituting relationships between classes, and the environs in which they lived. Baïf's nymph can identify the specific factory at fault: these were "poisons of your Gobelins," the upwardly mobile family dynasty of dyers whose workshops were on the banks of the Bièvre in the Faubourg Saint-Michel on the outskirts of Paris.[44] This identification of the human destruction that was at the heart of the river's despoliation is crucial to the poem's function as witness. Baïf's poetic response would seem to parallel a mode of response described as witnessing in modern trauma literature. Literary scholar E. Ann Kaplan has distinguished between modes of response to modern traumatic events that extend from overaroused emotions, such as shock, to a fleeting empathy for individual victims, through to witnessing, an act that entails an ethical and deliberate engagement that attempts to understand (and desires to amend) the broader context for the destructive event.[45] Baïf's poem is intended to achieve retribution and bring redress to the damage wrought. Thus, Bièvre pointedly condemns her attackers with vehemence:

May evil befall my enemies!
Who in wicked greed
Spoiling my clear running water
Place me thus in dishonor.[46]

Moreover Baïf sets the river's destruction in the wider context of the social and economic aspirations of his time, as the nymph cries out at "the shame of your wicked century."[47]

Baïf not only seeks to understand the causes for this act of natural world destruction, but also to serve as a catalyst for change. Catastrophe, as Baïf voices it here, is thus both devastating and potentially a productive turning point for the river. His articulation of this shocking act of feminine violation through the resulting feelings of shame for "the plaintive Nymph" is designed to move the poem's male readers to action.[48] Additionally, Baïf positions natural world destruction as moral injury and as sexual violence to an innocent female victim whose honor was understood by contemporaries to be the responsibility of elite men to protect and, failing that, to redress. After all, female sexual honor was, in the eyes of male contemporaries, a matter between men. Bièvre's highly charged emotive responses to her destruction aimed to motivate men to action:

Hear from a tearful Nymph
An unhappy and lamentable song [. . .]
Touched by this sorrow
Come embrace my vengeance.[49]

Bièvre's lack of agency translates in Baïf's work to a form of readerly and writerly agency. He calls upon his fellow poets to save her, including Pierre de Ronsard, Jean Dorat, Philippe Desportes, and Remy Belleau.[50] In their poetry Bièvre will live again:

May your band encourage each other
Against them with a just fury
As much that they resent their own faults
And, so well touched, repent
As that they will give me back my free course [. . .]
As they have shamed me so dirtily
[May they] be shamed with your help.[51]

The river's champions and saviors will be the courtly poets who can most skillfully and eloquently express its sorrows and resentments while manipulating the feelings of the reading public to fury and action.

A man speaking as a female entity expressed the shame of sexual violence in a way that was relatively radical for its time. Survivor accounts of sexual violence were rare, even in a century of widespread war.[52] War chronicles typically recounted distressing acts involving women (and only women) who had died, not those of women who survived to be integrated into faith communities in the aftermath.[53] Even in a modern context researchers find that victims are more likely to conceal sexual violence in settings where there is a high perception of shame surrounding the assault.[54] Indeed, Baïf productively employed his century's notions of female sexual dishonor to achieve his aims of social activism for the work.

Classical myths and poetic forms clearly frame important foundations for his work but there were also real-world contexts and events. Through the emotions of shame, honor, and revenge, Baïf conceptualized poetry as a moral force for natural world protection. His Bièvre is a vulnerable victim of male force, a rape survivor who demands that men restore her honor and her purpose. This was an emotionally—and morally—charged work for its specifically named male readership. In this poem, agency exists for the elite men who will speak for the Bièvre as a victim in order to protect and restore nature in crisis. Baïf charges his (male) readers with a moral responsibility to act.

Empathetic Witnessing of Nature in Crises

Just as Baïf had voiced the lament of the survivors of a catastrophic natural world event, so too did a natural philosopher whose work likewise stood as witness to nature in crises and whose victims could not be heard by other contemporaries. This nature too was a victim of human destruction that had wreaked devastation not only on its direct victims but also on the humans who heard its pain. Bernard Palissy, a self-taught Protestant natural philosopher, produced a series of texts in which he sought to reveal his understanding of God's mastery of nature, as it had been revealed to him by close contemplation of both the natural world and of God.[55] His observation and experimentation with nature reflected contemporary practices of natural philosophers but was conducted as an explicitly spiritual act. His works argued that his deeply personal engagement with the natural world enabled him to hear the feelings of nature perhaps nowhere more clearly than in the moments of unbearable pain of its desolation.

For those spiritually disposed to hear and see it, as Palissy claimed he was, the natural world was an expressive source. Grapevines that wrapped their leaves around budding fruit were "careful to protect their fruit, like a woman her infant."[56] Trees were social beings, responding to their arboreal community to prioritize their own interests: "Trees at the edge of the forest throw themselves out or incline themselves towards the edge of the islands, as if the other trees were their enemies."[57] Fruiting plants deserved human sympathy for their efforts, for, Palissy wrote, "nothing in nature produces its fruit without great effort, indeed, and pain."[58] Palissy's contemplation of nature, God's work, required not only recognition and interpretation of the feelings of nature but also a capacity to feel with the natural world, as an empathetic practice that brought him closer to the divine.

However, Palissy wrote of his style of empathetic contemplation of nature almost as a burden. He was, perhaps uniquely, capable of feeling the suffering and cries of pain of the natural world as it was destroyed, particularly due to human hands. Palissy reserved special criticism for the work of inexpert woodcutters who were uneducated by his terms and whose actions irreparably damaged trees: "I have seen the woodcutters here, cutting their coppice, leaving the stock or trunk that remains in the ground all hacked, wrecked and broken apart, not caring about the trunk. [. . .] I am amazed that the wood does not cry at being so villainously mauled. Do you think that the trunk that has be thus hacked and ripped out in various places does not feel the division and exaction that is done to it?"[59]

He envisaged the anger of nature, expressing his surprise "that the earth and the things produced in it do not demand vengeance against these ignorant and ungrateful maulers who do nothing other than destroy and dissipate the trees and plants daily, without any consideration."[60] Moreover it was a pain that he also experienced in empathy with nature: "The abuses that they commit every day to trees forces me to speak thus with passion."[61] Palissy's instructional text even has its interlocutor remark upon Palissy's unusual response: "You seem to take great pity on them; you say that the laborers murder them." Palissy's texts attest to a destruction whose victims were barely audible to most of his contemporaries, but whose destruction he had become deeply unsettled by himself through listening to and encountering nature.

Palissy's suffering from the desolation of the natural world was also the result of his perception that the human activity causing it represented a crime against God's natural system. He was not against productive interactions with nature if these respected his perception of divine creation and God's plan. To work the land ethically, laborers "must have some Philosophy, or otherwise they simply abort the earth and murder the trees."[62] This plan was dynamic but also acknowledged purposeful systems that human activity should not disrupt: "God did not create these things to leave them idle, thus each does its duty, according to the command given to it from God. The Stars and Planets are not idle, the sea travels from one side and the other, and is working to produce profitable things, the land is similarly never idle: what is consumed naturally in it is renewed and re-formed again, if not in one way, then in another."[63]

In the modern context, Robert Jay Lifton describes those who listen and converse with trauma survivors in their research as "survivors by proxy."[64] While Palissy's position appears similar in some respects to Lifton's concept, the nature of his suffering was not only that of an empathetic experience responding to the cries of natural world victims. For Palissy there was a two-fold suffering from his witnessing of nature in crisis: that of encountering the nonhuman beings who were its direct victims and that of his realization of humans' rejection of what he understood as God's path for them.

Like Montaigne, Palissy marveled at the diversity and fluidity of the framework of a natural world that God had set to "work, to engender, produce, come and go."[65] But his form of natural philosophy drove him to bear witness in his texts to the suffering of nonhuman victims and to feel their pain. This was coupled with his own sense of devastation and desolation at the misdirected actions of humans to destroy, rather than work with, God's beautiful design for nature.

Conclusions

Nature in crises could be both devastated and devastating. There is no question that destruction in nature could produce catastrophic consequences; that is, turning points for human populations that profoundly changed lives in their aftermath. However, the crises to which sixteenth-century texts attest were described within a range of conceptual frameworks that informed interpretation and guided responses ranging from the debilitating to the affirmative. Specific genres determined the expression of feelings generated by such events, including shame, profound sorrow, fear, or reassurance, as well as the contemporary practices for recovery these events elicited, practices such as acts of spiritual communion, of bearing witness to moral crimes, and of motivating action in others. They also governed whether such articulations were produced in the immediate aftermath of destruction, in the case of diaries, or were the result of longer-term reflections, such as essays, poetry, and agricultural texts. Faith positions, professional experiences, and a range of identity markers also shaped how individuals responded to these events and made sense of it for their future lives, for themselves and for their reading communities.

NOTES

This chapter has benefited from financial support of the Australian Research Council Centre of Excellence for the History of Emotions (CE110001011). I thank the editors and anonymous reviewers for their insights and advice.

1. Alix Cooper, "Environment and the Natural World," in *Oxford Bibliographies Online (OBO): Renaissance and Reformation*, ed. Margaret King (New York: Oxford University Press, 2014), DOI: 10.1093/OBO/9780195399301-0187; Randall Martin, *Shakespeare and Ecology* (Oxford, UK: Oxford University Press, 2015); Daniel Finch-Race and Stephanie Posthumus, eds., *French Ecocriticism: From the Early Modern Period to the Twenty-First Century* (Frankfurt: Peter Lang, 2017).
2. Timothy Morton, *Ecology without Nature: Rethinking Environmental Aesthetics* (Cambridge: Harvard University Press, 2007).
3. See, for example, Steve Mentz, "After Sustainability," *PMLA* 127, no. 3 (2012): 586–92; Craig Dionne, *Posthuman Lear: Reading Shakespeare in the Anthropocene* (London: Punctum, 2016).
4. Christian Pfister, Rudolf Brázdil, and Rüdiger Glaser, eds., *Climatic Variability in Sixteenth-Century Europe and Its Social Dimension* (Dordrecht: Kluwer, 1999); John

F. Richards, *The Unending Frontier: An Environmental History of the Early Modern World* (Berkeley: University of California Press, 2003); Wolfgang Behringer, *A Cultural History of Climate, trans. Patrick Camiller* (Cambridge, UK: Polity, 2010); Martin Knoll and Reinhold Reith, eds., *An Environmental History of the Early Modern Period: Experiments and Perspectives* (Münster: LIT Verlag, 2014). An excellent study in a different analytical mode is Peter C. Mancall, *Nature and Culture in the Early Modern Atlantic* (Philadelphia: University of Pennsylvania Press, 2018).

5. As Gwilym Jones has recently argued, continuing a push (in more nuanced terms) outlined by Keith Thomas, *Man and the Natural World: Changing Attitudes in England 1500–1800* (London: Allen Lane, 1983). See Gwilym Jones, "Environmental Renaissance Studies," *Literature Compass* 14, no. 10 (2017): e12407.
6. Vincent Nardizzi, *Wooden Os: Shakespeare's Theatres and England's Trees* (Toronto: University of Toronto Press, 2013); Jennifer Munroe and Edward J. Geisweidt, eds., *Ecological Approaches to Early Modern English Texts: A Field Guide to Reading and Teaching* (Farnham, UK: Ashgate, 2015); Martin, *Shakespeare and Ecology*; Finch-Race and Posthumus, eds., *French Ecocriticism*; Todd Borlik, ed., *Literature and Nature in the English Renaissance: An Ecocritical Anthology* (Cambridge, UK: Cambridge University Press, 2019).
7. Recent examples of this literature include Michael G. Madianos and Koukia Evi, "Trauma and Natural Disaster: The Case of Earthquakes in Greece," *Journal of Loss and Trauma* 15, no. 2 (2012): 138–50; Lauren Smith et al., "Coping with Vicarious Trauma in the Aftermath of a Natural Disaster," *Journal of Multicultural Counseling and Development* 42, no. 1 (2014): 2–12; Nancy P. Chin and Marta Talpelli, "'You Always Have to Struggle, So You Don't Have to Struggle': Community Trauma Recovery After a Landslide," *Journal of Loss and Trauma* 20, no. 2 (2015): 306–16; Damodar Suar et al., "Exposure, Resource Loss, and Posttsunami Trauma," *Journal of Loss and Trauma* 21, no. 5 (2016): 421–32; Leslie Dryud Furman et al., "Reflections on Collective Trauma, Faith, and Service Delivery to Victims of Terrorism and Natural Disaster: Insights from Six National Studies," *Social Work and Christianity* 43, no. 2 (2016): 74–94; Yaira Hamama-Raz et al., "Typhoon Survivors' Subjective Wellbeing—A Different View of Responses to Natural Disaster," *PloS ONE* 12, no. 9 (September 6, 2017): 1–11; Ma Jenna N. Nalipay, Allan B. I. Bernardo, and Imelu G. Mordeno, "Posttraumatic Growth in Survivors of a Natural Disaster: The Role of Social Axioms of Religiosity, Reward for Application, and Social Cynicism," *Journal of Positive Psychology* 12, no. 4 (2017): 342–53; Jean Ivey, "Hurricane Harvey: Trauma vs. Resiliency," *Pediatric Nursing* 43, no. 6 (2017): 265–74; Kim M. Anderson, "Posttraumatic Growth and Resilience despite Experiencing Trauma and Oppression," *Journal of Family Social Work* 21, no. 1 (2018): 1–4.
8. Anil Narine, ed., *Eco-Trauma Cinema* (London: Routledge, 2014).

9. Glenn Albrecht, "Solastalgia: A New Concept in Human Health and Identity," *Philosophy, Activism Nature* 3 (2005): 41–55.
10. Ruth Leys, *Trauma: A Genealogy* (Chicago: Chicago University Press, 2000), 7–8; Wulf Kansteiner, "Genealogy of a Category Mistake: A Critical Intellectual History of the Cultural Trauma Metaphor," *Rethinking History* 8 (2004): 193–221, esp. 194.
11. Kansteiner, "Genealogy of a Category Mistake."
12. Dominick LaCapra, *Writing History, Writing Trauma* (Baltimore: Johns Hopkins University Press, 2000); E. Ann Kaplan, "Global Trauma and Public Feelings: Viewing Images of Catastrophe," *Consumption, Markets, and Culture* 11, no. 1 (2008): 3–24.
13. Kansteiner, "Genealogy of a Category Mistake," 194.
14. Allan Young, *The Harmony of Illusions: Inventing Post-Traumatic Stress Disorder* (Princeton: Princeton University Press, 1997); Kansteiner, "Genealogy of a Category Mistake," 212–13.
15. Jean Céard, *La Nature et les prodiges* (Geneva: Droz, 1996; originally published in 1977); Lorraine Daston and Katherine Park, *Wonders and the Order of Nature, 1150–1750* (New York: Zone, 1998); Elaine Fulton and Penny Roberts, "The Wrath of God: Explanation of Crises and Natural Disaster in Pre-modern Europe," in *History at the End of the World? History, Climate Change and the Possibility of Closure*, ed. Penny Roberts with Mark Levene and Rob Johnson, 67–79 (Penrith, UK: Humanities-Ebooks, 2010); Alexandra Walsham, *The Reformation of the Landscape: Religion, Identity, and Memory in Early Modern Britain and Ireland* (New York: Oxford University Press, 2011); Susan Broomhall, "Disorder in the Natural World: The Perspective of a Sixteenth-century Provincial Convent," in *Religion, the Supernatural and Visual Culture in Early Modern Europe*, ed. Jenny Spinks and Dagmar Eichberger, 240–59 (Leiden: Brill, 2015); Jenny Spinks and Charles Zika, eds., *Disaster, Death and the Emotions, 1400–1700* (Basingstoke, UK: Palgrave Macmillan, 2016).
16. Susan Broomhall, ed., *Early Modern Emotions: An Introduction* (London: Routledge, 2016).
17. Susan Broomhall, "Narrating Experiences and Emotions of Distressing Events in the French Wars of Religion," and Andreas Bähr, "Remembering Fear: The Fear of Violence and the Violence of Fear in Seventeenth-Century War Memories," in *Memory before Modernity: Practices of Memory in Early Modern Europe*, ed. Erika Kuijpers et al., 253–67 and 269–82 (Leiden: Brill, 2013); Sarah Covington, "'Broken Verses across a Bloodied Land': Violence and the Limits of Language in the English Civil War," in *Aspects of Violence in Early Modern Europe*, ed. Jonathan Davies, 127–49 (Farnham, UK: Ashgate, 2013); Susan Broomhall, "Reasons and Identities to Remember: Composing Personal Accounts of Religious Violence in Sixteenth-Century France," *French History* 27 (2013): 1–20; Erika Kuijpers and Cornelius van der Haven, eds.,

Battlefield Emotions 1500–1800: Practices, Experience, Imagination (Basingstoke, UK: Palgrave Macmillan, 2016).

18. Erin Felicia Labbie and Allie Terry-Fritsch, "Introduction: Beholding Violence," in *Beholding Violence in Medieval and Early Modern Europe*, 1–14 (Farnham, UK: Ashgate, 2012), esp. 2.
19. Susan Broomhall and Sarah Finn, eds., *Violence and Emotions in Early Modern Europe* (London: Routledge, 2015); Spinks and Zika, *Disaster, Death and the Emotions.*
20. Erika Kuijpers, "The Creation and Development of Social Memories of Traumatic Events: The Oudewater Massacre of 1575," in *Hurting Memories: Remembering as a Pathogenic Process in Individuals and Societies*, eds. Michael Linden and Kryzsztof Ruthowski, 191–201 (London: Elsevier, 2013); Kuijpers et al., *Memory before Modernity*; Judith Pollmann, "Remembering Violence: Trauma, Atrocities, and Cosmopolitan Memories," in *Memory in Early Modern Europe, 1500–1800*, 159–85 (Oxford, UK: Oxford University Press, 2017); Erika Kuijpers and Judith Pollmann, "Turning Sacrilege into Victory: Catholic Memories of Iconoclasm, 1566–1700," in *Rhythms of Revolt: European Traditions and Memories of Social Conflict in Oral Culture*, ed. Éva Guillorel, David Hopkin, and William G. Pooley, 155–70 (London: Routledge, 2018).
21. Erika Kuijpers, "Expressions of Fear, Counting the Loss: Managing Emotions in War Chronicles in the Netherlands (1568–1648)," in Spinks and Zika, *Disaster, Death and the Emotions*, 93–111, esp. 105–6.
22. Cathy Caruth, *Unclaimed Experience: Trauma, Narrative, and History* (Baltimore: Johns Hopkins University Press, 1996), 7.
23. See the contributions in the section "The Non-Human World," in Broomhall, ed., *Early Modern Emotions*, 327–54.
24. Centre National de Ressources Textuelles et Lexicales, "Ortolang," http://www.cnrtl.fr/etymologie/Catastrophe, accessed March 15, 2018.
25. "Le 20, il a gelé, neigé et faict un temps aussi froid qu'à Noël, qui montre que Dieu est fort courroucé; les vignes commençoient à pousser fort, et tous les biens et fruits de la terre estoient au plus tendre, qui faict fort craindre que tout ne soit perdu," Joseph Garnier, ed., "Livre de Souvenance de Pepin, Chanoine de la Sainte-Chappele de Cette Ville [Dijon]," *Analecta Divionensia* 1, no. 2 (1864): 12.
26. "Le 13 février, il a faict fort froid le matin avec grand vent toute la nuict, et le jour a fort neigé, de sorte que par tous les greniers de Sainct-Fiacre y avoit de quatre grands doigts de neige par-dessus les monceaux de bled et avoine. [. . .] Le jour de la Purification, recommença la gelée et la froidure qui n'a cessé jusqu'qu 3 de mars, et a tous les jours gelé si impétueusement [. . .] mais le bon Dieu a tout bien gardé les biens de la terre qui n'ont esté gastés, et le 2 de mars on fit une belle procession générale," Garnier, 6.

27. "Il n'estoit memoire d'avoir vu, ne ouyr dire, ne avoir trouvé par escript telle perdicion des grains semez en terre comme il a esté ceste année, car en tout le royaulme la fortune fut [*sic*] qui espouventoit fort le peuple," Fernand Bournon, ed., "Chronique Parisienne de Pierre Driart," *Mémoires de la Société de l'Histoire de Paris et de l'Ile-de-France* 22 (1895): 85.
28. "La disposicion de ce present mois a esté la plus merveilleuse que oncques vivant n'avoit veu auparavant, car il pleust tous les jours, reservé le penultiesme jour, et en grande habondance," Bournon, 126.
29. "Seroit long à racompter tous les domaiges qu'ilz firent en plusieurs lieux," Bournon, 127.
30. "Il n'y avoit homme vivant qu'il dist l'avoir veu," Bournon, 133.
31. "Journal de ce qui s'est fait de plus remarquable au Parlement de Dijon depuis le 25 juin 1575 jusqu'à la fin de 1578," Joseph Garnier, ed., "Journal de Gabriel Breunot, Conseiller au Parlement de Dijon," *Analecta Divionensia* 1, no. 2 (1864): 165.
32. "Près de Soissons et la ville de Reims il est tombé de la gresle de si excessive grosseur, qu'il s'en est treuvé de la pesanteur de 35 livres, chose monstrueuse et prodigieuse; avec ce du feu du ciel est tombé qui a bruslé beaucoup de maisons, les fruicts entièrement perdus et plus de 1,200 personnes tuées," Garnier, 328.
33. "Dieu veuille avoir pitié de nous!" Garnier, 328.
34. Charles Cotton, trans., *The Essays of Montaigne (1686)*, ed. William Carew Hazlitt, 1877, Wikisource, https://en.wikisource.org/wiki/The_Essays_of_Montaigne/Book_I/Chapter_XXX.
35. Cotton, https://en.wikisource.org/wiki/The_Essays_of_Montaigne/Book_I/Chapter_XXV.
36. Cotton, https://en.wikisource.org/wiki/The_Essays_of_Montaigne/Book_I/Chapter_XXVI.
37. Michel Jeanneret, ed., *Perpetuum Mobile: Métamorphoses des Corps et des Oeuvres, de Vinci à Montaigne* (Paris: Macula, 1997).
38. See Narine, *Eco-Trauma Cinema*, 5.
39. Elizabeth Vinestock, "Myth and Environmentalism in a Renaissance Poem: Jean-Antoine de Baïf's *La ninfe Bievre*," *New Comparison* 27–28 (1999): 22–33; Louisa Mackenzie, "The Poet and the Environment: Naturalizing Conservative Nostalgia," in *The Poetry of Place: Lyric, Landscape, and Ideology in Renaissance France*, 121–45 (Toronto: University of Toronto Press, 2011).
40. "Aujourdhuy je me traine vile / Pour des teinturiers inhumains / Qui font de l'eau de mon ravage / Dans leurs chaudieres un lavage / De guesde & pastel meslangé: / Qu'apres dans mon sein revomissent / Et de leurs drogues me honnissent," Jean-Antonie de Baïf, *Euvres en Rime de Ian Antoine de Baif* (Paris: Lucas Breyer, 1573), 258r-v.

41. In the modern context, see G. B. Rahm, B. Renck, and K. C. Ringsberg, "Disgust, Disgust beyond Description: Shame Cues to Detect Shame in Disguise, in Interviews with Women who were Sexually Abused during Childhood," *Journal of Psychiatric and Mental Health Nursing* 13 (2006): 100–109; John P. Wilson, Boris Drozdek, and Silvana Turkovic, "Post-traumatic Shame and Guilt," *Trauma Violence and Abuse* 7, no. 2 (2006): 122–41; Terry F. Taylor, "The Influence of Shame on Posttrauma Disorders: Have We Failed to See the Obvious?" *European Journal of Psychotraumatology* 6, no. 1 (2015), doi:10.3402/ejpt.v6.28847.
42. "Tant de crein t'ofenser, honteuse / De mesler mon eau dans ton cours [. . .] Ainsi vilaine de je suis," Baïf, *Euvres en Rime*, 259r.
43. "Mon nom desia plus je ne porte, / que ces Gobelins m'ont osté. / Ma honte je cache pauvreté / Et mon nom, plus je ne regrete, / Puis qu'ils m'ont tolu ma beauté," Baïf, 259v.
44. "Des poisons de vos Gobelins," Baïf, 258v.
45. Kaplan, "Global Trauma," 20–21.
46. "Que mal viene à mes ennemis! / Qui par avarice méchante / Me gastans mon eau clair-coulante, / En deshoneur m'ont ainsi mis," Baïf, *Euvres en Rime*, 258v–259r.
47. "La honte / De vostre siecle tresmechant," Baïf, 258r.
48. "La Ninfe plaintive," Baïf, 258v.
49. "Race des hommes deploree, / Oiez d'une Ninfe éploree / Un grief & lamentable chant [. . .] Touchez de cette doleance / Venez embrasser ma vengeance," Baïf, 259r.
50. Baïf, 260r.
51. "Que vostre bande s'encourage / Contre eux d'une juste fureur. / Tant qu'ou leur fautes ils resentment, /Et si bien ateins se repentent, / Qu'ils me rendrent mon libre cours [. . .] Comme ils m'ont salement honnie, / Soyent honnie par vostre secours," Baïf, 260r.
52. Penny Roberts, "Peace, Ritual and Sexual Violence," in *Ritual and Violence: Natalie Zemon Davis and Early Modern France*, ed. Graeme Murdock, Penny Roberts, and Andrew Spicer, 75–99 (Oxford, UK: Oxford University Press, 2012).
53. Broomhall, "Reasons and Identities to Remember," section 5.
54. K. G. Weiss, "Too Ashamed to Report: Deconstructing the Shame of Sexual Victimization," *Feminist Criminology* 5, no. 3 (2010): 286–310; Maria Elena Vidal and Jenny Petrak, "Shame and Adult Sexual Assault: A Study with a Group of Female Survivors Recruited from an East London Population," *Sexual and Relationship Therapy* 22, no. 2 (2007): 159–71.
55. See Susan Broomhall, "Feeling Divine Nature: Natural History, Emotions and Bernard Palissy's Knowledge Practice," in *Natural History in Early Modern France: The Poetics of an Epistemic Genre*, ed. Raphaële Garrod and Paul J. Smith, 46–69 (Leiden: Brill "Intersections," 2018).

56. "Songneux de garder leurs fruits, comme la femme son petit enfant," Bernard Palissy, "Recepte Véritable," in *Oeuvres Complètes*, ed. Keith Cameron et al., (Paris: Champion, 2010), 190.
57. "Les arbres de la circonference de la forest se jettoyent & courboyent ou s'enclinoyent devers le costé des terres, comme si les autres arbres leur estoyent ennemis," Palissy, "Discours Admirables, de la Nature des Eaux et Fonteines," in *Oeuvres Complètes*, 527.
58. "Nulle nature ne produit son fruit sans extreme travail, voire et douleur," Palissy, "Recepte Veritable," 126.
59. "Veu que les buscherons de ce pays, en couppant leurs taillis, laissoyent la seppe ou tronc qui demeuroit en terre tout fendu, brisé, et esclatté, ne se soucians du tronc." . . . "Je m'esmerveille que le bois ne crie d'estre ainsi vilainement meurtri. Penses-tu que la seppe qui est ainsi fendue et esclattee en plusieurs lieux, qu'elle ne se ressente de la fraction, et extorsion qui luy aura esté faicte?" Palissy, 121–22.
60. "Que la terre et les natures produites en icelle ne crient vengeance contre certains meurtrisseurs, ignorans, et ingrats, qui, journellement ne font que gaster et dissiper les arbres et plantes, sans aucune consideration," Palissy, 109.
61. "Les abus qu'ils commettent tous les jours és arbres, me contraignent en parler ainsi d'affection," Palissy, 121–22.
62. "Il est requis, que les laboureurs ayent quelque Philosophie: ou autrement, ils ne font qu'avorter la terre, et meutrir les arbres," Palissy, 121.
63. "Dieu ne crea pas ces choses pour les laisser oisifves, ains chacune fait son devoir, selon le commandement qui luy est donné de Dieu. Les Astres et Planetes ne sont pas oisifves, la mer se pourmeine d'un costé et d'autre, et se travaille à produire choses profitables, la terre semblablement n'est jamais oisifve: ce qui se consomme naturellement en elle, elle le renouvelle, et le reforme derechef, si ce n'est en une sorte, elle le refait en une autre," Palissy, 132.
64. Robert Jay Lifton and Cathy Caruth, "Giving Death Its Due: An Interview with Robert Jay Lifton," in *Listening to Trauma: Conversations*, ed. Cathy Caruth 3–24 (Baltimore: Johns Hopkins University Press, 2014), esp. 18.
65. "Travailler à engendrer, produire, aller & venir," Palissy, "Discours Admirables," 289.

2

Historicizing Rape Trauma

Identification with the Aggressor in Early Modern Humoralism and *The Rape of Lucrece* (1594)

ZACKARIAH LONG

While the representation of rape has been a preoccupation of early modern literary and cultural studies for many years, the study of early modern rape trauma is a relatively recent phenomenon.[1] What is the difference between these two endeavors? On the simplest level rape is an act of aggression, whereas rape trauma is a psychological consequence of this act, and an interest in the former does not necessitate an interest in the latter. Indeed, as Diane Wolfthal points out, the history of criticism is replete with examples of scholars who have wittingly or unwittingly glorified aesthetic representations of sexual violence without considering their consequences, whether real or fictional.[2] The first thing an examination of early modern rape trauma implies, then, is an acknowledgment of the devastations of rape. At the same time, it must be acknowledged that an analysis of the effects of sexual violence does not an examination of rape trauma make. Since the late nineteenth century, "trauma" has referred to a profound disruption of the mind's ordinary mechanisms of defense, qualitatively different from even extreme states of distress.[3] Moreover experts on sexual violence have characterized rape trauma syndrome as a distinctive species of traumatic experience, similar to but also different from other kinds of posttraumatic stress.[4] An examination of early modern rape trauma therefore requires something more than sensitivity to rape-induced suffering; it requires attention to the ways that rape may disorganize one's ability to process and make sense of the world.

In this chapter I would like to contribute to our evolving understanding of early modern rape trauma by investigating the prehistory of a concept from modern trauma theory with roots in early modern humoralism as well as the literature of rape: "identification with the aggressor." First articulated by Sándor Ferenczi in 1932, identification with the aggressor is a defense mechanism whereby a victim of sexual assault responds not by lashing out against their attacker, but instead by internalizing the attacker's feelings of guilt and aggression, blaming themselves.[5] This is obviously a counterintuitive response, since under normal circumstances the mind's first reaction to external violence is resistance. However, Ferenczi notes that if an assault is sudden or overwhelming, then the mind may become paralyzed, leading to the splitting of consciousness and the dissolution of the ego; and in such a state of extreme vulnerability, the victim is contaminated not only by the aggressor's violent impulses but also by his guilt and self-loathing.[6] In the wake of such emotional invasion, the victim-survivor is naturally confused and yearns for catharsis. However, precisely because their ability to resist the aggressor has been shut down, this pent-up frustration must vent itself elsewhere, most tragically onto themselves—hence, the common impulse among victims of sexual abuse toward self-harm.

Of course early moderns did not speak of "identification with the aggressor" when discussing the perturbations of the mind. In a strict sense, then, there is no early modern equivalent to Ferenczian trauma theory. On the other hand, early modern writers on the soul and body did recognize a number of the phenomena that Ferenczi identifies and even discussed some of them under the same headings. In part 1 of this chapter I will examine just how far such resemblances extend, using Edward Reynolds's *A Treatise of the Passions and Faculties of the Soul of Man* as a case study.[7] My argument will be that although Reynolds did not constellate these ideas into the same patterns as Ferenczi, the potential for such linkages is there, and this fact was not lost on early modern writers. Indeed, as I shall demonstrate in part 2, Shakespeare recognized this potential, weaving a humoral conception of identification with the aggressor into his most profound exploration of the psychology of self-harm, *The Rape of Lucrece (1594)*. Of course as a context for examining *Lucrece*, Reynolds's treatise is admittedly inconvenient, for it was published after Shakespeare's poem. However, more than any other early modern psychological treatise I have identified, Reynolds brings together the materials necessary for a humoral account of identification with the aggressor, giving his text a heuristic advantage for those engaged in the project of historicizing trauma; moreover Reynolds's treatment of these materials is largely uncontroversial, since he hews closely to conventional ideas about the mind and body. Thus, even if Shakespeare would have had to cull these insights from other sources, they are precisely the kinds of insights he could have gleaned from many places. Attending to Shakespeare's innovative use of humoral theory not only illuminates the trauma of *Lucrece*'s titular character but also sheds light on the work's structure and poetics, which center on traumatic identification.

"This 'Softened and Unresisting Material'"

Why identify with the aggressor when the aggressor is the cause of one's suffering? The answer begins with terror. According to Ferenczi terror paralyzes the mind, leaving it vulnerable to the absorption of the aggressor's impulses. There are several factors that contribute to this response. First, rarely is there any warning of an attack, and "if a trauma strikes the soul, or the body, unprepared," then the mind is quickly overwhelmed: "In a moment of intense fright—or an attack of pain—the patient responds by summoning all of his psycho-physical resources in a tremendous effort" and, "for a time, all mental powers remain fully active, [as] all possible effort is made . . . to ward off the attack" (*CD* 69, 105, 6). However, such efforts are exhausting and "should the quality and quantity of suffering exceed the person's powers of comprehension, then one capitulates" (*CD* 170). Slipping into a paralytic state that "includes . . . the inhibition of perception and (with it) of thinking," the victim undergoes a kind of psychic "death," which Ferenczi analogizes to "the feigning of death in animals" (*FC* 240; *CD* 39, 104).

In describing traumatic shock in this way, Ferenczi builds on the insights of Freud, who also defined trauma as "an experience which within a short period of time presents the mind with an increase of stimulus too powerful to be dealt with . . . in the normal way," in addition to identifying "fright and the threat to life" as those experiences most likely to trigger such a response.[8] Indeed, behind many of Ferenczi's ideas lie Freud's ruminations on traumatic neurosis, from his emphasis on "the factor of surprise" to his characterization of trauma itself as a "breach" in the ego's "protective shield" that induces psychic paralysis by drawing resources away from one part of the psyche to another: when "cathectic energy is summoned from all sides to provide sufficiently high cathexes of energy in the environs of the breach . . . all of the other psychical systems are impoverished, so that the remaining [ones] are extensively paralyzed or reduced."[9]

Although Reynolds obviously does not speak of the ego but rather the soul, or about psychic energies but instead the spirits—those gossamer entities responsible for relaying messages between the soul and body—his description of the effects of terror map surprisingly well onto Ferenczi and Freud's accounts. We can see this in Reynolds's description of "*Suddenness of an Evil*" as a cause of fear, "when it seizeth upon (as it were) in the Dark":

> All Unacquaintance, then, and Ignorance of an Approaching Evil must needs work Amazement and Terror, as contrarily a foresight thereof Patience to undergo and Boldness to encounter it. . . . And there is good reason for this, because in a sudden daunt and onset of an unexpected evil, the spirits which were before orderly carried by their several due motions to their natural works are upon this strange appearance and instant Oppression of danger so disordered, mixed, and stifled, that there is no power left either in the Soul for Counsel, or in the Body for Execution: For as it is in the wars of men, so of Passions, those are more terrible which are by way of Invasion than of Battle, which set upon men unarmed and uncomposed, than those which find them prepared for resistance. (282–83)

In both of these modern and early modern accounts, terror is imagined as an assaultive force: a "breach" of the ego's "protective shield," on the one hand, or an "Invasion," on the other. Indeed, if, as Ruth Leys puts it, Freud describes trauma "in quasi-military terms" as an assault on the ego's defenses, then Reynolds makes such terms absolutely explicit, likening the mind's invasion by the irascible passion of fear to a surprise attack in "the wars of men."[10] Moreover both accounts connect terror's debilitating effects not only to the strength and scale of this invasion but to the circumstances within which it occurs and the mind's ability to combat it: we can see the former in both Freud's and Ferenczi's emphasis on the importance of fright, which shows up in Reynolds's description of how "Ignorance of an Approaching Evil must needs work Amazement and Terror," and the latter in Reynolds's comment that fright leaves "no power . . . either in the Soul for Counsel, or in the Body for Execution," which anticipates Freud and Ferenczi's account of traumatic paralysis. Of course, the psychological systems within which these accounts are embedded are profoundly different; however, because they both understand the soul or psyche as a system of limited resources, they observe a similar effect when those resources are overwhelmed. Structurally, then, if not substantively, they mirror each other in tracking the mind's response to terror.

As we consider the next element of identification with the aggressor, these structural parallels continue, although they begin to be marked by more significant substantive differences. According to Ferenczi two things happen in trauma-induced paralysis. First, the psyche's processes become disintegrated, leading to the splitting of the personality: "should the quality and quantity of suffering exceed the person's powers of comprehension, then . . . it is no longer worthwhile to combine these painful things into a unit, and one is split into pieces. . . . The individual components can suffer each by itself" (*CD* 170). Although in his *Clinical Diary* Ferenczi enumerates up to four different personality fragments created by such splits (*CD* 8–10), the prototypical split is into two: "a psychic being of pure knowledge that observes the events from the outside" (*CD* 104), on the one side; and a being that feels "pain without ideational content" (*CD* 30), on the other. Knowledge and affect are thus severed from one another.

The second consequence of terror-induced paralysis is that the mind takes on a special kind of impressionability: "Fear dissolves the rigidity of the ego (resistance) so completely that the material of the ego becomes as though capable of being molded *photochemically* . . . by external stimuli," like a photograph, and which he describes as a regression to an earlier "purely mimetic period" of being subject to external impressions (*CD* 111, 148, italics in original). It is into "this softened and unresisting material" that the aggressor's "alien will, born of hate and lust for attack" (*CD* 77) impresses itself, infusing the victim not only with his aggressive impulses but also his guilt, since most perpetrators of sexual abuse are not sociopaths but are internally divided themselves, made sick by their actions as much as they take pleasure in them. In this way not only are the contradictory feelings of the aggressor, but also his internal division, re-created within the mind of the victim-survivor—an insight that Ferenczi credits to one of his patients, who "arrived at the idea by herself that the total split in her father . . . has created a similar one in her: Dr. Jekyll and Mr. Hyde" (*CD* 193).

To what extent does Reynolds recognize these two consequences of traumatic terror, and how does he explain them? In *A Treatise of the Passions and Faculties*, Reynolds does not describe the neat division of consciousness and affect characteristic of Ferenczian splitting, although he does describe an analogous effect. Detailing how fear fosters "Weakness of the Faculties of the Mind and the Spirits of the Body" (299), Reynolds observes:

> As it is in the Civil State, so it is in the Moral Commonwealth of the Soul, that there are three principal ways to infer weakness: Foreign Incursions, Intestine Tumults, and an Emptying of the Parts, all which are to be seen in an Extremity of Fear. . . . For first there is a Confused and Unserviceable mixture of *Passion* and *Reason*, The *Passion* with too much outrage and assault breaking in and distracting the advices of *Reason*, which is *Foreign Incursion*. . . . Secondly, there is *Tumult* and Disorder amongst the Spirits, which is *Civil Dissension*. Thirdly, there is a Retiring of them to the Principal Castle or Fort, the Heart, whereby the Outward Quarters are left Naked and ungarrisoned, which though it be a strengthening for the better, yet it is a Weakening of the Major Part, and this answereth unto Emptying or Vacuity. By all which, both Reason is made unfit for Counsel (and the Conceits thereof being choked and stifled with a disorderly throng of Spirits and Passions) and the Body likewise is so benumbed, that though our discourse were entire, yet it could not be there seconded with any successful service. (300–301, italics in original)

In this analysis of fear Reynolds deploys the same language of military invasion to describe the workings of fear as he used in his analysis of sudden fright. However, this time he is more precise in characterizing its impact upon consciousness and affect, describing "a Confused and Unserviceable mixture of *Passion* and *Reason*, The *Passion* with too much outrage and assault breaking in and distracting the advices of *Reason*"—which if not identical to a division of consciousness and affect, at least runs parallel to it: after all, if reason is not identical to consciousness, it certainly requires it. So if an invasion of the mind by fear "distract[s] the advices of reason," then by definition it distracts consciousness too. The question is whether there is any analogy between this irascible "distraction" and Ferenczi's splitting of the psyche. The answer is yes, but one must go beyond Reynolds's account of fear to fully uncover it.

In the early chapters of his treatise, before he begins analyzing individual passions, Reynolds discusses "*Distraction*, or Confounding" as one of the "corruptions" of "vicious Concupiscence," processes by which passion attempts to subvert reason to achieve its desires (61, 57). Specifically, distraction is the corruption to which passion turns when it has been unsuccessful in undermining reason by direct and indirect means and has no choice but to try to interfere with its operations:

> If *Reason* will neither be *deluded* nor won over to the patronage of *Evil*, nor *diverted* from the knowledge and notice of Good, then doth *Passion* strive to *confound* and distract the Apprehensions thereof, that they may not with any firmness or efficacy of Discourse interrupt the Current of such irregular and headstrong motions. For, as things presented to the *Mind* in the nakedness and simplicity of their own Truth do gain a more firm Assent unto them, and a more fixed intuition on them, so, on the contrary side, those things which come mixed and troubled, dividing the intention of the *Mind* between *Truth* and *Passion*, cannot obtain any settled or satisfactory Resolution from the Discourses of *Reason*. (70, italics in original)

In short, distraction attempts to scramble reason's functioning—interrupting its course of thought, blurring ideas together it attempts to distinguish, dividing its attention between what it thinks and feels. The result is an unsettled and disordered consciousness—or, as Reynolds puts it, a "divi[sion of] the intention of the *Mind* between *Truth* and *Passion*." Of course this kind of concupiscent distraction has different origins than the irascible distraction Reynolds associates with overwhelming fear. In the former case it is passion's desire to satisfy its "Beastly and Sensual" appetite that provokes distraction, whereas in the latter case it is "a sudden daunt and onset of an unexpected evil" (62, 283). However, in both cases the "divi[sion of] the intention of the *Mind* between *Truth* and *Passion*" is traceable to the same source—the invasion of the mind by unruly passion—which the subject of the irascible and concupiscent passions suffers alike.

If we apply this notion of distraction to Reynolds's analysis of fear, then an analogy to Ferenczian splitting suggests itself, for distraction is also a division within the mind caused by powerful passions. The analogy is not perfect: rather than exhibiting a neat division of consciousness from affect, distraction is more accurately characterized by a division of consciousness *by* affect. Put differently, distraction privileges disorganization over dissociation. However, this difference should not be allowed to obscure the more profound resemblances between the two concepts, especially as we return to identification with the aggressor. For one of the striking things about Reynolds's parallel between concupiscent and irascible distraction is that it mirrors Ferenczi's idea that the split within the aggressor finds its corollary and sequel in the split within his victim, since any perpetrator of sexual assault is, by definition, driven by concupiscent desire. While not setting out to do so, Reynolds provides a psychological framework that not only explains the division of the survivor's consciousness but also the uncanny resemblance between the self-division of the aggressor and his victim.

What of the second part of Ferenczi's analysis, that in a state of terror the mind becomes vulnerable to impressions from without? Once again Reynolds seems to be aware of this possibility. Noting that "some great Commanders have caused their Scout-watches to be unarmed, that Fear might make them the more vigilant," he therefore concludes that "this Passion is the Instrument of Discipline, seasoning the Mind, as ground Colors do a Table, to receive those beauties and perfections, which are to be superinduced" (303). A "ground color" is a base coat of paint applied before a main coat. By describing the mind as a table and fear as a "ground color," Reynolds suggests that fear prepares the mind for "reception" by "superinduced" forces. Of course, in this example these forces are "beauties" and "perfections," but they needn't be. Indeed, in Reynolds's chapter on imagination, the faculty responsible for representing impressions from the outside world, Reynolds notes that one of its corruptions is "heaviness and sluggish fixedness . . . from which peremptory adhesion and too violent intention of the Fancy on some particular object doth many times arise not only a . . . kind of benumbedness of the Soul, but oftentimes madness, distraction, and torment" (29). Here, "too violent intension" and "peremptory adhesion" are not only associated with "benumbedness of the Soul"—precisely the kind of stupefaction caused by overwhelming fear—but also with the sort of mental fragmentation one would expect to result from trauma: "madness, distraction, and torment" (29).

Unfortunately, Reynolds does not provide an illustration of someone who identifies with an aggressor in a state of terror—or, rather, he does, although this is not what interests him about the example. In the midst of his discussion of how fear causes a "Tumultuary and distracted frame of mind," Reynolds quotes from Ovid's *The Art of Love*, "The Poet speaking of the Sabine Virgins, whom the Roman youth snatched away, and took to them for wives":

As weak and fearful Doves the Eagle fly,
And tender Lambs when they the Wolf espy:
So the affrighted Sabine Virgins run
Pale and discolored, Roman youth to shun.
Their Fear was One, but Fear had not One look,
Part here fit reav'd of sense, part there doth pluck,
And tear their hairs, One silent mourns, another
With a successless Outcry calls her Mother.
One moans, the fright another doth amaze,
One flies for Fear, for Fear another stays. (288)

Although Reynolds does not intend this passage as evidence of identification in a state of terror, the scene clearly illustrates it, with the Sabine women exhibiting the paradoxically binding-yet-disintegrating character of identification in group panic ("Their Fear was One, but Fear had not One look"). And had Reynolds been interested in such traumatic identifications, he could have found further examples in Livy's telling of this legend in *The History of Rome*, especially in the Sabine women's impulse to blame themselves for the war between their husbands and fathers.[11] For Reynolds, though, the Sabine women only serve a more general purpose: an "elegantly described" illustration of "this distraction of Fear" (288).

That Reynolds silently passes over the longer history of the Sabine women is not especially surprising—after all, he is not writing a theory of trauma, but a general treatment of the passions and faculties. Yet by invoking one of most foundational examples of identification with the aggressor in the Western heritage, and by doing so alongside his analyses of fright, distraction, and impressionability, Reynolds has ironically assembled all of the materials necessary for a humoral account of identification with the aggressor. All that is necessary is for someone to connect the dots. As we shall see in our next section, someone did.

"The Impression of Strange Kinds"

By the time Shakespeare wrote *The Rape of Lucrece* its heroine's suicide had been "a theme for disputation" for centuries.[12] At the center of debate was the fact that her suicide seemed misdirected: if Lucretia did not consent to Tarquin's desires, then she was unworthy of death; but if she did consent, then she was unworthy of praise. Some were content to seize one of the horns of this dilemma if only to turn it against Lucretia—thus, Augustine, in *The City of God*, exculpates Lucretia from the charge of adultery only to find her guilty of the sin of pride.[13] Others tried to escape this dilemma by reframing its understanding of innocence and guilt—thus, in *Declamatio Lucretiae*, Salviati's Lucretia kills herself not because she gives in to Tarquin's desires, but because his sexual violation involuntarily stirs her own, an experience she finds intolerable.[14] Whatever the appeal of such interpretations, there is something unsatisfactory about the way they resolve the paradox of Lucretia's suicide. In Livy's *History of Rome*, after securing from her husband and father the reassurance that ostensibly renders suicide unnecessary ("it is the mind that sins, not the body"), Lucrece declares, "Though I clear my self of the offence, my body shall feel the punishment," and then stabs herself.[15] Similarly, in Ovid's *Fasti*, before striking herself down Lucretia states, "The pardon you give . . . I myself refuse."[16] The weird power of these utterances is in the way they seem to get their signals crossed, applying the right action to the wrong person. Lucretia is innocent; therefore she is punished. Lucretia is pardoned; therefore she pays the penalty. It is as though Lucretia has confused herself with her rapist.

In *The Rape of Lucrece* Shakespeare suggests an explanation for Lucretia's suicide that puts this disturbing transposal at its center: Lucrece identifies with her aggressor. Drawing on humoral psychology, Shakespeare tracks how the trauma of rape makes Lucrece's mind vulnerable to invasion, allowing Tarquin's aggression and guilt to impress themselves into her consciousness. It is because of this subjective entanglement that Lucrece is unable to separate her feelings about Tarquin from her feelings about herself, leading her to kill herself for his crimes. Of course, in probing how rape trauma dissolves boundaries between perpetrator and victim, Shakespeare was not breaking entirely new ground. As Jocelyn Catty has shown, in the years leading up to *Lucrece* there was an efflorescence of complaint poetry featuring female speakers, often survivors of rape, that probed the complex and contradictory feelings of guilt and shame that attended sexual violation, so there was already a literary market for the kind of sexual psychodrama represented by *Lucrece*.[17] Similarly, Shakespeare was not the first writer of the late sixteenth century drawn to the transposed violence of Lucretia's suicide. In "An Apology for Poetry" Philip Sidney praises painters who are able to capture "the constant though lamenting look of Lucretia, when she punished in herself another's fault," and in "Euphues" John Lyly has his title character criticize Lucretia's "rigor to punish [Tarquin's] folly in her own flesh."[18] What distinguishes Shakespeare's treatment of these issues in *Lucrece* is the specificity of his psychological exploration and the evocativeness of the poetic style through which it is expressed.

To understand this poetics, though, one must first understand the subjective entanglement of the main characters in which it is based. As has often been noted, Shakespeare's poem is unprecedented in the amount of space it devotes to its heroine's subjectivity; less often noted is the space it affords to Tarquin's. Yet if Lucrece internalizes her aggressor, then an understanding of the latter is essential to understanding the former. Like the aggressors of Ferenczi's account, the most distinctive feature of Tarquin's character is that he is tormented by his desires. "Madly tossed between desire and dread" (173), Tarquin "holds . . . disputation / 'Tween frozen conscience and hot-burning will" (246–47), first articulating the reasons why his intended course of action is shameful, impious, and dangerous (190–238) before rejecting them (239–45, 253–80). This internal conflict is reinforced by the form of the poem, which assigns these speeches to different stanza groupings and which has Tarquin interrupt and respond to himself as though possessed by different voices. It is also reflected in the fact that Tarquin must recommit himself over and over to his dark purpose, availing himself of every resource to quiet his better angels.

Given the strenuousness of this effort, it makes sense that Tarquin should exhibit those corruptions through which Reynolds says passion attempts to subvert reason, especially distraction. As one will recall, distraction disrupts reason by dividing its attention between what it thinks and feels. This dynamic is captured nowhere so well in *Lucrece* as in the convoluted passage that describes Tarquin's state of mind as he makes his way to Lucrece's bedchamber:

> Within his thought her heavenly image sits,
> And in the self-same seat sits Collatine.
> That eye which looks on her confounds his wits;
> That eye which him beholds, as more divine,
> Unto a view so false will not incline;
> But with a pure appeal seeks to the heart,
> Which once corrupted takes the worser part. (288–94)

Editors have noted that ambiguity of reference makes it impossible to definitively say who is looking at whom in this passage.[19] While there are multiple ways of interpreting the scene, the one most suggestive for our purposes is to take the "eyes" of the passage as the eyes of Tarquin's mind. In this reading Tarquin's "thought" is dominated by two images, Lucrece and Collatine. Confusingly, these images are said to occupy "the self-same seat," as though superimposed atop each other; yet, also confusingly, they are imagined as the objects of two different eyes, as though Tarquin is afflicted with a case of mental exotropia and is gazing in different directions. The first eye looks at Lucrece, but this gaze "confounds his wits," making Tarquin unable to think clearly. Tarquin's second eye, meanwhile, beholds Collatine, but unto this view "will not incline," perhaps because doing so might dampen his desire. Instead this eye swerves to Tarquin's own heart, which the narrator, using Reynolds's preferred term, says becomes "corrupted." In the space of only a few lines, then, the narrator suggests how distraction enables Tarquin's crimes: because "dividing the intention of the *Mind* between *Truth* and *Passion*" allows him to look, and yet not fully look, at his victims.

This corruption of Tarquin's heart in a state of distraction has significant consequences, and not only for Tarquin himself, as its effects radiate outward toward Lucrece. This process begins inside Tarquin, when, in a groaner of a pun, his heart "*heartens up* his servile powers, / Who, flattered by their leader's jocund show, / Stuff up his lust" (295–97, emphasis mine)—that is, floods his members with blood and spirit—propelling him toward Lucrece's chamber. Or as the narrator puts it: "By reprobate desire thus madly led / The Roman lord marcheth to Lucrece' bed" (300–301). Of course by describing Tarquin's journey as a "march," his blood and spirits as "servile powers," and his heart as their "leader," the narrator weds the language of humoral physiology to the metaphor of the military invasion, already familiar from Reynolds—although, strikingly, Shakespeare uses this metaphor not to describe the mind's assault by its own fear, but the assaultive force of another's desire. This braided language intensifies when Tarquin arrives in Lucrece's chamber and pulls back the curtains surrounding her bed:

> His eye which late this mutiny restrains
> Unto a greater uproar tempts his veins.
>
> And they like straggling slaves for pillage fighting,
> Obdurate vassals fell exploits effecting,
> In bloody death and ravishment delighting,
> Nor children's tears nor mothers' groans respecting,
> Swell in their pride, the onset still expecting.
> Anon his beating heart, alarum striking,
> Gives the hot charge and bids them do their liking.
>
> His drumming heart cheers up his burning eye,
> His eye commends the leading to his hand;
> His hand, as proud of such a dignity,
> Smoking with pride, marched on to make his stand
> On her bare breast, the heart of all her land. (426–39)

The "servile powers" mustered by Tarquin's heart have now become "straggling slaves"; the "march" to Lucrece's bedroom has become a siege; and Lucrece's "bare breast" the "heart of all her land," which Tarquin invades. Moreover the reader can trace the steps by which this invasion is launched: Tarquin's imagination "corrupt[s]" his heart; his "drumming heart" cheers on his "burning eye"; that eye gives orders to "his hand"; and this hand "march[es]" to Lucrece's "heart." The effect is to conjure an image of a line running from Tarquin's heart to Lucrece's, the connection between them established at the moment that his hand touches her breast.

How telling, then, that at this moment the point of view of the poem changes. Indeed, the instant that Tarquin touches Lucrece, the "straggling slaves" of his passions disappear and we suddenly find ourselves inside Lucrece's body, observing how her "ranks of blue veins" respond to Tarquin's touch (440). Moreover, with this shift of perspective, the narrator draws our attention to a new chain of reactions, as the changes within Lucrece's body provoke changes in her mind. What does not change, however, is the metaphor that frames this encounter; we now just experience Tarquin's invasion from the perspective of those whose city is being attacked. This abrupt jamming together of perspectives is unsettling, as readers now find themselves looking at Tarquin's assault through two sets of lenses—invader and invaded—which has the effect of highlighting certain discomfiting symmetries and asymmetries between them:

His drumming heart cheers up his burning eye,
His eye commends the leading to his hand;
His hand, as proud of such a dignity,
Smoking with pride, marched on to make his stand
On her bare breast, the heart of all her land;
    Whose ranks of blue veins, as his hand did scale,
    Left their round turrets destitute and pale.

They, mustering to the quiet cabinet
Where their dear governess and lady lies,
Do tell her she is dreadfully beset,
And fright her with confusion of their cries. (435–45)

On the one hand, by figuring Tarquin's blood and spirits as an invading army and Lucrece's as a retreating guard, the narrator clarifies certain key differences between them. One such difference is their movement, since Tarquin's concupiscent passions surge outward whereas Lucrece's irascible passions retreat inward; another is their quality, as Tarquin's passions aim to rape and pillage whereas Lucrece's aim to counsel and warn. Yet one cannot follow the interaction between the two forces without also noting some disconcerting continuities between them. Consider, for example, the moment that Tarquin's hand touches Lucrece's breast: Tarquin may be the invader and Lucrece the invaded, but the instant that their ranks make contact, the surging force of Tarquin's passions is, in effect, taken over by Lucrece's, who charge the inmost sanctum of their lady's "cabinet" on his behalf, sowing "confusion." Moreover, within the tropology of the poem, the disorder wrought by this throng of forces resembles nothing so much as the "straggling slaves" of Tarquin's passions, who raise havoc within Tarquin before provoking it in Lucrece. To be sure, this effect is unintentional: the spirits throng their lady not to debilitate her, but to warn her, telling her that she "is dreadfully beset." However, in a revealing pun, these lines can apply as easily to the spirits themselves as to Tarquin: they are, after all, the *medium* of Lucrece's dread; in the most literal sense, *she* is beset by *them*. Reynolds's term for this danger is distraction—except whereas Tarquin's concupiscent distraction works to obscure his self-division, Lucrece's irascible distraction works to *create* hers by instigating enmity between her body and mind. The unavoidable conclusion is that Lucrece's soul may be in as much danger from her own fear as from Tarquin's desire, since it triggers the very distraction that leaves her vulnerable to identification with her aggressor.

What of the second constituent element, vulnerability to impression from without? As we pass from observing the effects of terror on Lucrece's body to its effects on her mind, the narrator also intimates that Lucrece may be at risk to such impressionability. Startled into consciousness by Tarquin's touch, Lucrece, "much amazed," "breaks ope her locked-up eyes" (446) yet is blinded by Tarquin's torch. The result is a kind of phantasmagoric night-vision, half composed of the impressions of Lucrece's senses and half composed of the figments of her "dreadful fancy" (450). Indeed, the narrator describes the dark shapes swirling before her eyes as a nightmare come to life:

Imagine her as one in dead of night
From forth dull sleep by dreadful fancy waking,
That thinks she hath beheld some ghastly sprite
Whose grim aspect sets every joint a-shaking;
What terror 'tis! but she in worser taking,
    From sleep disturbed, heedfully doth view
    The sight which makes supposed terror true.

Wrapp'd and confounded in a thousand fears,
Like to a new-killed bird she trembling lies;
She dares not look, yet, winking, there appears
Quick-shifting antics, ugly in her eyes.
Such shadows are the weak brain's forgeries;
    Who, angry that the eyes fly from their lights,
    In darkness daunts them with more dreadful sights. (449–62)

It is interesting that in describing the effects of terror and confusion in Lucrece's mind the narrator has recourse to an entirely different lexicon than that used to evoke the agitations of blood and spirit—not invading or retreating "ranks" but "ghastly sprite[s]" and "Quick-shifting antic[s]." However, the language that inflects these ghoulish apparitions shares a key characteristic with that of distraction: the difficulty of discerning whether a threat comes from inside or outside Lucrece. Consider, for example, the narrator's statement that it would be bad enough to take a nightmare for reality, but Tarquin is a "worser taking." Here the narrator plays on at least two meanings of "taking": first, a perception or apprehension (OED 1b) and second, an externally invading malignant force, in the sense of "taking ill" or even demonic possession (OED 4b).[20] The first sense merely means that seeing Tarquin is worse than a nightmare, but the second suggests that he has the power to possess Lucrece's mind. Similarly, with the narrator's description of Lucrece as "Wrapp'd and confounded in a thousand fears": "wrapp'd" can mean engulfed, evoking the enormity of Lucrece's terror, but it can also function as an aural pun on "rapt," in the sense of rapture or rape. As with "worser taking," the narrator seems to be suggesting that the hallucinatory intensity of Lucrece's fear-drenched perceptions not only has the power to disturb her mental tranquility but also the ability to forcefully penetrate her consciousness.

Before Lucrece is even fully awake, then, Shakespeare is already exploiting polysemy to suggest that terror has made her vulnerable to impressions from without. What, however, are those impressions? Despite her fright at being awakened by Tarquin's hand on her breast, Lucrece manages to ask "under what color he commits this ill" (476). In response Tarquin offers two answers that will prove important to understanding her reactions in the wake of the rape. First, he replies:

> The color in thy face,
> That even for anger makes the lily pale
> And the red rose blush at her own disgrace,
> Shall plead for me and tell my loving tale.
> Under that color am I come to scale
>   Thy never-conquer'd fort: the fault is thine,
>   For those thine eyes betray thee unto mine. (477–83)

In other words, Tarquin blames the victim. However, no sooner does this excuse pass Tarquin's lips than he changes course, admitting his intended course of action is wrong and goes against his better judgment:

> I see what crosses my attempt will bring;
> I know what thorns the growing rose defends;
> I think the honey guarded with a sting;
> All this beforehand counsel comprehends.
> But will is deaf, and hears no heedful friends;
>   Only he hath an eye to gaze on beauty,
>   And dotes on what he looks, 'gainst law or duty.
> [. . .]
>
> I know that repentant tears ensue the deed,
>   Reproach, disdain, and deadly enmity;
> Yet I strive to embrace mine infamy. (491–97, 502–4)

By articulating these opposite positions in such quick succession, Tarquin not only exhibits his internal division before Lucrece but also displays the distraction that allows him to momentarily overcome this division. As before, this distraction is figured as a kind of sensory disorder, except now instead of an internally divided single sense—one eye separated from the other—it is imagined as a division between the senses—sight separated from hearing: "will is deaf and hears no heedful friends; / Only he hath an eye to gaze on beauty." This deafening of the will is apropos, for in a moment Lucrece will attempt to dissuade Tarquin by reminding him of the claims of "law or duty," hoping to reactivate his internal conflict. However, after listening to her for over eighty lines, Tarquin finally cuts her off: "'No, more,' quoth he, 'by heaven I will not hear thee'" (667). Indeed, he not only stops Lucrece's mouth, so he cannot hear her, but he also extinguishes his torch, so he cannot see her ("For light and lust are deadly enemies," the narrator observes, "Shame folded up in blind concealing night" [674–75]). And then: he rapes her.

Of all Tarquin's words and deeds, this is obviously the worst, and the one that seals Lucrece's trauma. Yet Ferenczi makes it clear that the dissimulations and erratic behaviors of the aggressor—from treating the victim as though they did something to deserve their assault to simply exposing them to their own emotional volatility—can be just as harmful as the sexual assault itself, for these behaviors supply the material out of which the victim-survivor's destructive identifications are formed. In this respect Tarquin's victim-blaming and distraction are just as important to explaining Lucrece's trauma as the fact of her rape. And in light of these harmful effects, two aspects of Lucrece's thought and action in the wake of her rape assume special significance. First, she experiences terrible guilt, despite the fact she has done nothing wrong; and second, she is driven to self-harm. Both reactions are unexpected given what we know of Lucrece, but both are explicitly associated with identification with the aggressor and with Tarquin. Moreover, through a series of rhetorical and poetic techniques, the narrator encourages the reader to notice how they have been transposed from Tarquin to Lucrece.

As evidence of this transposition, consider the sequence of paired descriptions by which the narrator sketches Tarquin and Lucrece's responses in the immediate aftermath of the rape. One such pairing—"He thence departs a heavy convertite; / She there remains a hopeless castaway" (743–44)—creates a template of structural complementarity set off by semantic contrast—a contrast that, in this case, confirms our expectations of what is appropriate to each character, with Tarquin predictably regretting his act and Lucrece having to deal with the consequences. In the lines that follow, however, this pattern abruptly shifts, as qualities we have previously seen in Tarquin now reappear in Lucrece:

He in his speed looks for the morning light;
She prays she never may behold the day.
"For day," quoth she, "night's scapes doth open lay,
  And my true eyes have never practiced how
  To cloak offences with a cunning brow.

"They think not but that every eye can see
The same disgrace which they themselves behold;
And therefore would they still in darkness be,
To have their unseen sin remain untold.
For they their guilt with weeping will unfold." (745–56)

While Tarquin regrets his deed of darkness and so "looks for the morning light," Lucrece "prays she never may behold the day," lest her "offences" and "guilt" be revealed—a prayer that not only does not make sense, since Lucrece has done nothing wrong, but that explicitly recalls Tarquin's act of extinguishing his torch and the narrator's accompanying maxim that "light and lust are deadly enemies: / Shame folded up in blind concealing night" (674–75). Yet the fact that this prayer is inapplicable to Lucrece and is the kind of thing her rapist would say is precisely the point: it is not properly hers at all. Instead Lucrece sounds like Tarquin in the midst of his distraction, when he admits that "shame," "sorrow," and "repentant tears" will "ensue [his] deed," but then plunges into darkness anyway (499, 502). It is in this same darkness of distraction that Lucrece now wishes to remain, lest the light of day and her "weeping" betray the "guilt" of her "unseen sin."

A very similar dynamic unfolds with respect to the other compulsion from which Lucrece suffers in the aftermath of the rape: the impulse to self-harm.

Once again, in introducing this impulse the narrator uses a parallel construction to establish a contrast between Tarquin and Lucrece but then suddenly reverses course to draw attention to an unexpected congruence between them:

> He like a thievish dog creeps sadly thence;
> She like a wearied lamb lies panting there;
> He scowls and hates himself for his offence;
> She, desperate, with her nails her flesh doth tear. (736–39)

The narrator's first paired description of Tarquin as a "thievish dog" and Lucrece as a "wearied lamb" establishes the familiar pattern of contrastive juxtaposition identified in the last paragraph; we therefore expect the lines that follow to adhere to the same pattern. And, at least initially, it seems they will: Tarquin has committed a terrible deed, after all, so it makes sense that he "scowls and hates himself for his offence." Lucrece, however, is guilty of no such crime, and so we expect the next line to describe a contrasting attitude and action—perhaps something like, "She, desperate, with her voice his name doth tear." However, the expected contrast never materializes. Instead Lucrece *attacks herself*, exhibiting synonymy with Tarquin where we expected antimony; instead of *lashing out*, Lucrece *lashes in*, surprising us with aggression directed not against Tarquin but against herself. And yet this inward-directed violence follows a certain twisted logic if one recalls Tarquin's words to Lucrece about her beauty: "The color in thy face . . . / Shall plead for me and tell my loving tale / . . . the fault is thine, / For those thine eyes betray thee unto mine" (477–83). If it was Lucrece's beauty that invited Tarquin's attack, then it deserves to be punished. Indeed, the guilt that Lucrece has introjected from Tarquin demands it.

These twin impulses—guilt and self-harm—are woven throughout Lucrece's tortured reflections for the remainder of the poem and climactically come together in Lucrece's suicide, which, like identification with the aggressor itself, is epitomized by two images.[21] The first is contained within Lucrece's final words. Like her antecedents, Shakespeare's Lucrece is careful to both declare and elicit from her male audience an affirmation of her mind's purity before plunging her knife into her body; and also like her antecedents, when she turns that knife on herself, she conflates herself with Tarquin. However, this conflation works a little differently in Shakespeare's poem. Whereas Livy's Lucrece declares her innocence before stabbing herself and Ovid's Lucrece rejects her audience's pardon, Shakespeare's Lucrece attributes her suicide to Tarquin himself: "He, he, fair lords, 'tis he, / That guides this hand to give this wound to me" (1721–22).[22] At once an image of internalized aggression, self-harm, and demonic possession, Tarquin's "guidance" of Lucrece's hand crystallizes one side of identification with the aggressor: the vulnerability to impression from without. However, balancing this disturbing image is another, equally haunting, emblem: the stream of blood that issues from Lucrece's wound, dividing into "two slow rivers" that "circle her body on every side" (1738–39). This image of the two rivers—one black, one red; one corrupted, one pure—is the ultimate figure for the other side of identification with the aggressor, the splitting of the mind. Together the two images express the paradox at the center of traumatic identification: the fact that its victim is simultaneously both more and less than they were before, their identity having been riven in two and then supplanted by an alien will.

Of course just because Shakespeare had the insight to recognize such psychological dynamics does not mean that he possessed a conceptual framework for uniting them. Reynolds, after all, did not. Besides the narrator's strategic puns and rhetorical patterning, is there any evidence that Shakespeare, like Ferenczi, thought of these phenomena as part of a unified scheme?

Roughly halfway through the long final stretch of the poem during which Lucrece unpacks her suffering, she calls to her maid for assistance. Although the maid has no idea what has happened, as soon as she sees her mistress's tears she begins crying spontaneously, "enforced by sympathy" to share in her lady's woes—a tendency, the narrator remarks, common to women (1229). However, the narrator then abruptly pivots from the mutual contagiousness of women's emotions to their vulnerability to impression by men:

> For men have marble, women waxen, minds,
> And therefore are they formed as marble will;
> The weak oppressed, the impression of strange kinds
> Is formed in them by force, by fraud, or skill.
> Then call them not the authors of their ill,

No more than wax shall be accounted evil
Wherein is stamped the semblance of a devil.
[. . .]

No man inveigh against the withered flower,
But chide rough winter that the flower hath killed:
Not that devoured, but that which doth devour,
Is worthy blame. O, let it not be hild
Poor women's faults, that they are so fulfilled
With men's abuses: those proud lords, to blame,
Make weak-made women tenants to their shame.
(1240–46, 1254–60)

As we have seen, Ferenczi's preferred metaphor for the process by which the traumatized victim is impressed by the feelings of the aggressor is taken from photography (*CD* 111). The narrator's metaphors are obviously early modern, but the animating idea is still very much the same, especially the image of women's "waxen minds" "stamp'd" by "the impression of strange kinds." Of course, as Katharine Maus has noted, this vision of women as "pure malleability," if taken to its logical conclusion, means not only that women's minds are vulnerable to men but that they are vulnerable to everything, such that they scarcely can be said to possess wills at all.[23] Yet whatever the narrator's logical blind spots, there are signs that he understands such impressionability is not simply a fact of nature but has a special relation to sexual trauma. For immediately after describing how women are "fullfilled with men's abuses," the narrator invites the reader to view this "precedent . . . in Lucrece" (1261), whose terror was the crucible for her trauma: "Such danger to resistance did belong / That dying fear through all her body spread; / And who cannot abuse a body dead?" (1265–67). It was precisely the intensity of Lucrece's fear that made her vulnerable to "the impression of strange kinds." Whether the narrator understands exactly how such impressions come about, be it "by force, by fraud, or skill," it is clear that he perceives a connection between them and terror. So, we can assume, did Shakespeare, who manages once again to be ahead of his time while remaining firmly within it.

NOTES

1. On rape in early modern literature and culture, see Mercedes Camino, *"The Stage Am I": Raping Lucrece in Early Modern England* (New York: Edwin Mellen, 1995); Jocelyn Catty, *Writing Rape, Writing Women in Early Modern England: Unbridled Speech* (New York: St. Martin's, 1999); Diane Wolfthal, *Images of Rape: The "Heroic" Tradition and Its Alternatives* (Cambridge, UK: Cambridge University Press, 1999); Elizabeth Robertson and Christine Rose, eds., *Representing Rape in Medieval and Early Modern Literature* (New York: Palgrave, 2001); Barbara Baines, *Representing Rape in the English Early Modern Period* (Lewiston NY: Edwin Mellen, 2003); Amy Greenstadt, *Rape and the Rise of the Author: Gendering Intention in Early Modern England* (Farnham, UK: Ashgate, 2009); Lee Ritscher, *The Semiotics of Rape in Renaissance English Literature* (New York: Peter Lang, 2009); Lisa Starkes-Estes, *Violence, Trauma, and Virtus in Shakespeare's Roman Poems and Plays: Transforming Ovid* (Houndmills, Basingstroke, UK: Palgrave, 2014). Of these studies, only Catty, Robertson and Rose, and Starkes-Estes grapple explicitly with historicizing early modern theories of trauma in connection with rape.
2. Wolfthal, *Images of Rape*, 2.
3. Cathy Caruth, *Unclaimed Experience: Trauma, Narrative, and History* (Baltimore: Johns Hopkins University Press, 1996), 3; Judith Herman, *Trauma and Recovery* (New York: Basic, 1992), 9; Ruth Leys, *Trauma: A Genealogy* (Chicago: University of Chicago Press, 2000), 3–4.
4. Annette Burgess, "Rape Trauma Syndrome," in *Rape and Society: Readings on the Problem of Sexual Assault*, 239–45 (New York: Westview, 1995); Sharon Wasco, "Conceptualizing the Harm Done by Rape: Applications of Trauma Theory to Experiences of Sexual Assault," *Trauma, Violence, & Abuse* 4, no. 4 (2003): 309–22.
5. The paper in which Ferenczi formulates identification with the aggressor is "Confusion of Tongues Between Adults and the Child: The Language of Tenderness and of Passion," reprinted in *Contemporary Psychoanalysis* 24 (1988): 196–206, although Ferenczi also discusses it extensively in his *Clinical Diary*, published as *The Clinical Diary of Sándor Ferenczi*, ed. Judith Dupont (Cambridge: Harvard University Press, 1985), and assorted papers collected in *Final Contributions to the Problems and Methods of Psycho-Analysis*, ed. Michael Balint (New York: Routledge, 2018). For the sake of convenience, in parenthetical citations I hereafter abbreviate these titles as *CT*, *CD*, and *FC*.
6. Following Robin Field in *Writing the Survivor: The Rape Novel in Late Twentieth-Century American Fiction*, 21–25 (Clemson University Press, 2020), I use several different terms--"victim," "survivor," and "victim-survivor"—to describe the person harmed by sexual assault, "depending on the larger circumstances of the situation or

narratological focus of the depiction" (22). Because Shakespeare's Lucrece commits suicide shortly after her assault and describes her motives in various and contradictory ways, the straightforward application of any of these terms to her situation is inevitably problematic from one direction or other. For further discussion of these matters, see note 22.

7. Edward Reynolds, *A Treatise of the Passions and Faculties of the Soule of Man: A Facsimile Reproduction with an Introduction by Margaret Lee Wiley* (Gainesville FL: Scholars' Facsimiles & Reprints, 1971). Spelling and punctuation from Reynolds have been silently modernized. Please note: In the original edition of Reynolds's text, there is a pagination error that begins on page 193, which is corrected in the facsimile edition. For all citations in this chapter, I use the corrected facsimile pagination.
8. Sigmund Freud, *Introductory Lectures on Psycho-Analysis*, trans. and ed. James Strachey (New York: Norton, 1966), 340–41, and Sigmund Freud, *Beyond the Pleasure Principle*, trans. and ed. James Strachey (New York: Norton, 1961), 35.
9. Freud, *Beyond the Pleasure Principle*, 11, 34.
10. Leys, *Trauma*, 23.
11. Livy, *The Roman History Written by T. Livius of Padua*, trans. Philemon Holland (London, 1600), 10.
12. William Shakespeare, "The Rape of Lucrece," in *Narrative Poems*, ed. Jonathan Crewe (Hammondsworth, UK: Penguin, 1999), 822. All subsequent parenthetical citations are to this edition. On the literary and commentary tradition on Lucretia, see Ian Donaldson, *The Rapes of Lucretia: A Myth and Its Transformations* (Oxford, UK: Oxford University Press, 1982); Stephanie Jed, *Chaste Thinking: The Rape of Lucretia and the Birth of Humanism* (Bloomington: Indiana University Press, 1989); Camino, *"The Stage Am I"*; and Melissa Matthes, *The Rape of Lucretia and the Founding of Republics: Readings in Livy, Machiavelli, and Rousseau* (University Park: Pennsylvania State University Press, 2000).
13. Saint Augustine, *The City of God* (New York: Modern Library, 1950), 25.
14. Salviati, *Declamatio Lucretiae*, trans. Jed, in *Chaste Thinking*, 151.
15. Livy, *The History of Rome*, translated by William Painter in *The Palace of Pleasure*, *"The Second Novel,"* in *Narrative and Dramatic Sources of Shakespeare*, vol. 1 (London: Routledge, 1957), 198.
16. Ovid, *Fasti*, trans. Anne and Peter Wiseman (Oxford, UK: Oxford University Press, 2013), 39.
17. Catty, *Writing Rape*, 55–74.
18. Sir Philip Sidney, "An Apology for Poetry," in *Sir Philip Sidney's Apology for Poetry and Astrophil and Stella: Texts and Contexts*, ed. Peter Herman, 54–126 (Glen Allen VA: College, 2001), 68; John Lyly, "Euphues: The Anatomy of Wit," in *An Anthology*

of Elizabethan Prose Fiction, ed. Paul Salzman [83–150] (Oxford, UK: Oxford University Press, 1987), 116.

19. Katherine Duncan-Jones and H. R. Woudhuysen, eds., *Shakespeare's Poems* (London: Arden, 2007), 296.
20. "taking, *n.*" OED Online, Oxford University Press. Updated September 2020. https://www.oed.com/view/Entry/197174?rskey=41ct1t&result=2&isAdvanced=false#eid.
21. On Lucrece's sense of guilt, see lines 807–12; 825–26; 1058–59; 1074–75; 1208; and 1342–44; on self-harm, 759–61; 1135–39; and 1174–76.
22. Lucrece's insistence that Tarquin "guides" her hand raises serious questions about the limits of her agency and her suicide's significance as a political and symbolic gesture. Earlier in the poem Lucrece describes her suicide as a redemptive act that will restore her stained honor and secure her future reputation ("So of shame's ashes shall my fame be bred; / For in my death I murder shameful scorn: / My shame so dead, mine honor is new born" [1188–90]). She also clearly anticipates its significance as a spur to vengeance ("How Tarquin must be used, read it in me: / Myself thy friend will kill myself thy foe; / And for my sake serve thou false Tarquin so" [1195–97]). While these motivations are not canceled out by her parting words, the fact that she accedes agency to Tarquin in her final moments does suggest that other, far murkier, motives lie behind the act as well. For a sampling of the ways that modern feminist critics have understood the psychological and social constraints that inform Lucrece's suicide, see Coppelia Kahn, "The Rape in Shakespeare's *Lucrece*," *Shakespeare Studies* 9 (1976): 45–72, esp. 64–67; Janet Newman, "'And Let Mild Women to Him Lose Their Mildness': Philomela, Female Violence, and Shakespeare's *The Rape of Lucrece*," *Shakespeare Quarterly* 45, (1994): 304–26; and Greenstadt, *Rape and the Rise of the Author*, 57–82.
23. Katharine Maus, "Taking Tropes Seriously: Language and Violence in Shakespeare's Rape of Lucrece," *Shakespeare Quarterly* 37, no. 1 (1986): 75.

3

The Trauma of Self

Hannah Allen and Seventeenth-Century Women's Spiritual Writing

AMELIA ZURCHER

The subject of this chapter is an early modern narrative, Hannah Allen's *A Narrative of God's Gracious Dealings with that Choice Christian Mrs. Hannah Allen*, which by twenty-first-century standards almost demands to be read as traumatic. Published in 1683 in London, told in first person, Allen's narrative recounts in about seventy-five pages a young woman's struggle with a powerful urge toward despair. The story is framed as a conflict with Satan and shares several conventions of Protestant nonconforming women's spiritual life-writing from the period, but it also contains vivid markers of what in the twenty-first century we would call trauma. Allen agonizes over a dissociation from her own thoughts that persuades her she is incapable of laying claim to intention or sincerity; she starves herself and inflicts multiple other harms on her body in a repetitive cycle of despair and anger; and she constructs a narrative that is formally disrupted by switches of perspective and temporality. Historians resist, for good reason, attempts to diagnose early modern characters, even those who are ostensibly historical, as if they were real people, and to apply modern assumptions about psychological subjectivity and health to personae constructed hundreds of years ago. Trauma theory, though it has begun to emerge as one of our most capacious cultural narratives, rests on assumptions about the value of individual agency and autonomy that would have been foreign to devout seventeenth-century English women and indeed to most seventeenth-century people. In part for these reasons, much recent scholarship on trauma in early modern anglophone culture has avoided analyses of individualized or psychologized suffering, using trauma theory instead to make visible broad traumatic patterns in early modern cultural and historical narratives, particularly repetition and closure postponed or denied.[1] A micro-history such as Allen's, however, seems to require that we reclaim the individual as the paradigmatic subject of trauma. And it calls for what Zackariah Long describes as a "local analysis" of her represented experience, a careful negotiation of the linguistic, conceptual, and contextual differences between her discourses for suffering and our own.[2] Such an analysis offers the occasion not only to discern traumatic patterns in early modern narrative but also, more fundamentally, to consider whether and how a theory of subjectivity relying on post-Enlightenment constructions of the autonomous, narratively constructed subject can illuminate pre-Enlightenment experiences of suffering—and, conversely, how early modern accounts of suffering might shape our own conceptions of trauma.

Contemporary trauma theory is a highly mobile discourse that takes many different forms in different disciplines. For many psychoanalytic theorists, from Freud through Lacan to Laplanche, traumatic experience is constitutive of subjectivity, universal among humans who have succeeded at entering the linguistic or sexual order. For others, trauma is the response to a particular extraordinary event, one so violent and disruptive that the subject cannot integrate it into ordinary experience.[3] At one end of this analytic spectrum everyone is traumatized to some degree; at the other, trauma is reserved for those who have undergone the extraordinary. By its nature trauma also makes it difficult to perceive the causal link between precipitating event and traumatic consequences. Whether universal or extraordinary, one of its hallmarks is the production of a split or fissure in the subjectivity of the sufferer. For the traumatized subject, the original traumatic experience is not recoverable to ordinary memory and becomes available for use or understanding only belatedly, through traumatic repetition and other symptoms. As a result, accounts of trauma are often characterized by disruptions in temporality and perspective that make traditional historical reconstruction difficult. And, of course, interpreting absence becomes ever more difficult as historical distance increases. In reading Allen's *Narrative* through the lens of trauma, I will take as common ground that trauma is an experience of suffering. I will assume, too, that in degree traumatic suffering is outside the norm, beyond that experienced by every person in the course of ordinary existence, and that it is the result of an event or circumstance in the world rather than organic dysfunction alone.

Trauma has an inherently dilatory function with respect to suffering, extending its temporal duration and concentrating our focus on it. One strain of trauma theory presents this mainly as a problem to be solved for the subject, but for others it offers space for certain kinds of ethical resistance.[4] One reason to dwell on traumatic suffering is to honor the pain of those who undergo more than their share. Another is that trauma's power to delay closure might open the space to create more generous and inclusive modes of resolution. As Mary Jacobus points out, quoting Geoffrey Hartman, those who read accounts of trauma, like those who theorize it and those who suffer it, learn to "'stay longer' (to tarry) in a negative realm," and such tarrying in the negative can constitute a counterweight to the pressure for ideological resolution.[5] Recent historians of early modern trauma have emphasized the distinction in trauma theory between narratives of trauma worked through, what Mathew Martin in the context of early modern drama calls "tragic mimesis," in which the subject achieves coherence and closure or a stance of distanced "reflection" or even redemption, and narratives (much less likely over the course of time to become canonical) in which the subject, whether character or culture, remains inside trauma.[6] Though in most clinical settings the production of the first kind of narrative remains the goal, under the assumption that the healthy subject is relatively autonomous and unbound by its past, theorists and scholars have emphasized the potential in the second kind of narrative for liberatory resistance—pushback against new early modern cultural pressures toward coherent selfhood, or against the ideological foreclosure characteristic of classic tragedy. If culturally dominant history, as Martin says in a revision of Fredric Jameson's dictum, is "the denial of what hurts," narrative that delineates trauma takes us back before that denial, to the recognition of historical suffering.[7] Representations of unworked-through trauma—what I will call traumatic narrative—seem to offer access to traces of something like the Lacanian real, experience less mediated than ordinarily by the ideological closure common to most culturally dominant modes of representation and of normative subjectivity. Such access, if perhaps ethically useful in hypothesis, is only fantasy; elements of Allen's history that feel still traumatic, for instance, turn out to be also conventional, tropes that recur regularly in seventeenth-century conversion narratives. As trauma theory reminds us, we can never return to origins, and experience communicated through language is always already configured in ideological form. But traumatic narrative might be more useful than other kinds for pausing the story and letting us dwell on its constituent parts. As an analytic lens it might loosen the ideological knot of the autonomous, agentive self and help us to recognize more clearly other, less privileged kinds of subjects.

The theory of trauma has strong structural analogues in early modern discourses of religion and the self. Trauma and Christian typology, to name one analogous discourse, construe history in strikingly parallel ways. As Heather Hirschfeld points out, although typology privileges the subsequent event over the original, while trauma at least by some accounts gives the original event primacy, in both schemes the original event is only dimly apprehended even as it gives meaning to the subsequent one.[8] Both are also organized by the premise of a historical event of splitting between past and present. As so canonically set forth by Augustine's *Confessions*, the experience of Christian conversion in some ways echoes this structure, incorporating within the historical narrative of the individual the typological relation of past and present. At the moment of conversion there is subjective rupture, at which moment, as Allen's contemporary Mary Rich describes it, "I am not I," and then in the light of that rupture the self casts its newly reflective eye backward over the past self to give it meaning as a type (or antitype) of the present.[9] As typology does, and arguably as trauma theory does too, conversion narratives redeem past experience from across the gap of rupture by making it a means toward present understanding. Paradoxically, in all three paradigms the past experience loses the integrity of its otherness even as it gains usable meaning in the present. "What we take to be flare-ups of memory," as Pierre Nora says of the process of integrating experience into shared cultural narrative, "are in fact its final consumption in the flames of history."[10] As theorists of autobiography have long recognized, the model for autobiography that becomes canonical in the West, the Enlightenment narrative of the consolidation of a coherent and autonomous self, also participates in this conversion structure. Like the conversion narrative, it privileges climactic moments of insight that resolve suffering or confusion, and with typology it takes as its task the representation of past experience from the perspective of the reflective present self.

Clearly conversion is a master trope in Western accounts of the subject, both religious and secular. As another, more limited account of the self, trauma theory shares some of Christian conversion's structural logic, and in the theological context of post-Reformation seventeenth-century England, for reasons I will delineate, the two paradigms were especially close. In Allen's *Narrative* they are presented as all but identical. From a historical distance it is most likely impossible to disentangle the traumatic logic of conversion from other kinds of trauma in the account of any given subject. Perhaps the often painfully split self that was prescribed to nonconforming women in seventeenth-century England was conducive to trauma, or perhaps the splitting of conversion was a repetition of another kind of trauma we cannot recover, whether universal or particular. What seems crucial is that trauma of the kind in Allen's *Narrative* is not just an analogue to religious conversion and the struggle to secure one's faith, but is instead represented, and presumably lived, through that struggle. In her well-known argument about the traumatic structure of revenge in *Hamlet*, Hirschfeld calls for us to understand early modern religious discourse "alongside, rather than in opposition to," the psychoanalytic discourse of trauma.[11] I would argue, more strongly, that in Allen's *Narrative* trauma does not exist parallel to the subject's relation with God but is configured by that relation, each constitutive of the other.

In considering Allen's depiction of her suffering, her modest readership has also wrestled with what relation her *Narrative* bears to the discourse of madness.[12] Women's religious life-writing from this period is full of symptoms—depression, dissociation, self-harm, the drive to suicide—that signify illness in modern contexts. In the early modern period such symptoms were understood as the result of women's inherent susceptibility to madness, their "unstable and precarious" sanity, as Katharine Hodgkin says, depending on an "unruly physiology" that shaped all of their experience, religious included.[13] This misogynist characterization was often leveled against women's public religious speech, for instance, that of the prophet Anne Wentworth, who in her printed *Vindication* rejects that move and reclaims the language of madness for spiritual authority. If "I am a person beside myself," she ringingly proclaims to the detractors who have dismissed her prophecy as madness, "I confess my self to be beside my self to God."[14] We risk repeating that pathologization in reading women's religious struggles as expressions of illness—but on the other hand, to write madness out of these accounts may be to miss significant dimensions of their experience, dimensions they themselves may have owned. Allen offers a way to negotiate this problem in her *Narrative*, when her aunt tries, not with hostile but with sympathetic motives, to pathologize Allen's spiritual convictions as emotional disorder. Hoping that her niece might understand her misery as the effect of melancholy—in early modern terms, a disorder whose etiology is in the individual—and thus stop interpreting it as the sign of God's deliberate estrangement, Allen's aunt exclaims in frustration, "Would you but believe you were melancholy it might be a great means to bring you out of this condition." "Melancholy," retorts Allen, "I have Cause to be melancholy," given that she is "assuredly Damn'd."[15] In Allen's view there is no barrier to accepting both explanations: melancholy does not compete with God's judgment as an explanation for her suffering but is a natural correlative. The anonymous prefacer to her *Narrative*, cooperating with Allen's view, offers a materialist analogy to explain why this should be so. One's soul is put at risk both by disordered humors, which in keeping the body "in frame and tune" act as the "Souls Organs," and by "the immediate impressions of God's wrath upon the Soul," pressing on it as if wrath and soul were substances (D1r-v). The mind and spirit in this model of health and disorder are not qualitatively distinct from the bodily but occupy the same functional space, and threats from the inside and outside are of similar kinds. To be "beside oneself" may be at once an expression of psychic disorder and clear reasoning; it may even be, as Wentworth suggests, a means toward resolution in the ultimate sense. Trauma is a particularly apposite model here, in that it describes that situation in which a fundamental philosophical problem of self or identity is expressed viscerally, as a problem of mind, spirit, and body in one.[16]

To the extent that they participate in traumatic logic, Augustinian conversion and that strand of Enlightenment autobiography proceeding from it are mostly not traumatic narratives in the sense in which I used it earlier, but narratives of trauma worked through, of subjects who have resolved their painful split in self.[17] Spiritual life-writing from seventeenth-century

England rarely proceeds to this resolution, but instead devotes its energies to the expression of suffering. Partly this refusal of narrative resolution may owe to the fact that these texts tend to be written by subjects who do not speak from a position of cultural dominance, whether because of gender or social status or theological opinion, and thus have fewer of the resources that make individual agency possible. More significant, as I previously suggested, is the nature of seventeenth-century Protestant theology. Amid the great variety of terminology and belief across sects and decades in early modern England, there was a general and important distinction between what many called "belief," being "called" or "justified" in faith, which tended to happen early in life, and theological "assurance" of God's grace.[18] In the intermediate state between the two, which could last years or even a lifetime, the soul was open to temptations of despair, the lapse into a conviction that one was, after all, reprobate. Many narratives by women recount the search for and hopeful meditation over "promises," scriptural passages that they believed targeted them personally as they struggled to feel the assurance of grace. Often the promises would seem to recede from the subject's grasp, and a convention in many spiritual narratives of the period is the anxiety that one has committed the "one unpardonable sin," the sin against the Holy Ghost (Matthew 12:31–32), and thereby lost God's grace.

The unpardonable sin has varying interpretations in seventeenth-century theology, but essentially it is the deployment of faith (or, as it reveals itself to be, merely ostensible, false faith) in one's own interest, rather than God's. So in *Grace Abounding* the preacher John Bunyan defines his unpardonable sin as "selling Christ," while the popular theologian William Perkins identifies it, more broadly, as the temporary faith of the reprobate who merely flatters himself with his own assurance.[19] The term most often used to capture the unpardonable sin is "hypocrisy," or false profession, which applies regardless of intention, whether the subject means to deceive or instead is deceived by her own mistake. This latter possibility, that what one thought was faith is at best wishfulness, instigates a sort of anti-conversion, in which all that one thought one knew, all the ground of one's soul, might get swept away. There is no defense against it but denial, or God's mercy. According to the theological tenet of grace, mercy is bestowed freely rather than as recompense for any deed or impulse of the soul, indeed without even the cooperation of the will, and those spiritual narratives that find some resolution to their predicament of doubt are thus not organized by the subject's agency.[20] Rather, the subject remains passive, and the account of the resolution is accordingly perfunctory. Protestant theology in this period, then, disables the possibility of working through trauma in the modern sense: the subject either remains split, vacillating between moments of hypothetical assurance and the conviction of despair, or she is lifted out of her traumatic narrative into a different kind, in which the theological dangers of her trauma simply dissipate.

In its anxieties about promises gained and lost, Allen's *Narrative* hews closely to these conventions. When she was a girl, Allen says, her soul already experienced "earnest breathings after the ways of God" (2), but she was also subject to melancholy from the beginning. After the early death of her beloved first husband she falls into "black humour" (7), and as her "temptations" increase, she fears that she is a hypocrite making overly hasty claims to faith: "I am just as if two were fighting within me" (8), she complains, as she feels herself slipping again and again from the ground of assurance. Her conviction that she has committed "the Unpardonable sin" (4) hardens (she does not define it), and her loving family gives her "Physick" (10) and moves her from place to place in the hopes of breaking the hold of her melancholy—from her mother's to her aunt's, then to London to stay with her uncles and brother, then to the house of a kinswoman in London because her brother travels too often. But without the hope of grace she feels that she is on the brink of death every day, and she begins to devise ways of killing herself, by overdosing on opium, smoking spiders (apparently perceived to be poisonous when vaporized), secreting herself in her aunt's attic for days without water, reopening her veins after she has been bled. "That which I prayed against in hypocrisie," she concludes in the midst of her sufferings, "God had brought upon me in reality" (40). For page after vivid page she describes debates with her family and friends, including several clergy, whose arguments to her mind are no match for her "nimble . . . Answers" (63); her extravagant conviction that in her sinfulness she is "unparallel'd," "the Monster of the Creation" (23, 43); and her prolonged effort to starve herself till she is only "Skin and Bones" (64). Suddenly, however, in the space of a few sentences and without any narrative motivation or cause, after a minister Shorthose and his wife come to talk to her (she has visited them before, to no effect), her "bodily distempers abated" and "my spiritual Maladies also," and God convinces her without any struggle that Satan, not her own unregeneracy, has been the author of all her misery (72). The book ends immediately afterward with a list of the scriptural "Promises" that at moments during her years of suffering seemed to apply particularly well to her predicament. She had been able to use them, she says now in retrospect, for reassurance.[21]

Although the *Narrative*'s resolution may seem underwritten to us, its sudden brevity at the moment of conversion and its vagueness about causality fit the nonconforming Protestant theology of grace, and indeed may have been psychologically comforting to readers who, like Allen, felt as an impasse the division in self between a part that is terrified it has been cast out of God's grace and another that in its persistence in "earnest breathings after God" counters the self's incipient despair. In this way Allen's *Narrative* is not unusual; what is remarkable is the intensity with which she experiences her split self and the difficulty of sustaining it alive. Whoever made the decision to print the *Narrative* may have intended the lesson to be, as the title says, the reliability of God's grace, but the energy of the account is in Allen's suffering, which Job-like threatens to escape its moral trajectory and in so doing opens a space for the expression of spiritual struggle as trauma.[22]

Like many Protestant spiritual narratives of the period, Allen's focuses on scripture as the ground for her relationship to God, and on her own reading and writing practices as the tools with which to live out that relationship. It is a historical commonplace that as Reformed theology is fundamentally logocentric, so post-Reformation spiritual crises center on the often-fraught relation between the subject and the word, or the book. In *Grace Abounding*—now singularly canonical even though in the context of similar, much less read narratives of the period it was quite conventional—Bunyan struggles again and again with the words that present themselves to his mind, unsure whether they are God's promise of grace or Satan's temptation to sin.[23] He pores over scripture, trying to reconcile those passages that seem to promise his own particular damnation with others that offer assurance. Words have a material force as they "break" and "bolt" into his mind, where they have the power to "lie all day long, all the week long, yea, all the year long in my mind, and hold me down."[24] Language seems almost willful, an agent of its own in the temporal world as it conveys the tangible presence of God and his enemy. The great challenge for the subject is not to harness words' power, as in humanist pedagogical theory—making words an instrument of the self would be prideful—but rather to scrutinize them for their likely source and thus their intention. To give another, quite disparate example, Mary Rich, Countess of Warwick, was far from a Quaker, but she was deeply troubled, as she recounts often in her diaries, by her husband's "swearing" during his protracted and sometimes agonizing bouts with gout, by which she probably meant his speaking God's name in complaint rather than humble acceptance.[25] Her objection is more general than the Quaker opposition to oaths, which was based on the troubling assumption implicit in oath-taking that ordinary language had correspondingly less stringent requirements for sincerity. But it almost certainly stemmed from a similar aversion to pride in the face of God, and a similar anxiety about words' power as the engine of that pride. The Quaker Mary Pennington (whose son-in-law William Penn founded Pennsylvania) remembers that when she first tried to pray as a young girl, she realized with dismay that "an ungodly person could use as well as I" to merely "read one out of a book." It was not until "it came into my mind that I would write a prayer of my own composing," though she could still barely form letters, that she was able to open her mind to God and pray in good faith.[26] At the far end of the dissenting spectrum, Pennington was unable to certify to herself that her prayers were imbued with her own intention, and thus truly received from and directed toward God, unless the words were hers alone. Like most Quakers she insisted on a connection to God unmediated by language that had been adulterated and compromised by its implication in the world.

Words are the medium of the person's relation to God, and insofar as that relation is uncertain and likely to be sabotaged, they are fraught with danger and power. As such, they are at the center of the persistent anxiety characterizing religious writing in this period. In her *Narrative*, Allen's distress, too, is focused by books and writing, through her deep Bunyanesque unsureness about whether she can recognize or claim God in the words she reads and speaks. Her family and friends and the ministers she associates with are Presbyterian, not Quaker, but there are Quaker lineaments to her terror, when she writes and reads, that she cannot take the words in her mind as her own, that she is unable to profess or even to ingest them with sincerity.[27] Like many girls and women, early in her life she keeps in shorthand a book of prayers, praises, and promises as a kind of spiritual account, but as she becomes more melancholy she seems to split into two parts: one part who uses language ordinarily in the world, and another, standing aside, who is ironically estranged from all that the first part says and begins to recast her writing as a sort of challenge to God, "to see what God will do with me" (18). At the height of her preoccupation with death she imagines that all the lights in other houses at night, which signify others reading around her, are tiny devils, mocking her because in her own earlier reading "I proved such an Hypocrite" (34). Disgusted and horrified that as a reader she once accepted as applicable to herself godly comforts that she now knows she never truly believed in, she cannot endure "to hear the sound of reading, nor the sight of a Book or Paper; tho' it were but a Letter, or an Almanack," and when she receives letters from friends trying to comfort her in her distress, she tears them up without reading them (58). At times, she confesses miserably, she "would strike the Horn-book out of my Childs hand," not to protect her child but because she is so enraged by the estrangement from her own sincerity that reading signifies. "It had been happy for me if I had been born blind," she concludes, never to have "seen book, or learned letter" (59). Albeit unwittingly, she has "medled" with the Word and sacraments of God (51), a term that suggests tampering and adulteration, and the only way she can think of to forbear from this sin is through another one, to exile herself even from the medium of her relation to the divine. At one odd moment she hears books "cryed" in the streets, presumably booksellers advertising their wares, and she is struck with the idea that soon she will be the subject of a book herself, and of similar "dreadful" calls, imagining that "I should be called Allen that Cursed Apostate" (46–47). A book here becomes not just the means but the symbol of her estrangement from God and self, her sin hypostatized and encapsulated within someone else's words.

If, then, Allen's tormented relationship with written words finds a context in Protestant and specifically dissenting theology of the period, it is also part of a chapter in the complex early modern history of reading and representation, which encompasses and recontextualizes theological reading practices. Women readers and writers of spiritual narratives in the later seventeenth century are inheritors of a long tradition that construes reading and viewing of representations not as a conversation between representation and reader or viewer, but as an act of occupation, as it were, by the representation. In effect the representation replaces the ordinary world in the viewer's or reader's mind with the world it conjures. In the model's negative manifestation, thought to apply particularly to weak readers such as women and the uneducated and considered most perilous in secular genres that foregrounded pleasure, the audience risks losing itself. The dissociation from the real or from the self prepares the ground for naïve identification, according to which the self might become implicated in and even one with the thing it sees. Anxiety about naïve identification recalls an earlier history of Reformation debates about idolatry, among other loci. It is also at the heart of anti-theatrical protests in the late sixteenth century, which denounce plays for their power to confuse truth and fiction in the minds of their viewers, and of the early modern hostility to prose romance and other forms of what we would call escapist fiction.[28] In seventeenth-century conversion stories, as part of their turn toward belief, women almost formulaically renounce or disavow the reading of "plays and romances." As Mary Rich's brother Robert Boyle, himself a youthful devotee of romance, argues in his memoir, such dangerous genres train the mind to mimic their undisciplined form and extreme affect and thereby to reject both God and reason.[29]

This identificatory model of reading has positive implications too, particularly for humanists and other relatively elite readers thought to have the skills and sophistication to harness identification for good. The medieval "mirror for princes," a genre of political writing offering to rulers images of men like themselves for emulation or avoidance, is picked up first by sixteenth-century humanists and then by aristocratic seventeenth-century prose romance, the readers of which, as John Barclay says in his 1621 *Argenis*, for example, will first "love" the fiction "as not concerned in it," but as they read more deeply "shall meet with themselves, & as in a Looking-glasse, shall see the face and merit of their owne fame."[30] Reading does not just offer exemplars for observation but enlists its subjects in the active construction of them. In psychoanalytic terms we might see the process of recognizing oneself in a positive fictional exemplar as something like the incorporation of an ego ideal. Such a process runs the risk of self-flattery, to return to early modern terminology, for those too quick to see the ideal as a faithful mirror, but for virtuously humble readers it motivates what we might call "strenuous identification"—that is, an intentional and self-conscious effort to complete the mirroring relation—and leads not to a loss of self but to an augmentation of it. To make such work less onerous, the book offers among other pleasures the narcissistic delight of meeting oneself in an ideal other, who is projected into and seemingly extant already in the world. The ideal is thus aspirational but also self-confirming: the reader is already inside, a direct addressee of the word.

It would be illogical to call scriptural promises ego ideals, but fascinatingly, seventeenth-century women seem to have searched for and collected promises with a very similar identificatory goal. In spiritual narratives women record combing scripture for promises "sutable to [their] condition" and keeping a "daily account" of promises that fit the particular "frame of [their] heart[s]." One young woman, even as she joys at hearing sermons that seem as if "onely concerning my particular," is reluctant to "apply . . . to my selfe" the apparently more demanding affirmation of some promises she "highly priced," for fear that she does not yet merit "interest"—here, something like implication or participation—in them.[31] In much the same way that Bunyan struggles to discern in *Grace Abounding* whether the scriptural passages that come into his consciousness have been sent by God, women query whether the promises they read are meant to speak directly to them — whether the words in their minds are part of the promises, or they themselves participants in the voice that speaks those promises. To feel confirmed personally by promises is to experience oneself as named by the scriptural text, integrated into the divine. Of course Protestant theology makes assurance a very high bar to clear and offers little mechanism for the inclusion of unregenerate experience in the confirmed or assured self. To the extent that it defines the difference between being saved and lost as absolute, such a theology may itself conduce to the traumatically split subject. Hypocrisy, as used by good Protestants in this period, describes essentially a desire that cannot be met: the self projects its incorporation in the ideal but cannot experience it as real, and in its failure it becomes insufficient to itself, its intention rendered pointless. Scripture is a text that promises, but like all texts also fails to deliver. And the practice of identificatory engagement with scripture, insofar as it tends toward the end not only of temporary, temporal pleasure but toward a guarantee of eternal life, makes that refusal traumatizing.

For Protestant women, then, the stakes of identificatory reading of scripture are absolute. The ideal is the only option, and for women who are taught to make their spiritual status the main preoccupation of their lives, the failure to feel it as achieved renders them insufficient to their sense of self. Faced with this prospect of a traumatic split, Allen makes a choice that is on the face of it obviously self-destructive but also, within this traumatic paradigm, self-enabling. If she cannot be absolutely identified with the ideal, she decides, she will instead be absolutely divergent, absolutely fallen and absolutely, materially dead. Early in her life when her melancholy tempted her to believe that "never any was like me," she let herself be corrected by reading in books of spiritual guidance that "treated on my Case" (4–5). As she grows estranged from books and writing, however, she increasingly sees herself as "unparalleled," unexampled by anything she encounters outside herself (23). Convinced that she has committed, as she says, not only the one "Unpardonable sin" but a sin greater than any committed by anyone before, that she has not only been possessed by the devil but become the devil himself, she declares herself "the Monster of the Creation." Tellingly, and disarmingly, she adds that "in this word I much delighted" (43): there is a pleasure for her in subject consolidation even at the negative pole, in the relatively coherent identity offered by monstrousness. To be monstrous is to be whole, if only in a negative sense, as a gross compensation for the incoherence of her suffering. Allen knows that outside of God's grace the devil is calling her every day to "dye by the way," and her repeated attempts to kill herself can be seen as an attempt to express or instantiate this literally. When her mother tries to put her in a coach to London for a change of scene, Allen reminds her that she is still dying as always, and then asks indignantly, "Do you think people will like to have a dead Corps in the Coach with them?" (28). This bid to have her suffering taken literally is complex. If she is in part self-ironizing, she is also desperately sincere: she and her mother both know there will not be a corpse in the carriage at the end of the trip, but even if her mother only imagines herself as a passenger in a coach riding alongside a corpse, perhaps she will begin to glimpse the uncanny intrusions of outrageous pain that Allen must endure all the time. Her trauma now is no longer her distance from the ideal but the contradiction of persistent life within a self that is already dead. As a monster who might literalize on her body her felt sense of absolute separation from God, she recasts the ideal in the negative. If she cannot become one with God, then like Milton's Satan she will find consistency through renouncing him. That she ironizes this gesture toward heroism, aware even in the midst of it that it cannot repair her loss of God, is one of the saddest aspects of her account, and a testament to the rigors of her traumatic predicament.

In the last section of this chapter I want to bring in one more set of terms, a set common in Protestant women's spiritual writing and one through which they negotiate some accommodation with spiritual trauma. Allen's failure to identify with God might also be expressed as a failure of allegory, or more precisely as the experience of a tendency always inhering in allegory to proceed to a dead end. In following the imperative toward identification with God, Allen participates in an ancient Christian tradition of allegorical hermeneutics, which understands the universe as an enormous network of analogous meanings, a nearly infinite number of cases and significations all in harmony with one another in their relation to the all-encompassing divine. In her non-signifying literality or her monstrousness Allen would seem to be the opposite, the purely singular instance. But the structural equivalence between God and monster that she posits is telling, pointing as it does to the risk always inhering in allegory's drive toward unity, of obscuring or strangling dissent and difference. Instead of a glorious network of multiple meanings, allegory always potentially yields one simple, tyrannical idea. The subject in such an allegorical world, if we define it as having or seeking integrity in and of itself, has no good options. To say yes to the divine is to lose its integrity; to say no, to be exiled from all relation and thus to lose its boundaries in another way. In a revealing study of Bunyan's take on marriage, Thomas Luxon draws a distinction between the progressive deployment of "allegorical hermeneutics" to point out correspondences and analogs, a practice he associates with Milton, and the kind of totalizing, simplifying allegory he sees at work in Bunyan. When Bunyan writes marriage between man and woman as a mere type of the relation between God and (specifically) man, what Luxon describes as his "all but narcissistic" projection of "oneness with the risen Christ," the Protestant preacher is using allegory to cancel out women and assorted troublesome others, along with the "paradox, anxiety, or even tension" that come with relation to them.[32] For Luxon, Bunyan's struggle toward identification with God as it is represented across all of his work is radically simplifying of the world he encounters. Allegory does not know what to do with difference that wants to sustain itself as different without entirely leaving the stage, but it is the respect for difference that will save it from collapsing in on itself, and save too the dissenting subject.

Allegory shares a major aspect of traumatic narrative, an obsessive repetition of its one simple story. Though it wants to present itself as wide-ranging and generous, welcoming all comers in its polysemic multiplicity, in marshaling them within its coherent structure it quickly turns "daemonic," to use Angus Fletcher's word, zeroed in on its unilinear trajectory.[33] But in its representations of the literal, it might also retain resistant traces of difference—traces whose integrity, paradoxically, might be preserved by allegory's rush past them toward the idea. Mary Jacobus reads traumatic narrative in an interestingly similar way, arguing that though in its symptomology trauma might seem demonic, it actually contains within itself its own undoing, and thus perhaps its cure. In a discussion of Pierre Nora's "*lieux de mémoire*," those fossilized, public "sites of memory" that attempt to rationalize and justify complex living memory, Jacobus identifies an "excess of signification—memory, as it were, in the wrong place," that cannot be assimilated into the dominant historical narrative. As if despite themselves, *lieux de mémoire* frustrate their own drive to monumentalize. Such traumatic excess, Jacobus adds, also "tends to accompany the literary representation of historical trauma." For new, historically different readers of those representations, whether monuments or texts, traumatic excess opens a hermeneutic door, "making it possible," she concludes, "to generate new meanings and unforeseeable connections from the accidents of memory."[34] Traumatic excess is a force that opens the monopolistic singular to variety and possibility, in much the same way that allegory preserves its own undoings. It would be overly simplifying to identify allegorical with traumatic narrative, but in its structurally analogous tendency toward reductive repetition and its preservation of hermeneutic excess, allegory offers itself as an early modern vehicle for the expression of trauma, and perhaps too even as a method for mitigating it.

In its emphasis on God's grace over human agency, it is fair to say, most later seventeenth-century Protestant women's life-writing does not offer much of a road map toward the narrative resolution of spiritual trauma. But in closing I will consider two examples of allegory's conceptual efficacy in texts by women, Jane Turner's 1653 spiritual manual *Choice Experiences of the kind dealings of God before, in, and after conversion* and Mary Rich's *Occasional Meditations*. Turner devotes her manual, "whereunto is added a description of true Experience," to a detailed explanation of how women "can truly wait for the accomplishment of Promises."[35] Her solution is what she calls "close walking with God," which she defines by a particularly daunting list of customary feminine spiritual practices: "meditation, self-examination, self-watching, self-judging, self-humbling and prayer" (185). Unlike other writers, though, Turner leans hard on the concept of "experience," which she elevates to equal importance with what she calls "knowledge" of scripture. Experience is not a vehicle to that knowledge so much as the set of practices that bring the subject into relation with it: "All experience," she says, "is either an effect of knowledge, or by it we learn knowledge" (200). Turner certainly desires assurance, but her own history of conversion and uncertainty has taught her to fill the space of waiting with practice, a "walking with" rather than an insistence on achievement of or possession by the divine.

Women's spiritual writing, to the modern reader, may look repetitive and formulaic, offering little insight into the individual psyche, but formulaic repetition, Turner reminds us, was precisely the point. For the subject who could trust in experience, the writing and rewriting of promises and meditations was not traumatic repetition but the approach to God. We have tended to think of trauma as blocked narrative, and to assume the value therefore of reasserting narrative flow and resolution, but Turner suggests the value of practice and experience, not as means to another end but in themselves. In her argument for "true experience" over false, the Baptist Turner is also keen to refute the Quaker reliance on mere inward apprehension of God, which she denounces as "allegorical notions" without any ground, the mere "vision of their own brains" (163, 202). In part Turner wants to assert the value of the literal, the text of scripture, which Quakers famously subjugated to their own direct experience of the divine. But her correction is both broader and more pointed than that. When Quakers and others focus on mere "allegorical notions," ideas in their own minds, then "things come and go with them" (206). But those who engage in "serious observation and meditation" (206)—that is, "true experience"—fix those things as present, rescue them from ephemerality, or rescue their minds from the tendency to make things so. In this way they construct an anchor to presence and the real where Allen could conceive only absence.

Not merely coincidentally, seventeenth-century philosophers beginning to construct what would become modern scientific method at this time were dedicating themselves to very similar rigors of "serious observation." The rationale, and the challenge, here too was to discipline the mind's excesses. Robert Boyle, to give one famous example, struggled as a young man with what he called "raving," an intellectual and emotional distraction brought on, so he believed, by his identificatory reading of romances and other unserious literature. He cured himself by a practice very much like Turner's (though broader in scope to match men's greater liberty in subject matter), learning to fix his mind by "attentive observation of the Objects wherewith he [was] conversant." The record of his acquiring this discipline is his large body of published "Occasional Reflections," his analogue to women's spiritual writing, encompassing not only "Theological" but also "Political . . . Oeconomical, or even . . . Physical" matters.[36] The analogy I am suggesting between empiricist and spiritual habits of thought is brought home by the fact that Boyle's literary sister Mary Rich wrote her own large collection of "Occasional Meditations," which discern in ordinary objects and events—"a gloworme," "an hour glass," "sealeing a lettar," "my Lady Anne Baringtones childes weaneing"—moral and spiritual significance.[37] In her diaries Rich explains that she employed her practices of conceiving, writing, and reviewing her meditations as an antidote against the spiritual "dulness" through which she experienced her separation from God. Her meditations, that is, along with her other spiritual practices, were very much in line with Turner's "close walking."[38] This discipline of attentive observation of "things," for all three writers, grounds the mind, countering its tendency to indulge in the excess of pure thought while softening and expanding its field of vision. As an idea it recuperates allegory, rescuing it from mere "allegorical notions" by restoring the literal and material to significance. For Turner and others who subscribe to "close walking" as a practice, allegory becomes not just a one-way linear narrative toward pure idea, but a way to make idea and referent simultaneously available to the mind—a ground for meditative practice, we might say, rather than a means to accomplished identification with the ideal.

Allen's contemporaries help frame what is usual and unusual in her writing. If she pursues the logic of her despair with extraordinary rigor and persistence, she is entirely ordinary within the context of early modern women's spiritual life-writing in her perception of a split in self and her suffering because of it. One crucial implication of this ordinariness is that early modern women were not outside the main historical trajectory for subjectivity but right at its center. In her book on early modern trauma, Cynthia Marshall posits that imaginative identification with representations of the traumatized, shattered subject was transgressively pleasurable for the reader or spectator, as a sort of release valve for the cultural pressure toward an increasingly coherent, consolidated model of subjectivity. But women, she suggests, at least somewhat exempt as they were from this pressure, may not have felt the same pleasure.[39] For women, that is, trauma was less of a challenge to the normative self because the normative self was not firmly enough in place to be challenged. Allen, and Turner and Rich as well, would differ. In fact, as their spiritual writings and those of their contemporaries suggest, it seems to have been women's cultural duty at this time to manage challenges to the coherent self. Their spiritual writing practice was a means of tending to the spiritual split in self—experiencing it and also, by the same techniques, mitigating it, because the spiritual habits that conduced to the traumatic recognition of distance from God, as Turner shows, also contained it. Perhaps this daily negotiation with the threat of trauma was even a necessary correlative to the emergent fantasy of the autonomous, narratively complete subject, the mirror image against which it found its identity.

NOTES

1. For examples, see James Robert Allard and Mathew R. Martin, eds., *Staging Pain: Violence and Trauma in British Theater* (Burlington: Ashgate, 2009); Patricia A. Cahill, *Unto the Breach: Martial Formations, Historical Trauma, and the Early Modern Stage* (New York: Oxford University Press, 2008); Heather Hirschfeld, "Hamlet's 'first corse': Repetition, Trauma, and the Displacement of Redemptive Typology," *Shakespeare Quarterly* 54 (2003): 424–48; Mathew Martin, *Tragedy and Trauma in the Plays of Christopher Marlowe* (Burlington: Ashgate, 2015). Zackariah C. Long offers a summary of scholarly approaches to early modern trauma in "'Uncollected Man': Trauma and the Early Modern Mind-body in *The Maid's Tragedy*," in Allard and Martin, *Staging Pain*, 31–46.
2. Long, "Uncollected Man," 31.
3. Cathy Caruth, *Unclaimed Experience: Trauma, Narrative, and History* (Baltimore: Johns Hopkins University Press, 1996), offers a summary of psychoanalytic trauma theory. For the alternative view, common in most contemporary clinical approaches to trauma and presupposed by such concepts as post-traumatic stress disorder (PTSD), see, for example, Bessel Van der Kolk, *The Body Keeps the Score* (New York: Penguin, 2014).
4. For a succinct account of these two strains in trauma theory, see R. Clifton Spargo, "The Rhetoric of Trauma," *Reading On* 1, no. 1 (2006): 1–21, esp. 2–3.
5. Mary Jacobus, *Psychoanalysis and the Scene of Reading* (New York: Oxford University Press, 1999), 132. Jacobus quotes Hartman, "On Traumatic Knowledge and Literary Studies," *New Literary History* 26 (1995): 537–63, esp. 547.
6. Mathew R. Martin, "'This Tragic Glass': Tragedy and Trauma in *Tamburlaine Part One*," in Allard and Martin, *Staging Pain*, 15–29, 16; Martin, *Tragedy and Trauma*, 10–16.
7. Martin, *Tragedy and Trauma*, 20; Fredric Jameson, *The Political Unconscious: Narrative as a Socially Symbolic Act* (London: Methuen, 1981), 102.
8. Hirschfeld, "Hamlet's 'first corse,'" 446.
9. Mary Rich, "Some Specialities in the Life of M Warwicke," in *The Autobiography of Mary Countess of Warwick*, ed. T. Crofton Croker (London: Percy Society, 1848), 24.
10. Pierre Nora, "Between Memory and History: *Les Lieux de Memoires*," trans. Mark Roudebush, *Representations* 26 (Spring 1989): 7–24, esp. 13.
11. Hirschfeld, "Hamlet's 'first corse,'" 427.
12. See especially Katharine Hodgkin, "Mad Unto the World: Spiritual and Mental Disturbances" in *Madness in Seventeenth-Century Autobiography* (London: Palgrave Macmillan, 2007), 86–101; also, Allen Ingram, ed., *Patterns of Madness in the Eighteenth Century: A Reader* (Liverpool: Liverpool University Press, 1998), 29–35; Elaine

Hobby, *Virtue of Necessity: English Women's Writing, 1649–88* (Ann Arbor: University of Michigan Press, 1989), 92–93.

13. Katharine Hodgkin, "Dionys Fitzherbert and the Anatomy of Madness," in *Voicing Women: Gender and Sexuality in Early Modern Writing*, ed. Kate Chedgzoy, Melanie Hansen, and Suzanne Trill (Keele, UK: Keele University Press, 1996), 69–90, esp. 73–74.
14. Anne Wentworth, *A Vindication of Anne Wentworth* (1677), 8.
15. Hannah Allen, *A Narrative of God's Gracious Dealings with that Choice Christian Mrs. Hannah Allen* (London, 1683), 60–61. All further parenthetical references are to this edition.
16. My reading of Allen's crisis, and of Protestant women's spiritual struggles in general, differs here from that of Elspeth Graham, "Authority, Resistance, and Loss: Gendered Difference in the Writings of John Bunyan and Hannah Allen," in *Trauma and Transformation: The Political Progress of John Bunyan*, ed. Vera J. Camden, (Palo Alto: Stanford University Press, 2008), who argues that Allen suffers from the failure of her religious framework to explain her distress and her abhorrence of relationship with others.
17. For now-canonical examples, see William Wordsworth, *The Prelude* (1798, 1805); Benjamin Franklin, *The Autobiography of Benjamin Franklin* (1793); Olaudah Equiano, *The Interesting Narrative of the Life of Olaudah Equiano* (1789); and Frederick Douglass, *Narrative of the Life of Frederick Douglass* (1845). For an overview of the history and centrality of the "conversion framework" in American and European autobiography, see Peter Dorsey, *Sacred Estrangement: The Rhetoric of Conversion in Modern American Autobiography* (Pennsylvania: Penn State University Press, 1993), esp. chaps. 1–2, pp. 17–86.
18. See Mary Morrissey, "Narrative Authority in Spiritual Life-writing: The Example of Dionys Fitzherbert (fl 1608–1641)," *The Seventeenth Century* 15, no. 1 (2000): 5–7.
19. John Bunyan, *Grace Abounding to the Chief of Sinners*, ed. Roger Sharrock (Oxford, UK: Clarendon, 1963), paras. 135–36; for Perkins, see Morrissey, "Narrative Authority," 6.
20. Morrissey, "Narrative Authority," 8, discusses this convention.
21. Elizabeth Skerpan-Wheeler, the editor of Allen's *Narrative* for *The Early Modern Englishwoman: A Facsimile Library of Essential Works*, notes that pages 75–78 of the *Narrative*, the bulk of Allen's list of Promises, are missing in all seven known exemplars of the work (*Life Writings, II: Printed Writings 1641–1700*, series II, part 1, vol. 2 [Burlington: Ashgate, 2001], introductory note, xii–xiii). W. Carew Hazlitt, *Bibliographical Collections and Notes on Early English Literature* (London, 1903), however, records in its entry for Allen's *Narrative* a colophon on H7 that lists a printer different from the title page, Richard Baldwin rather than John Wallis, and a dedication "by Hannah

Hatt to the Lady B[aker]" (176). (John Hatt, as Allen's *Narrative* notes, was Allen's second husband, whom she married after the time discussed in the *Narrative*.) This record suggests Hazlitt may have seen another, more complete copy.

22. The author of the preface to Allen's *Narrative*, who signs him- or herself "Thy Soul-friend and Servant for Jesus Sake" and dates the preface as 1681 rather than 1683 as on the title page (xi), is unknown. His or her reference to Allen as a "Now-glorified Soul" (v) indicates that Allen was already dead in 1681.
23. For a discussion of Bunyan's conventionality within the context of spiritual life-writing during the seventeenth century, see Maria Magro, "Spiritual Autobiography and Radical Sectarian Women's Discourse: Anna Trapnel and the Bad Girls of the English Revolution," *Journal of Medieval and Early Modern Studies* 34, no. 2 (Spring 2004): 412–33, esp. 423–26.
24. Bunyan, *Grace Abounding*, paras. 145, 206, 262.
25. Mary Rich, *Memoir of Lady Warwick, also her Diary, from A.D. 1666–1672* (London: Religious Tract Society, 1847), for example, 97, 104, 115, 125, 229, 237, 253.
26. Mary Pennington, *Some Account of Circumstances in the Life of Mary Pennington, printed from her manuscript, left for her family* (London, 1821), 3–4. The manuscript survives in a copy at the Haverford College Quaker & Special Collections; see "An Abstract from the Life of Mary Pennington, formerly Springett," TriCollege Libraries, accessed November 15, 2020. https://archives.tricolib.brynmawr.edu/repositories/5/resources/974.
27. See Hodgkin, *Madness in Seventeenth-Century Autobiography*, 98, for Allen's Presbyterianism.
28. Amelia Zurcher, *Seventeenth-Century English Romance: Allegory, Ethics, and Politics* (New York: Palgrave Macmillan, 2007), 2–3.
29. For plays and romances, see, for example, Rich, *Some Specialities*, 4, 21; Rich, *Memoir of Lady Warwick*, 129, 221, 259. Robert Boyle, "An Account of Philaretus During His Minority," in *Robert Boyle by Himself and His Friends*, ed. Michael Hunter (New York: Routledge, 1994), 1-22, 8, 12.
30. John Barclay, *John Barclay His Argenis*, trans. Robert Le Grys (London, 1628), 131.
31. "Sutable," in *Imitation and Caution for Christian Women, Or, the Life and Death of that Excellent Gentlewoman, Mrs. Mary Bewley* (London, 1659), 10; Allen uses the same phrase, *Narrative*, 8. "Daily account" and "frame of my heart" in Richard Baxter, *A Treatise of Death . . . preached at the Funerals of Elizabeth, the late wife of Mr Joseph Baker . . . with some few passages of the life of the said Mrs Baker* (London, 1660), 239–40. Sermons and promises "highly prized" in Edmund Staunton, *A Sermon Preacht at Great Milton . . . on Mrs Elizabeth Wilkinson . . . Whereunto is added a Narrative of her Godly life and Death* (Oxford, UK, 1659), 29–30.

32. Thomas Luxon, "One Soul Versus One Flesh: Friendship, Marriage, and the Puritan Self," in *Trauma and Transformation*, 81–99.
33. Angus Fletcher, *Allegory: The Theory of a Symbolic Mode* (New York: Cornell University Press, 1964).
34. Jacobus, *Psychoanalysis*, 123, italics in original; Nora, "Between Memory and History," 7.
35. Jane Turner, *Choice Experiences of the kind dealings of God before, in, and after conversion* (London, 1653), 104.
36. Robert Boyle, "An Account of Philaretus During his Minority," in *Robert Boyle by Himself and His Friends*, ed. Michael Hunter (New York: Routledge, 1994), 8; Boyle, *The Works of Robert Boyle, Electronic Edition*, ed. Michael Hunter and Edward B. Davis, 14 vols. (Charlottesville: InteLex, 2003), vol. 5; Boyle, *Occasional Reflections Upon Several Subjects*, 1–180; Boyle, "Attentive observation," 32; "Theological . . . ," 30.
37. Mary Rich, *The Occasional Meditations of Mary Rich, Countess of Warwick*, ed. Raymond A. Anselment (Tempe: Arizona Center for Medieval and Renaissance Studies, 2009), 64, 74, 83, 131.
38. Rich, *Memoir of Lady Warwick*, for example, 121, 143, 147, 163, 180, 195, 200.
39. Cynthia Marshall, *The Shattering of the Self: Violence, Subjectivity, and Early Modern Texts* (Baltimore: Johns Hopkins University Press, 2002).

4

Early Modern Ciphering and the Expression of Trauma

KATHERINE ELLISON

Messages written in cipher describe significant emotional experiences, often while they are occurring: violence, entrapment, starvation, wounding, mourning, dying. The discipline of cryptography has long occupied a special status as a confessional system, and ciphers record the limitations of human languages to communicate the traumas of war, famine, plague, imprisonment, and genocide. In 1685, after the death of Charles II and in a gesture of loyalty to James II, John Falconer would describe cryptography as a "consecrated art" in *Cryptomenysis Patefacta: Or the Art of Secret Information Disclosed Without a Key*.[1] "By means of Secret Intelligence," Falconer explains, "*not only* Armies, *but* Kingdoms and Crowns *have been* lost" (4 italics in the original). Though he does not cite specific historical events, his dedication to fellow Royalist Charles, Second Earl of Middleton, indicates Falconer's bitterness about the execution of Charles I and his warning to the court of James II that they must be savvy in their knowledge of ciphering. In one example drawn from a contemporary conflict Falconer does not name, the writer ciphers an urgent request using a simple substitution method:

Y pb vdgrts id ztte ixt Hdafytgh
Idcb wofr rihm obr rihm rxfh
Dfaawi fd zc espi gtww cpfzwe ez
Cqn Nwuxg bynnmrtg. qibc.

I am forced to keep the Soldiers
upon hard duty and hard diet:

Supply us, or they will revolt to
the Enemy speedily. Hast. (20)

Falconer does not explain how he has obtained this cipher or verify its authenticity; he assumes an audience intimate with the recent political trauma that motivates his publication of *Cryptomenysis*, who will read its pathos, collectively, as a call to action. Similarly, when Napoleon Bonaparte's more famous encrypted letter of October 20, 1812, to Foreign Minister Hugues-Bernard Maret was finally deciphered, its command, to destroy the Kremlin, was an act of desperation. Napoleon writes: "My cavalry is in tatters, many horses are dying." "This letter is an incredible insight," writes Jean-Christophe Chataignier, who auctioned the letter in 2012. He notes that "we've never seen Napoleon emotively speaking in this way before" and that "this letter is unique" because "it's the first time we see this different Napoleon."[2] In both ciphers readers see behind the glory of war; there is the sense that this suffering, organizational and bureaucratic, is the real battle. Soldiers and horses starve and mutiny without provisions.

Real world ciphers, like Falconer's example and Napoleon's plea, provided modes of expression for generations experiencing great upheaval in their political, social, theological, and scientific worldviews. As cryptography historians have long noted, ciphering has been prevalent in times of war and in situations of personal and collective crisis that require secrecy to survive. Gustavus Selenus (pseudonym for Augustus, the Duke of Brunswick-Lüneburg) explains, in *Cryptomenytices et Cryptographie* (1624), that "though to some this whole subject may seem the invention of an idle man and even childish trifling, contributing neither to private nor to public utility, still, let one be as sensible in his own person as he may, if he will not or cannot understand the importance that there is, especially in war-times and at other times of stress, in this safe method of conveying a secret."[3] As Selenus and others note, writers without the status of Napoleon have also been eager to learn how to cipher and decipher their communication even during relatively peaceful times, whether to disguise personal tragedy, commercial secrets, or romantic correspondence or to better understand messages circulating around them.[4] Cryptography instructional manuals, like Falconer's *Cryptomenysis*, have provided that guidance. During and after the Wars of the Three Kingdoms (1639–51) the genre flourished and was popular with both specialist and nonspecialist readers. It would not be as popular again, instructionally, until World War I. Composing in cipher and forging through the computational problem-solving processes of deciphering were presented by cryptographers as pedagogical strategies for processing trauma and circumventing and conventionalizing the communication and reading of suffering. Rarely studied and often devalued, late seventeenth- and eighteenth-century cryptography manuals negotiate nervousness about perception and interpretation during the Wars of the Three Kingdoms and the Restoration, exegetical but also social, cultural, political, and scientific, through computation and metaphorical thinking. This instruction of the seventeenth and early eighteenth centuries provided wide, everyday audiences with direction for how to cipher and decipher using a range of simple and complex methods, and those manuals articulated a crisis of interpretation and expression that was bound up in uncertainty about emotional authenticity. In other words, the manuals documented ciphering as the language of trauma.

Cryptography is the study of secret writing and cryptology is of the hidden word, but truer to the etymology of each, they are also studies of the crypt—the vault or cavern, or the burial space. As Falconer stresses, ciphering is an art of consecration. Selenus, too, calls a cipher a "citadel" and an "inner sanctuary."[5] Petrus Meyderlinus, overseer of the Evangelical College of Augsburg in 1624, says of ciphering that "there has been found the art that cryptographically reveals the secrets of the heart,—mystic, godlike, sacred."[6] Yet unlike the buried dead, the protected messages interred in ciphers are designed to be resurrected by chosen readers. Ciphers both "defy and demand our witness."[7] They are secrets that resist reading yet entice and even demand that they be examined slowly, with the care and analysis necessary to decipher them. In medieval and early modern cryptography, deciphering is not a desecration of the dead or the lost but a ceremonious dedication to service, a quest for truth. They even promise a revelation or awakening. Ciphers used during actual emergency situations, too, like Falconer's example and Napoleon's letter, are elevated in status as sacred objects capable of testifying to truths that non-ciphered writing cannot. Cryptographers like Selenus and his English contemporary, John Wallis, describe moments during which they take ciphers into their private chambers and deliberate upon them for hours, and sometimes weeks, until the message's meanings are unlocked and help can either be sent or plans can be foiled.

Ciphered letters are circulating questions; they are open-ended invitations for answer in the form of interrogation. Cathy Caruth argues that a question that communicates a crisis "can never be asked in a straight-forward way, but must, indeed, also be spoken in a language that is always somehow literary: a language that defies, even as it claims, our understanding."[8] As I will describe in this chapter, ciphers are certainly literary in that way. In a dedication to Selenus, Georg Ramus Remus notes that "by the subtle strength of the vigorous mind, was found the art of arts,—verily an art of the most ingenious kind,—which, by change of letters, numbers, figures, shows well the Mode of writing hidden thoughts."[9] They rely upon analogic representation, and even in their plaintext form when solved they are often poetic and still ambiguous as they tell the stories of their writers. This analogic mapping that is necessary to reach the plaintext occupies the mind with a series of steps. The methodical, even computational, problem-solving process is not a diversion from emotional acknowledgment of the experience but a multimodal and multisensory expression of it.

As my reference to Caruth's findings indicates, this chapter is informed by the tradition of trauma studies in literary scholarship, forged by the Yale School of which Caruth is a part, yet it is also attentive to postcolonial studies, the rhetoric and composition studies community, and recent work in affect theory and the history of science by Ruth Leys.[10] In postcolonial studies, the push against generalizations of traumatic experience and resistance to assumptions that different cultures experience similar symptoms of and responses to trauma regardless of traditions, time, or place, is useful in historical study.[11] As I will note, emotion, for example, is not historically static, nor are activities like calculation and computation presumed in all cultures and times to be antithetical to more visibly emotional responses in traumatic situations, such as artistic expressions. Similarly, rhetoric and composition scholars have helpfully focused on student confrontations with the emotion and affect required to read and write about traumatic narratives; the disciplinary challenge to literary studies from within rhetoric and composition concerns the role of the individual witness, foregrounding unique personal experience and its ownership and warning pedagogues against universalizing, stereotypical, and assimilating representations of survivors and their experiences.[12] Historian of science Ruth Leys has attended to the ways in which cultural responses to trauma may change over time. She uses the Foucauldian form of the genealogy to trace a historical progression from the nineteenth century to the present, finding that Western civilization has shifted from the rhetoric of guilt, or regret for what one did, to shame, or regret for who one is.[13] She argues that the Caruth model of Freudian repetition—that victims go over past trauma repeatedly in their minds, reliving the event in an attempt to recover what cannot be processed—does not adequately account for the lived experience of all victims; rather, Leys's genealogy reveals that the history of trauma theory itself has oscillated between the mimetic model, in which the victim unconsciously identifies with and copies an aggressor or oppressor and compulsively reenacts the event, and the anti-mimetic model, in which the victim may imitate an aggressor or reenact the experience yet does so consciously, perceiving and controlling their own actions as if looking in from the outside. Leys aligns the mimetic model with guilt and the anti-mimetic model with shame.[14]

Similar to Erin Peters, who finds that the politics of memory during the early modern period was a "genuinely multimedia affair," my appeal to recent scholarship on trauma is motivated by my interest in multilinguistic and multimodal responses to the contemporary perception that early modern England was suffering an exegetical crisis during and after the Wars of the Three Kingdoms.[15] As James Bono and Robert Markley have persuasively argued, the civil wars and aftermath of the 1640s and 1650s were both result and reflection of communication breakdown in politics, crises of interpretation in theology, and debates about the authority of systematic methods of experimentation and problem solving in the new sciences.[16] For early linguists, many of whom were cryptologists, political corruption was tied to corruption of human language, the obscurities of specialist jargon, and subjective interpretations of scripture that could not be negotiated. Ciphers were narratively proposed as the answer to the biblical Curse, or the division of human communication into countless regional and professional languages. Ciphers were recognized at that time as metaphorical and relational in nature, and they were valued because of their ability to centralize both the medium and mode of expression as a means of survival. As I argue elsewhere, cryptography emerged as a means of systemizing metaphorical relationships.[17] Within the context of early modern cryptography, that association is conscious and not accidental. Cryptographers looked to poetics, rhetorical traditions, narrative, and literary genres as well as to mathematics and early linguistics for their strategies. This intertextuality of ciphering has not been discussed. The scholarship of emotion and affect has privileged the crafted word, literary and poetic, but it also offers a space for the use of other languages, modes of expression, or media as important in the communication of the passions or of trauma.[18] These modes can be and often are accessed *during* an ongoing crisis, and their purpose is to bring help to the writer or someone the writer cares about or, conversely, to bring harm to an enemy. They are mimetic, in that they are reproductions of the words of another, perhaps even requiring that an oppressor or combatant's own thought process be replicated by potential victims. This reenactment or mirroring may be compulsive, as cryptologists often describe a kind of addiction to or insatiable drive toward working long hours until a cipher is solved. Yet the reproduction is also highly controlled. Patterns must be tested methodically. Algorithmic instructions must be discovered and followed with precision.

In this way Leys's counter to Caruth's interpretation of the repetition compulsion is helpful because it provides a framework for the ways in which both ciphering and deciphering are active, conscious, controlled repetitions, especially as they take place during a traumatic experience, yet it is also limited. Because ciphers attempt to intervene in the trauma, they complicate Leys's line of reasoning as representing regret for who one is; if the decipherer fails to solve the message, there might certainly be regret for what one did, or did not do, but the manuals do not deal with that possibility. What is most important about the manuals is that they allow for the possibility that one *can* represent and express traumatic experience. The nature of the testimony in cipher is largely present and futurist: it is about making sense of what is happening now, how to escape what is happening, and how to influence future events to prevent or change an outcome rather than about what is already done and can only be endured. There is the sense that prevention, revision, and expression of the event are possible. And in cryptography manuals, the example ciphers serve yet another function, which is to anticipate crisis and provide a proactive language with which to communicate the crisis *before it happens*. Ciphers are projected, by Selenus, John Wilkins, Wallis, Samuel Morland, Noah Bridges, Falconer, and Philip Thicknesse, to provide a means of communicating impending—but preventable or revisable—disaster without writing about it directly. For this reason the authenticity of the examples they use—whether they are from actual, lived situations or are composed by the authors to fit their lessons—is less relevant than it would be if their project was to recount history or map the successes of specific past ciphers. They want their readers to stay grounded in the present of the problem solving and the future of its application, as well as to acknowledge that the past can never be fully remembered, though it can be revised. In Samuel Morland's *New Method of Cryptography* (1666), for example, a machine called the Cyclologica Cryptographica mediates the expression of a painful realization that may or may not be from his own archives as a decipherer: "bfd***ytzdtihkfqdymblnofl****" means "yourbrotherbetrayesyou."[19] His focus is on how to use the machine to reach this heartbreaking conclusion, not on who was betrayed.

Leys's conscious anti-mimetic model challenges Caruth's discussion of *aporia*, or the unsolvable paradox of the direct experience of an event so emotionally powerful that the mind cannot process and remember it. What I find in working with early modern ciphers is that both insights apply. *Aporia*, or direct observation without understanding, poignantly describes what it is like to see a cipher—like Falconer's "qibc," decrypted as "hast" or Morland's cipher with the asterisks marking nulls—that may communicate an urgent plea or warning but can only belatedly be broken, and the breaking of the cipher is an emotional and physical release, like a wound opened. As Roger Luckhurst notes, "trauma is a piercing or breach of a border that puts inside and outside into a strange communication."[20] Ciphers are "broken," and codes are "cracked." This breaking, though, is through a conscious, controlled act of deciphering, and it is possible that the event can be expressed, read, understood, and acted upon. My goal, then, is not simply application of Freudian psychoanalysis or Foucauldian genealogy to works that long predate them but recognition of a type of language that had been developed almost solely for communicating crisis and, yet, has been misunderstood as a computational attempt to remove emotion, affect, and imaginative expression from the experience of trauma. Pedagogy—the teaching that takes place within the manuals—is central to this "strange communication" of the cipher as it puts inside and outside in contact with one another. Central in this chapter, too, is the erroneous assumption that computation is disconnected from suffering; writings in early modern mathematics, and the instructional works I investigate here, reveal that the act of computing—whether of numbers, alphabets, symbols, geometries, or other multimodal expressions—was itself motivated by the desire to express the inexpressible. This is precisely what Morland's Cyclologica Cryptographica was designed for.

Conceptually, seventeenth-century cryptographers sought to recover a loss: the pure global language gifted to Adam and Eve before the Fall. Falconer references the curse of the seventy-two languages at the beginning of his introduction, and John Wilkins notes in chapter 13 of *Mercury, or The Secret and Swift Messenger* (1641), the first English manual, that this linguistic division is the impetus for his research in cryptography. The punishment for sin, for seeking forbidden knowledge, was multilingualism, a linguistic decentralization or polyglot chaos, in which populations separated geographically could not communicate with a common language and, further, no human could adequately express the depth of their own emotional and intellectual experiences. This curse was seen to have stifled the potential of human achievement, yet Wilkins, in particular, believed it might be possible to create a new language—the language of cipher—to reclaim what had been lost. Seeking a universal language that would unite all cultures, he desired a single character system that would allow "every one" to "express his own meaning."[21] Selenus did not share Wilkins's interest in a universal, or real, character, but his manual of 1624, after first marveling that alphabetic language could communicate so much about the human experience, does acknowledge that a special language is needed that expresses "other occasions" in which there is danger, daring, and even promiscuity.[22]

While Wilkins's 1641 *Mercury* taught skills that would be useful during the ongoing Wars of the Three Kingdoms, fellow cryptographer John Falconer wrote *Cryptomenysis* in 1685, immediately after the death of Charles II and the political turmoil surrounding the ascension of James II. A Scottish clergyman, Falconer supported unification and the recognition of James II as the one true king of England, Scotland, and Ireland. Falconer notes that "tho' the *Tongue* was confounded, the Curse extended not to the *Brain*: *Reason* remained entire, which by help of that great School-master, *Experience*, taught them an useful piece of Philosophy, *That the World is but a large Society of Men, link'd together by a Chain of Wants almost of infinite Variety*" (B2 italics in the original). Falconer, too, is concerned about polyglossia and laments the global as well as local conflict that results from poor communication; however, he does not share Wilkins's hope that ciphers will heal the wounds of the Fall. Writing after the civil wars, during which the ciphers of Charles I were intercepted and published, Falconer is frustrated with the prevalence of ciphering and the tendency it has not to unite the nation but to divide it. He teaches deciphering, not ciphering, so that everyday citizens might prevent further trauma of civil war: "if a private Sentinel, by decyphering an intercepted Epistle, should save an Army, etc., 'tis no Crime, I hope, that he be more clear sighted than his Superiours" (B4). Unlike Wilkins's example ciphers, which often depict writers pleading for help (see figures 3, 5, 6, and 7), many of Falconer's ciphers are acts of aggression against which the reader must learn to defend himself. The cipher "Xlh Hqhph mw mq kvhdx gmwrvghv, idoo ysrq xlhp doo hashgmxmrq," for example, means "The Enemy is in great Disorder, fall upon them with all Expedition" (3). Another long example, entirely in numbers, ends with the command that "*we must not now delay the surprize of the Castle, when things are just ripe for Execution*" (13 italics in the original).

Wilkins's grand vision for cryptography is of a unifying, civilizing language that will reverse the Curse, while Falconer's postwar interest in deciphering is more cynical, even arguing that cryptography is a corruption of manners that can only be countered by educated citizens ready to save armies through decryption. Both, however, discuss past military victories that were made possible because of cryptography. At first glance this may seem a small point and for marketing purposes only—Wilkins, especially, needs to establish that cryptography works and has practical value. Yet what is noteworthy about Wilkins's historical survey is that he devalues the glory of the military celebrity, the historical figure one had been educated to admire, and suggests that real military victory was—and in fact always had been—the result of rational counsel and calculation, such as sending enough supplies so that soldiers do not starve.[23] Falconer presents a similar historical sketch. This would support Albert O. Hirschman's theory of the mid-seventeenth-century Wars of the Three Kingdoms that political imperative caused a significant ethical and anthropological revision of the passions, whereas previously, in the feudal economy, military glory had been the motivation and goal of conflict. Hirschman sees this replaced by a science of politics in which countering passions—glory as opposed by rationalism, boastful aggression as opposed by protective survival—push and pull against one another and drive the emotional community. The pedagogy of ciphering in the manuals of the seventeenth century, at least from Wilkins in 1641 to Falconer in 1685, assumes a reader invested in modest self-preservation and self-interest.[24] Cryptography is proposed as a civilizing language and enacts this push and pull through its potential to also be corrupting; the decryption of a cipher, unlike the charge across a hillside on horseback with swords and muskets, is a humble, private individual effort to save oneself or the cause or, in Falconer's examples, to disrupt the system. Ciphering is not a regulation of passion, or of the profound emotions of war, but it offers a medium through which the passions—and specifically, the sensations of pleasure (through ciphered love letters, for example) and pain (such as the ciphers cited, in this chapter, about starvation and entrapment)—can be negotiated and parsed through rational problem solving.

This rational problem solving is central in the manuals. Their instruction attempts to mediate—not minimize—the passions and to create a readership able to seek help and to provide assistance through reenactments of communication during crisis. Controlled reenactment here is a form of practice to improve one's craft, not an unconscious compulsion as Leys describes. Falconer borrows his examples, for the reader's training, directly from a recent Scottish plot against King William's life, foiled because of successful decipherers. Wilkins does not note where his examples come from, but their messages seem current. Figure 1, for example, uses a biform cipher. This means that it uses two handwriting styles, and only letters written in the key style are part of the solution:

FIG. 1. A biform cipher in Wilkins's *Mercury* (1641). Courtesy of the National Cryptologic Museum.

Wilkins does not explain whether this message is from an actual historical situation or can be found in the archives from which he works for his study. Before the example he directs the reader to "write an Epistle of an ordinary matter."[25] At first glance this message appears to console the reader: all is well, we do not need assistance. The handwriting is inconsistently flourished, but it might not raise suspicion as it is circulated. Wilkins has already provided the key that would need to be on hand (or ideally memorized) by the intended recipient (fig. 2), identifying the second alphabet as the plaintext typography:

FIG. 2. The key to the biform cipher in Wilkins's *Mercury* (1641). Courtesy of the National Cryptologic Museum.

Both the writer and the reader, working under great stress, must orchestrate and notice small variations in the typography of two alphabets, directing their focus toward the text and its penmanship rather than toward the event. Attention to serifs, slant, spacing, and other flourishes is necessary to distinguish between the two alphabets in the ciphered message that reports that the writers prosper. That problem-solving process leads to the solution (fig. 3):

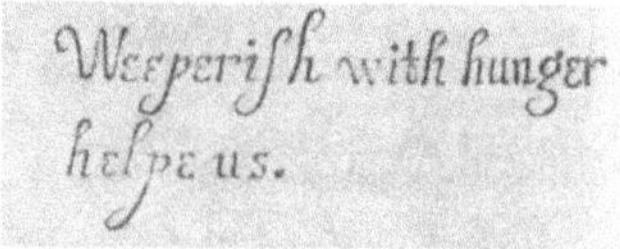

Weeperish with hunger helpe us.

FIG. 3. The solution to the biform cipher in Wilkins's *Mercury* (1641). Courtesy of the National Cryptologic Museum.

The plaintext, the real message behind the apparent confirmation of contentment, reveals the emergency at hand. Wilkins's interest is in the ways in which ciphers require a new mode of reading, as I have argued in other publications.[26] The biform, bilateral cipher, or "mixed writing" as he calls it, provides a means of expressing *omnia per omnia* (anything about anything), Wilkins notes, borrowing Francis Bacon's term in *Of the Advancement and Proficience of Learning*. For Wilkins, this method is "the highest degree of Cyphering."[27] It is mimetic, in that the decipherer must replicate the cipherer's original plaintext, but the process itself is not an exact copy. The decipherer must be creative, observant, and in full conscious control of the wide graphic field of the message and its context. Wilkins is determined that the reader must understand the potential of mixed writing for practical, urgent use, and he spends more time and detail working through the examples of this method than he does others. In a second example (fig. 4) Wilkins provides a longer ciphered message, which uses the same key as the previous lesson:

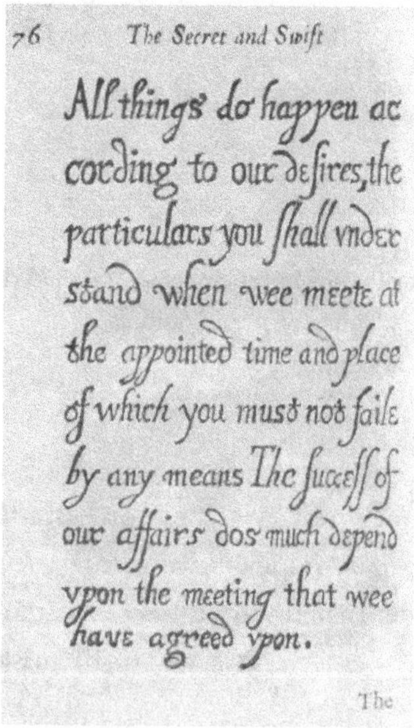

76 The Secret and Swift

All things do happen according to our desires, the particulars you shall understand when wee meete at the appointed time and place of which you must not faile by any means The successe of our affairs dos much depend vpon the meeting that wee have agreed vpon.

The

FIG. 4. A more ambitious biform cipher example in Wilkins's *Mercury* (1641). Courtesy of the National Cryptologic Museum.

The tone of this message is affirming yet pleading. In this visible layer of the writing, the author expresses a mutual goal, a "desire," that requires more conversation and negotiation of details. Punctuation is inconsistent, making the language seem breathless, but the length of the letter implies that it is written at leisure. The tone is decidedly not urgent. The obvious variations in the handwriting, if they are not a giveaway to the presence of a cipher, at the least give the impression of a meticulously crafted text. The plaintext communication, however, is quite the contrary (fig. 5).

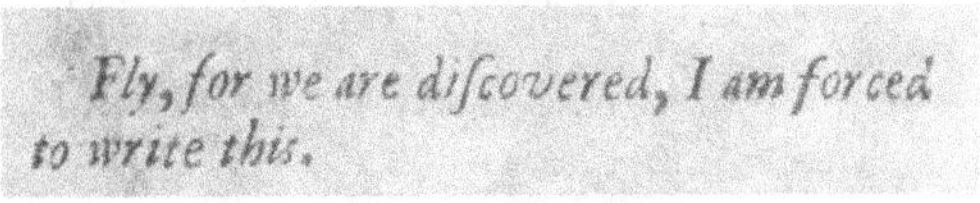

Fly, for we are diſcovered, I am forced to write this.

FIG. 5. The solution to the longer biform cipher example in Wilkins's *Mercury* (1641). Courtesy of the National Cryptologic Museum.

The cipher translates as a brief, panicked message, and the calm leisure of the disguise, written after one has been captured and is under restraint and probable threat to life, suddenly reveals the immediate danger of the situation. Wilkins is not instructionally concerned with the contextual information that is or is not provided by the solution; he immediately settles into the problem-solving process required to move from the problem message—the cipher saying the plan is still in play—to the sad conclusion—that all is lost, the writer is captured and under force, the reader must flee. *Mercury* thus reenacts the focused, controlled replication of steps that deciphering requires; it proceeds from one instructional lesson to another without pause for reflection, the amateur audience propelled forward by examples that increase in complexity and demand for attention.

Across the genre of the cryptography manual, the problem-solving and computing process mediates the recognition of danger and loss. Morland's *New Method*, written personally for the protection of Charles II after his restoration, illustrates this through an especially creative series of detailed directions.[28] In his introduction to the efficiency of the Cyclologica Cryptographica, a series of interlocking cipher disks that can be programmed according to predetermined decisions, Morland presents a scenario in which one receives the following intelligence: "Dear Cozin, I do not a little wonder at your long silence, and am exceeding fearfull, that some accident has befallen you since your arrival."[29] This particular cipher is in quadruplex, which means that it requires four different geometric figures (in this case a rectangle parallelogram, a rhombus, a rectangle triangle, and a trapezium) in four series of configurations (upright columns, horizontal lines, diagonal, and alternative diagonal), which entails reading in four different directions (descending vertical, ascending horizontal, left to right descending diagonal, etc.). Morland's directions are clear and easy to follow even given the complexity of his methods. If Charles II and his court follow the steps carefully, labeled with 1, 2, 3 accordingly, they will reach the solution: "Sir, Look to your Self; for this Night your Person is to be seized, And the Castle to be delivered up to the Enemy by your own Souldiers."[30] Morland does not comment upon the concern in this plaintext, but his recent assistance to Charles II—Morland helped Charles reclaim the throne, though he had also been previously loyal to the Protectorate—suggests that he was drawing from likely recent correspondence. The purpose of the mechanical mediation, and the ambition for more efficiency in ciphering and deciphering, is precisely to allow correspondents to express and quell their worry. The concentration that both ciphering and deciphering demands illustrates a preoccupation with "steps," and these steps are repeated and even *require* a repetition compulsion that forces the interpreter to go over the cipher multiple times to solve it if they are not careful in their first attempt. Many of the examples in early manuals like Wilkins's, too, are repeated in later instruction. Wilkins's bell, torch, and knot ciphers are taken up by Thicknesse in *Treatise on the Art of Decyphering* (1774), for instance, as is Wilkins's plea to flee in figure 5.[31]

The typographic and computational experimentation, "mixed writing," and other types of multimodality described in the manuals across the seventeenth and early eighteenth centuries emphasize that the expression of trauma is and necessarily must be a whole-body experience; trauma is not an inherently literary or narrative construction that takes place only within alphabetic language. Wilkins acknowledges that every visual, sonic, or tactile occurrence is communicational and has patterns that can be quantified, such as the length of a person's stride. As the human experience of suffering and triumph involve all the senses, the ideal secret language, Wilkins concludes, must thus be as multimodal as possible, involving sound, sight, numbers, and alphabets (131). His preferred system uses moving light and bells capable of five distinguishable sounds. In one example torches held by either the right or left hand communicate HASTEN.

The right hand.		The left hand.
II	H	3
I	A	1
IV	S	3
IV	T	4
I	E	5
III	N	3

FIG. 6. Explanation of a multimodal cipher in Wilkins's *Mercury* (1641) that uses torches. Courtesy of the National Cryptologic Museum.

In another, bells and lights together convey starvation: VICTUALS.

A. B. C. D. E. F. G. H. I. K. L. M.
aa. ab. ac. ad. ae. ba. bb. bc. bd. be. ca. cb.
N. O. P. Q. R. S. T. V. W. X. Y. Z.
cc. cd. ce. da. db dc. dd. de. ea. eb. ec. ed.

V. I. C. T. U. A. L. S.
de. bd. ac. dd. de. aa. ca. dc.

FIG. 7. The key for a multimodal, bilateral substitution cipher in Wilkins's *Mercury* (1641) that could use bells, light, or other media. Courtesy of the National Cryptologic Museum.

Deciphering is taught as a kind of awakening of all the senses. In some cases it is depicted as a sudden revelation, as an aha moment at which the pattern of the cipher becomes instantly apparent to the ingenious reader who can make the connections. In other cases it is a gradual recognition, a fogginess that slowly becomes clearer after a long process of trial and error. Elizabeth Mazzola finds, in her analysis of Mary Stuart's expert ciphering, that "exploiting the many gaps between type and script, for instance—much like a piece of needlework that could contain spot motifs, band designs, and the alphabet—Mary's codes included Greek letters, Arabic and roman numerals, French, and her own apparent set of designs." Mary Stuart's ciphering required the kind of multimodal openness that Wilkins showcases, which in some instances demanded concentrated problem solving or, in other contexts, a simple, quick understanding that "a woman's 'X' on the page," for example, "more frequently taken as the most convincing proof of her illiteracy, in Mary's hands has the power to raise legions and unseat queens."[32]

Whether quick or laborious, computation and calculation are required to work through the language as it appears in new multimodalities, the form of the language combining the alphabetic, numeric, and often even graphic, tactile, sonic, and gestural. Cryptography manuals throughout the seventeenth century are thus formally experimental and can even be read as examinations of form itself. Form, Henry S. Turner remarks, "marks a point of convergence between three distinct moments: the act of recognizing the mere being of a thing, as defined by its form; the act of judging the significance of a thing, as again defined by its form; and the act of coming to some kind of knowledge about that same thing—because one can know only what one can recognize and endow with significance."[33] Form is often discussed in one of four ways: at the level of style and poetics (diction, figurative language, etc.), as structure (genre and its parts), as physical materiality (the book as object), and as social organization (kinship, class, political structure, etc.). Turner adds a fifth, which he calls mathematical form, that is predominantly geometric. He finds that "in the late sixteenth century, mathematical notions of form that were primarily structural, spatial, and quantitative began to compete with rhetorical notions of form that were primarily linguistic, stylistic, and qualitative."[34] Indeed, figuring out the form of a cipher is the essential first step in decryption. John Davys includes examples in his edited collection of John Wallis's deciphering methods in *An Essay on the Art of Decyphering* (1737), and though the messages are often emotionally poignant and are from actual historical documents from the Wars of the Three Kingdoms, it is the *form* of the ciphers that fascinates him.[35] "Towards the End of the Account of the *Rye-house* Conspiracy we find a very remarkable Letter from *Scotland*," Davys notes (46 italics in the original). One might expect Davys to marvel at the situation of the letter and the information it provides about the attempted assassination of King Charles II and his brother James in 1683, but instead he is intrigued by its linguistic, stylistic, qualitative, structural, and quantitative characteristics: "There are in it a few *Cant* Words, and some others in *Figures*, but the main Contrivance for *Secrecy* lies in the artful Transposition of Words plainly written" (46 italics in the original). Davys challenges Turner's theory of formal competition, in fact: In ciphering and deciphering, what is remarkable is that style and poetics, structure and genre, physical materiality, social organization, and mathematical form clearly work together. The mathematical and the rhetorical depend upon one another to communicate trauma.

The seventeenth-century interest in mathematical form as complementary to and, ideally, working in collaboration with, the alphabetic requires that modern readers suspend judgment of the apparent emotional distance in the cryptography manuals as they narrate trauma through example ciphers. Susan J. Matt has noted that emotion is historically and culturally bound and that the terms, gestures, and objects that express emotion can and do change over time.[36] Similarly, Daniel M. Gross points out that emotions were and are "contested terms negotiated in a public sphere where power is distributed unevenly."[37] Glen McGillivray looks to seventeenth- and eighteenth-century acting styles and notices that today's theater scholars "still betray a Stanislavskian realist bias"; in other words, modern readers assume that in order to be moved, audiences of the past required the same emotional realism, using the same semiotics of voice and gesture, that audiences do today. McGillivray explains that it is difficult to imagine a performance style that uses poses, set rhetorical gestures, and vocal conventions as highly affective, yet recorded contemporary reactions reveal that they indeed were.[38] Further, emotion—a term not used commonly during the period—and feeling were not interchangeable concepts at that time. Passion, too, was a connected yet distinct notion. It is not the work of this chapter to outline the differences between emotion, feeling, and passion, but it is worth keeping in mind that formulaic behaviors, like rhetorical acting or even mathematical computation, were not experienced as antithetical to emotion during the period. In fact, as Aleksondra Hultquist argues, the idea that the computational *relieved* the mind of emotion, distancing it from the emotional in any way, is a post-eighteenth-century construction; during the period, reasoning and feeling were reciprocal. "Feeling was not separate from action, movement, cognition, or rationality for an eighteenth-century mind," Hultquist notes.[39] Morland, Wilkins, Davys, and other cryptographers of the period may appear to ignore the emotional contexts of the messages they decipher, not musing over the sadness of starvation or wondering about the fate of the imprisoned, then, but their immediate turn to rational problem solving is itself an affective response.

Mercury posits a kind of literacy in which readers should pay more, not less, attention to human emotion and the ways in which the body expresses it, and as Hultquist finds, computation is one of many expressive multimodal practices. Ciphering does not *remove* messages about trauma *from* the personal subjective space of emotion but rather allows for a reciprocal relationship between emoting and reasoning. To further stress this potential, Wilkins proposes what he calls "philosophical numbers," which can represent "any such measure, whereby we judge the differences betwixt severall substances" (107). Philosophical numbers represent for Wilkins a new way of appreciating the emotive potential of the computational. Noah Bridges would, in *Stenographie and Cryptographie* in 1659, develop a similar mathematic idea but using the term "transmutation" to mean a symbolic system to articulate the magnitude or scale of the inexpressible in rational numbers, which is a foundational principle of early trigonometry.[40] Morland looks to geometry as a system of relations in a larger interconnected network that can most adequately structure and express human emotion.

I have focused on this pedagogy of ciphering and deciphering in accessible textbooks, in my long-term research agenda, because the self-reflexive theory of communication articulated in these manuals reveals a conscious effort, on the part of thinkers like Selenus, Wilkins, Morland, Falconer, Davys, and others, to create a codified system for the expression of trauma. Dominick LaCapra cautions that scholars must distinguish between the criticism of identification and the criticism of empathy to avoid making indistinguishable the experience of those who experienced the trauma and those who witness or participate in the narrative of that survivor's ongoing experience of it.[41] In other words, a scholarly distance must be maintained. This is, in a sense, what the instructional manuals are doing as they provide ciphers as exercises working through the expression of suffering. The manuals can maintain a critical distance in order to further the conversation about trauma and its communication all while engaging directly with the suffering that those conversations are about. The manuals taught contemporary readers to practice critical multimodal literacies. They taught their generation that what they may perceive as a dramatic break between their past and their present, as a sudden interruption or change, may simply be a shift in *perspective* accessible through new modes of observation. The manuals teach today's readers that we must be cautious not to assume that the engagement with computation is itself an avoidance of emotion. Earla Wilputte argues that it is during the early eighteenth century that literary critics, in particular, began to question the ability of written language—and the poetics of the seventeenth century—to communicate "the passions."[42] My research finds that dissatisfaction and the active development of alternative models much earlier, though not within traditionally literary forms. My motivation for bringing seventeenth- and eighteenth-century ciphering into conversation with recent trauma studies is therefore not to posit some new way of knowing the historical period of the broad early modern era but to recognize within it an ongoing conversation that influenced the culture's experience of suffering. The assumption that ciphers reveal the emotional identity of otherwise unknowable historical figures like Napoleon—and that emotional identity is perhaps even the true identity—is admittedly a problematic one. Yet if the beginnings of trauma studies are grounded in questions about the imaginative uses of language to express the inexpressible, both the pedagogies and real practices of cryptography provide examples of what kinds of communication were inexpressible long before trauma studies and how a particular culture, at a specific historical moment, sought creative means of leveraging analogic thinking to create new linguistic and narrative frameworks to seek help.

The hope with which Wilkins and his colleagues embraced cryptography as a language finally able to express the anguish, desperation, and even triumph of their contemporary emotional community was, however, short lived. Ciphering and deciphering would largely rhetorically operate, from the late eighteenth century to the present, as computational languages of the state and of mercantilism detached from the emotional contexts of their use. Though certainly there was widespread domestic ciphering as well, it was no longer *rhetorically* marketed as the answer for polyglossic and inexpressive human communication that resulted from the Fall. Only recently has the cryptography community begun to seriously reconsider the ability of algorithms, codes, and ciphers to understand and communicate emotion as they were first conceived during the seventeenth century. Affective computing, or "affect recognition," is perhaps the future of the digital.[43] The goals of this movement, however similar to the goals for governments and businesses during the eighteenth century, are predominantly security and profit. Affective computing seeks to predict user behaviors based on online emotional cues to prevent disaster and collective trauma (to identify the characteristics of a potential terrorist, for example), in one sense, but also to better manipulate consumers and voters. Affective machines will work multimodally, reading user facial expressions, body language, voice, sounds, touch, and other media to calculate future behavior, treating the human face, for example, as a cipher to be broken. Cryptography is still an essentially preventative language, but its function as a confessional system in the expression of trauma has become ancillary to its economic and political potential.

NOTES

1. John Falconer, *Cryptomenysis Patefacta: Or the Art of Secret Information Disclosed Without a Key* (London, 1685), A3. All further parenthetical references are to this edition.
2. "Napoleon dynamite—letter ordering destruction of Kremlin to be auctioned," *The Guardian*, November 30, 2012, https://www.theguardian.com/world/2012/nov/30/napoleon-code-letter-russia-auction. Chataignier's conclusion that this letter is unique because Napoleon is "emotively speaking" here and not in other letters is not accurate. Numerous letters are archived between Napoleon and Josephine de Beauharais that reveal that he often wrote emotively. At least one was even intercepted and published in London, to use his emotional attachment and vulnerability to attack his character. Since 2002 the Fondation Napoléon has published volumes of approximately 33,000 letters.
3. Gustavus Selenus, *Cryptomenytices et Cryptographie*, trans. John William Henry Walden (Lunaeburgi: Exscriptum typis & impensis Johannis & Henrici fratrum, der Sternen, bibliopolarum Lunaeburgensium, 1624), 10–11. References to *Cryptomenytices* are from Walden's English translation, composed around 1900, which is unpublished and not dated. All that is known about this translation is that it appeared in George

Fabyan's collection of cryptography resources at the Riverbank Laboratory, and it is now in the Fabyan collection at the U.S. Library of Congress. It is a meticulous, thorough translation.

4. See Elizabeth Mazzola, "The Renaissance Englishwoman in Code: 'Blabbs' and Cryptographers at Elizabeth I's Court," *Critical Survey* 22, no. 3 (2010): 1–20; Katherine Ellison, *A Cultural History of Early Modern English Cryptography Manuals* (New York: Routledge, 2016).
5. Selenus, *Cryptomenytices*, 11.
6. Quoted in Selenus, *Cryptomenytices*, 24.
7. Cathy Caruth, *Unclaimed Experience: Trauma, Narrative, and History* (Baltimore: Johns Hopkins University Press, 1996), 5.
8. Caruth, *Unclaimed Experience*, 5.
9. Selenus, *Cryptomenytices*, 15.
10. See also Shoshana Felman, "Education and Crisis, or the Vicissitudes of Teaching," in *Testimony: Crises of Witnessing in Literature, Psychoanalysis, and History*, eds. Shoshana Felman and Dori Laub, 1–56 (New York: Routledge, 1992). Felman's essay was also published in *Trauma: Explorations in Memory*, ed. Cathy Caruth, 13–60 (Baltimore: Johns Hopkins University Press, 1995).
11. See the 2008 special issue of *Studies in the Novel* as well as: Roger Luckhurst, *The Trauma Question* (New York: Routledge, 2008); Irene Visser, "Trauma Theory and Postcolonial Literary Studies," *Journal of Postcolonial Writing* 47, no. 3 (2011): 270–82; Irene Visser, "Trauma and Power in Postcolonial Literary Studies," in *Contemporary Approaches in Literary Trauma Theory*, ed. Michelle Balaev, 106–29 (London: Palgrave Macmillan, 2014).
12. See the special issue on "Trauma and Rhetoric" in *JAC: A Journal of Rhetoric, Culture, & Politics* 24, no. 2 (2004); Lynn Worsham, "Going Postal: Pedagogic Violence and the Schooling of Emotion," *JAC: A Journal of Rhetoric, Culture, & Politics* 18 (1998): 213–45; Shane Borrowman, ed., *Trauma and the Teaching of Writing* (Albany: State University of New York Press, 2005).
13. Ruth Leys and Marlene Goldman, "Navigating the Genealogies of Trauma, Guilt, and Affect: An Interview with Ruth Leys," *University of Toronto Quarterly: A Canadian Journal of the Humanities* 79, no. 2 (2010): 656–79.
14. Thomas P. Anderson articulates the Caruth-Leys debate in an endnote of *Performing Early Modern Trauma from Shakespeare to Milton* (New York: Routledge, 2016), 14n14. Anderson notes that Leys reads Caruth's theory of trauma as history too literally, and he provides a helpful summary of Shoshana Felman's response to Leys and defense of Caruth's remarks about perpetrators as also affected by past trauma. Anderson rightly notes that the stakes of trauma studies are high; it concerns itself with fundamental questions about morals, normalization, and guilt.

15. Erin Peters, *Commemoration and Oblivion in Royalist Print Culture, 1658–1667* (New York: Palgrave Macmillan, 2017), 5.
16. James Bono, *The Word of God and the Languages of Man: Interpreting Nature in Early Modern Science and Medicine* (Madison: University of Wisconsin Press, 1995); Robert Markley, *Fallen Languages: Crises of Representation in Newtonian England* (New York: Cornell University Press, 1993).
17. Ellison, *Cultural History*, 94.
18. See A. T. McKenzie, *Certain Lively Episodes: The Articulation of Passion in Eighteenth-Century Prose* (Athens: University of Georgia Press, 1990), 16.
19. Samuel Morland, *A New Method of Cryptography* (London, 1666), 11.
20. Roger Luckhurst, *The Trauma Question* (New York: Routledge, 2008), 3.
21. John Wilkins, *Mercury, or The Secret and Swift Messenger* (London: I. Norton for John Maynard and Timothy Wilkins, 1641), 106.
22. Selenus, *Cryptomenytices*, 39.
23. The logistics of warfare has begun to attract more scholarly attention. See John A. Lynn, *Feeding Mars: Logistics in Western Warfare from the Middle Ages to the Present* (Boulder CO: Westview, 1993), and Martin van Creveld, *Supplying War: Logistics from Wallenstein to Patton* (Cambridge, UK: Cambridge University Press, 2004).
24. Albert O. Hirschman, *The Passions and the Interests: Political Arguments for Capitalism Before Its Triumph* (Princeton: Princeton University Press, 1977), 13.
25. Wilkins, *Mercury*, 90.
26. See Ellison, *Cultural History*, and Katherine Ellison and Susan Kim, eds., *A Material History of Medieval and Early Modern Ciphers: Cryptography and the History of Literacy* (New York: Routledge, 2017).
27. Ellison, *Cultural History*, 92. Francis Bacon, *Of the Advancement and Proficience of Learning; or, The Partitions of Sciences* (London, 1640).
28. *New Method* is rarely cited in cryptography histories, and one of the only known copies is at the Folger Shakespeare Library and has been digitized for the *Early English Books Online* database (https://search.proquest.com/legacyredirect/eebo), making it now more accessible for those with a subscription.
29. Morland, *New Method*, 9.
30. Morland, 8.
31. Philip Thicknesse, *Treatise on the Art of Decyphering and of Writing in Cypher with an Harmonic Alphabet* (London, 1774), 38, 48.
32. Mazzola, "Renaissance Englishwoman in Code," 8.
33. Henry S. Turner, "Lessons from Literature for the Historian of Science (and Vice Versa): Reflections on 'Form,'" *Isis* 101, no. 3 (2010): 582–83.
34. Turner, "Lessons from Literature," 581.

35. John Davys, *An Essay on the Art of Decyphering, in which is inserted a discourse of Dr. Wallis. Now first publish'd from his original manuscript in the publick library at Oxford* (London: L. Gilliver and J. Clarke, 1737).
36. Susan J. Matt, "Current Research in History, or, Doing History from the Inside Out," *Emotion Review* 3, no. 1 (2011): 117–24; see also William M. Reddy, *The Navigation of Feeling: A Framework for the History of Emotions* (Cambridge, UK: Cambridge University Press, 2001).
37. Daniel M. Gross, *The Secret History of Emotion: From Aristotle's "Rhetoric" to Modern Brain Science* (Chicago: University of Chicago Press, 2006), 110–11.
38. Glen McGillivray, "Motions of the Mind: Transacting Emotions on the Eighteenth-Century Stage," *Restoration and Eighteenth-Century Theatre Research* 28, no. 2 (2013): 5–34, esp. 6.
39. Aleksondra Hultquist, "New Direction in History of Emotion and Affect Theory in Eighteenth-Century Studies," *Literature Compass* 13, no. 12 (2016): 764.
40. Noah Bridges, *Stenographie and Cryptographie: or, The Arts of Short and Secret Writing* (London: J.G. for the Author, 1659).
41. Dominick LaCapra, *Writing History, Writing Trauma* (Baltimore: Johns Hopkins University Press, 2001), 21.
42. Earla Wilputte, *Passion and Language in Eighteenth-Century Literature: The Aesthetic Sublime in the Work of Eliza Haywood, Aaron Hill, and Martha Fowke* (New York: Palgrave Macmillan, 2014), 1.
43. The term "affective computing" was coined by Rosalind W. Picard, director of the Affective Computing Research Group at MIT, in *Affective Computing* (Cambridge MA: MIT Press, 1997).

5

Soliciting Sympathy

The Search for Psychological Trauma in Petitions from Seventeenth-Century Maimed Soldiers

ISMINI PELLS

In recent years, the psychological impact of the seventeenth-century civil wars in Britain and Ireland has drawn increasing attention from historians. A handful of well-known cases of potentially traumatized soldiers and civilians has been included in military histories of the wars, while David Appleby has considered the impact of mental health problems among disbanded soldiers in his analysis of veteran politics in the Restoration.[1] In a more extensive analysis Erin Peters has examined how traumatic experiences appeared in popular print during the seventeenth century and how this illustrates a contemporary awareness of nonphysical war wounds and the palliative effects of trauma narration.[2] However, it is still the case, as Mark Stoyle remarked in 2003, that "a huge amount of work remains to be done."[3]

Much of the scholarly reticence in engaging with this subject can be attributed to the methodological problems associated with identifying and analyzing trauma in the past. While modern psychologists have recognized that trauma resulting from human violence has a long and repeated history over many millennia, the circumstances and environment of combat can cause complex and unique responses.[4] As a result traumatic war experiences manifest in numerous symptoms, and those associated with the condition most familiar to modern society—post-traumatic stress disorder (PTSD)—represent only some.[5] In what follows, caution will be exercised in identifying cases of potential psychological suffering and the emphasis will be on the language and forms used to (re)present psychological wounds in the petitions, quite apart from attempting to determine whether a particular soldier was suffering trauma. Indeed, "the psychological notion of trauma is one that has been constructed by humans, over time, and that is connected to the cultural ethos in which people pay attention to those affected by traumatic events."[6] Consequently, Nigel Hunt encourages historians to pay particular attention to the language employed to describe the condition and the sociocultural context in which it was used.[7]

To explore this concept in relation to the civil wars, this chapter will investigate numerous petitions submitted by, and on behalf of, maimed soldiers to English quarter sessions in order to claim financial relief from the state. While demonstrating the difficulties faced by historians in making positive identifications of combat-related trauma in the past, these petitions do contain tantalizing references to troubled emotions potentially indicative of such a condition. They also provide an avenue through which the language used to describe distressed states of mind can be explored in some detail. While contemporaries understood that psychological distress could result from combat experiences and that such conditions required support with financial relief, the difficulties of explaining how psychological wounds hindered a veteran from earning a living prompted them to describe their condition with carefully selected words that often appeared alongside descriptions of physical wounds. Moreover, petitioners, who had to appear in person before the court, were astutely aware of the power of performance. Their petitions often contained strong emotive appeals to their audiences that impressed upon them the graphic realities of their combat experiences and its consequences, certainly to secure a positive outcome but perhaps also to fulfill a need to testify to the distressing past.

The maimed soldiers' petitions are also useful to understand local political culture in the aftermath of the civil wars. As Appleby notes, there has been a renewed interest in the localities among historians of the Restoration, which he attributes to collaborations between historians and social scientists working in the field of post-conflict culture.[8] Thus, in addition, this chapter will investigate collective petitioning to the quarter sessions concerning potentially traumatized veterans to elucidate how the language used reflected the interrelationship between individual and shared responses to the wars and to examine what this might reveal about the post-conflict society of both Interregnum and Restoration England.

Maimed soldiers had been able to claim financial relief from the state since the 1593 Act for Relief of Soldiers created a system of parochial taxation. This was administered on a countrywide basis by county treasurers and the money distributed by justices of the peace (JPs) at the quarter sessions.[9] The act was amended in 1598 and again in 1601, when rates were increased.[10] In response to petitioning from the New Model Army, parliament passed three ordinances in 1647 that supplemented the 1601 act: rates were again increased, pensions were denied to royalists, and claimants had to show that they were "disabled in body for work."[11] Pensions were also made available to the widows and orphans of those who had died in parliament's service. To qualify for a pension, maimed soldiers had to obtain a certificate from their regimental commander, return to their home parish, and present it to two JPs. The JPs would order relief until the next sessions, when the magistrate would withhold or award a payment upon the soldier's petition.[12] At the Restoration, royalist claimants began to petition the quarter sessions and in 1662 parliament passed an act that raised the rates once more and officially denied pensions to parliamentarians. This act lapsed in 1679, and while the 1601 act was still in force, the increased rates were no longer valid. The pension scheme became largely ineffectual, though some soldiers continued to petition and receive pensions.[13]

Most petitions were submitted directly to the JPs, though some claimants appealed to borough corporations, the county committees set up to coordinate parliament's war effort, military governors, or even to leading figures such as Oliver Cromwell. These petitions were usually then referred to the relevant county quarter sessions, with a note of endorsement if the petitioner was lucky. Among these surviving petitions exist alluring glimpses of veterans that potentially experienced psychological trauma as a result of their civil war experiences. As early as 1646 Margaret Buckler petitioned the Dorset committee on behalf of her son, who "hath byn a souldier for the Parlyamt and is now lunatiq." Margaret had already lost both her husband and another son in parliament's service and could not afford to maintain her surviving son on her own.[14] In Devon in 1663 Captain William Hooper provided a certificate to accompany the petition of Philip Luccombe, in which he not only testified to Luccombe's service in Sir Edmund Fortescue's Regiment of Foot but also to the service of John Chudde of South Huish in the same regiment. According to Hooper, Chudde had "received a shott ag[ains]t Plymouth which hath disablinge [sic] him not so much in body as senses."[15] Nearly twenty years later in the West Riding of Yorkshire, a petition was presented to the quarter sessions held at Wakefield in October 1681 by one Elizabeth of Horbury on behalf of her husband. The document is now so severely damaged that even Elizabeth's surname is illegible; however, it is worth citing what is available in full:

> That your peticon[e]rs husband is aged and fallen into a sad [cond]icon by reason of his former Hurts in his ma[jes]t[i]es late service and is much troubled in [damaged] that he should be soe slighted for his great losses and imprissonments that he suffored [damaged] the late rebellious warr never changeinge his principalls that we dare not venture him to [damaged] but is forst to have one to looke after him he out ?stoote us and went to wakefeild [damaged] likely have beene lossst [sic] when goeinge over a bridge, and I cannot follow any thinge for [damaged] after him and I am not able to doe it my charge is soe great and to lett it be Knowne [damaged] trouble to me that my condicon should be knowne to any but your wor[shi]ps I have beene lame [damaged] my selfe and had my brest cutt of w[hi]ch hath disinabled me much to doe that [damaged] formerly I had done for him or els I would not be soe troublesome to your w[?orships] cannott indure to let my Condicon be Knowne to any but your selfes
>
> My humble desire is that yow would be pleased to ?give him some quarterly or monthly Pention for and towards his maintenance whilest he live from ?the head constable assement w[hi]ch I believe will not be longe in his condicon.[16]

This petition, though frustratingly damaged at crucial parts of the text, can certainly be interpreted to suggest that Elizabeth's husband was suffering from psychological problems that she has attributed to his combat experiences.

Indeed, in these three petitions it is difficult to accurately isolate and identify trauma from a broader range of psychological conditions. It also should not be assumed (except perhaps in Chudde's case) that these veterans' mental states were solely a result of their wartime experiences. However, Margaret,

Captain Hooper, and Elizabeth portray the subjects of their petitions as suffering psychologically at least partly as a consequence of their military service, and, significantly, they believed that the quarter sessions might concur with this interpretation. This reveals two important points: first, contemporaries understood that external experiences could cause psychological injuries; and second, that such injuries were deemed to be serious enough to require support with financial relief.

Mental problems (both illness and intellectual impairment) were recognized by contemporaries as physically disabling conditions.[17] For example, the legal theorist Michael Dalton directed JPs that those eligible for poor relief included "the person naturally disabled, either in wit, or member, as the Ideot, Lunaticke, Blind, Lame &c."[18] Nevertheless, it must have been more difficult for veterans to explain how mental wounds made them "disabled in body for work." Maimed soldiers were most successful when they related how their military service rendered them incapable of maintaining themselves and their families by their civilian occupation.[19] Hands, arms, and legs (the most crucial bodily parts in manual labor) were those most often mentioned by petitioners, while many argued that their disability prevented them from practicing their specific trade, rather than from working generally.[20] Henry Fowler of Chard, for instance, petitioned the quarter sessions at Taunton, Somerset, in 1652 explaining how the wound he received in his thigh at the capture of Jersey prevented him from carrying out his trade as a serge weaver.[21] Moreover, medical practitioners were increasingly brought in to assist with the assessment of disability.[22] Therefore petitioners were possibly more likely to mention psychological conditions only if they could couple this with a physical disability, such as was perhaps the case for John Cooley of Ware. Cooley petitioned the quarter sessions at Hertford shortly after the Restoration. He had served Charles I in Scotland and later fought at the siege of Colchester. Cooley claimed that "through often watchinge and lyinge upon the ground in the aforesaid services and by the Cariagde of great Burthens yo[u]r petic[i]on[er] is growne very Lame and Crazye."[23] Cooley's use of the word "crazy" is intriguing. To modern readers this might imply that Cooley was suffering from mental difficulties; however, the reality is more complex. "Crazy" was originally defined as "full of cracks or flaws; damaged, impaired, unsound;

liable to break or fall to pieces; frail, 'shaky.'" Within a medical context this meant "Having the bodily health or constitution impaired; indisposed, ailing; diseased, sickly; broken down, frail, infirm."[24] In this sense it is possible that Cooley was simply referring to his physical frailty. Nevertheless, "crazy" as a state of "unsound mind; insane, mad, demented, 'cracked'" was a definition also recognized in the seventeenth century.[25] Interestingly, Jennifer Evans has found evidence to suggest that by the mid-seventeenth century, "crazy" was a word used to describe *both* physical and mental torment, and that often linked the two conditions together.[26]

Cooley's petition raises two further important points: first, that historians must beware the fact that psychological trauma might be hidden behind language where the meaning has changed over time; and second, that petitioners chose their words very carefully. It is important to remember that the whole purpose of petitioning was to secure a pension. Petitioners competed not only with each other but also with routine administrative affairs, and they had to persuade the busy magistrates to part with limited county funds.[27] Therefore the act of hearing a petitioner's case before the quarter sessions became something of a courtroom drama, in which claimants ensured that their scripts included words especially selected for the performance. Geoffrey Hudson notes that while supplicants wore "a mask of deference," they knew how to manipulate the system in their favor, while David Appleby highlights how petitioners' cultural and political awareness informed their decisions on which aspects of their story to emphasize and which to palliate.[28] Furthermore, scholarship on the performance of traumatic events has emphasized that "literary texts of any given period do not simply or even primarily reflect established historical practices; instead, they embody the desires, often otherwise unexpressed, of writers and their projected audiences."[29] Cynthia Marshall appealed to historians not to forget that early modern audiences may have actually taken pleasure in violent episodes or tales of woe.[30] It was crucial that petitioners engaged, even entertained, their audiences, and therefore it must be considered that they deliberately employed violent images or motifs to achieve this.

These points are illustrated by the dramatic petition of John Cornelius of Bishopsteignton to the Devon quarter sessions in 1672. He had served as a royalist soldier "from the begining unto the last period" of the civil wars.

He had been commissioned as a lieutenant and during his service received "two sev[er]all Shotts in his side; One Shott in his neck, One other shott in his legg, and a cut in his head." He had also been imprisoned by the enemy. After the king had surrendered himself to the Scots in 1646, Cornelius had been forced to flee for his safety to Flanders, "where he remained above two yeares in great indigency and misery." Returning to England he was "soe hunted and vexed by the Adverse p[ar]tie" that he was forced to leave for Barbados. He remained there until the Restoration, when he returned home and had "ever since remained in a very sad and mahaymed condic[i]on." He was maintained by his parents until they could no longer bear the burden. By 1672 he was "not only decripate, But hath alsoe lost the use of his reason, by his greife."[31] Cornelius's mental distress, to the extent of losing rationality, is indicated clearly. His use of "grief" is illustrative of the fact that this word, as it was understood in the seventeenth century, covered a much wider range of emotions than it does in modern English. The seventeenth-century term included conditions that today would be labeled depression and post-traumatic stress. The effects of grief were understood to be felt deeply, to the extent that death might be the result of those whose grief became excessive and all-consuming.[32]

In early modern England, "sadness" also reflected "a more acutely worrying state of mind than it does now." It could be understood as "an extremely dangerous illness that potentially might lead to suicide."[33] Similar to Cornelius's petition, several petitions of maimed soldiers mention sadness. For example, in his petition to the Ely quarter sessions in October 1662, Edward Gill of Wisbech claimed that while in the Oxford garrison and "severall Fights" in royalist service, he had received "severall wounds" that had weakened his limbs and rendered him incapable of work. As a result, he was "brought into A very meane and Sad Condic[i]on."[34] Former royalist soldier Henry Travis petitioned the quarter sessions at Wigan in October 1674, begging the JPs to consider his "sad distress" and to supplement his existing pension while he was "in this sad and Miserable Condic[i]on."[35] At Skipton in July 1675 Samuel Constantine of Kettlewell claimed that he had been "a great and sadd sufferer" for the king and not only had he spent his whole estate for this cause but had also "rec[eive]d soe manie severall wounds; That yo[u]r poore Petic[i]oner is altogether soe disabled, as that he cannot take anie paines or Imploym[en] ts where by he may or canne releeve himselfe; soe that yo[u]r Petic[i]on[e]r (at pr[e]sent) is in a verie sadd and poore condic[i]on."[36]

It is difficult to tell if the "sad condition" mentioned by these petitioners was genuinely reflective of some form of mental anguish or simply an attempt to pull on the heartstrings of the presiding JPs. Furthermore, few petitions were written by the supplicants themselves. Most were drafted by local scribes, such as parish clergy or schoolmasters, who were educated men and familiar with the classical format of petitions by virtue of their grammar school education.[37] These scribes had to reorder and refocus what petitioners told them into a coherent argument that included all the deferential formulae that may appear hollow to modern readers but would have been a huge breach of etiquette if forgotten.[38] Such men would have been well aware of what made a powerful petition and could have manipulated what the petitioner told them in "a carefully contrived effort to dismantle the composure of those who read, watched or listened."[39] Thus, there is room to suspect that it might have been the scribes who were inserting words about the petitioner's "sad condition" when the petitioner was not in fact suffering from mental distress. That said, even if this is the case, it reveals that traumatic language was regarded as helpful to a petition's success, indicating a broader contemporary sympathy for psychological wounds.

Nevertheless, as Robert Houston maintains, "Amanuenses articulated what petitioners told them rather than invented their narratives, which are sufficiently distinctive in content to be described not merely as individualised, but as individual."[40] Indeed, Mark Stoyle argues that scribes appear to have determined the precise wording of the texts, did their best to ensure that the petitions would impress, and chose the conventional formulae with which the documents began and ended. Yet the crucial central passages of the petitions relied upon the testimony of the veterans themselves.[41] Consequently, it seems that the claims being made in the petition largely came from the petitioner, even if those claims were contrived.[42]

In accepting this it is possible to view these documents in the context of the vast scholarship on the acts of testimony and witness. Testimonies "occupy a place within a field of tension between memory and judicial procedures, between a desire for justice and political rationality."[43] While it was the JPs' task to ascertain the factual criteria required by the current legislation, many petitioners seemed to have relished the opportunity to tell their stories. As Shoshana Felman observes, "To testify . . . is more than simply to report a fact or an event or to relate what has been lived, recorded and remembered. Memory is conjured here essentially in order to *address* another, to impress upon a listener, to *appeal* to a community."[44] The "imperative to tell and to be heard" is a phenomenon commonly identified among modern trauma survivors and might perhaps be detected in the maimed soldiers' petitions.[45] Stoyle illustrates how the central passages in the Devon royalist petitions contain detailed descriptions of veterans' wartime experiences that perhaps reflect this imperative to tell. Many narrate the harsh realities of military campaigning, including the pervasiveness of hunger, cold, and sickness; the torment of imprisonment; and the dominance of skirmishes and sieges over pitched battles, though the latter are graphically depicted when they occur.[46] Stoyle's discovery is mirrored in petitions from the rest of the country.

In Derbyshire the frantic atmosphere of a skirmish at Shallcross Hall is strikingly apparent in the petition of parliamentarian soldier John Cawverd, while John Radige of Hasland could still remember vividly in 1687 how he had been imprisoned "without any manner of satisfaction" after his mare was shot from underneath him.[47] In Wiltshire the hard usage that Edmund Stephens received at the hands of the Cornish, who had stripped him naked, had seared itself into his memory; and later Philip Goldston regaled the bench with tales of his escape to a wood, where he lay for many days in the cold, after being defeated in a skirmish at Salisbury during Penruddock's Uprising.[48]

Modern research has demonstrated that in the telling of their own stories veterans can find "significant cathartic relief."[49] Constructing a narrative "re-externalizes" the traumatic event and enables the survivor to reassert "the hegemony of reality" through which process they may historicize the event and thus gain some closure.[50] Erin Peters demonstrates that some civil war veterans certainly recognized the benefits of putting their traumatic experiences into narrative forms and the utility of what is now termed "narrative exposure therapy" or "testimony therapy."[51] This is not to imply that veterans who described their military experiences in detail were experiencing trauma as it might be medically defined but that there are more widespread forms of mental suffering that are often more difficult to detect. Indeed, these petitioners may not have been consciously attempting to divest themselves of their reactions to distressing events but instead may have involuntarily lapsed into doing so.

Stoyle also notes that royalist petitions in Devon almost all portrayed "a sense of unbending personal allegiance to the crown," a phenomenon likewise found by Appleby in royalist petitions from Essex.[52] In one sense this is unremarkable, as the 1662 act specifically stated that pensions would only be awarded to those who had served Charles I "out of their sense of their duty and allegiance."[53] Petitioners may have merely been anxious to comply with the terms of the act. Yet it is perhaps worth considering that petitions could also reflect what has been termed "philosophies of trauma," the need to attach meaning to difficult past experiences and convince oneself and others that it was not all in vain.[54] During the Interregnum those who suffered as a result of royalist service had been ignored while their parliamentarian counterparts had been awarded pensions. Research in modern societies has shown that the effects of victimization continue to resonate for many years, often for generations in the family systems of people who have been discriminated against.[55] Is it possible, then, that clichéd phrases concerning the "blessed" or "glorious" memory of the late king might mask a deeper sense of suffering and victimization that could be alleviated through attachment to wider popular royalism, now vindicated at the Restoration?

It is perhaps pertinent to note petitions that are conspicuous in their royalism. Stoyle notes that most of the Devon petitioners avoided using harsh language to describe either their former enemies or the conflict itself. However, he points out that seven (a very small minority) referred to "the Rebellion" or "the late Rebellious times."[56] Petitions to the Ely quarter sessions are particularly marked in their vituperative vocabulary. Thomas Kilborne claimed that, "Dureinge the Tyme of the Late Rebellion . . . [he] Did for the Defence of his Said Sacred Ma[jes]ties parson his Crowne and Dignities with manie hazards venture his Lyfe."[57] Mary Saby petitioned for maintenance for her grandchildren, whose father had "by the blood thirsty people of the late tymes [been] unjustly put to Death and murdered," while the inhabitants of Wimblington who testified on behalf of William Thomason noted that he had been imprisoned several times and had his goods taken away "by ye Late usurped power."[58] These last two petitions are a reminder that traumatic war experiences were not confined to the soldiery. It may have been easier to express overt royalist sentiments in Ely, which since the outset of the wars had been an enclave of royalist support, now bolstered by the return to power in 1660 of Bishop Matthew Wren.[59] However, in Devon over half the Interregnum Bench continued serving at the Restoration, but this was not enough to put off the few who used virulent language to describe parliamentarians, and, incidentally, they still secured pensions.[60]

On the other hand, veterans suffering from psychological problems may have been put off from petitioning for relief because of ignorance about the required procedure, or the stigma of becoming a burden on the community, and subsisted by their own means or by the charity of relatives and friends.[61] Such men would only come to the attention of the authorities if they became disruptive to wider society. In 1652 the inhabitants of Enville petitioned the Stafford quarter sessions about "a very Troublesome neighbor," Roger Fellowes. Fellowes was "a Constant Breaker of the Sabboth day by bodily labour," a "Com[m]on swerer" and had threatened to "smoke all the p[ar]ish Except 3 or 4 houses for a souldier he had bin, & a souldier he would bee."[62] Fellowes had a history of antisocial behavior and quarrels with his neighbors stretching back to 1648, but there is simply not enough evidence to prove that he was suffering from psychological trauma induced by his previous military service.[63] Nevertheless, that Fellowes cited his military experience as the reason for his threat indicates that it must be considered a possibility that his behavior was linked to his past service.[64] It is perhaps significant that he was "a Constant Breaker of the Sabboth," as feelings of anger at God and stopping attendance at religious services are common among modern veterans.[65] It is difficult to establish if the spiritual changes recognized in modern veterans were shared by their civil war counterparts (who, it must be remembered, resided in a religiously permeated society), though further research may be revealing.

Homecoming is often a difficult time for modern veterans, when they are no longer fully immersed in the collective body of the military, yet not fully reintegrated into the civilian community, and the experience of a jarring return has been identified as a contributing factor in the onset of trauma.[66]

Homecoming seems to have caused problems for Raph Rishton. In 1661 John Hogle, overseer of the poor in Haslingden, Lancashire, petitioned the quarter sessions at Preston that "one Raph Rishton hath for sev[er]all yeares last past beene a soldier & about three weekes since came into Haslingden whoe is since distracted & distempered."[67] In another case Appleby draws attention to a man he identifies as a traumatized soldier, John Horne of Buckland in Kent.[68] Horne's wife petitioned the East Kent quarter sessions in 1662 that her husband was "a distracted man and in his madness did sett on fire and burne his owne house whereby his sayd wife is destitute of a dwelling house."[69] Horne was described as a husbandman and nowhere does it say that he had been a soldier. However, the JPs ordered the treasurer for maimed soldiers, William Russell, to pay Horne's wife twenty nobles.[70] This suggests that Horne may have spent time soldiering in the civil wars and that the JP considered that this past experience accounted for his present condition. It also raises the enticing possibility that other "distracted" men described in quarter sessions records by their civilian occupation may have served in one of the civil war armies. While it is possible that Horne's wife was granted maimed soldier funds simply because funds were available, it is worth pointing out that Restoration Kent was burdened with such overwhelming numbers of pensioners that JPs were forced to restrict the value of pensions and desperately sought alternative sources of income.[71]

Fellowes, Rishton, and Horne were all ultimately removed to local prisons.[72] In locking up these men, it appears that the public benefitted more than the traumatized veterans. The latter seem to have received little, if anything, in the way of care, while their neighborhoods were relieved of their threatening presence. Research into modern post-conflict societies has shown that communities that have experienced war become highly sensitive to any perceived threat in their environment.[73] This is a phenomenon that appears reflected in the three petitions. The Enville inhabitants informed the JPs that they wished to "live in peece & quietnesse" but Fellowes's behavior put them in "danger of their lives" and risked "the losse of their estates."[74] Rishton provided the embodiment of the problem of the wandering soldier, a problem that the Restoration government, faced with large numbers of disbanded soldiers, was anxious to police.[75] Horne was a liability to his wife but also, in setting fire to his house, a threat to his community as fear of fire was "a very real and constant factor" in early modern settlements.[76]

Theorists have remarked how trauma sufferers have usually experienced that which is unimaginable to others, and that witnesses to testimonial encounters are often deeply unsettled by the memories and residues of the traumatic incident.[77] Yet very few contemporaries would not have experienced distressing incidents during the civil wars for themselves in some way or other.[78] Many may have preferred to avoid interacting with mentally distressed veterans as this might have forced them to reengage with their own upsetting memories. Indeed, Shosana Felman and Dori Laub argue that large-scale modern traumatic events can become a "cultural secret" kept through "various forms of communal or of personal denial, of cultural reticence or of cultural canonization."[79] If we accept the possibility that a culture of reticence was developing, it is all the more interesting to note that the labels used to describe the psychological condition of Fellowes ("Troublesome"), Rishton ("distracted & distempered"), and Horne ("distraction" and "madness") were all words used as euphemisms for the civil wars. For example, Stoyle notes how several Devon petitioners referred to "the Troubles" in describing the wars.[80] In a summons directed to the Scottish Privy Council in December 1642, the king claimed military assistance "to raise this miserable distemper and distraction in this kingdom."[81] "Madness" was associated with opposition to the king but was also used in reference to the radical sects that emerged during the civil wars in order to invalidate their claims.[82] In many ways there was nothing unusual in the vocabulary used by the petitioners from Enville, Haslingden, and Buckland. Peters suggests that after the civil wars, the effects of psychological trauma on the individual were transposed onto the national psyche and there was "a high level of fluidity" between the conceptualization of individual and collective trauma.[83] This worked to create "a publicly available trauma narrative" in which individual traumatic experiences of the wars became "incorporated on a collective scale into narratives and memories of the nation's past, influencing the manner in which they are represented in the present."[84]

In the immediate aftermath of the civil wars, collectively agreed euphemisms for that conflict may have provided a ready source of language for the petitioners to describe the state of mind of the potentially traumatized. Sybille

Kramer and Sigrid Weigel claim that survivors of traumatic events are viewed as "the bodily trace" of those events, and perhaps to the petitioners, Fellowes, Rishton, and Horne were reminiscent of the disrupted state of the country during the wars.[85] The connection between the state of mind of the potentially traumatized individuals and the turmoil of the civil wars was probably not one deliberately invoked by the petitioners, though it should be borne in mind that the lower social orders were certainly aware of the political implications of certain phrases, and so the ostensibly apolitical presentation of grievances in petitions should not necessarily be taken at face value.[86]

Imprisoning Fellowes, Rishton, and Horne removed them from their communities, but it created a financial burden through the cost of their incarceration. The Enville inhabitants expressed their irritation at the expense of continually hauling Fellowes before the JPs and implored the JPs to enforce a warrant ordering Fellowes to give financial security for good behavior.[87] Hogle lobbied for the cost of Rishton's imprisonment to be borne by the hundred (the wider division of the county) rather than just the town of Haslingden, "ye Town being verie Little & ye Charge soe great," while the inhabitants of Buckland subsequently petitioned that they were unable to pay the five shillings a week toward Horne's maintenance in prison and that the bill had to be picked up by the treasurer for maimed soldiers.[88] Whether the inhabitants of Enville, Haslingden, and Buckland were genuinely suffering economic hardship, or whether they merely wished to extricate themselves from the burden of paying for Fellowes, Rishton, and Horne's incarceration, remains unknown. However, it was the responsibility of men like Hogle, who had presumably faced opposition in his attempts to collect poor relief rates, to convince the JPs of their communities' inability to pay.

It was commonly argued that charity should not be measured in terms of private suffering but with regard to the problems of the wider community. Furthermore, relief was deigned to help preserve order and confirm "neighborliness." The extent to which contemporaries were aware of such issues is often apparent in petitions.[89] By persuading the JPs that the community felt threatened by the mentally distressed veterans and (even unintentionally) using language that juxtaposed the veterans' psychological conditions with the disrupted state of the nation during the civil wars, the petitioners may have persuaded the JPs that swift action was necessary to prevent an escalation into wider disorder. In turn this served as a reminder to the magistrates that for many, the legacy of the conflict was still very real.

Petitions were not only a medium for the lower orders to engage in political matters but also, for those in authority, an important source of knowledge about current opinions among their social inferiors.[90] As the three examples show, petitions often claimed to speak for the whole community.[91] Naturally, these petitions might not have been as representative of the community as they claimed to be.[92] Nevertheless, petitions were seldom created by one person but were the product of collaborative activity: petitioners probably discussed their case with family, friends, and local officials, as well as with the scribe who wrote the document.[93] Consequently, petitions played a role in constructing a public identity for those upon whose behalf they claimed to speak.[94] Moreover, petitions formed a staple part of how people received their news and could be used to manipulate popular opinion.[95] At the quarter sessions the public paid to view proceedings from the gallery, while back home the local community awaited the verdict.[96]

Gary Rivett recently demonstrated how some contemporary authors were adamant that the civil wars had to first be remembered before peace could be achieved.[97] As a result conflicting narratives emerged that attempted to shape the debates surrounding the peace process and legitimize a partisan vision for the future.[98] Rivett's work focuses on a well-known text (Joshua Sprigge's *Anglia Rediviva*), but his arguments might just as well apply to the petitions in this study. Reflecting the voices of predominantly illiterate authors, and narrated before audiences comprising a wide cross-section of the local community, it is worth considering the impact that the stories narrated in these petitions had in shaping both the public memory of the wars and the collective vision of their post-conflict society. As Matthew Neufeld maintains, although the 1660 Act of Indemnity and Oblivion called for public pardon and forgetting, it also provided the opportunity to promote narratives of the civil wars that conformed to the official Restoration image of the righteousness of the royalist cause.[99] This is apparent in post-Restoration petitions, especially in the conspicuously royalist petitions previously discussed. A similar opportunity was available for parliamentarian petitioners during the Interregnum. For example, Anthony Baker of Salisbury, Wiltshire, referred to Penruddock's 1656 royalist uprising as the "late insurrection and rebellion."[100] Even when the partisanship of petitioners was not immediately apparent, such as in the petitions relating to Fellowes, Rishton, and Horne, the message could not be clearer. There may have been a reluctance to fully face up to it, but ordinary Englishmen and -women were not, despite the official rulings, ready to forget the civil wars.

Maimed soldiers' petitions from the British civil wars provide a useful opportunity to examine how the language used to describe mental distress has changed over time, while also offering an example of how it may be affected by the context in which it was being used. Although contemporaries were receptive to claims based on the disabling nature of combat-related psychological conditions, the need to prove unfitness for work may have prompted the selection of words, like "crazy," that linked mental conditions to physical conditions, while words like "grief" or "sad" were no doubt effectual in eliciting sympathy from the presiding JPs. At the same time, while skepticism might suggest that petitioners (with the help of their scribes) exaggerated or perhaps even fabricated a distressed mental state, the detailed narratives and overt expressions of allegiance in some petitions may have fulfilled a veteran's simultaneous needs both to appeal to audiences and to testify to past horrors. The public and performative nature of the petitions makes these documents ideal for examining these issues, while the lessons learned from this case study may be applied more widely to other source-types. Few, if any, documents were ever intended to be truly private, but the subject and style were shaped by social and cultural conventions and the expectations of the intended audience, as well as by authorial aspirations. Indeed, testimony is pervasive and implicated, sometimes unexpectedly, in almost every kind of writing.[101]

In drawing attention to the significant changes in how emotions were expressed over time, Michael Braddick argues that these changes were closely related to the ways in which collective emotions and political life intersect.[102] Likewise, Thomas Anderson contends that "significant cultural loss alters normative modes of expression and representation," and thus "the early modern period uses a specific vocabulary with which to talk about the relationship of history, memory, progress, and loss."[103] This view is conceivably reinforced by the petitions concerning Fellowes, Rishton, and Horne. The connection between the words used to describe the mental conditions of the three men and the euphemisms for the civil wars may not have been deliberately invoked, but it is reminiscent of the interchangeability of the vocabulary used to conceptualize individual and collective trauma argued for by Peters. Furthermore, the maimed soldiers' petitions highlight the role of manuscript sources and oral narration in shaping the collective memory of the civil wars for a wide cross-section of local society.

Whether the petitioners from Enville, Haslingden, and Buckland consciously drew comparisons between the psychological states of their veterans and the civil wars in order to play upon JPs' fear of disorder is a moot point. Yet the sensitivity to threat known to exist in modern post-conflict societies is seemingly apparent, and JPs who were dismissive of parochial concerns often found that disorder resulted.[104] For these petitioners the memory of the violent past had seemingly become part of their sociocultural memory, and the presence of mentally distressed veterans within their communities represented "the bodily trace" of these events.[105] Perhaps this is unsurprising. Certainly by 1660 the maimed, the bereaved, the indigent, and, it seems, the traumatized "were everywhere to be seen, visible reminders of the troubled past," and thus "the idea that the Restoration somehow represented a return to 'normality' is bizarre."[106]

NOTES

1. Charles Carlton, *Going to the Wars: The Experience of the English Civil Wars, 1638–1651* (London: Routledge, 1992), 224–25; Peter Gaunt, *The English Civil War: A Military History* (London: I. B. Tauris, 2014), 237; David Appleby, "Veteran Politics in Restoration England, 1660–1670," *The Seventeenth Century* 28, no. 3 (August 2013): 334, doi:10.1080/0268117X.2013.823101.
2. Erin Peters, "Trauma Narratives of the English Civil War," *Journal for Early Modern Cultural Studies* 16, no. 1 (Winter 2016): 78–94, doi:10.1353/jem.2016.0008.
3. Mark Stoyle, "'Memories of the Maimed': The Testimony of Charles I's Former Soldiers, 1660–1730," *History* 88, no. 2 (April 2003): 205, doi:10.1111/1468-229X.00259.
4. Debra Hyatt-Burkhart and Lisa Lopez Levers, "Historical Contexts of Trauma," in *Trauma Counselling: Theories and Interventions*, ed. Lisa Lopez Levers, 23–46 (New York: Springer, 2012), esp. 23–24; Roger Buck, "The Impact of War on Military Veterans," in Lopez Levers, *Trauma Counselling*, 434–53, esp. 434.

5. Buck, "Impact of War," 436.
6. Hyatt-Burkhart and Lopez Levers, "Historical Contexts of Trauma," 39.
7. Nigel Hunt, *Memory, War and Trauma* (Cambridge, UK: Cambridge University Press, 2010), 14.
8. David Appleby, "The Restoration County Community: A Post-Conflict Culture," in *The County Community in Seventeenth-Century England and Wales*, ed. Jacqueline Eales and Andrew Hopper, 100–24 (Hatfield, UK: University of Hertfordshire Press, 2012), esp. 101–2.
9. Geoffrey Hudson, "Disabled Veterans and the State in Early Modern England," in *Disabled Veterans in History*, ed. David Gerber, 117–44 (Ann Arbor: University of Michigan Press, 2003), esp. 118–19.
10. Hudson, 122.
11. Charles Firth and Robert Rait, eds., *Acts and Ordinances of the Interregnum, 1642–1660* (London: H. M. Stationery Office, 1911), 1:939.
12. Firth and Rait, *Acts and Ordinances*, 1:938–40, 997, and 1055; David Appleby, "Unnecessary Persons? Maimed Soldiers and War Widows in Essex, 1642–1662," *Essex Archaeology and History* 32 (2001): 210; Hudson, "Disabled Veterans," 122.
13. Appleby, "Unnecessary Persons?," 216; *Journal of the House of Lords* (London: H. M. Stationery Office, 1767–1830), 10:405; Hudson, "Disabled Veterans," 122.
14. Charles Herbert Mayo, ed., *The Minute Books of the Dorset Standing Committee* (Exeter: William Pollard, 1902), 80–81. I am very grateful to David Appleby for this reference.
15. Certificate for Philip Luccombe, 1663, QS 128/125/1, Devon Heritage Centre (hereafter DHC); Mark Stoyle, "Remembering the English Civil Wars," in *The Memory of Catastrophe*, ed. Peter Gray and Kendrick Oliver, 19–30 (Manchester: Manchester University Press, 2004), 21.
16. Petition of Elizabeth of Horbury, October 1681, QS 1/20/9/6/4, West Yorkshire Archive Service, Wakefield (hereafter WYAS).
17. Geoffrey Hudson, "Disability in the Early Modern West," in *The Encyclopedia of Disability*, ed. Gary L. Albrecht, 855–58 (Thousand Oaks CA: Sage, 2005), 855.
18. Michael Dalton, *The Countrey Justice* (London, 1618), 76.
19. Appleby, "Unnecessary Persons?," 213.
20. Geoffrey Hudson, "Arguing Disability: Ex-Servicemen's Own Stories in Early Modern England, 1590–1790," in *Medicine, Madness and Social History*, ed. Roberta Bivins and John Pickston, 105–17 (Basingstoke, UK: Palgrave Macmillan, 2007), 108; Hudson, "Disabled Veterans," 129–30.
21. Petition of Henry Fowler of Chard, 1652, Q/SR/99/4, Somerset Heritage Centre.
22. Hudson, "Disability in the Early Modern West," 857.

23. Petition of John Cooley, c. 1661–64, QSR/12, fol. 232, Hertfordshire Archives and Local Studies.
24. "Crazy, adj.," Oxford English Dictionary, accessed May 19, 2017, http://www.oed.com/view/Entry/44007?isAdvanced=false&result=2&rskey=cZtr9t&.
25. "Crazy, adj.," Oxford English Dictionary.
26. Jennifer Evans, "'I am still very crazy, my pains not suffering me to stir abroad': Male patients' experiences of pain in early modern England" (paper presented to the Social History Society 41st Annual Conference, UCL Institute of Education, April 4, 2016). I am very grateful to Dr. Evans for discussing this concept with me.
27. Appleby, "Unnecessary Persons?," 212.
28. Hudson, "Arguing Disability," 117; Appleby, "Unnecessary Persons?," 215.
29. Cynthia Marshall, *The Shattering of the Self: Violence, Subjectivity, and Early Modern Texts* (Baltimore: Johns Hopkins University Press, 2002), 8–9.
30. Marshall, 5.
31. Petition of John Cornelius, 1672, QS 128/10/2, DHC.
32. Clodagh Tait, "'Whereat his wife tooke great greef & died': Dying of Sorrow and Killing in Anger in Seventeenth-Century Ireland," in *Popular Culture and Political Agency in Early Modern England and Ireland*, ed. Michael Braddick and Phil Withington, 267–84 (Woodbridge, UK: Boydell, 2017), esp. 272.
33. R. S. White, "Language of Emotions," in *Early Modern Emotions: An Introduction*, ed. Susan Broomhall, 33–36 (Abingdon: Routledge, 2017), esp. 33.
34. Petition of Edward Gill, 1662, EDR. E10, Cambridge University Library (hereafter CUL).
35. Petition of Henry Travis, October 12, 1674, QSP 424/29, Lancashire Archives (hereafter LA).
36. Petition of Samuel Constantine, July 13, 1675, QS 1/14/5/6/1, WYAS.
37. Appleby, "Unnecessary Persons?," 211; Robert Houston, *Peasant Petitions: Social Relations and Economic Life on Landed Estates, 1600–1850* (Basingstoke, UK: Palgrave Macmillan, 2014), 73.
38. Houston, *Peasant Petitions*, 77–78; Appleby, "Unnecessary Persons?," 213.
39. Marshall, *Shattering of the Self*, 2.
40. Houston, *Peasant Petitions*, 78.
41. Stoyle, "Memories of the Maimed," 210.
42. Appleby, "Unnecessary Persons?," 209.
43. Sybille Kramer and Sigrid Weigel, "Introduction: Converging the Yet-Separate Theoretical Discourses of Testimony Studies," in *Testimony/Bearing Witness: Epistemology, Ethics, History, and Culture*, ed. Sybille Kramer and Sigrid Weigel, ix–xli (London: Rowman and Littlefield, 2017), xxiv.

44. Shoshana Felman and Dori Laub, *Testimony: Crises of Witnessing in Literature, Psychoanalysis, and History* (London: Routledge, 1992), 204.
45. Felman and Laub, 78.
46. Stoyle, "Memories of the Maimed," 211–19.
47. Petition of James Cawpard [Cawverd], undated, Q/SB2/647, Derbyshire Record Office (hereafter DRO); Petition of John Radige, October 4, 1687, Q/SB/2/627, DRO.
48. Royal Commission on Historical Manuscripts (hereafter HMC), *Report on Manuscripts in Various Collections* (London: H. M. Stationery Office, 1901), 1:123 and 128.
49. Buck, "Impact of War," 449.
50. Felman and Laub, *Testimony*, 69–70.
51. Buck, "Impact of War," 449; Peters, "Trauma Narratives," 83 and 87.
52. Stoyle, "Memories of the Maimed," 224; Appleby, "Unnecessary Persons?," 217.
53. Stoyle, "Memories of the Maimed," 224.
54. Christine Hallet, "Portrayals of Suffering: Perceptions of Trauma in the Writings of First World War Nurses and Volunteers," *Canadian Bulletin of Medical History* 27, no. 1 (Spring 2010): 77 and 81, doi:10.3138/cbmh.27.1.65.
55. Hyatt-Burkhart and Lopez Levers, "Historical Contexts of Trauma," 26–27.
56. Stoyle, "Memories of the Maimed," 223–24.
57. Petition of Thomas Kilborne, 1662, EDR. E10, CUL.
58. Petition on behalf of William Thomason, 1662, EDR. E10, CUL; Petition of Mary Saby, 1662, EDR. E10, CUL.
59. Clive Holmes, *The Eastern Association in the English Civil War* (London: Cambridge University Press, 1974), 54–55 and 73.
60. Ronald Hutton, *The Restoration: A Political and Religious History of England and Wales 1658–1667* (Oxford, UK: Clarendon, 1985), 129; Stoyle, "Memories of the Maimed," 223–24.
61. Appleby, "Unnecessary Persons?," 210–12.
62. Articles of misbehaviour against Roger Fellowes, April 1652, Q/SR/276/19, Staffordshire Record Office (hereafter SRO).
63. Articles of misbehaviour against Francis Devy, April 1652, Q/SR/276/17, SRO; Warrant to the constables of Enville, September 5, 1648, Q/SR/276/18, SRO.
64. For an interesting discussion of this case, see Owen Rees, "The Use of Psychological Science in History: Theory and Practice" (MA Dissertation, University of Nottingham, 2010), 19.
65. Buck, "Impact of War," 448.
66. Lucy Robinson, "Explanations of Post-Traumatic Stress Disorder in Falklands Memoirs: The Fragmented Self and the Collective Body," *Journal of War and Culture Studies* 5, no. 1 (2012): 97.

67. Petition from John Hogle concerning Raph Rishton, 1661, QSP/210/7, LA.
68. Appleby, "Veteran Politics," 334.
69. East Kent Quarter Sessions Order Book, 1653–71, Q/SO/E1, fol. 90, Kent History and Library Centre (hereafter KHLC).
70. East Kent Quarter Sessions Order Book, 1653–71, fol. 90, KHLC.
71. Appleby, "Veteran Politics," 335–36.
72. Petition by inhabitants of Enville, July 1652, Q/SR/277/23, SRO; Petition from John Hogle concerning Raph Rishton, LA; East Kent Quarter Sessions Order Book, 1653–71, fol. 90, KHLC.
73. Elaine Hanson and Gwen Vogel, "The Impact of War on Civilians," in Lopez Levers, *Trauma Counselling*, 412–33, esp. 421.
74. Articles of misbehaviour against Roger Fellowes, SRO.
75. Appleby, "Veteran Politics," 334–35.
76. Penny Roberts, "Agencies Human and Divine: Fire in French Cities, 1520–1720," in *Fear in Early Modern Society*, ed. William Naphy and Penny Roberts, 9–27 (Manchester, UK: Manchester University Press, 1997), esp. 9.
77. Kramer and Weigel, "Introduction," xvi; Felman and Laub, *Testimony*, xvi, 48, and 58.
78. Michael Braddick, *God's Fury, England's Fire: A New History of the English Civil Wars* (London: Penguin, 2009), 389–97.
79. Felman and Laub, *Testimony*, xix.
80. Stoyle, "Memories of the Maimed," 222.
81. Edward Hyde, Earl of Clarendon, *The History of the Rebellion and Civil Wars in England*, ed. William Dunn Macray (Oxford, UK: Oxford University Press, 1888), 2:406.
82. Jonathan Sawday, "'Mysteriously Divided': Civil War, Madness and the Divided Self," in *Literature and the English Civil War*, ed. Thomas Healy and Jonathan Sawday, 127–43 (Cambridge, UK: Cambridge University Press, 1990), 128.
83. Peters, "Trauma Narratives," 80.
84. Peters, 80 and 85.
85. Kramer and Weigel, "Introduction," xi–xii.
86. Appleby, "Unnecessary Persons?," 213.
87. Petition by inhabitants of Enville, SRO.
88. Petition from John Hogle concerning Raph Rishton, LA; East Kent Quarter Sessions Order Book, 1653–71, fols. 57, 90, and 93, KHLC.
89. Appleby, "Unnecessary Persons?," 211.
90. Richard Hoyle, "Petitioning as Popular Politics in Early Sixteenth-Century England," *Historical Research* 75, no. 190 (November 2002): 366, doi:10.1111/1468-2281.00156; Houston, *Peasant Petitions*, 106.

91. Mark Knights, *Representation and Misrepresentation in Later Stuart Britain: Partisanship and Political Culture* (Oxford, UK: Oxford University Press, 2005), 114.
92. David Zaret, "Petitions and the 'Invention' of Public Opinion in the English Revolution," *American Journal of Sociology* 101, no. 6 (May 1996): 1523, doi:10.1086/230866.
93. Appleby, "Unnecessary Persons?," 211; Houston, *Peasant Petitions*, 86.
94. Knights, *Representation and Misrepresentation*, 111 and 140.
95. Knights, *Representation and Misrepresentation*, 111; Zaret, "Petitions," 1521–26.
96. Appleby, "Unnecessary Persons?," 212.
97. Gary Rivett, "Revivifying and Reconciling the State: Peace-Making and Narrative Hegemony in Post-Civil-War England, 1646–1647," in *Civil War and Narrative: Testimony, Historiography, Memory*, ed. Karine Deslandes, Fabrice Mourlon, and Bruno Tribout, 175–90 (Basingstoke, UK: Palgrave Macmillan, 2017), 175.
98. Rivett, 186–87.
99. Matthew Neufeld and Rachel Hatcher, "Civil-War Stories in Lands of Commanded Forgetting: Restoration England and Late Twentieth-Century El Salvador," in Deslandes, Mourlon, and Tribout, *Civil War and Narrative*, 191–210, esp. 202–3.
100. *Report on Manuscripts in Various Collections*, HMC, 1:131.
101. Felman and Laub, *Testimony*, 7.
102. Michael Braddick, "Political Revolutions," in Broomhall, *Early Modern Emotions*, 185–88, esp. 188.
103. Thomas Anderson, *Performing Early Modern Trauma from Shakespeare to Milton* (Aldershot, UK: Ashgate, 2006), 3–4.
104. Appleby, "Unnecessary Persons?," 209.
105. Kramer and Weigel, "Introduction," xii.
106. Appleby, "Restoration County Community," 123.

6

Hans Sloane and the Melancholy Slave

PETER WALMSLEY

In Hans Sloane's "Miscellanies" catalog for his private museum the following entries are scattered:

> 1090: A manati strap for whipping the Negro slaves in the Hott W. India plantations
>
> 1623: A noose made from cane split for catching game or hanging runaway negros
>
> 1796: A bullet used by the runaway Negros in Jamaica made of pewter dishes & lead in a thimble.
>
> 1966: A coat of the runaway rebellious negros who lived in the woods of that Island made of the Mahot bark.[1]

These relics of slavery, given to Sloane by his Jamaican contacts Robert Millar and Henry Barham, sit oddly among Sloane's other ethnographic artifacts. His "Miscellanies" catalog is, for the most part, a list of exotic *objets de vertue*, elaborately ornamented examples of Indigenous handiwork that typically filled cabinets of curiosity. By contrast these simple, even ugly artifacts of slavery find a place on Sloane's shelves because, by their very apparent improvisation, they evoke a scene of desperation and violence. Sloane's extraordinary inclusion of these items registers his culture's emergent understanding of, and disruptive attraction to, the generative scenes of trauma that animate the Caribbean colonial project. Signaling the extreme violence meted out to Black bodies by which slavery is sustained, they stand as silent, uncanny witnesses to Jamaica's ongoing war between master and slave, perpetrator and victim. Some of these objects made their way into the new British Museum, along with Sloane's botanical specimens, but they have now all disappeared, either winnowed out over the years by curators, or simply turned to dust. Curiously, these empty clothes and these memorials of slave punishment and rebellion do bear some similarities to the specimens in Sloane's natural history collections: the shells, the husks and dried leaves, the fossils and bones. They evoke, first and foremost, absent bodies, even life itself, which seems perpetually to elude the collector.

This chapter pursues the problem of the spectral body and the elusive psyche of the slave in Sloane's collections and writings—Sloane's clear obsession with the traumatic experience of the Jamaican slave, and his just as obsessive evasions of this trauma. This dynamic, I argue, is compellingly evident in an entry in his Jamaican medical journal, which he publishes as part of the introduction to the first volume of his *Voyage to Jamaica* (2 volumes, 1707, 1725). Here he offers a case history of a house-slave named Rose, whom he diagnoses as suffering from melancholy. While Sloane's record of his examination and treatment of Rose replicates the violence of master/slave relations in Caribbean chattel slavery, it also offers some rare evidence of the psychic suffering of a slave and captures a moment of slave resistance—Rose's presentation with debilitating melancholy proves a serious challenge to the plantation's cycles of coerced labor. Through Rose's case history I consider the possibilities of reading for trauma in late seventeenth-century Caribbean life, and the extent to which early modern diagnoses of melancholy can be illuminated by recent trauma theory. Reading such theory in dialogue with period writings on melancholy by Thomas Sydenham and Robert Burton, I map the common ground of trauma and melancholy. Both conditions are distinguished by dissociation, a lack of agency, and a loss of interest in life, but simultaneously both offer an authoritative disruption to the status quo. The early modern melancholic and the late modern trauma survivor bear powerful, if sometimes unwelcome, messages about what cannot be accepted, assimilated, and forgotten.

To understand historic slave trauma, I draw upon the recent turn in postcolonial, Black, and feminist/queer theorizings toward reading for trauma in the domain of the everyday.[2] Slave trauma does not unfold along the lines proposed in classic formulations of trauma, which propose a singular, elusive moment of damage that haunts the survivor over years. Rather, since chattel slavery can only be maintained through regular displays of force, by the ritual repetition of scenes of power, slave trauma is recurrent, ever renewing, always imminent. While there are variations in these scenes—confinement in the hold, public whippings and execution, chaining and coffling—the object of violence, the Black body, is always the focus. Sloane's intrusive observation and treatment of Rose's body, I argue, is just one such scene in the reiterative theater of enslavement. Dominick LaCapra argues that to be a secondary witness of historic trauma is to become entangled in trauma's "dissociation of affect and representation": ethical witnessing is the struggle to balance "judgment, and self-preservation" with "empathetic unsettlement."[3] Sloane, however, refuses the affective invitation of Rose's suffering; the empiricism that informs his distinctively "modern" practice of both medicine and natural history enables him to approach her treatment with what LaCapra calls a "numbing 'objectivity'" and an "extreme objectification."[4]

Much postcolonial critique has read melancholy as the presiding affect of the Black Atlantic, and my reading of Rose's case history complements Ramesh Mallipeddi's recent explorations of eighteenth-century slave melancholy as a form of resistance.[5] But I am equally mindful that melancholy—always a fluid and inclusive diagnosis—has shifted radically over the centuries. Recent deployments of melancholy tend to work in the wake of Freud, for whom melancholy appears as a debilitating and pathological version of the more explicable and socially acceptable work of mourning.[6] Freud certainly informs Mallipeddi's reading of slave melancholy as nostalgia, a suffering bound up with homesickness, forced mobility, and dispossession.[7] Shifting away from postmodern senses of melancholy as absence and incoherence, I seek to recover melancholy as a diagnosis and discourse in the late seventeenth century, when it was both psychic and somatic and connected with imagination and memory, more consonant with trauma than with loss and mourning.

Sloane's Voyage to Jamaica and Slavery

Hans Sloane visited Jamaica from 1687 to 1689 as physician to the new, and short-lived, governor of the island, Christopher Monck, Second Duke of Albemarle. Even before he left England, Sloane had a growing medical practice and a large botanical collection. The trip to Jamaica was an opportunity to expand both. Twenty years later he produced the first volume of *A Voyage to Jamaica*, with original engravings illustrating the flora and fauna of the island. The appearance of this volume in 1707, dedicated to Queen Anne, marked an upturn in Sloane's fortunes. By 1712 he was physician extraordinary to the ailing queen, a role he continued as physician-in-ordinary to Georges I and II. He was created baronet in 1716, president of the Royal College of Physicians in 1719, and president of the Royal Society in 1727, having served as first secretary since 1695. In Jamaica Sloane met his future wife, Elizabeth Rose, whom he married in 1695, by that point the widow of a slave importer whose widow's portion included a one-third share of several Jamaican plantations.[8] In the British Library Sloane manuscripts, there are letters from Jamaica suggesting that, if not directly involved in the overseeing of his wife's plantations, he kept an eye on her properties and investments. And he certainly received large regular shipments of sugar as profits from her estates.[9]

The scientific value of Sloane's *Voyage* has long been recognized, based as it is on his firsthand observation of living plants in Jamaica and the substantial collection of botanical specimens that accompanied him on the return voyage. In studying the flora of Jamaica, Sloane worked hard to weed out taxonomic duplications, and he achieved many "inventions"—a first description and naming of a species. His botanical mentor John Ray wrote to Sloane: "I cannot byt admire your industry and diligence in collecting & describing so many species in so short a time."[10] But for all the seriousness of Sloane's commitment to the project of bringing the plants of the world into one vast taxonomy, his *Voyage* also seeks to satisfy a wider curiosity about life in the newly established Caribbean plantations, and particularly the slave labor that made these ventures so profitable. In the rambling 150-page introduction to the *Voyage* Sloane covers such topics as Jamaican weather, topography, and trade in no particular order, and mixed in with this is a good deal of pastoralizing ethnography of sugar plantation slave life: how the slaves sleep on the floor on mats, how their thatched huts are constructed, their funeral ceremonies, their laws surrounding adultery, their festivities and music. Sloane visited Jamaica at a moment of rapid expansion for the island's sugar industry, on its way to surpassing that of Barbados, with three thousand African slaves imported annually in the 1680s.[11] In the introduction Sloane recounts a slave sale in neutral language, and describes the punishment meted out to criminal or rebellious slaves in more sensational terms: "After they are whip'd till they are Raw, some put on their Skins Pepper and Salt to make them smart: at other times their Masters will drop melted Wax on their Skins, and use several very exquisite Torments."[12] As Mallipeddi has pointed out, Sloane's descriptions of slave torture are strikingly affectless: a "detached, unemotional account," "just another ethnographic fact."[13] Sloane's final verdict on these tortures puts him squarely on the side of the masters: "These punishments are sometimes merited by the Blacks, who are a very perverse Generation of People" (lvii). James Delbourgo considers Sloane's attitudes to slavery as of a piece with his general attitude to the natural world—his collection of slave artifacts is not a product of "moral or political concern" or even a scientist's interest in race, but as a matter, more than anything else, of early modern curiosity, a fascination with the prodigious, the wondrous, and the novel. For Delbourgo the *Voyage* is "an ambiguous text" where it comes to slavery, and he suggests this is, in fact, typical of pre-abolition writings about slavery—when attitudes were not yet polarized—and typical also of pre-Victorian encounters with other races, before race became a matter of scientific fact.[14] But recent scholarship has stressed that there was, in fact, a vigorous critique of Caribbean slavery in late seventeenth-century England. While there was a widespread acceptance of Greek and Roman practices of slavery as the natural product of conquest—enemies captured in a just war could fairly be enslaved in exchange for the sparing of their lives—many recognized that something quite different was afoot in the burgeoning transatlantic slave trade. As Robin Blackburn has shown, "the thoroughly commercial character of most New World slavery" seemed to set it apart from its Roman predecessor for most late seventeenth-century observers.[15] Both planters and their slaves understood that they were now dealing with a new order of human interaction: slavery was centrally about work, the extraction of labor from bodies that had been paid for and were now owned. For the slave this made work avoidance central to resistance, while for the master this made the surveillance of work and the exemplary punishment of dilatoriness crucial. Chattel slavery's new dispensation was thus deeply disruptive to understandings of traditional work relationships in English life—between master and servant, mistress and maid, guildsman and apprentice. These conventional bonds between unequals were built on a well-understood set of reciprocities, including loyalty, service for wages, membership in a "family," and an exchange of knowledge, reciprocities that slavery did away with. Travelers to the Caribbean reacted strongly to this transformation of the realm of work and came back with accounts of the cruelties of plantation labor. Thomas Tryon's *Friendly Advice to the Gentlemen-Planters of the East and West Indies* (1684) gives voice to the slave forced to labor beyond his natural strength, suffering "in continual drudgery, till our Heart-strings crack, and our Nerves are enfeebled, and our Marrow is exhausted."[16] Warren Chernaik, in his study of Aphra Behn's depiction of slavery in *Oroonoko*, shows that much nascent antislavery rhetoric turned upon the character of white slave owners as embodying a new, heartless economic order: Behn calls them "rogues and runagates, that have abandoned their own countries for rapine, murders, thefts and villanies," while Richard Baxter wrote that they "are fitter to be called incarnate Devils than Christians."[17] Sloane's visit to Jamaica thus corresponded with the emergence of a highly charged moral condemnation of Caribbean slavery.

While Delbourgo is right to identify a fundamental ambiguity in Sloane's attitudes to slavery, I would argue that more is at work here than the virtuoso's omnivorous curiosity, that there is a pattern of concealment and avoidance in Sloane's collecting of slave artifacts and writing about slave life.[18] More than this, at the heart of the *Voyage* there is a gap, a hollowing out of the living core of the imperial engine—the working body of the slave is nowhere to be seen. This seems particularly odd since Sloane himself is otherwise so obsessed with work, so eager to portray himself as a tireless and industrious botanist and physician. To invoke Ian Baucom's *Specters of the Atlantic*, Sloane is perfectly exemplary of the "phenomenal busy-ness" and banality of global rule, as he spends his time productively employed while strenuously avoiding the violence all around him.[19] Sloane has almost nothing to say about the daylong, dangerous, grinding labor that Jamaican slaves had to perform. To read the *Voyage* is to become increasingly aware of this absence, so much so that it becomes a spectral presence. Some of this becomes evident in the botanical descriptions. Sloane works to isolate, in word and image, the plant as a perfect species, distinct from all others. But so many of the plants he exhaustively describes are food plants—cassava, peppers, maize, plantains—from the slaves' own gardens, where Sloane would have had to go to make his observations and gather specimens. Sloane chooses to ignore the role these plants play in sustaining the bodies who work the sugar fields, rendering them instead as autonomous productions of nature and discrete objects of study. The spectral slave similarly haunts the last fifty pages of the introduction, in which Sloane prints the medical journal he kept during his eighteen months on the island. Over this time Sloane found himself increasingly in demand outside of Albemarle's household, called upon to treat not just planters and their families but their slaves as well.

The Case History of Rose

Of the 128 case histories reproduced in the *Voyage*'s introduction, eighteen clearly deal with slaves of African descent, and of these the most extensive recounts the treatment of Rose:

> A *Negro* Woman of [Mr. Fletcher's] called *Rose*, who us'd to be about the House, and attend Children, grew Melancholy, Morose, Taciturn, and by degrees fell into a perfect Mopishness or stupidity. She would not speak to any Body, would not eat nor drink, except when forc'd, and if she were bid to do any thing she was wont to do, before she had gone about it, she would forget what her Commands were. If one brought her out to set her about any thing, she would stand in the Posture she was left, looking down on the Ground, and if one further, as for instance, put a Broom in her Hands to sweep the House, there she stood with it, looking on the ground very pensive and melancholy. She had fallen into this the Full Moon before I saw her, and afterwards her Exacerbations always on the Full or Change. I had her Cupt and Scarified in the Neck, ordered her a very strong Purge of *Extr. Rud*, to be forc'd down her Throat. This does not work. I gave her six Ounces of *Vin. Emet.* telling her it was a Dram, which wrought pretty well with her. I gave her also, several days very strong Doses of *Diagridium*, or Jalap amongst her Victuals, which sometimes wrought none at all, and at other times would work pretty well. In a months time there was much

> alteration for the better, so that she was concluded not to be bewitched by her own Country people, which was the Opinion of most saw her. This happens very often in Diseases of the Head, Nerves or Spirits, when the Symptoms of them are extraordinary, or not understood, to be attributed by the common People to Witchcraft, or the Power of the Devil. *Assa foetida* is used in Exorcisms, which I take to be more proper for Hysterick or Nervous disorders of those to be Exorcis'd, than to offend the Nostrils of the Devil. I blistered her Neck, gave her now and then *Vin. Emet.* to six Ounces, or *Merc. Vit.* to eight or nine Grains, she being very hard, as all mad People are, to work on. She had some white Pustles rose all over her Skin, and by the use of these Medicines alternatively, she came to her self, went about her business, and was well. (cxiv–cxv)

Sloane included his medical journal in the first volume of the *Voyage* for publicity purposes, as a way of demonstrating his competence and success as a physician. Like so many entries in the medical journal, Rose's case history exemplifies the physician's virtues of attentiveness and diligence. Sloane pits his knowledge and perseverance against a stubborn mental illness, and a cure is effected. Sloane was trained by Thomas Sydenham, and he shows Sydenham's emphasis on experience and circumspection in diagnosis: diseases are species, consistently revealing a pattern of distinguishing symptoms over time. Rose's case history shows a practice of ongoing observation followed by the sequential experimental use of treatments that distinguishes Sloane as a modern, one who is adapting the methods of the new science to physic. That said, Sloane like Sydenham still works within a Galenic tradition, the conventions of which are also clear in Rose's case. It was not typical for physicians to touch patients in Sloane's day, and diagnosis proceeded from a careful observation of a clothed patient and a conversation with the patient about the complaint, often with observations sought from other members of the patient's family: in this case Sloane is clearly relying on evidence provided by the Fletchers, Rose's owners. From the patient's body shape, disposition, and complexion, Sloane would determine the general humoral imbalance at play, characterizing a patient as manifesting an excess of one humor resulting in a temperament that is sanguine, choleric, phlegmatic, or melancholic.

Sloane clearly understands Rose's illness as falling under a general diagnosis of melancholia from an excess of black bile.

From one angle, then, Sloane's case history of Rose is striking for approaching an African slave's illness with the same medical assumptions and methods applied in his treatment of Europeans. Indeed, Sloane's medical diary, which mixes white bodies and black bodies in one long catalog, seems to offer a model of scientific objectivity, even in matters of race. It has been read in this way by Wendy Churchill, who argues that "Sloane transgressed categories of gender and race by diagnosing and treating all his patients according to the same medical ideology."[20] Churchill observes that where many colonial physicians believed both that diseases manifested differently in the tropics and that slaves of African descent were subject to disorders that did not affect white colonists, Sloane did not.[21] But despite the seeming impartiality of the journal, there are some significant differences when it comes to Sloane's treatment of slaves, differences that are evident in his case history of Rose. While acknowledging, with Saidiya Hartman, "the impossibility of fully reconstituting the experiences of the enslaved," I take up Hartman's challenge to "struggle within and against the silences imposed by the nature of the archive," reading against the grain of the *Voyage to Jamaica* for evidence of the ways both Rose and Sloane are entangled in slavery's brutal dynamics.[22] Informing my reading, too, is the central fact that the Black body is the site on which slavery was effected and articulated: as Mallipeddi puts it, "the two features of Atlantic slavery—commodification and punishment—are fundamentally concerned with transformations of the body, with the subjection of the raced body to the regimes of the market and to plantation discipline."[23]

The sustaining violence of slavery is perhaps most obvious in the medicines and interventions Sloane prescribes. While Galenic physic aimed for balance, it often sought to do so by shocking the body, and in this Sloane is conventional, relying on purges, emetics, and diuretics, and routinely recommending bloodletting in one form or another, all to eliminate morbific matter from the body.[24] So his treatment of Rose is not discontinuous from his approach to white patients with a range of disorders, and indeed Sydenham recommends "large evacuations by Bleeding and Purging" for madness, though he also urges caution in cases of patients with weakened constitutions.[25] But in working on a slave body, Sloane is quick to resort to extreme measures, dispensing with the circumspection he typically exhibits in treating white patients. As Dorothy and Roy Porter have shown, the early modern patients were discerning and self-determining when it came to their care, seeking advice, often from several quarters, and choosing treatments according to their own understandings.[26] Physicians, apothecaries, and surgeons all relied on a satisfied clientele and word-of-mouth for a healthy practice and a steady income. In this context a physician's advice was inevitably couched within an understanding of the patient's preferences and comfort in mind, and treatment was often a matter of negotiation. In this Sloane is no exception: fresh from London and part of the governor general's retinue, he brings a high professional standing and authority, but he finds himself surrounded by competitors, including Black doctors, in Jamaica's medical marketplace. He is frequently frustrated when patients take their own paths, preferring the advice of another practitioner or misrepresenting their conditions. Others "would not observe Rules" (xcvi), modifying his prescriptions or self-medicating, usually with alcohol. In his case histories for white patients, Sloane typically proceeds with caution, starting with mild or tried-and-true treatments, and avoiding distressing interventions save in the most serious situations.[27] In the case of Rose, however, he is being paid by her master, and the sole purpose of her treatment is that she might return to work.

In this reconfigured relationship between patient and practitioner, Sloane opts from the start for a wide array of more drastic measures, subjecting Rose to a battery of painful treatments. These include doses of cathartics—medicines that purge by irritating the lining of the bowel—that Sloane admits are dangerously large: he gives her "a very strong purge" of *extractum rudii* (a blend of two potentially deadly botanicals, colocynth and black hellebore) and then for several days "very strong doses of *Diagridium*" (a purgative gum resin from the roots of convolvulus scammonia) or jalap (from another convolvulus, *exogonium purga*). He also prescribes an emetic in the form of *vin émétique* (typically white wine with an infusion of antimony) that causes violent and prolonged vomiting, accompanied by sweating and purging, alternating this with liquid mercury, a treatment for syphilis in the period recognized for its toxicity and serious side effects, which caused heavy salivation.[28] On top of these oral medicines, Sloane orders that Rose be "Cupt and Scarified in the Neck," a fairly common form of localized bleeding where shallow incisions are made in the skin and heated glass cups are applied to draw out the blood.[29] He also has her blistered in the neck, a recognized treatment for madness involving the application of a powder or ointment (typically of cantharidin, derived from blister beetles). The blisters resulting from the chemical burn would then be lanced and drained. Both bleeding and blistering would leave scars, and those of scarification would likely be permanent, a fact that resonates troublingly with Sloane's own attention to the scarring of slave skin throughout the introduction to the *Voyage*. He notes that "there are few *Negros* on whom one may not see a great many Cicatrices or Scars"; some of these are the result of medical treatments—slaves working as doctors in Jamaica often bled their patients, scarifying and cupping with calabashes—and some are made "for Ornament"—Sloane's interpretation of the facial scarring practices common among West African peoples to signal family ties and to mark rites of passage. He also records in detail the torture of recalcitrant slaves, particularly how "for Negligence, they are usually whipt by the Overseers with Lance-wood switches, till they be bloody . . . the Cicatrices are visible on their Skins for ever after." Those slaves that bear "the marks of their severe Corrections . . . are not very saleable" (liii–lvii). By Sloane's accounting, then, scars in slave culture signify in multiple ways, as a consequence of medical care and as ornament but also as punishment. Slave scars are at once sites of cultural expression, self-assertion, and white discipline. Above all they serve as tokens of value within a chattel slavery economy that constantly seeks to render people into commodities. In marking Rose's neck through scarification and blistering, Sloane is applying accepted medical procedures, but he is doing so in a context where such marking inevitably evokes the regular and ritual violence by which slavery is sustained in Jamaica.

Overall, in Rose's case Sloane proceeds without the constraints and the deference with which he treats his white patients, implicitly adopting and exploiting the imbalances of power between master and slave. Where typically he would offer two or three medicines, here he seems to feel he has license to unleash his full pharmacopeia. Nor does he seek Rose's consent to these medicines, or prepare her for their alarming effects, but proceeds by violence and deception, forcing purges down her throat or mixing them with her food, telling her an emetic was just a "dram." That he records this treatment in such detail suggests he is offering it to us, in part, as a successful experiment in the treatment of madness, but one that could, given its extremity, only be risked on a slave body.

Galenic physic was highly personalized, not just in its attention to the patient's humoral disposition but also in its assumption that life habits and behaviors are common causes of the imbalances that bring disease. Seventeenth-century physicians diligently inquired into such things as diet and sleep patterns, looking for irregularities, overexertions, and overindulgences, and in this Sloane was no different.[30] Most of Sloane's white patients are, in Sloane's opinion at least, victims of their own excess. Indeed, his disapprobation and dismay are everywhere evident in his account of white Jamaican culture: "I believe People here [are] more debauch'd than in *England*" (xxxi). Sloane judges that most of his white patients, men and women, caused their illnesses through immoderate habits, including binge drinking, late hours, overeating (such as indulging in hot peppers, mushrooms, and shellfish), and, of course, "venery" (cxxii). In one case he had to treat two participants in a drinking competition who had rendered themselves comatose (cxvii). The journal confirms the picture offered by many accounts of colonial Jamaica as a place of excess with a fragile social fabric.[31] It is striking, then, that in his account of Rose's madness, as in all his case histories for slaves, he makes no inquiry into the possible personal causes of their illness. In fact in Rose's case he tentatively seeks an external cause, suggesting her madness might have been brought on by the full moon, invoking an older and by this point relatively suspect understanding of lunacy. And yet at the same time he makes an elaborate point of rejecting the slave community's spiritual accounting for Rose's condition: she was determined "to be bewitched by her own Country people, which was the Opinion of most saw her." This is, in fact, one of the few places in the *Voyage* where Sloane registers the influence of Obeah in Jamaican slave culture, with its blend of secretive religious and medical practices. Obeah was widely feared by planter society for its associations with poisons and hexes and its ability to elude surveillance.[32] Sloane the scientist is predictably dismissive, pitting his own empirical medical practice against the superstitions of "common people," ironically enough, given that the secularization of madness in England had only occurred relatively recently: as late as the mid-seventeenth century even the educated could attribute mental illness to demonic possession.[33]

If, then, as Churchill argues, Sloane does not accept the common view that different races are prone to different diseases, race is nonetheless a factor when it comes to his approach to diagnosis and treatment. He consistently avoids investigating the habits and constitutions of his Black patients when seeking the causes of their illnesses, something he prioritizes for his white patients. The reasons are, perhaps, obvious: the hardships faced daily by a plantation slave—backbreaking labor, long hours, little or bad food—are a given, and these conditions of life are irremediable. Sloane is paid to cure slaves only that they might return to the intolerable circumstances that almost certainly caused their illness in the first place. If his white patients are knowable as individuals, and indeed typically culpable for their own suffering, Sloane has nothing to say of the lives of his Black patients. Baucom observes of the slave trade "that among other violences it inflicted on millions of human beings was the violence of becoming a 'type': a type of person, or, terribly, not even that, a type of nonperson, a type of property, a type of commodity, a type of money."[34] By failing to explore the personal causes of his Black patients' complaints, or to consider that they might be caused by their enslavement, the conditions of their work, or the quotidian violence they both experience and witness, Sloane implicitly participates in this spectralization of the slave, treating her not as an individual but as a type.

Sloane's case history of Rose is marked, then, by evasions and disavowals as much as by violence. His examination and extended treatment of Rose would have brought the white elite Briton and the Black slave into an extraordinary intimacy. If white Jamaican culture strove to segregate and objectify its others, Black Jamaican culture sought out myriad forms of resistance. In treating Rose, Sloane enters a charged and contested realm, called upon to attend to a humanity that is otherwise strenuously ignored. Moreover, the nature of Rose's disorder presented challenges of its own to a seventeenth-century physician. Mental illness had only relatively recently been medicalized, and there were no accepted traditions of practice attending it. Where most of the illness Sloane deals with is bodily and localized, with patients gladly describing their symptoms, madness is more elusive. Nervous disorders manifest in behavioral symptoms, rather than physical ones, and demand interpretation. For her part, Rose remains uncommunicative about her condition. For all these reasons Sloane would have found his encounters with Rose disorienting. And while his primary response is a signal failure of his trademark curiosity, it is possible nevertheless to read in the language of Rose's case history evidence of Sloane's own uncertainty, and even an implicit recognition of the complex personhood of his patient. This is perhaps most evident in his diagnosis, which is at once slippery and excessive: Rose grew "Melancholy, Morose, Taciturn, and by degrees fell into a perfect Mopishness or stupidity" and appeared to all to be "pensive and melancholy." He later associates her with "all mad People" as being hard to treat, and that when cured "she came to her self." This language recognizes Rose's mental interiority: "pensive," silent, and forgetful, she has turned away from the world, revolving her own thoughts. It also registers her complex emotional state: "morose" suggests a sullenness and irritability, "melancholy" a deep and fixed sadness.

In diagnosing Rose as melancholic, Sloane seeks, as far as possible, to give her a specific diagnosis, but melancholy brings with it, of course, considerable cultural baggage. Melancholy's cachet in the early modern period looked back to Aristotle, who in his *Problems* had registered the fact that all those "who have become extraordinary in philosophy, politics, poetry, or the arts are obviously melancholic": where in some black bile produces "apoplexy or torpor or spiritlessness or fear," in others it fires boldness and inspiration.[35] This marriage of mental suffering and genius informs Shakespeare's melancholics (Hamlet, Jaques), and similarly structures Robert Burton's vast *Anatomy of Melancholy* (1621–38), which insists on the role of imagination in the disease. Even one as skeptical of authorities as Sydenham feels obliged to concede, from his own experience, that "*Aristotle* was in the right, when he said that Melancholy People are most ingenious."[36] Burton defines melancholy as "*a perpetuall anguish of the soule, fastned on one thing*" and "*a kinde of dotage without a feaver*"; the melancholy are "bashfull, suspicitious, solitary" and suffer from excessive "feare and sorrow" and a "wearisomenesse of life."[37] While the early moderns accepted melancholy as a physiological condition, an excess of black bile that could be brought back into balance by common treatments like bloodletting and purging, they equally believed that its causes were, more often than not, spiritual, psychic, and social. Burton himself is particularly interested in thwarted love, religious doubt, and excessive study as triggers for the disease; interestingly for Rose's case, Burton also identifies excessive labor, servitude, and loss of liberty as causes as well.[38] Reading Rose's case history in the context of Burton's compendium of the rich cultural discourses of melancholia opens up implications for Sloane's diagnosis, implications that he himself refuses to explore but would have been evident to his readers. As the *Anatomy* makes clear, melancholy is not simply a nervous disorder, but a primary site for core debates in seventeenth-century English life regarding such things as mortality, grief, sinfulness, love, imagination, and sociality. As Roy Porter puts it, "to melancholize was human."[39] And Aristotle's link between melancholy and genius remained strong. Like sensibility a few generations later, melancholy was a mark of spiritual depth, of the examined life, of a capacity to grieve, to empathize, to see life's fragility. Not surprisingly, a member of England's educated urban elite is more likely than a rural day laborer to be diagnosed as melancholic. Moreover, as Joseph Addison and George Cheyne make clear, melancholy was increasingly being claimed in this period as a particularly English malady; as Addison puts it, "Melancholy is a kind of Demon that haunts our Island, and often conveys her self to us in an Easterly Wind."[40] In this context the figure of the melancholy Caribbean slave is disruptive, laying claim to an interiority and emotional complexity that was seen as properly belonging to England's white ruling class.

Melancholy and Trauma

Seventeenth-century melancholy's capaciousness, its multiple kinds and causes, makes it troublesome for physicians like Sydenham and Sloane who are committed to precise diagnosis.[41] Its amorphousness likewise makes it less legible to twenty-first-century medicine. For Jennifer Radden, Burton's *Anatomy* is concerned with what modern psychiatry calls mood disorders, such as anxiety or depression, and she mines Burton for his insights about the role of mental habit in creating and sustaining depressive states of mind.[42] But it could equally be argued that Burton's account of melancholy captures some of what we would now identify as psychic trauma. Particularly resonant is his understanding of the genesis of melancholia, in which the imagination and memory work together, driven by the "Passions and Perturbations of the Minde," to become obsessed with a past distressing scene or experience:

> To our imagination commeth, by the outward sense or memory, some object to be knowne (residing in the foremost part of the braine) which he, misconceiving or amplifying, presently communicates to the Heart, the seat of all affections. . . . If the imagination be very apprehensive, intent, and violent, it sends great store of spirits to, or from the heart, and makes a deeper impression, and greater tumult. . . . [Imagination] rageth in melancholy persons, in keeping the species of objects so long, mistaking, amplifying them by continuall and strong meditation, untill at length it produceth in some parties reall effects, causeth this and many other maladies.[43]

Burton illustrates with the story of a gentlewoman who saw a hog butchered and became obsessed by the scene, applying it to herself: "Shee could not forget it, or remove the object out of her sight" but finds she must "dreame and continually thinke of it."[44] Burton's attention to melancholy's debilitating fixation on a feared or hated object, which returns in thought and dreams but is never mastered, aligns with trauma theory's account of the patient's struggle with an incomprehensible and unassimilable scene of horror, in Cathy Caruth's words, "a crisis that is marked, not by a simple knowledge, but by the ways it simultaneously defies and demands our witness."[45] Burton also seems to capture what we recognize as trauma's circularity, rendering the sufferer apparently static, cut off from the world and buried in the past: "Sorrow is both Cause and Symptome of this disease." Importantly, Burton comes close to describing melancholy as a primarily psychic rather than physiological disorder: "Why was *Hecuba* said to be turned to a Dogge? *Niobe* into a stone? but that for griefe she was senseless and stupid."[46] Nor was he alone in this: if seventeenth-century physicians often speculated about material and somatic causes for melancholy (overeating and heavy drinking were favorites), most also conceded that personal losses and the trials of life had a large role. For Sydenham melancholy becomes entrenched and dangerous with "Adversity, Care, or Trouble of mind."[47] Caruth follows Shoshana Felman and Dori Laub in stressing that trauma is social, even communicable, in its demands for difficult witness, something that similarly distinguishes early modern melancholy, which in both theater and life developed a conventional set of gestures and words to share its peculiar pains.[48] As Drew Daniel has argued, Shakespeare's "Jaquis understands melancholy as a multiplicity, an expressive array of materials and postures and cases distributed across a social surround"; for Daniel "melancholy joins together its sufferers and its witnesses into tenuous perceptual communities."[49] Burton's *Anatomy* is a fulsome testament to melancholy's elaborate rhetoric and the resulting communities of suffering it produces, recognizing the relief that comes from sharing—"the best way for ease is to impart our misery to some friend, not to smother it up in our owne breast."[50]

Can contemporary trauma theory enlighten the experience of seventeenth-century slavery? More particularly, is it helpful to read Rose's case history as a trauma narrative? Scholars such as Jane Kilby and Stef Craps have registered the Eurocentric biases of much trauma theory, the need to "understand trauma as a global phenomenon, as something experienced throughout the world and by any number of peoples and communities," and the dangers attendant on such a reimagining.[51] The archetypical trauma survivor is the white middle-class European or North American, one whose subjectivity and sensibility is a given and readily legible to those who inhabit similar positions. Trauma studies typically have not attended to the experiences of trauma outside the West, so to write of the trauma of a woman of West African descent risks assuming the universal applicability of European psychiatric models and flattening cultural differences. But linking trauma and melancholy as I have done crosses temporal boundaries as well: the diagnosis of trauma is an invention of twentieth-century psychiatry and is, in many ways, shaped by the moment of its birth. As Craps points out, "Definitions of trauma and recovery . . . have developed out of the history of Western modernity," and "they often favour or even prescribe a modernist aesthetic of fragmentation or aporia as uniquely suited to the task of bearing witness to trauma."[52] To reach into the deeper past of the late seventeenth century, long before the modernist articulation of trauma, riskily assumes a continuity of psychic life across centuries. That said, there are some rich affordances to pushing beyond the borders of space and time that have typically bound the study of trauma. Not least among these is the weight and recognizability that the diagnosis of trauma carries in modern life: to treat events as traumatizing and subjects as traumatized is to make those experiences and subjects available for concern and to grant them importance. Nor can it be denied that trauma has proved its explanatory power over time, illuminating a pattern of psychic suffering that manifests widely. Trauma theory has proved illuminating, for example, in more recent work on the afterlives of slavery in contemporary Black American life and on intergenerational trauma among North American Indigenous peoples.[53] To pursue the inter-illuminations of early modern melancholy and late modern trauma is to register the ways each serves as a focal point for understanding mental suffering, and likewise how each is elaborated into a rich cultural discourse, attracting both a complexity and an authority in their respective cultural moments.

It is a challenge to know Rose through Sloane's language—whatever she might have said for herself is lost—but even through this limiting lens she is clearly legible as both melancholic and traumatized. Her extreme dissociation and detachment are certainly symptomatic of trauma in our contemporary sense: "pensive" and turned inward, she seems fixated, haunted, static, rooted in an unknowable, unassimilated violence or loss. Trauma and melancholy alike are marked by a lethargy that embodies a failure of agency and rejects the busyness of the quotidian and the normal. Trauma theory looks for the causes that Sloane, for all his diligence, refuses to ask about—the events that might have brought Rose to this place of utter debility and despair. The possibilities, of course, are legion for a woman slave in the Caribbean: crushing labor, perennial surveillance, sexual violence, the death or sale of children. Indeed, the multiple and repeated violences of slavery have exposed some of the limitations of classic trauma theory, which assumes a single event as trauma's genesis.[54] So Craps proposes a supplementary model of postcolonial trauma "which—unlike the traditional individual and event-based model—can account for and respond to collective, ongoing, everyday forms of traumatizing violence."[55] Caribbean chattel slavery is a trauma engine, extraordinary in its violence, and the more so because it is equally inexplicable to both perpetrator and survivor. Caruth's insight that trauma is in many ways an epistemic crisis suggests that trauma theory is particularly relevant to slavery, which—with its defiance of human feeling and natural law—baffles any attempt at comprehension.

Slave Resistance

Bringing trauma theory to bear on early modern melancholy is valuable, too, for helping us read for the political. Centered as it is in Holocaust testimony, trauma is understood as inherently political: trauma stories, no matter how personal, are always cast as stories of injustice, illuminating abuses of power and showing the human capacities for both cruelty and suffering. Trauma also foregrounds the possibilities of resistance. Fundamentally it registers the mind's inability to assimilate an experience or scene of horror; while debilitating in itself, it paradoxically marks the mind's native and self-protecting resistance to admitting what should never have to be known, a refusal to accept and move on. I would argue that trauma can help remind us of the politics of early modern melancholy, which are not always obvious: melancholy can seem reclusive, even quietist, to twenty-first-century eyes. But the seventeenth-century melancholic is, more often than not, a malcontent, repudiating the pervasive emptiness of the mundane, unable to acquiesce in the collective cheer by which the social is sustained. It is likewise commonly a madness that comes from a refusal to suffer fools. And melancholy is, as Drew has shown, richly rhetorical and performative, a discontent that seeks the affirmation of an audience. Returning to Jamaican slavery, and Rose in particular, it is possible in this light to read her melancholic stance as resistant, even subversive. Caribbean slavery was sustained not just by violence but by a complex theater, where planter performed unflinching and absolute authority, and slave performed willing compliance and contentedness. Cheerfulness is adopted by the enslaved as a way of deluding planter authority and deflecting its more violent expressions.[56] Rose's melancholy—the very antithesis of slave cheerfulness—violates the script by which master/slave relations are managed. That Sloane underscores Rose's silence—"Taciturn," "She would not speak to any Body"—shows the extent to which it compounds the problem. An inability to speak is a recognized sign of trauma; Felman and Laub note the "bewildered muteness of the survivors of the holocaust," a response to the genocide's "historical unspeakability."[57] But in the case of Rose it is further a refusal to show deference, to register her acceptance of orders, to answer to a name that is inevitably not her own.[58] This is a passive defiance, of course, all the more effective because implicit, careful not to elicit white ire and punishment. Sloane's examination of Rose perversely replicates the spectacle of the auction block, the public stage on every plantation where the Black body comes under intense visual scrutiny, assessed for health and work readiness—evidence of which Rose does not supply. Katherine McKittrick establishes how slave women's bodies were subject to constant public surveillance, becoming "seeable sites of wealth, sexuality, and punishment." In this visual economy "black subjects" become simultaneously "hidden and on display," spectacular and absent, seen and unseeable. Rose's distinctive mental absence is not unlike Harriet Jacobs's garret hiding place, her "loophole of retreat," which McKittrick reads as resisting the "patriarchal logic of visualization," allowing Jacobs to "eras[e] herself from the immediate landscape."[59] There is a similar fugitivity to Rose's turn inward. Like the slave artifacts in Sloane's collection, Rose's body seems an empty shell, offering only the vestiges of a runaway slave.

Slave resistance in the Caribbean took many forms, everything from songs covertly mocking masters to open and armed rebellion, but it most commonly manifested in the disruption of work, with strategies ranging from dilatoriness to the sabotage of millworks. In his medical treatment of other slaves, Sloane is intensely conscious of feigned illness as a way of avoiding work. His account of a footman named Emanuel is a case in point. Emanuel had been ordered to guide some of Albemarle's soldiers across the island. He immediately took sick, groaning and unable to speak, which Sloane judged to be mere dissembling: "to frighten him out of it, I told the Standers by, that in such a desperate condition as this 'twas usual to apply a Frying-Pan with burning Coals to the crown of the Head, in order to awake them thoroughly, and to draw from the Head, and that it was likewise an ordinary method to put Candles lighted to their Hands and Feet, that when the flame came to burn them they might be awaked" (cxlii).

Emanuel shortly comes to himself, and with the threat from Sloane that "he should have due Correction" if he refuses to get up, he goes about his errand. Sloane casts himself as a canny enforcer for the planter class, able to see through slave ruses, and potentially willing to resort to violence. And this story seems to be offered in part for our entertainment, what might be referred to as a "frolic" in the day, though in all else Sloane seems a deeply humorless person. Emanuel's case reflects interestingly on Sloane's treatment of Rose: Sloane judges her to be genuinely ill, though, as I have suggested, his treatment exhibits some of the coercion and deception that distinguishes the elaborate theater of medical torture that he devises for Emanuel. Both cases foreground the way work is the prime site of contest between master and slave. Slavery's urgent labor economy is reflected in the image of Rose with her broom: "If one brought her out to set her about any thing, she would stand in the Posture she was left, looking down on the Ground, and if one further, as for instance, put a Broom in her Hands to sweep the House, there she stood with it, looking on the ground very pensive and melancholy" (cxiv). Sloane, in this carefully rendered moment, registers that Rose's melancholy is a problem only insofar as it interferes with her labor, and clearly the Fletcher family experimented with trying to set her to work despite her illness. Holding her broom but not moving, just gazing downward, Rose stands in dumb-show, a tableau of *not* work, of work evaded or refused, a message underscored by the menial tool she holds, itself an emblem of (slave) women's labor. Rose's posture at once displays and defies slavery's insistence on work above all else. Seeming no longer quite human, a broken machine, she embodies the very logic of slavery, turning herself into a mere object, a property.

As chief benefactor of both the British Museum and the Chelsea Physic Garden, Sloane has consistently attracted the kind of civic celebration that Britain reserves for its Enlightenment patriarchs. In 2010, for example, to celebrate the International Year of Biodiversity, the Physic Garden created a special Jamaican Garden to honor Sloane, who was by coincidence having a 350th birthday. The promotional brochure cheerily proposes that the "Jamaican garden . . . highlights how the exchange of plants from country to country has shaped the cultures of people throughout the world. The Jamaican Garden will include palms, cotton, bamboo, banana, papaya, ackee, avocado and sugar cane."[60] When I visited that July, the avocados were clearly not enjoying the English summer, and there was, predictably enough, no mention that any of these were slave crops. So it is perhaps not surprising that historians of science, even those who have attended to Sloane's Jamaica sojourn and his sticky entanglement with sugar and slavery, have handled him gingerly: for Delbourgo, Sloane is an exemplar of a questing scientific curiosity; for Churchill, a physician who treated master and slave with the same dispassionate eye, dispensing health to both. My consideration of Sloane's case history of Rose, which attends to the evidence of the physician's implication in slavery's violence and the slave's refusal of that oppression, tells another story. Like the slave objects in Sloane's collections, his narrative of Rose's melancholy can be read for the traces it bears of slave trauma and, ultimately, for the witness it offers of slave resistance.

NOTES

Italics in quotations throughout this chapter are in the original.

1. British Museum, Department of Ethnography, Sloane MSS, "Miscellanies," fols. 2–152v. In reproducing Sloane's text, I have preserved for accuracy historical racial terms that are now understood to be offensive. In Sloane's day, well before the emergence of scientific racism in the nineteenth century, "negro" was a relatively neutral term, commonly interchanged with "African."
2. See, for example, Ann Cvetkovich, *An Archive of Feelings: Trauma, Sexuality, and Lesbian Public Cultures* (Durham NC: Duke University Press, 2003), 19–20.
3. Dominick LaCapra, *Writing History, Writing Trauma* (Baltimore: Johns Hopkins University Press, 2001), 42, 78.
4. LaCapra, 78–79.
5. Ramesh Mallipeddi, *Spectacular Suffering: Witnessing Slavery in the Eighteenth-Century British Atlantic* (Charlottesville: University of Virginia Press, 2016), esp. 146–79. See also Paul Gilroy's influential exploration of the melancholic denial of imperial legacies in the twentieth century, *Postcolonial Melancholia* (New York: Columbia University Press, 2006).
6. For Freud, both mourning and melancholy seem to be responses to the loss of a loved object, but melancholy is distinguished by self-reproach: "In mourning it is the world which has become poor and empty; in melancholia it is the ego itself." "Mourning and Melancholia," in *The Standard Edition of the Complete Psychological Works of Sigmund Freud, Volume XIV (1914–1916): On the History of the Psycho-Analytic Movement, Papers on Metapsychology and Other Works*, trans. and ed. James Strachey et al., 237–58 (London: Hogarth, 1964), esp. 246. Freud links such self-berating to the subject's covert discontent with the lost love object: "the self-reproaches are reproaches against a loved object which have been shifted away from it on to the patient's own ego. . . . the reactions expressed in their behaviour still proceed from a mental constellation

of revolt, which has then, by a certain process, passed over into the crushed state of melancholia" (248). Both Douglas Trevor and Lisa Starks-Estes have productively negotiated the terrain between early modern and Freudian understandings of the melancholic. Trevor stresses the extent to which early modern melancholy was taken up by writers as an opportunity for self-scrutiny, *The Poetics of Melancholy in Early Modern England* (Cambridge, UK: Cambridge University Press, 2004). In her study of Shakespeare's deployment of the raw sexual violence of Ovid's "Metamorphoses," Starks-Estes establishes the connections between love melancholy, trauma, and early modern subjectivity, *Violence, Trauma, and Virtus in Shakespeare's Roman Poems and Plays: Transforming Ovid* (London: Palgrave Macmillan, 2014).

7. Mallipeddi, *Spectacular Suffering*, 147–48, 169–70.
8. James Delbourgo calls Sloane "a gentleman entrepreneur" and describes his personal profits from Jamaican slavery, "Slavery in the Cabinet of Curiosities: Hans Sloane's Atlantic World," The British Museum, accessed November 10, 2020, http://www.britishmuseum.org/pdf/Delbourgo%20essay.pdf, 8.
9. See, for example, the letter from his brother-in-law Francis Rose of September 19, 1716, British Library Sloane MSS 4044.
10. British Library Sloane MSS 4036, fol. 160.
11. Herbert S. Klein and Ben Vinson III, *African Slavery in Latin America and the Caribbean*, 2nd ed. (Oxford, UK: Oxford University Press, 2007), 55.
12. Hans Sloane, *A Voyage to the Islands Madera, Barbados, Nieves, S. Christophers and Jamaica, with the Natural History . . . of the Last of Those Islands*, 2 vols. (London: Hans Sloane, 1707, 1725), liii, lvii. Subsequent references are to this edition.
13. Mallipeddi, *Spectacular Suffering*, 2.
14. Delbourgo, "Slavery in the Cabinet of Curiosities," 3–4, 8–10. Roxann Wheeler has shown how in the early eighteenth century Britons tended to conceive of human difference in terms of dress, commerce, and religion rather than skin color, *The Complexion of Race: Categories of Difference in Eighteenth-Century British Culture* (Philadelphia: University of Pennsylvania Press, 2000), 1–21.
15. Robin Blackburn, *The Making of New World Slavery: From the Baroque to the Modern, 1492–1800* (London: Verso, 1997), 501.
16. Thomas Tryon, *Friendly Advice to the Gentlemen-Planters of the East and West Indies* (London: A. Sowle, 1684), 87–88.
17. Warren Chernaik, "Captains and Slaves: Aphra Behn and the Rhetoric of Republicanism," *The Seventeenth Century* 17 (2002): 100–102.
18. My approach to Sloane the physician parallels work by Kay Dian Kris on Sloane the natural historian. Kris reads the copperplate engravings of flora, fauna, and artifacts that illuminate the *Voyage* as expressive of the violence of the Caribbean contact zone: she finds in Sloane's work a "conflict . . . between the act of forgetting and the

resurfacing of repressed and usually violent memories," in "Curiosities, Commodities, and Transplanted Bodies in Hans Sloane's 'Natural History of Jamaica,'" *William and Mary Quarterly* 57, no. 1 (2000): 45.

19. Ian Baucom, *Specters of the Atlantic: Finance Capital, Slavery, and the Philosophy of History* (Durham NC: Duke University Press, 2005), 5.
20. Wendy Churchill, "Bodily Differences?: Gender, Race, and Class in Hans Sloane's Jamaican Medical Practice, 1687–1688," *Journal of the History of Medicine and Allied Sciences* 60, no. 4 (2005): 391.
21. Churchill observes that Rose "was treated by Sloane for madness with scarification, blistering, purges, juleps, and mercury, all methods he commonly used in treating white men and women for diseases of the head," evidence of what she calls his "non-racial understanding of the body" (432, 435).
22. Saidiya V. Hartman, *Scenes of Subjection: Terror, Slavery, and Self-Making in Nineteenth-Century America* (Oxford, UK: Oxford University Press, 1997), 11.
23. Mallipeddi, *Spectacular Suffering*, 3.
24. He administers quinine, by 1688 an established if expensive treatment for fevers, and also favors crabs' eyes, live millipedes, and an electuary made with powdered steel, the latter one of Sydenham's preferred prescriptions. See Thomas Sydenham, *The Whole Works of that Excellent Practical Physician Dr. Thomas Sydenham*, trans. from Latin by John Pechy (London: R. Wellington, 1696), 455.
25. Sydenham, 60–61.
26. Dorothy Porter and Roy Porter, *Patient's Progress: Doctors and Doctoring in Eighteenth-Century England* (Cambridge, UK: Polity, 1989), 70–95.
27. Compare, for example, his treatment of a white woman, Mrs. Fuller, who is suffering from hysteria with "a great many incoherent and troublesome Fancies and *Chimaera's* in her thoughts" and who had already been given purges on the advice of several doctors. In this instance Sloane focuses on slowing down her bowels with "a very gentle Opiat," followed by a steel electuary and encouragement of good diet and exercise (cix–cx). Likewise he treated a white farmer named Barret who was a hypochondriac with a simple steel electuary (cxxxviii).
28. Sloane elsewhere expresses reservations about prescribing mercury (cii).
29. For Robert Burton bloodletting is a given in cases of melancholy: "*Cupping-glasses* with or without scarification . . . worke presently, and are applied to several parts, to divert humours, aches, winde, &c," in *The Anatomy of Melancholy*, ed. Nicholas K. Kiessling et al., 5 vols. (Oxford, UK: Clarendon, 1990), esp. 2:237.
30. Churchill, "Bodily Differences?," 429.
31. On the wildness of Jamaican planter life, see Ned Ward, *A Trip to Jamaica with a True Character of the People and Island* (London, 1698).

32. Julie Chun Kim notes that Sloane would have gleaned extensive knowledge about Obeah from Henry Barham's *Hortus Americanus* in "Obeah and the Sources of Atlantic Medicine," in *From Books to Bezoars: Sir Hans Sloane and his Collections*, ed. Alison Walker, Arthur MacGregor, and Michael Hunter, 99–104 (London: British Library, 2012), esp. 102–3.
33. Roy Porter, *Madness: A Brief History* (Oxford, UK: Oxford University Press, 2002), 19–25.
34. Baucom, *Specters of the Atlantic*, 11.
35. Aristotle, "Problem XXX," in *Problems*, ed. and trans. Robert Mayhew, 2: 277–91, 2 vols. (Cambridge: Harvard University Press, 2011), esp. 2: 277, 287.
36. Sydenham, *The Whole Works*, 445.
37. Burton, *Anatomy of Melancholy*, 1:162, 2:206–7.
38. Burton, 1:341–44.
39. Roy Porter, *Mind-Forg'd Manacles: A History of Madness in England from the Restoration to the Regency* (London: Athlone, 1987), 29.
40. Cheyne: George Cheyne, *The English Malady: or, a Treatise of Nervous Diseases of all Kinds* (London: G. Strahan, 1733). No. 387, *The Spectator*, ed. Donald F. Bond, 5 vols. (Oxford, UK: Oxford University Press, 1965), 3:454.
41. Sydenham, a specialist in fevers and epidemic diseases, found himself well outside his comfort zone when writing about nervous disorders: "A Day would scarce suffice to reckon up all the symptoms belonging to Hysterick Diseases, so various are they, and so contrary to one another" (*The Whole Works*, 446).
42. Jennifer Radden, *Melancholic Habits: Burton's* Anatomy *and the Mind Sciences* (Oxford, UK: Oxford University Press, 2017), 273–91.
43. Burton, *Anatomy of Melancholy*, 1:246–50.
44. Burton, *Anatomy of Melancholy*, 1:335. Sydenham confirms that the melancholy are afflicted with nightmares: "only Funerals and Apparitions of their Friends deceased are represented in [their] Dreams" (*The Whole Works*, 445).
45. Cathy Caruth, *Unclaimed Experience: Trauma, Narrative, and History* (Baltimore: Johns Hopkins University Press, 1996), 5.
46. Burton, *Anatomy of Melancholy*, 1:256–58.
47. Sydenham, *The Whole Works*, 445.
48. For Felman and Laub the act of listening to Holocaust testimony generates "an existential crisis in all those involved," a "crisis of experiencing their boundaries, their separateness, their functionality, and indeed their sanity, at risk," in *Testimony: Crises of Witnessing in Literature, Psychoanalysis, and History* (New York: Routledge, 1992), xvi.
49. Drew Daniel, *The Melancholy Assemblage: Affect and Epistemology in the English Renaissance* (New York: Fordham University Press, 2013), 5, 7.
50. Burton, *Anatomy of Melancholy*, 2:104.

51. Jane Kilby, "The Future of Trauma: Introduction," in *The Future of Memory*, ed. Richard Crownshaw, Jane Kilby, and Antony Rowland, 181–90 (New York: Berghahn, 2010), esp. 181; Stef Craps, *Postcolonial Witnessing: Trauma Out of Bounds* (Houndmills, UK: Palgrave Macmillan, 2013), 2–3. Ann Cvetkovich proposes "alternative genealogies of melancholy that foreground the presence of colonialism and race in its Western historical lineages"; "a full picture of this history must include racism's connections to more chronic and low-level feelings, such as those associated with depression" in *Depression: A Public Feeling* (Durham NC: Duke University Press, 2012), 116, 120.
52. Craps, *Postcolonial Witnessing*, 2.
53. See, for example, Hartman, *Scenes of Subjection*; Christina Sharpe, *In the Wake: On Blackness and Being* (Durham NC: Duke University Press, 2016); and Peter Menzies, "Developing an Aboriginal Healing Model for Intergenerational Trauma," *International Journal of Health Promotion and Education* 46, no. 2 (2008): 41–48.
54. So LaCapra observes how historic traumatic events like the Holocaust and Hiroshima have accrued, in their "absolute uniqueness," an "epiphanous, sublime, or sacral quality" (*Writing History*, 80).
55. Craps, *Postcolonial Witnessing*, 4.
56. On how Black cheerfulness was taken up in early twentieth-century sociology, see Rhett S. Jones, "Proving Blacks Inferior: The Sociology of Knowledge," in *The Death of White Sociology*, ed. Joyce A. Ladner, 114–35 (New York: Random House, 1973), esp. 125.
57. Felman and Laub, *Testimony*, xix.
58. "Rose" is a typical example of the perverse renaming by which masters exerted ownership in the Black Atlantic world and demeaned those who were enslaved to them. Often mock-heroic, such renaming ironically ascribed power to those who had none (Caesar, Prince, Psyche) while denying ties to African and diasporic cultural traditions. Rose's name, invoking as it does the ideal of European fairness as beauty, is similarly meant cruelly.
59. Katherine McKittrick, *Demonic Grounds: Black Women and the Cartographies of Struggle* (Minneapolis: University of Minnesota Press, 2006), xxx, 43, 44.
60. "Chelsea Physic Garden: 2010 International Year of Biodiversity at London's Oldest Botanic Garden," (London: Chelsea Physic Garden, 2010).

7

Representations of Loss and Recovery in Unca Eliza Winkfield's *The Female American*

MELISSA ANTONUCCI

As Kathleen Brown-Rice notes, in the 285-year span between Columbus's voyage to America and the birth of American independence in 1776, the numbers of North American Indigenous populations sharply declined amid the violence of land theft, disease, and war, which constituted widespread destruction of native rituals and relationships.[1] The exact numbers of population decline and growth among Indigenous peoples, resulting from European contact and expansive practices of colonialism, are difficult to come by.[2] Brown-Rice, however, has put the loss of Native American population at some 95 percent.[3] During European exploration, settlement, and colonization, Native economic systems were disrupted, the accumulation of knowledge—cultural, religious, and medicinal—was a "casualt[y] of warfare and disease," and the systematic removal from and loss of homelands, which "provided familiar sources of sustenance," led to "severe spiritual and psychological injury."[4] The ubiquity of such trauma has led numerous Native American scholars to conclude that Europe's ethnic cleansing of America was indeed a holocaust.[5] Just as the trauma of the Holocaust has been argued by scholars as transmissible to generations of Jewish people removed from the actualities of World War II through a process of historical trauma, so too have Native American scholars debated the ways in which modern Native populations continue to suffer from the legacy of colonialism. Allison Crawford, writing about her research on the Inuit in Nunavut, Canada, highlights the "*contemporary collective*" nature of historical trauma that results in present "*distress or mourning*" and its "*cumulative*" impact, "which is theorized to be passed along to other members of the group and to future members through *intergenerational transmission*."[6] Exploring the transference of such trauma, Alison Landsberg relies on the phrase "prosthetic memory" to explain how "it has become possible to have an intimate relationship to memories of events through which one did not live."[7] Landsberg's particular focus centers on the commodities culture of the twenty-first century, more specifically on mass media technology, and how our experiences with such technologies create personal, yet artificial, memories of past events or narratives distributed through various types of and experiences with media.[8] It is possible that the cumulative nature of historical trauma might be in part the result of information transference that produces traumatic memories of past events and shapes how we identify with our present environment. In other words, prosthetic memories shape how we interpret our present experiences in relation to that which we know occurred in the past.

Bonnie Duran, Eduardo Duran, and Maria Yellow Horse Brave Heart refer to intergenerational experiences of trauma as the "soul wound," a "spiritual injury" inflicted on a collective psyche by loss and the inability to fully grieve such loss.[9] This conception of the soul wound emerged as a clinical term in the field of psychiatry based on Yellow Horse Brave Heart's own experiences as a Lakota woman and her investigation into Lakota psychology and modes of healing. Despite the relatively small research sample size, Duran, Duran, and Yellow Horse Brave Heart nonetheless claim that "many Native American people understand their problems in contemporary life by reference to the traumatic events of the past."[10] Others, however, such as Laurence J. Kirmayer, Joseph P. Gone, and Joshua Moses, question the application of "holocaust" to describe Native experiences of colonial destruction, and as such challenge the existence of intergenerational trauma among Native American descendants. Their concern stems from a fear of creating universalist tendencies to describe systematic trauma and approaches to healing. Rhetorical choices such as these, Kirmayer, Gone, and Moses claim, are reductive and obscure the role political, social, economic, cultural, linguistic, and spiritual structures play in affecting how individuals and communities experience trauma and work toward reconciliation.[11]

Noting years of research and debate, Irene Visser echoes a similar dissatisfaction with a one-size-fits-all discourse to trauma studies, claiming in 2015 that Freudian psychoanalytic approaches to negotiating trauma in postcolonial texts and communities had been "discarded."[12] What has taken its place is an overture to inclusivity—a theory that acknowledges trauma, particularly as it relates to the political, economic, and ethnic upheavals and violence of colonialism, not as a single blow, whose symptoms are postponed by a period of latency, followed by repetitive cycles of acting out traumatic memories via nightmares or hallucinations, for instance, but as a phenomenon that persists through the entrenched machinery of colonialism that continues to act in the present upon colonized peoples.

For postcolonial scholars, psychoanalytic approaches to trauma are "problematic" in that they tend to emphasize "weakness, victimization, and melancholia."[13] By doing so, psychoanalysis restricts the available modes of exploring and coming to terms with methods of reconciliation, recovery, and the "dynamics of life-affirming and activist processes" utilized by postcolonial subjects.[14] Thus, as Visser has described, "'decolonizing' trauma studies" involves "a reorientation towards narratives that are forward looking, striving for subversion of the traumatic experience rather than its containment in melancholia."[15] Her claims echo Roger Luckhurst, who, in *The Trauma Question*, unpacks with a rather bemused incredulity the seemingly unstoppable pervasiveness of trauma as a condition of modern life—discussions ranging anywhere from the atrocities of wars, natural disasters, violence, and terrorism, to terminal illness, death, and popular culture.[16] The speed at which trauma has beset the milieu of everyday life corresponds directly with the complexity and contradiction the term has engendered. Luckhurst seems to suggest that trauma is at once everywhere and nowhere; thus its meaning continues to push and challenge our boundaries of understanding. Trauma's pervasiveness corresponds also to the many competing disciplines whose heuristics intersect with trauma studies. Although such an intersection informs and complicates our understanding of trauma, it has also created an "unappetizing" argument as to who has the rights over our conceptions of trauma.[17] To counter this Luckhurst points to Bruno Latour's theory of the knot, which instead of privileging one way of knowing over others, posits that disciplines are not arranged hierarchically but intersect and overlap with one another.[18] In thinking about disciplines as entanglements and accumulations of knowledge, Luckhurst argues that a similar multidirectional approach is needed in our considerations of trauma as well.

Despite the challenges and controversies surrounding discussions of historical and intergenerational trauma, I would like to once again return to Duran, Duran, and Yellow Horse Brave Heart's conception of the soul wound. Informed by psychoanalytic theories of traumatic expression, the soul wound does not consistently account for the varied experiences of Indigenous people, whose lives cannot be described accurately by one overarching narrative. Nonetheless it provides a useful heuristic for exploring the colonial trauma experienced by America's first peoples, particularly because of its focus on the various mechanisms at play in both the past and the present. Native-Euro encounters signal not only a loss of and removal from land but also a degradation of the connections between Native American communities and their ancestors, customs, and rituals as new frameworks were, and continue to be, thrust upon them. Many of the texts produced between early British contact with Indigenous populations and the Indian Removal of 1830 refer to Native Americans only as a function to create and underscore an English identity.[19] While Samson Occom, Logan, Tecumseh, and Pontiac might be some of the mostly widely recognized Indigenous voices of the mid- to late eighteenth century, very few Native voices persist from that period. And none represent the experiences of Native women. *The Female American*, published in 1767, is an attempt to account for that lack.[20] In the years following Michelle Burnham's 2001 edition of the novel, scholars have written a great deal about it. Often, they have been most concerned with the relationship between the female protagonist's hybridity and the nature of her religious mission. Scholars have questioned the novel's authorship and source materials, analyzed it through the lens of a variety of theoretical approaches including postcolonialism, deconstructionism, and performativity, and paid particular attention to describing the main character, Unca Eliza, as a hybrid heroine to explore how the text questions established power structures within the expanding British empire. A major thread of inquiry has repeatedly attended to issues of colonialism and the ways in which Unca Eliza's hybridity acts as a liberating fantasy for women and Native Americans, an interpretation first initiated by Betty Joseph.[21]

As of yet no one has explored the novel through a lens of trauma theory. It is my hope that this chapter will provide a starting point for further investigation into the ways in which *The Female American* can shape our understanding of early modern trauma among America's Indigenous populations. In keeping with Duran, Duran, and Yellow Horse Brave Heart, along with Luckhurst and Visser, I have attempted to expand the scope of trauma theory's application to account for trauma's cumulative and multidirectional aspects. A decolonized approach to identifying trauma and its various expressions, coupled with the theory of the soul wound, lends itself not only to recognizing the structures underscoring victimization but also how they intersect with, challenge, and perhaps even support recovery as well. My intent here is not to claim that the novel is consciously attuned to exploring trauma, but instead that a reading of the novel focused on trauma theory allows us to test the bounds of these entangled theoretical approaches, especially in regard to an early modern text written before a clinical explanation of trauma was available. In other words, this text demonstrates the limitations of psychoanalytic constructions of trauma and instead highlights the entangled ways in which culture, economics, and religion collide and accumulate, leading to experiences of collective and individual disruption.

Describing her first moments of exile, Unca Eliza, the protagonist of *The Female American*, writes that "thus disconsolate, and alone, I sat on the seashore. My grief was too great for my spirits to bear; I sunk in a swoon on the ground: how long I lay in this senseless state I know not, or whether I might ever have recovered, had not a wave . . . broke over . . . [and] awaked me" (56). The somatic and psychological responses she describes to her forced banishment on a deserted island underscore the novel's representations of the acute trauma associated with experiences of exile—the physical, mental, and emotional movement away from, and the loss of, one's homeland, family, and possessions. When studied through the lens of trauma, the novel highlights the experiences of forced displacement that results from cultural exchange and assimilation as well as from physical movement away from sites designated as home. As a young woman who claims both Native and English heritage, yet finds herself unable to acclimate fully to either culture, Unca Eliza bears the protracted trauma that results from the collision of disparate cultures—specifically, first contact among Europeans and Indigenous communities of North America—which inevitably alters the structures and symbols individuals rely upon to make sense of themselves and their environment. Thus, her island exile serves to uncover and magnify her earlier trauma of loss that functions as a manifestation of displacement.

However, the novel demonstrates that traumatic markers can operate as modes of rehabilitation as well. Eliza's exile and eventual reintegration into Native society intersect at both the point of trauma and of recovery: the unnamed island on which she is exiled. In recognizing this intersection we can focus on the symptoms of traumatic exile while remaining attenuated to her process of moral and spiritual regeneration. *The Female American* is concerned with a young woman's struggle to overcome physical, psychological, and spiritual wounds to find meaning in her life. The novel explores how a woman transforms a scene of abandonment into a home of harmony and acceptance with a nearby Indigenous community, overcoming suffering, reconceptualizing her moral responsibilities, and re-creating that which she lost as a young girl. Her involvement with the Native community, informed at least in part by her experiences on the island, hint at what Dominick LaCapra has referred to as processes of acting out, or the repetition of "traumatic memory," and working through, "a countervailing force" of trauma, whereby an individual "tries to gain critical distance on a problem and to distinguish between past, present, and future."[22] LaCapra has longed argued that acting out and working through should not be seen as two separate, independent processes where one begins after another ends, but instead as "interacting processes."[23] The simultaneity of these processes comes into relief more distinctly during Unca Eliza's time on the island. When she explores the island, observes animal interactions, and learns of the Native community, she exhibits tendencies that align with LaCapra's notion of working through. When she spies the approach of European sailors on the island of her exile, Unca Eliza avows to protect her new companions, who she believes will suffer horribly if discovered by Europeans. This moment highlights the novel's engagement with and subversion of the violence of trauma, resulting from dynamic cultural disruptions that settle into permanence and replicate across generations with reverberating effect. She reflects on what she knows of the violent past interactions between Natives and Europeans, and she relies on her prosthetic memories of the past, experienced via eighteenth-century media—stories told to her by her English uncle, the knowledge gained from her sophisticated English education, books, and, the novel suggests, cabinets of curiosity or perhaps even fairground displays—all of which shape her understanding of the past and what is necessary of her future actions.[24] Although Unca Eliza eventually brings English values to bear on her new community, perpetuating/acting out her own form of trauma through the partial erasure of an Indigenous society's spiritual practices, she strives nonetheless to subvert colonial violence that follows in the wake of a European presence that has scarred her own life.

For Unca Eliza, European settlement destabilized her sense of self and her conception of home. With the Natives, she attempts to rebuild and replace that which she has lost—a community that supports and accepts her two distinct selves. She interprets the spiritual change she brings as good for both her and the Natives. Unca Eliza once lived in a space that, despite having undergone a disruptive shift in culture and religion, accommodated the differences among Natives and Europeans. What destroyed this community was violence initiated by a European presence. Although it was Unca Eliza's aunt who murdered her mother, the jealously her aunt experienced—the jealously that drove her to murder—was precipitated by the existence of European explorers in the New World. On the island, Unca Eliza embraces both her Native and English ancestries because she has discovered a place that will allow for the incorporation of both. It is not the commingling of disparate cultures that Unca Eliza hopes to block, but the violence and its intergenerational effects that are consequences of such encounters (103).

Fictionalizing the common occurrences that characterized European exploration, Native-Euro relations, and missionary activities, the novel offers a glimpse of early modern experiences of traumatic displacement and exile. No matter how far away Unca Eliza is from the epicenter of European society, she cannot escape its ideological residue. In the novel, that moment of first contact sparks a cultural and religious displacement from which generations of Native peoples cannot return. In refusing to leave her island exile when the opportunity arises, Unca Eliza enacts a departure of a different kind—a departure from the cruelty and violence perpetuated by Europeans against Indigenous peoples. Her eventual refusal to return to England, then, signifies her passage home.

The Soul Wound

During one particular excursion across the island of her exile, Unca Eliza observes an animal unknown to her, who instead of hunting its prey with stealth, giving chase when required, invites rodents to dine on the bugs and parasites feeding on its own fur. Observing what she believes to be a symbiotic relationship between these animals, Unca Eliza is abhorred to learn that this is not a relationship that benefits both species. She watches as the larger animal deploys deception and trickery to devour an entire community of mice, and concludes: "I cannot think that it was the original design of the Almighty, that animals should at all destroy one another. I suppose it rather to be one of the unhappy consequences of the general corruption of nature" (103). This moment recalls an earlier one in Unca Eliza's narrative—one that involves Native-European contact. In telling the story of her familial history, she includes her uncle's admonition to her father, William Winkfield, before the latter left for the New World: "We have no right to invade the country of another," her uncle cautions, "and I fear invaders will always meet a curse; but as your youth disenables you from viewing this expedition in that equitable light that it ought to be looked on, may your sufferings be proportionally light!" (37). His warning is prophetic. Unca Eliza's future maternal grandfather, the Indian chief Powhatan, captures the English explorers, including Winkfield, and questions their motives: "We know you not, and have never offended you; why then have you taken possession of our lands, ate our fruits, and made our countrymen prisoners? Had you no lands of your own? Why did you not ask? we would have given you some" (38). Receiving no satisfactory answers, he orders them executed. In a scene reminiscent of the mythic story of John Smith and Pocahontas, Unca Eliza's mother interrupts the executioner and delivers Winkfield his life at the last possible moment. While she rarely directly speaks of the violence perpetuated by Europeans against Indigenous populations, this passage presages others in the novel that suggest Unca Eliza knows of the venality that characterizes such encounters among disparate peoples.

Powhatan's speech to the Europeans here also anticipates such Indigenous orators as Logan, Red Jacket, and Tecumseh, all of whom decry their people's treatment by the English, at times even advocating for retributive violence.

Often locating the initial injustice perpetuated against Native communities during the time of their forefathers, they tap into the intergenerational trauma of first contact. Red Jacket, for instance, in his reply to the missionary Jacob Cram, argues, "There was a time our forefathers owned this great island. . . . The Great Spirit had made it for the use of Indians. . . . But an evil day came upon us. Your forefathers crossed the great water and landed on this island. . . . At length their numbers had greatly increased. They wanted more land; they wanted our country. Our eyes were opened, and our minds became uneasy. Wars took place. . . . and many of our people were destroyed.'"[25]

Red Jacket traces the arc of relative peace his forefathers experienced before first contact to underscore the destabilizing upheavals borne by Europeans. These cataclysmic events altered both the Native American historical timeline and the Indigenous collective psyche. The intergenerational trauma of which Red Jacket laments is not limited only to the Europeans' theft of Indigenous land but also to the pestilence of liquor, the manipulation of Native nations that turned communities into agents of war who fought one another instead of their European enemies, and the disruptions to Native religious traditions. This is the soul wound—the trauma of not just one acute event but consistently evolving economic, social, religious, environmental, physical, and spiritual injuries that persist through generations by becoming enmeshed into the framework of everyday life, thus altering the trajectory of individual and cultural evolution.

For Unca Eliza the soul wound appears as a symptom of her exile. The unfamiliarity of the island and the absence of cultural symbols from which to make meaning and to understand herself in that environment lead to the somatic and psychological symptoms she experiences. It is exile that magnifies her wounded psyche, bringing into focus that general corruption of humanity that has infiltrated to varying degrees her relationships with others and the environments in which she found herself prior to her abandonment.

Exile

After the death of her father when she is twenty-four, Unca Eliza leaves America and boards a ship for England, believing she no longer has any ties to the country of her birth. Traveling alone with only her loyal Native American slaves, six men and two women, she is accosted daily with marriage proposals by the ship's captain.[26] Keenly aware and afraid of the precarity of her situation—a wealthy single woman traveling alone—Unca Eliza has no recourse against the captain except to delay her answer through humor. Enraged by her reticence the captain threatens to abandon her on a nearby island and leave her "prey to wild beasts" (54). When her slaves learn of the captain's threat, they intervene but are injured or brutally murdered: one "was hung up alive at the yard-arm, bleeding as he was, there to perish by hunger, thirst, and heat" (55). Unca Eliza is no stranger to violence, but she has been removed from the immediacy of such grotesque witnessing. Despite the trauma of her mother's murder, a brutal, treacherous act of sororicide—a moment the young Unca Eliza did not witness—her understanding of violence between Europeans and Indigenous populations was formed mostly from stories told to her by her father and uncle. What she sees and what she hears aboard the ship metamorphoses concepts of violence into reality. She sees firsthand the bodily damage inflicted by pistols and cutlasses. She sees the debauchery of human nature and experiences the powerlessness engendered by acts of bloodshed. Unca Eliza humiliates the captain who vents his dissatisfaction through the infliction of pain and suffering, not to Unca Eliza immediately but to her proxies, who are even more powerless than she. Although she begs the captain to remove her tortured slave from the yardarm, and later refers subtly to this event in her narrative, much of the trauma she experiences in this moment, and during her exile, results from a realization that as much as she believes she is in control of her life—that she has the power to make her own choices—she is, in fact, not. The captain removes the façade, proving she has little power over her own life.

Allowed no time to comprehend the violence perpetuated against her and to mourn the death of her slaves, Unca Eliza is precipitously exiled on an uninhabited island—punishment for refusing to bow to the whims of a white man. Writing of her exile, Unca Eliza notes the overwhelming sense of grief and senselessness she sustained (56). Grappling with the trauma and initial confusion of exile, Unca Eliza wavers between periods of fainting and sustained moments of intellectual clarity and spiritual cognizance. Writing of the trauma associated with migration and exile, Leon Grinberg suggests that acts of departures accompanied by farewells and good-byes strengthen bonds between people by "establish[ing] 'protective borders.' . . . The traveler who leaves without saying goodbye is spurred on by impatience, a state of uneasiness, and apprehension."[27] These symptoms manifest themselves in Unca Eliza: disoriented by the lack of sensory familiarity and an absence of people, she finds her "grief . . . too great . . . to bear" and faints (56). When she regains consciousness, she runs immediately to higher ground and takes in the various scenes before her. Stirred by a sense of agitation and impatience, she expresses those sensations unconsciously through physical movement that challenges her body in familiar ways. From atop a hill, she gains not only a panoramic view of the island, which helps her calculate her future actions, but also mental clarity that shifts her focus from her own misery to God's mercy. This tranquility is fleeting, however. When she returns to sea level, she once again suffers the bodily effects of fear. Narrating the moment in her journal, Unca Eliza describes the hesitation she experienced while standing at the entrance of the cave: "I looked, I stopped, I prayed, and then I moved again; thus strangely divided between hope and fear, I still kept going forward, and in an inexpressible agitation got close up to it, almost insensibly" (57). These scenes demonstrate how fear catalyzes many of her initial actions on the island. The loss of bodily control underpins her earlier experiences of powerlessness. She is paralyzed by fear, yet concomitantly forced to move because of fear. She runs to higher ground and descends into caves. She loses consciousness, and even when conscious she moves insensibly from place to place.

These initial scenes of Unca Eliza's exile challenge more traditional approaches to understanding trauma. Hers is not an ahistorical reliving of the terror aboard the ship; it is a soul wound inflicted by environmental change, social isolation, and a loss of self-identification that follows in the wake of her exile. The violent, involuntary rupture from recognizable landscapes, social networks, and material belongings to a space devoid of familiar and cultural symbols injures Unca Eliza's psyche. That psychological injury—the injury to her soul, her sense of belonging and understanding—is manifested through an inability to exert full control over her body because she cannot yet understand her body in this new environment. The small world in which she now lives is terrifying in its unfamiliarity, and her lack of sensory and physical connection with this space forces a detachment from the physicality of her own body.

Even after finding shelter and later a hermit's manuscript—a guide to procuring the basics needed for survival—Unca Eliza continues to exhibit the effects of her trauma as she wavers between composure and instability. These almost instantaneous mental fluctuations occur within her psyche yet manifest physically through both unconsciousness and debilitating physical volatility: "I raved, I cried, I laughed by turns. I soon became so weak, that I was scarce able to crawl . . . and with as much resignation as I could, laid me down to die" (66). The frantic workings of her mind that result from an inability to control her surroundings translate into physical manifestations that inhibit her ability to perform basic functions of survival.

Unfamiliarity with her new environment, however, is not the only component of exile contributing to Unca Eliza's trauma. Exile also disallows the "protective borders" established by saying good-bye. Instead it demarcates physical borders that restrict her movements and signal the impossibility of return to her previous life. The island's restrictive boundaries constitute the only world she will ever know, and what becomes known of her disintegrates into nothingness. No one, besides the captain and his men, will know what has happened to her. She ceases to exist to and in the world beyond the borders of her island prison. Although the captain did not kill her, as he did Unca Eliza's slaves, his ruthless actions insinuate that she is disposable.

This experience is Unca Eliza's first tangible encounter with violence, but a similar brutality also defined her early life. Her narrative highlights the instability she suffered from transcontinental mobility, the ever-present specter of death, and encounters with others through exploration and resettlement. As in life, these periods are marked with moments of levity; however, they nonetheless comprise the bulk of her experiences, entrenching themselves within her very core. Her exile, then, operates as a metaphor for the soul wound and the chronic trauma of loss it signifies. Unca Eliza is a product of the collision of two cultures, and the trauma of this encounter is seared on her psyche, not because trauma is transmittable genetically, but because she was born into a community that was irrevocably altered at the moment of first contact and continued to be so as these interactions endured.[28]

Having lost her mother, displaced in some sense from her Native community, finding herself a token of exoticism and mystery among the English despite having converted to Anglicanism, Unca Eliza is at times ill at ease in both cultures of which she claims heritage. Her ancestral in-betweenness disallows full immersion and social participation in these cultures. The social barriers she encounters prior to exile function similarly to the geographic boundaries of the island. By magnifying her isolation, the island becomes a symbol of the entangled knot of experiences described by postcolonial scholars. Overlapping and intersecting religious, social, and economic trajectories converge, altering the orbit of Unca Eliza's life, and lead to her exile. Her actions on the island demonstrate how the tensions created from the entanglement of different power structures and philosophies shape one's sense of self and transform her worldview, her interactions with others, and her environment. Although the soul wound materializes as a debilitating condition only after her abandonment on the island, her exile hints that it has always existed since the moment of first contact, which led to jealousy, murder, and Unca Eliza's physical and cultural displacement.

Recovery

For Unca Eliza, her sensations of trauma are often coupled with somatic paralysis of some sort—falling into bouts of unconsciousness, fearing to take one step forward, and becoming so ill she cannot walk. Because exile functions in this novel as both an acute experience of trauma and a metaphor for her continued experiences of loss, recovery must also take multiple forms. To overcome these traumas she must learn to control those forces that infect her mind and body, which she accomplishes via two distinct yet similar courses of action—physical and spiritual exploration. When Unca Eliza converts the unknown landscape into a familiar space by undertaking excursions across the island, her actions bespeak a working through of her physical exile. She couples these daily expeditions with contemplative spiritual explorations to find motivation for and purpose in her life—all of which help her to gain a semblance of control over herself and her new environment.

In the early days of her exile, Unca Eliza discovers the island has had one inhabitant—a hermit who lived in isolation there for decades and left a manuscript of his life. In this manuscript the hermit describes how to start a fire, how to create a light source from the shell of a particular fish and the fat of indigenous goats, and how to hunt and fish more skillfully. It also includes information about the island's human visitors—a nearby Indigenous community whose pilgrimage brings them to the island once a year to worship at the oracle of their sun god. In its most basic form, the manuscript is a how-to manual for survival. Survival is not recovery, however, and Unca Eliza continues to suffer from the somatic effects of her traumatic displacement. She spirals into a state of worry and becomes gravely ill: "I sat dissolved in sighs and tears, and indulged my melancholy, till the night drew on, when I laid me down, but not to rest; and so greatly was my mind afflicted, that it brought on a violent fever, attended with a delirium" (66). This delirium anticipates a physical sickness that is so severe she expects to die.

Desperate for sustenance she crawls on hands and knees to the river's edge and satisfies her thirst but unexpectedly falls into the water. After dragging herself to shore, she suckles milk from a goat, "vomit[s] violently," and falls into a deep sleep, continuing to wrestle with bouts of unconsciousness (67). Unlike the scene of her initial abandonment when she awakes after fainting and runs insensibly to higher ground, Unca Eliza emerges from her sleep and moves slowly with precision, giving her body the time it needs to recover. Reflecting on the physical hardships she experienced during her illness, she recognizes that her fever was a consequence of "those anxious corroding cares that had arisen in my mind concerning my future subsistence" (69). She comes to understand the symptoms of her trauma—her descent into delirium and illness—as physical manifestations of her fractured soul. During her physical recovery, then, she spends much of her time devoted to cognitive and spiritual concerns as well. While her ability to reflect on her condition and to use her mind to push back against the somatic effects of her trauma is not inherently unique to Unca Eliza, it is effective for *her* exactly because she is dissociated from any social or cultural interactions and violence. The absence of people and the culturally neutral space of the island allow her to reflect on her situation with intellectual and religious clarity.

For Michelle Balaev landscape, geography, and environment, alongside personality traits that individualize people and their experiences, also shape experiences of trauma and how an individual or a community attempts to work through it. "The term 'place,'" Balaev suggests, "refers to a physical environment that is inhabited or imagined by a person who attaches and derives meaning from it. . . . Place is not only a location of experience, but is also an entity that organizes memories, feelings, and meaning for the individual and for groups."[29] Initially a place devoid of meaning with no recognizable symbols or cultural accoutrements, the island undermines Unca Eliza's sense of self. D. W. Meinig reiterates the importance of place on an individual or communal psyche, describing it as "a mental imposition of order" that makes sense of geographical location to those who have assigned it social value.[30] But the island has no value initially—there is no imposition of order from which to derive meaning. Unable to establish sensory connections with what she sees on the island, Unca Eliza is forced inward, tapping into her spirituality for psychological succor.

By linking herself to a religious collective identity, Unca Eliza stymies the somatic manifestations of her trauma and isolation. Because her identity is entangled with Anglican values and mores, the collective with which she identifies is a European one: she imagines conferring with her uncle, an Anglican minister and the person responsible for her education. While rooting her to a familiar past, her fictional meditations with her uncle also allow her to consider her abandonment objectively: "How preferable is your condition to that of those consigned to slavery for life! forced to bear with accumulated evils, utterly unknown to you! slaves to a tyrant, and the subjects of unrelenting cruelty! Ah, Eliza! would we but compare our sufferings with those of others, where would the wretch be found who would not have something wherewith to console himself. How many have voluntarily quitted the advantages of society, to avoid the temptations of it, in a worse retirement than yours?" (70). This meditation on the plight of others reminds Unca Eliza to position herself and her experiences within a broader timeline of human trials and tribulations—an awareness that will direct the course of her life on the island. Reestablishing her spiritual core, Unca Eliza moves also from melancholia—bemoaning and grieving the condition of exile—to mourning the sinfulness of her melancholia, which denied the presence of God in her life. Such a shift, according to LaCapra, initiates recovery. Whereas melancholia is "an arrested process in which the depressed, self-berating, and traumatized self . . . is possessed by the past[,] . . . mourning brings the possibility of . . .

achieving a reinvestment in . . . life that allows one to begin again."[31] Through the process of mourning—working through her trauma via religion—the protagonist gains a "measure of critical distance, change, resumption of social life, ethical responsibility, and renewal."[32]

Clinical studies of trauma note the benefits between one's capacity for self-reflection, which Unca Eliza's meditations provide, and the ability to "reconstruct a vision of self and reality . . . [that] provides a more coherent and meaningful worldview in which the trauma becomes a source of psychological and social lessons."[33] Forced to juxtapose her trauma against the collective suffering of others, she determines to value her life and enact what she believes to be her moral and religious imperatives to live purposefully, "thereby transforming anxiety into meaning."[34] Via these mental activities Unca Eliza "endeavour[s] to fortify my heart, and to learn patience and resignation to the dispensations of providence; nor were my attempts in vain; nor did I ever again suffer such anxious cares as those from which I was just now delivered" (71). This tableau of mental and emotional rebirth marks her transition from suffering the effects of displacement and exile toward the act of recovery and reconciliation.

Overcoming the somatic symptoms of trauma is only the beginning of her journey toward recovery, however. Motivated to live purposefully Unca Eliza searches to improve and enhance her life on the island specifically through physical exploration. As confidence in her physical and mental potential gives way to curiosity, Unca Eliza explores the island farther inland and in the process acquires knowledge of the island's terrain, its animal inhabitants, and the Native community whose ancient relics pepper the landscape. Her treks across the island provide a multitude of physical and mental benefits. They give her confidence, increase her strength and endurance, and occupy her mind. Exploration is also about her learning to understand this new environment—to make it familiar. Familiarity with the island transforms it from a threatening, alien space to a place of possibility. Her spiritual recovery reminds her of the generous dispensations of the Lord, which enable her to reorient the experience of exile, not as abandonment but as an example of God's divine providence and thus ripe with opportunity to prove herself worthy. At its core the novel's primary concern—Unca Eliza's path from suffering to happiness—is informed by Protestant providentialism, which for centuries espoused suffering as evidence of God's presence.[35] More specifically it was how God communicated with an individual and was supposed to be met with gratitude and fortitude. It is possible then that experiences modern readers might today refer to as traumatic were often understood in the long eighteenth century as spiritual tests to help people focus on living well and doing good. As is the case in *The Female American*, working through this divine suffering depends on personal agency and is not always considered a private matter only.[36] Unca Eliza's imperative to live a meaningful life is enacted in part by her excursions on the island: she moves with purpose and care—she seeks knowledge and understanding of her new world and her place in it. And it is during these excursions in which she learns of a community of people with whom to build that more meaningful life. As a product of the collision between emerging narratives of religion and moral philosophy, *The Female American* pivots on Unca Eliza's fellow-feeling for the Natives she meets as a mode of achieving happiness.

When her explorations take her to the Natives' site of worship, Unca Eliza encounters cultural symbols on the island that draw out her own Indigenous cultural knowledge and English education. She climbs into the head of the sun idol and descends fearlessly into the dark caverns. She learns of the community's "priests of the sun . . . his age, and the time of his death" and "virgins of the sun, consecrated to the service of the temple" (74). She happens upon drawings of animals painted in traditional Native characters, uncovers mummies, and learns of the community's burial rituals. Here she finds comfort in the familiarity of Native symbols and languages, transforming her physical exploration of the Natives' ancient relics into memory-work. Recalling events from her past, Unca Eliza relies on them to shape her understanding of the present and plan for her future just as she did with her surveillance of the unknown animal's predatory deception. A similar response occurs after she examines the ancient relics. Despite earlier claims that the island is a culturally neutral space, the presence of the Indigenous community's temples invalidates this assumption. What she learns of the Natives is rooted to their religious and spiritual practices. Having reconnected with her own religiosity while exiled on the island, and having determined to live morally and purposefully, Unca

Eliza discovers a way to join the community and rebuild her life that pivots on her and the Natives' spirituality, if its members will have her.

Departure

Grinberg has written that experiences of exile differ vastly from those of migrants specifically because the prospect of return is often impossible for those who have been cast out of their communities.[37] As Unca Eliza transitions into a member of the Indigenous community, the possibility of departing the island, of returning to England, dissipates. The culture she creates with her husband, John—Unca Eliza's cousin and Anglican minister who arrives on the island years later in search of her—and the Natives symbolizes a departure from an inhumane, brutal world to a stable, accepting home, reconstituting, in essence, what she lost as a young girl—the idyllic paradise she enjoyed with her parents in Virginia before her mother's brutal murder.

When she encounters the Indigenous community, she recognizes an opportunity that will not only ensure her survival, but also allow her to live a life of purpose. In joining the community Unca Eliza puts her recovery into action. When she finally introduces her physical form to the Natives—she has only ever spoken to them via their sun oracle—she assumes the guise of a female prophet, recalling for readers the animal who employed trickery to ensnare the mice. Dressed in ornate clothing and adorned with jewels she discovered among the Natives' relics, Unca Eliza presents herself as a celestial being sent to right a religious wrong.[38] But her motivations for doing so differ greatly from the animal she observed and from European explorers who wreaked havoc on Native communities and relationships. Her deception is rooted in her desire to join the community and relies upon the knowledge she has of Indigenous peoples and what she has learned of this group while exploring their spiritual sites. She is not there to destroy them, to steal their land, or to make them slaves. Instead, as other scholars of the novel have noted, Unca Eliza attempts to construct a new home blended with aspects of both Native and European cultures—a home where she values not only the knowledge she brings to it but what the Natives bring as well.[39] In envisioning such a community, Unca Eliza believes that she might lead "a much happier life, and . . . [do] abundantly more good, than I had the least reason to think I should ever effect during the whole course of my life" (84).

The European values she hopes to bring to the community come in the form of spiritual guidance: she converts the Natives to Christianity and only then can she participate as a member of their society. Her desire to spread Christianity demonstrates the difficulties of negotiating the collision of cultures and boundaries of intersecting power structures. By altering the spiritual symbols that Natives use to make sense of themselves and their environment, Unca Eliza transmits a cultural disruption similar to that which she too experienced. For many contemporary readers of the novel, Unca Eliza's religious mission, the destruction and theft of pagan relics, would have been seen as appropriate actions. When examined through the lens of trauma, we recognize this as a residue of European hegemony, imposed through colonization of Native lands and social structures. Having internalized some European ideals concerning Native spirituality and temperament, Unca Eliza uses them to reproduce Anglican religious structures, repeating what seems to be a similar shift in power dynamics that precipitated her own cultural and familial fissure. Her desire to replicate the Anglican religious values with which she was inculcated occurs simultaneously with her community-building mission. She recognizes changes must follow in the wake of new social encounters, but her time on the island has provided her the knowledge necessary to usher in such changes with empathy: the changes she institutes are not forced; debates are logical, rational, and convincing.

At the start of her third year with the Indigenous community, Unca Eliza encounters one final obstacle that threatens the safety and well-being of her new home—the surprising appearance of European sailors on the island of her exile. When she first sees them advance toward the sun idol, she immediately fears their presence and determines to shield her companions from the violence and destruction a European occupation will surely bring: "My next fear was for the poor Indians, who would come in the evening, and not finding me by the shore, as usual, would no doubt come upon the island, in search of me, and be taken for slaves. . . . their country might be discovered, and probably invaded, and numbers of the people carried away into slavery, and other injuries committed" (121). The palpable fear she experiences for their welfare underscores her commitment to their livelihood and security. This is a pivotal moment in Unca Eliza's recovery: she refuses to allow evil to befall her new home. Although she interacts with the sailors, she keeps the presence of her community hidden. Her avowal of the exploitation, oppression, and death that is possible if Europeans were to discover the community underscores the historical and intergenerational consequences of trauma. Recollecting what she knows of the interactions between Native peoples and Europeans, she roots her fear not to some outlandish speculation, but instead to specific moments of historical violence that have shaped her family history and redirected the course of her life.

In their rejection of psychoanalysis as an effective framework for exploring trauma among colonized people, postcolonial scholars such as Visser contest the conception of intergenerational trauma. This distinction between scholarship, however, is not irreconcilable. Visser's rejection of intergenerational trauma is not a rejection of trauma or its effects but is instead an acknowledgment that the trauma caused by colonialism, which is itself ongoing, persists into the present. In other words, intergenerational trauma signifies the aftereffects of a traumatic event; postcolonial scholarship claims that colonialism has no end date. The trauma experienced by a postcolonial subject is not a delayed response to an earlier event, but is a response to a present condition. However, as Laura Murphy has noted, Marianne Hirsch's research on postmemory among second-generation Holocaust survivors suggests that those removed from the immediacy of traumatic events can nonetheless still suffer from the effects of those moments because they may "feel compelled to 're-member, to re-build, to re-incarnate, to replace, and to repair.'"[40] Thus, it seems feasible that despite colonialism's lack of an end date, moments of earlier experiences of colonialism can persist through generations while those same generations suffer from the present reach of colonialism. Murphy has highlighted the duality of trauma—that it is "both an immediate experience, a wounding, and the belated effects of that wound."[41] The effects of colonialism share a similar duality. The aftermath of colonial projects is immediate, yet because colonialism concerns the consistent evolution of material, social, cultural, economic, and religious frameworks, its consequences persist throughout generations. Unca Eliza cannot stop fully the transmission of trauma to her new community, but determined to live a life of purpose, she chooses a life devoted to protecting others.

NOTES

1. Kathleen Brown-Rice, "Examining the Theory of Historical Trauma among Native Americans," *The Professional Counselor* 3 (2013): 117.
2. Russell Thornton, "The Demography of Colonialism and 'Old' and 'New' Native Americans," in *Studying Native America: Problems and Prospects*, ed. Russell Thornton, 17–39 (Madison: University of Wisconsin Press, 1998).
3. Brown-Rice, "Examining the Theory," 118.
4. Bonnie Duran, Eduardo Duran, and Maria Yellow Horse Brave Heart, "Native Americans and the Trauma of History," in Thornton, *Studying Native America*, [60-78], esp. 62–63.
5. Duran, Duran, Yellow Horse Brave Heart, 64.
6. Emphasis in original. Allison Crawford, "'The trauma experienced by generations past having an effect in their descendants': Narrative and historical trauma among Inuit in Nunavut, Canada," *Transcultural Psychiatry* 51 (2014): 343, doi:10.1177/1363461512467161.
7. Alison Landsberg, "Prosthetic Memory: The Ethics and Politics of Memory in an Age of Mass Culture," in *Memory and Popular Film*, ed. Paul Grainge, [144-61] (Manchester, UK: Manchester University Press, 2003), esp. 148. Although I make use of Landsberg's phrase "prosthetic memory" throughout this chapter, it was Gregg M. Horowitz who first coined "memory's prosthesis" to describe how the past is artificially transferred to generations via history, Horowitz, *Sustaining Loss* (Stanford CA: Stanford University Press, 2001), 21.
8. Landsberg, "Prosthetic Memory," 148–49.
9. Duran, Duran, and Yellow Horse Brave Heart, "Native Americans," 64.
10. Duran, Duran, and Yellow Horse Brave Heart, 64.
11. Laurence J. Kirmayer, Joseph P. Gone, and Joshua Moses, "Rethinking Historical Trauma," *Transcultural Psychiatry* 51 (2014): 299–319, doi:10.1177/1363461514536358.
12. Irene Visser, "Decolonizing Trauma Theory: Retrospect and Prospects," *Humanities* 4 (2015): 253, doi:10.3390/h4020250.
13. Visser, 254.
14. Visser, 254.
15. Visser, "Trauma Theory and Postcolonial Literary Studies," *Journal of Postcolonial Writing* 47 (2011), 279, doi:10.1080/17449855.2011.569378. "Decolonizing trauma

studies" was first proposed by Michael Rothberg in his article "Decolonizing Trauma Studies: A Response," *Studies in the Novel* 40 (Spring and Summer 2008): 224–34.

16. Roger Luckhurst, *The Trauma Question* (London: Routledge, 2008), 2.
17. Luckhurst, 14.
18. Luckhurst, 14.
19. Conceptualizing their mission in the colonies as one of a religious nature, the English often imagined Indigenous populations in ways that spoke more about the English themselves than the communities with which they interacted. For instance, Joseph Caryl's fictitious tableaus of spiritual transformation occurring among the Natives, captured in his *A Late and Further Manifestation of the Progress of the Gospel*, weaves together figurative language of nature and wilderness with that of economics and finance: "O let old England rejoyce . . . that our brethren . . . have Planted themselves in the Indian Wildernesses . . . to Plant the Indians as a spirituall Garden, into which Christ might come and eat his pleasant fruits. . . . This gaine of soules is a Merchandize worth the glorying in upon all the Exchanges, or rather in all the Churches throughout the world." See also Laura M. Stevens, *The Poor Indians: British Missionaries, Native Americans, and Colonial Sensibility* (Philadelphia: University of Pennsylvania Press, 2004), 34. Unpacking Caryl's varied themes and terminologies, Stevens suggests that by couching economic gain within the context and language of holy work, Caryl's "apparent disowning of greed merely brackets the real object he was selling: a sense of belonging, through shared desire and emotional response, to a transatlantic community" (36–37). Cathy Rex, in her article "Indians and Images," provides interesting insight into issues of colonial identity and the figure of the Native American as imagined by Puritans. Tracking the changes of the Native figure on the Massachusetts Bay Colony Seal between 1629 and the 1690s, Rex juxtaposes representations of Indigenous peoples on the seal to the real-life figure of James Printer, a Praying Indian, and demonstrates that the seal signifies an imagined Native whose otherness underscores the imagined identity of the English colonists, "Indians and Images: The Massachusetts Bay Colony Seal, James Printer, and the Anxiety of Colonial Identity," *American Quarterly* 63 (2011): 61–93. In a similar vein, Kristina Bross explores the transatlantic currents of early American colonization and the importance of England and the figure of the Native American, particularly the figure of the Praying Indian, in the formation of colonial identity in *Dry Bones and Indian Sermons: Praying Indians in Colonial America* (Ithaca: Cornell University Press, 2004). Highlighting England's criticism of the lack of Indian conversions in the New World, Bross argues that the early history of New England is strongly associated with contemporary English culture and politics. Wanting to retain their Englishness, colonists engaged in missionary work, in part, to prove their worthiness to English society. Similar discussions and uses of Native Americans as figures whose sole purpose is to spotlight English and later American

righteousness continue into the Jacksonian period of American politics and literature. Catherine Maria Sedgwick's *Hope Leslie; or, Early Times in the Massachusetts*, 1827, ed. Carolyn L. Karcher (New York: Penguin, 1998), for instance, laments the vanishing Indian while concomitantly recognizing the inevitability of their disappearance to ensure America's manifest destiny.

20. Unca Eliza Winkfield, *The Female American; or, The Adventures of Unca Eliza Winkfield*, 1767, ed. Michelle Burnham (Peterborough ON: Broadview, 2001).
21. See the dissertations of Adrienne DuVall, "The Ethics of Enterprise: Imagining Colonization in Eighteenth-Century Novels of Colonial Encounter" (PhD diss., University of Oregon, 2009), ProQuest (3370143); Keely Susan Kuhlman, "Transatlantic Travel and Cultural Exchange in the Early Colonial Era: The Hybrid American Female and Her New World Colony" (PhD diss., Washington State University, 2006), ProQuest (3221799); Keely McCarthy, "'Reducing them to Civilitie': Religious Conversions and Cultural Transformations in Protestant Missionary Narratives, 1690–1790" (PhD diss., University of Maryland, College Park, 2000), ProQuest (9982812); Jennifer Aimee Mills, "Navigating Between Two Worlds: How Portrayals of the Americas in Eighteenth-Century Novels Influenced British Identity" (PhD diss., Baylor University, 2011), ProQuest (3469367); and Elizabeth J. Thompson, "The Princess, the Convert, and the Schoolgirl: Indian Girls and Anglo Desire in American Literature, 1595–1934" (PhD diss., University of Tulsa, 2008); and Betty Joseph, "Re(playing) Crusoe/Pocahontas: Circum-Atlantic Stagings in 'The Female American,'" *Criticism* 42 (2000): 317–35.
22. Dominick LaCapra, *Writing History, Writing Trauma*, (Baltimore: Johns Hopkins University Press, 2001), 142–43.
23. LaCapra, 144.
24. When Unca Eliza enters one of the many ancient rooms she discovers as part of a subterraneous network of Native ruins on the island, she narrates, "The first room I entered, I found surrounded with mummies, like those I have read of in the histories of Egypt, and one of which I once saw in England" (Winkfield, *The Female American*, 73). Her phrasing here situates her as a female reader and purveyor of material culture. The British Museum opened in 1753, fourteen years before the publication of *The Female American*. However, since the novel is set in the seventeenth century, Unca Eliza might have seen such sights at a semiprivate collection, a cabinet of curiosities, or a fairground display. See Troy O. Bickham, *Savages within the Empire: Representations of American Indians in Eighteenth-Century Britain* (Oxford, UK: Clarendon, 2005), esp. 34–51.
25. William Leete Stone, *The Life and Times of Red-Jacket or Sa-go-ye-wat-ha: Being a Sequel to the History of the Six Nations* (New York: Wiley and Putnam, 1841), 190–91.

26. When she was presented with these slaves as a young woman in America, she gave them their freedom, but she claims that they refused it (Winkfield, *The Female American*, 53).
27. Leon Grinberg, *Psychoanalytic Perspectives on Migration and Exile*, trans. Nancy Festinger (New Haven: Yale University Press, 1989), 156.
28. Fascinating work, however, by Patrick O. McGowan and Moshe Szyf, among others, suggests that there might be some link between trauma and epigenetics. See, for instance, McGowan et al., "Epigenetic regulation of the glucocorticoid receptor in human brain associates with childhood abuse," *Nature Neuroscience* 12 (2009): 342–48, doi:10.1038/nn.2270.
29. Michelle Balaev, *The Nature of Trauma in American Novels* (Evanston IL: Northwestern University Press, 2012), xv.
30. Quoted in Balaev, xv.
31. LaCapra, "Trauma, Absence, Loss," *Critical Inquiry* 25 (Summer 1999): 713.
32. LaCapra, 713.
33. Michael Christopher, "A broader view of trauma: A biopsychosocial-evolutionary view of the role of the traumatic stress response in the emergence of pathology and/or growth," *Clinical Psychology Review* 24 (2004): 87.
34. Christopher, 87.
35. Alexandra Walsham, "The Happiness of Suffering: Adversity, Providence, and Agency in Early Modern England," in *Suffering and Happiness in England 1550–1850: Narratives and Representations*, ed. Michael J. Braddick and Joanna Innes, 45–64 (Oxford, UK: Oxford University Press, 2017).
36. Walsham, see especially 60–61.
37. Grinberg, *Psychoanalytic Perspectives*, 157.
38. Unca Eliza directs the Natives' focus from the sun, which they believe to be their god, to the Anglican God.
39. The tensions at the core of Unca Eliza's ancestral and spiritual hybridity have been investigated thoroughly by a number of scholars included in endnote 21. Their work covers a breadth of literary interpretations that range from gender and religious performance to the geopolitics of transatlantic trade and Anglican missionary practices, all of which pivot to some degree on the novel's exploration of cultural amalgamation.
40. Laura Murphy, "The Curse of Constant Remembrance: The Belated Trauma of the Slave Trade in Ayi Kwei Armah's *Fragments*," *Studies in the Novel* 40 (Spring and Summer 2008): 53.
41. Murphy, 53.

Part 2

Recognizing Early Modern Trauma

8

Stories of Trauma in Early Modern Ireland

EAMON DARCY

A memorandum of grievances compiled in 1622 described the turmoil caused by the confiscation of land in the Irish midlands and its redistribution to "loyal" servants of the Crown and New English Protestant parvenus at the expense of traditional Irish Catholic elites. The effect of this profound transformation of landownership and of local sociopolitical power structures in County Longford on its inhabitants was clear: "Diverse of the poor natives or forever freeholders of that county after the loss of all their possessions, or inheritance there, some run mad, and others died instantly for very grief." One reported story is worthy of note: "James McWilliam O'Ferrall of Cloonard and Donogh McGarrett O'Ferrall of Quillagh and others . . . who in their death beds were in such a taking that they by earnest persuasion caused some of their family and friends to bring them out of their said beds to have abroad the last sight of the hills and fields they lost in the said plantation, every one of them dying instantly after."[1] Two issues emerge from this vignette of the Irish past that require further investigation: First, the authors of this memorandum of grievances used the imagery of death and the language of grief to explain the psychological impact of these disempowering events. Second, they believed that this story had polemical value and could be used to sway the minds of those in power, the colonial administration based in Dublin Castle, to encourage them to accommodate former landowners aggrieved by plantation schemes.

The use of trauma narratives to influence politics prompted Ana Douglass and James E. Young to advise scholars to investigate trauma in terms of "*what happened* and *how it passed down to us* and *what are we doing with it now*."[2] Constraints of space prevent a detailed analysis of *what happened* in Ireland, but a consideration of the circulation and appropriation of stories of trauma is possible. Rather than the modern term "trauma narratives," this chapter uses the phrase "stories of trauma." The term "trauma narratives" has particular connotations today, for it refers to a means of rehabilitating people affected by trauma and, usually, has an emphasis on the victims' deliberate act of *writing* words as opposed to those *performed* or *spoken* as a means of processing their experiences. "Stories of trauma" takes inspiration from Hannah Arendt's pioneering work on the role of stories and storytelling in shaping collective identities. It reflects key modes of identity formation in the early modern period that relied on oral and literate means of communication, and emphasizes the organic and ever-changing nature of early modern responses to traumatic events.[3] The 1622 memorandum of grievances was one of a number of notable communications between local elites and Crown officials about the plantation scheme in Longford. Thus, this story of trauma contributed to a "national" or "public" conversation about political events and formed part of a dialogue between elites and their subordinates about politics.[4] This was particularly problematic as Irish "publics" were divided by ethnicity and religion.[5] Nevertheless, if stories of trauma are taken as a focal point of investigation, it is possible to gain insight into other phenomena such as the relationship between the individual and the early modern state, the formation of collective identities, and political participation. How were stories of trauma in the past appropriated in early modern Ireland?

Studies of trauma caused by European colonialism in North America have shown the long-term, intergenerational impacts on the colonized.[6] Early modern Ireland may add a useful comparison as it, too, witnessed extensive violence, depopulation, exile, land appropriation, and cultural genocide as a result of policies pursued by English colonists. It is important to avoid, however, retrospective diagnoses of trauma. "We have to understand," Richard McNally argues, "how trauma was viewed from their perspective, not our own."[7] Underpinning work on trauma is the need to understand what Clifford Geertz termed the "webs of significance" from which people interpreted and drew meaning from their worlds.[8] For example, work by Christina Weber and

Allan Young reminds us that trauma is stitched into the fabric of everyday lived experiences and shaped by contemporary social and cultural values that invested trauma narratives with meaning.[9] The imagery and language employed to describe and explain the emotional impact of these events will form part of this inquiry as contemporary responses were fundamentally shaped by cultural norms.[10]

Early modern Ireland experienced a series of changes, evolutions, and revolutions that radically altered its demography, economy, social power structures, and topography.[11] After the advent of religious reform, those who traced their ascendancy in Ireland to the original twelfth-century English invasion remained loyal—after a period of ambiguity in the sixteenth century—to both the English Crown and their Catholic faith. They became known as the Old English. Throughout early modernity the Old English became more closely aligned politically to Irish-speaking natives because they too, for the most part, remained Catholic. The failure to convert local elites to the newly established Anglican-inspired Church of Ireland was mitigated by the promotion of English-born Protestant officials (the "New English") at the expense of both the Old English and the Irish. Matters were not helped by the emergence of sectarian tensions that could be exacerbated by events in England, Scotland, and Europe, adding an international dimension to the equation. By 1691 these newcomers would own over 80 percent of Irish lands, a clear indication of their wealth and power. This was the net result of a series of plantation schemes in Munster and Ulster, as well as the Cromwellian and Restoration land settlements. At the same time many Irish Catholic gentry and nobility were forced into Continental exile, the key event being the Flight of the Earls (1607). At the local level the transformation of Irish landholding was accompanied by an influx of English and Scottish tenants of various faiths, which meant that Ireland became even more culturally, ethnically, and religiously mixed. Such profound change was both prompted and precipitated by episodes of extreme violence: the Desmond rebellions (1569–73, 1579–83); the Nine Years' War (1594–1603); the Irish rebellion, Confederate wars, and Cromwellian conquest (1641–53); not to mention the heavy reliance on martial law, even in peacetime.[12] From a historiographical perspective, however, the focus on widespread dislocation, exile, transplantation, violence, and war and its impact on demography overlooks ordinary peoples' experience of these phenomena and the scars carried by the individuals who survived.[13]

What emerged in Ireland in the seventeenth century were two speech communities: most of the population spoke Irish and were largely Catholic. The other speech community were English speakers who mostly identified as Protestant, with bilingual brokers mediating between the two. Both communities told stories of trauma that were highly selective and partisan. Crucially, these stories were told and retold to reinforce contemporary politico-religious divides and could later be forgotten or suppressed. A key goal of this chapter therefore is to begin a conversation about the social construction of trauma in early modern Ireland. It will investigate the articulation of, and cultural frameworks deployed in, early modern Irish stories of trauma and their subsequent polemical use by both English and Irish speech communities. While our early modern Irish counterparts may not have used modern pathologies and terminologies associated with trauma, they nonetheless recognized that the turmoil of the time had a significant emotional and psychological impact on ordinary people, what is now considered to be trauma.

The Flight of the Earls and the Ulster Plantations: Trauma of Dislocation?

Due to Tudor political and religious reform movements, the exercise of English power in Ireland increased dramatically over the course of the sixteenth century. This transformation both relied on and precipitated violence, most notably the outbreak of the Nine Years' War (1594–1603). This campaign cost the English royal coffers almost £2 million sterling and was Elizabeth I's most expensive war. Two of the key leaders in the Irish war effort, Hugh O'Donnell (known as "Red Hugh") and Hugh O'Neill, sought help from the Spanish monarchy, offering the kingdom of Ireland to a Habsburg prince. The defeat of Irish and Spanish forces at the battle of Kinsale (Winter 1601–2) effectively ended the resistance, culminating in the Treaty of Mellifont (March 1603). Much to the annoyance of English soldiers and administrators who fought O'Neill, he received favorable terms from the newly crowned James VI of Scotland and I of England. It soon became clear, however, that the Stuart regime was intent on implementing English Common Law and on transforming traditional power structures at the local level in Ulster, the patrimony of the O'Donnell and O'Neill families. The appointment of Arthur Chichester as lord deputy (the official representative of the English Crown in Ireland), the expulsion of Catholic priests and the ban of Catholic education in Ireland, and the establishment of permanent garrisons further undermined O'Donnell's and O'Neill's authority. Deprived of their political influence and honor status, both Hugh O'Neill and Rory O'Donnell (Red Hugh's brother and successor) suffered a form of what Orlando Patterson, drawing on the work of Zygmunt Bauman, would later describe as social death.[14] On September 4, 1607, fearing the intentions of James I and Chichester, O'Neill left Ulster with O'Donnell and approximately one hundred others.[15] This event was immediately dubbed the Flight of the Earls and is now seen as an epochal event in Irish history although their permanent exile was not a foregone conclusion when they left.[16]

The earls availed of extant expatriate Irish clerical, mercantile, and military networks on the Continent. Over the course of the seventeenth century significant numbers of Irish joined them as a result of various colonization schemes as well as religious and political persecution back home. This exile of the Irish to Europe prompted much intellectual introspection among the expatriate community. Irish colleges on the Continent, established after the ban on Catholic education in Ireland, trained new generations of Catholic priests imbued with post-Tridentine ideas. A printing press at Louvain produced a small number of Irish-language texts to promote the Catholic faith in Ireland. The exile of the Irish lords and the growth of an expatriate Irish clerical, merchant, and military community in Europe meant the Old English and native Irish slowly began to adopt a common identity based on their shared faith and fatherland. This was a direct response to the renewed vigor of English colonialism in Ireland and the development of an early modern Irish diaspora with strong ties back home.[17]

One product of this broader cultural development was the compilation of a manuscript anthology of poetry now known as the "Book of the O'Conor Don." This volume was compiled for Captain Somhairle Mac Domhnaill, a relation of Randal MacDonnell, the Catholic earl of Antrim, and comprises 341 poems (making it, by far, the largest Irish *duanaire*). Mac Domhnaill fled Ireland in the summer of 1616 after antagonizing Sir Thomas Phillips, a planter in Ulster. He later became a captain in the Spanish army, serving in Flanders, and lobbied for Spanish military intervention in Ireland.[18] At some point in 1631 he was in Ostend and procured the services of the scribe Aodh Ó Dochartaigh. Ó Dochartaigh selected (or was told to gather) a selection of verses, which one scholar has called the "golden oldies" of Irish literature.[19] These poems, celebrating the traditional ruling families in Ireland, were normally kept in a dedicated family poem book or *duanaire*. Included with these historical and family poems was a collection of poems that chronicled the plight of the Irish since the battle of Kinsale.[20] These poems were probably performed before audiences of Irish expatriates in the Spanish Netherlands, which might suggest that this volume was a key manuscript in shaping contemporary understandings of the turmoil of the early seventeenth century. The collection suggests a growing national identity in Ireland, one that transcended traditional local, familial loyalties.[21] Crucially, for the purposes of this chapter, similar themes, most notably the emasculation of the Irish aristocracy and the Irish victimhood at the hands of English cultural genocide, emerge in some of the key pieces.

Lochlainn Ó Dálaigh's "Cáit ar ghabhadar Gaoidhil?" (Where have the Gaels gone?) contrasts the former glory of Ireland, replete with brave soldiers and warriors, with the contemporary population ruled by upstarts. It keenly notes the destruction of Irish cultural, social, and political traditions. One of the earliest uses of the loanword "acraibh" (acres) appears as planters divide the lands of Ulster among themselves and redistribute them in English acres ("Roinnid í eatorra féin . . . nach bhfoil 'na acraibh agoinn") replete with English-style hedged enclosures ("creasa tar fhaithche d'fhál air").[22] There is a considerable disparity portrayed between the brave militaristic Gaels of bygone years with what has been left behind as a result of English colonization. The author laments the expulsion of "Óig Laighean, laochraidh Mhuimhneach" (the young warriors of Leinster, [and] the heroes of Munster) as a result of the Ulster and Munster plantations. These men of aristocratic honor were replaced by "dírim uaibhreach eisiodhan" (an arrogant impure crowd). The effect of this social inversion on those who remained in Ireland is portrayed in suitably dramatic terms. "Ní fhaic aoinneach d'fhuil Ghaoidhil ní ar bioth lé mbí forbhfaoilidh" (No one of the blood of the Gaels sees anything at which to rejoice). The demise of Ireland's traditions robbed those remaining of their souls, "gadaidh asda a n-anmanna," and leaves them resembling half-dead corpses, "cuirp bheómharbha a mbaramhuil."[23] Here can be seen how the effect of English colonization on ordinary people was measured and explained by the imagery of death and the language of grief.

Another poem contained in the same volume, "Anocht is uaigneach Éire" (Tonight, Ireland is desolate) followed the emerging pattern of describing the effect of the Flight of the Earls on those in exile and on those left behind through the language of grief: "do-bheir fógra a fírfhréimhe/ gruaidhe a fear 'sa fionnbhan flioch" (the banishment of [Ireland's] true race has left wet-cheeked her men and her fair women). The author of the poem, Eoghan Ruadh Mac an Bhaird, also traveled to the Continent to join the earls and was part of O'Donnell's entourage in Flanders. The poem was recorded in two Irish manuscripts on the Continent, the *Book of the O'Conor Don*, and the poem book of Nuala O'Donnell. Nuala was the half sister of both Red Hugh and Rory O'Donnell, which suggests that this poem circulated among, and its message resonated with, those in exile. There are numerous references to grief, sorrow, and lamentation ("tuirsi," "airc," "cumha") as a result of the banishment ("díobairt") of O'Donnell and O'Neill.[24] Four stanzas in the middle of the poem describe the loss in bleak terms. Children deprived of laughter, no feasting, no poetry, no banqueting, no learning—all celebrated tenets to Irish aristocratic culture. This left the Gaels without joy at any tidings ("ní bhiadh feasda forbhfaoilidh") and full of sorrow ("fada leanus an léan dáibh").[25] In the final stanzas in the version of the poem contained in the *Book of the O'Conor Don*, the exiled Irish are compared to the Israelites under Egyptian bondage in the book of Exodus.[26] Their plight stripped the author of his soul: "fa bhroid troim ag goid ar n-anma asoinn." There is a significant difference in the version of this poem contained in the poem book of Nuala O'Donnell as it contains sixteen additional stanzas. These extra verses provide guidance to the expatriate Irish on how to remedy their situation. It does not seek vengeance; rather it calls for the exiles to take heed of their own sins and repent. This would assuage God's anger and result in their restoration to their former glory—a possible coping strategy for the poem's audience to work through the trauma and understand contemporary events.[27]

The *Book of the O'Conor Don* and Nuala O'Donnell's poem book were two of a small number of Irish-language manuscripts that were compiled on the Continent in the seventeenth century. Another anthology, the *Book of O'Gara*, compiled between 1655 and 1659, originated in Lille with a brief sojourn in Brussels. An Augustinian scribe, Fearghal Dubh Ó Gadhra, transcribed the volume in his spare time after his expulsion from Ireland at the hands of the Cromwellians, a context that shaped its composition. Although this volume was a personal anthology for Ó Gadhra, its eventual return to Ireland in the late seventeenth century meant that its contents became known to a wider literary circle and had a profound impact on manuscript production there.[28] Ó Gadhra included a lament for Sir Phelim O'Neill, a key leader of the Irish rebellion of 1641, which contains a mournful passage on how the Irish have not prospered and have been oppressed since the exile of the Irish ("ní mor ágh aoínfhir dár bhfonn / Gaoídhil do ládh fá leatrom").[29] Ireland's plight clearly affected Ó Gadhra. At one point, on February 12, 1656, he stopped transcribing and confessed that his depression would not lift until "acht amhain go mbearuinn áon amharc ar Eirinn," he saw Ireland again—a clear sign of the psychological impact of exile. Ó Gadhra also included a copy of "Cáit ar ghabhadur Gaoidhil?" (Where have all the Gaels gone?) and confessed "Cáit, nescio" (Where, I do not know).[30]

One of the more pertinent poems for this discussion was written by a poet who remained in Ireland after the Flight of the Earls, Eochaidh Ó hEódhusa, and is called "Beg mhaireas do mhacraidh Ghaoidheal" (Few of the youths of Ireland survive). Ó hEódhusa's poem reminds us of the transnational dimension to contemporary Irish culture and captured in descriptive detail the effect of the Flight of the Earls and the prospects of those left behind: "ge mhairid ni mairenn síad," (although they survive they do not live). The Irish have now been emasculated and lack their usual ferocity in battle: "Do dermaid síad a sen gnatach a ngrain catha a cleasa luidh." Ó hEódhusa captured the deep psychological scars felt by those abandoned by the earls: "geall re bas a mbetha gnath" (their normal life is like death), "Tuccsat uallcha ar inntinn ccuthail 's cétfadh ar muich malairt clé" (They have exchanged pride for a subdued mind and [high] spirits for a subdued mind). To put it simply, Ó hEódhusa claimed that the Irish were not a living people: "ní daoine beó amlaidh iad."[31] This dire situation prompted another Irish cleric, Seathrún Céitinn (alias Geoffrey Keating), on the Continent to ponder whether the Irish should leave Ireland altogether and join their fellow exiles to escape English oppression.[32]

To what extent, therefore, can poems from these three volumes provide evidence of trauma? The use of Irish literary evidence, such as that previously discussed, as a historical source is hotly debated.[33] On the one hand, most contemporary poets were trained in the Irish literary tradition in bardic schools. Students spent six years or more learning the complex rules governing Irish verse. Therefore, many motifs, meters, and tropes appear time and again. So much so that in some instances it is difficult to determine whether a poem was written in the twelfth or the seventeenth century, such is the consistency of language and imagery use. As the poets were patronized by local leaders much of their work used ornate and hyperbolic imagery to describe concepts such as kingship and sovereignty. Thus, when a ruler behaved correctly, the land was bountiful and, if not, the land was barren. With the departure of leading local figures, therefore, several poets reused these motifs to explain the turbulent events of 1607. Thus, this poetry may not indicate a significant rupture from the past, but a *continuity*.[34] On the other hand, it could be argued that the poets relied on well-known cultural constructions to demonstrate trauma. The scars of dislocation were personified in descriptions of Ireland as a barren land, with its aristocratic men emasculated and its warriors silenced; all well-known tropes that were employed to portray a troubled kingdom. Furthermore, the descriptions of ordinary people wandering aimlessly in a state between life and death suggest that the poets recognized that a significant rupture had occurred.

Notably, the articulation of an Irish identity based on stories of trauma that responded to the political needs of the expatriate community and spoke to those left behind in Ireland in the seventeenth century illustrates the dynamic forces that influenced Irish intellectual outputs. The collection of anthologies of Irish poetry was part of a broader robust cultural response to the consequences of expanding Stuart rule in Ireland. For example, Geoffrey Keating united old ethnic divisions between the Old English and the Irish in "Foras Feasa ar Éirinn" (A compendium of knowledge of Ireland) and propagated a shared identity based on a common faith and fatherland. This history reached a wide audience in Irish manuscripts and in English translations.[35] Furthermore, a printing press at Louvain provided necessary religious materials in Irish to support the practice of Catholicism at home in the face of episodic religious persecution. What is remarkable, therefore, about the trauma of dislocation is the sheer volume of materials produced both at home and abroad. Can it be argued that Irish literati were working through the trauma of the early seventeenth century in very public ways?

The Social Trauma of the 1640s: Revenge, Revenge, Revenge

The causes of the Irish rebellion of 1641 were hotly debated by contemporaries. Decades of colonial misgovernance, land appropriation, and religious persecution coupled with harvest failures sparked an uprising in the northern province of Ireland, Ulster, and soon spread to the rest of the country. Some believed that the rebellion was a premeditated massacre of Protestant settlers by their Catholic neighbors. Evidence collected by eight Church of Ireland clergymen, now known as the 1641 depositions, from settlers affected by the outbreak of violence confirmed these suspicions. Whether or not a widespread massacre occurred was the subject of intense debate that affected Irish politics sporadically in the centuries that followed. The controversy hinged on the reliability of the testimonies contained in 1641 depositions. Catholic apologists decried them as based largely on hearsay and rumor while their Protestant counterparts pointed either to the sheer size of the archive of over eight thousand statements, or to the social status of the deponents, as proof. Although in modern scholarship the depositions have been used to glean greater insight into Irish society, politics, and economy, there is still considerable scope to investigate the depositions from the perspective of the history of emotions and trauma.[36]

One of the most fascinating examples among the depositions is the testimony of Elizabeth Price. Having been left to fend for her safety and that of her five children after her husband, a military captain, was presumably press-ganged into service, Price was captured by Sir Phelim O'Neill, a nephew of Hugh O'Neill and a key instigator of the 1641 rebellion. Price knew O'Neill personally as her husband had purchased lands from him prior to the rebellion.

After the outbreak of the rebellion, Price, along with her children, were imprisoned and were later offered safe passage to England; perhaps lacking the financial resources to travel, Price stayed in Ireland. While her children were supposed to be conveyed to safety, they were, instead, forced into the River Bann where it flowed through Portadown; approximately one hundred people were killed in this atrocity. As well as losing her children Price was also tortured, being "thrice hanged up to confess moneys and after . . . had the soles of her feet fried and burned . . . and was often scourged and whipped." Instruments of torture, a block and hatchet, were displayed as a reminder of the "engines of their deaths." Despite their status as prisoners to be traded or used as leverage in war, Price and her fellow inmates received poor rations "only a quart of oatmeal amongst six [people] for 3 days and not half water enough." They were reduced to breaking a window of the prison to grasp for grass and weeds outside.[37] The return of Irish soldiers imbued with Continental rules of war, most notably Owen Roe O'Neill, ameliorated their plight.[38] Owen Roe publicly castigated Sir Phelim "for his odious and merciless cruelties" and threatened to mete out equally severe punishments to those who mistreated prisoners.[39]

Based on Price's vivid account of the emotional turmoil she experienced as well as the loss of her five children, one could be tempted to diagnose trauma, especially when considering what transpired after the atrocity. Price visited the scene after hearing stories of ghostly apparitions there. One evening at twilight she saw "a vision or spirit assuming the shape of a woman waist high upright in the water naked with elevated and closed hands, her hair disheveled very white, her eyes seeming to twinkle in her head, and her skin as white as snow which spirit or vision seeming to stand straight upright in the water divulged and often repeated the word Revenge Revenge Revenge."[40] A small number of other deponents also testified that they witnessed similar apparitions at the Portadown bridge and that they were a hot topic of conversation among locals. Katherin Cooke, for example, witnessed the ghost and heard stories of "visions and apparitions there and much screeching and strange noises heard in that river at times afterwards."[41] Deponents and perpetrators alike interpreted the ghosts as a providential sign, with the latter fearing its message of vengeance.[42] Two "rebels" allegedly confessed their concerns of the ghosts' cries "for vengeance and blood against the Irish that had murdered their bodies there."[43] These stories of trauma circulated outside the local nexus of communication in Portadown and became conflated with other stories of atrocities and ghostly apparitions.[44] The violence and butchery that characterized the opening months of the rebellion, particularly in Ulster, left deep psychological scars on the locality and among the broader Protestant community as they attempted to make sense of the turmoil.

Price's story of trauma quickly became part of a broader print narrative that emphasized the butchery of Irish Catholic rebels and Protestant victimhood. In the beginning Church of Ireland clergy struggled with the theological implications of these visions due to their Catholic connotations. Henry Jones, the head of the deposition commission, carefully negotiated an acceptable interpretation. Such visions were not like Catholic attempts to "ground belief of the most ancient truth with new miracles"; rather, these stories were evidence of divine providence and "God's displeasure" toward the Irish rebels.[45] This legitimated the publication of testimonies that alluded to the appearance of ghosts and allowed contemporaries to utilize Price's story of trauma to full polemical effect. John Temple, the master of the rolls, incorporated Price's story into his official history, *The Irish Rebellion* (London, 1646). By presenting his account as a history and framing his narrative with quotations from the book of Ezekiel, Temple shaped the stories into a broader godly and providential narrative. *The Irish Rebellion* equated the plight of Irish Protestants with the Israelites, thereby reinforcing Irish Protestant identity and providing an interpretative framework for the events of the 1640s.[46] Quoting Ezekiel, Temple assured his readers that God "will certainly in his own time execute great vengeance upon them with furious rebukes."[47] Temple assured his readers that the victims of the rebels died "gloriously" and that their deaths were more fitting for a martyrology.[48] Samuel Clarke accepted Temple's informal challenge and adapted the *Irish Rebellion* into his broader history of Protestant persecution, the *General Martyrology* (London, 1651). Clarke made subtle but telling alterations to Temple's history reinforcing its utility as a godly narrative. Clarke argued that the stories of ghosts at Portadown were further evidence of God's damnation of the Irish. Those rebels who rejoiced in their butchery were now either struck down by war or the plague, which devastated Ireland in 1650: "they either shall be humbled for their horrid sins, or be they utterly consumed from the face of the earth."[49]

Depending on the audience, Clarke's and Temple's accounts of the Irish rebellion of 1641 became the key sources for later publications that were rapidly recharged with polemical energy at a time of political crisis.[50] In an English context, with a small number of exceptions, Clarke's portrayal of the martyrdom of Irish Protestants was the most common inspiration. Crude reprints of Clarke's section on the outbreak of the 1641 rebellion appeared at times of rising sectarian tensions such as the Great Fire of London (1666), the Popish Plot (1678–81), and the Exclusion Crisis and Williamite Wars (1685–91).[51] Nathaniel Crouch, writing under the pseudonym R.B., used Clarke's *General Martyrology* as the source for his discussion on the ghosts at Portadown. Reflecting undoubtedly on William's success in Ireland, Crouch argued that the ghosts' desires for vengeance were realized: "it was not long, ere divine justice overtook them [the Irish rebels]."[52] In an Irish context, however, if such crude lines can be drawn, Temple's *Irish Rebellion* provided the main inspiration to future generations of commentators. Both manuscript and printed histories were deeply indebted to Temple, particularly to his section containing edited abstracts from the depositions.[53] Edward Gibbon's unpublished *Short Survey* of the 1641 rebellion contained copies of testimonies that described the ghosts at Portadown; at least one reader, presumably a kinsman, John Gibbon, heavily annotated these testimonies.[54] A small number of printed sermons, delivered on the newly enshrined day of thanksgiving for God's deliverance (October 23) by the Church of Ireland, used Temple's history as evidence for the cruelties, atrocities, and ghost stories of the 1640s. William Lightburn warned in 1661 that the stories of the ghosts of Portadown proved that Protestantism and Catholicism were incompatible: "If Protestants stand, Rome must fall, but if Rome stand, Rome will still be contriving to our fall."[55] Stories of ghosts seeking vengeance became a part of broader narratives that accentuated Catholic butchery both in print and at the pulpit, hinting at their polemical valency. At times of heightened fears of Catholic aggression official histories and unofficial stories of the 1641 rebellion could recirculate and provide further evidence of Irish Catholic perfidy, suggesting that the trauma of the 1640s left deep psychological wounds that could be reopened to suit political needs.

While the centrality of the memory and commemoration of the 1641 rebellion to collective Protestant identities in Ireland is well known, often the individual experiences of ordinary people, like Elizabeth Price, are overlooked in broader historical analyses. Her story became a key component to later retellings both at the pulpit and in print. Rather than offer a retrospective diagnosis of trauma based on Price's (and others') sworn testimony of seeing a ghost, what can be argued is that once again the imagery of death and the language of grief provided the necessary tools for Price to articulate her emotional pain. She and her contemporaries spun this ghost story within a providential web that was later embellished and refined by contemporary commentators in print and on the pulpit, having successfully negotiated an acceptable theological veneer. Through the medium of print, Price's personal story of trauma reached a broader audience both geographically and chronologically. The reprinting of older histories and the (re)writing of sermons at times of political crises, that used Price's story, suggests that they had a powerful valency as polemical tools to denigrate Irish Catholics.

The Silence of Trauma: Ireland after Cromwell

While the *articulation* of the trauma of the mid-seventeenth century underpinned English-language Protestant narratives, there is one striking characteristic of the Irish-language response: silence.[56] After the execution of Charles I, the English Civil War effectively spilled over to Ireland as parliamentarian forces, led by Oliver Cromwell, sought to root out a conglomeration of English and Irish royalists. What is now called the Cromwellian conquest lasted from 1649 until 1653 (although Cromwell only served in Ireland for nine months) and wrought significant devastation. Cromwellian forces committed many atrocities, most notably the sack of Drogheda and Wexford towns. Upon the defeat of royalist forces, the Cromwellian regime embarked on a campaign of unprecedented social change by the transportation of thousands to England's Atlantic colonies, the transplantation of Catholic landowners to the western province of Connaught, and the further exile of others, especially soldiers, to the Continent.[57] Over the course of the mid-seventeenth century it is believed that the population of Ireland declined by 41 percent as a result of violence, war, and famine, meaning that the Irish front was significantly more violent than England or Scotland during the Wars of the Three Kingdoms.[58] Although scholars cannot be certain about the extent to which contemporary Irish manuscripts were destroyed during this time, what can be determined is that during the wars of the mid-seventeenth century, Irish literati offered some commentary of events. Afterward, however, few surviving poems attempt to capture or portray contemporary trauma and its effect on ordinary people or even to comment on contemporary politics. Thus, it appears that the trauma of the 1640s and the 1650s is measured by the silence of the Irish literati in the 1660s and 1670s.

A small number of poems from the 1640s and 1650s describe the consequences of the wars and the Cromwellian regime's impact on Ireland.[59] Some criticized their political opponents within the confederate Catholics of Ireland (the government of the Irish "rebels" after 1642) or lamented the lack of unity within Irish Catholicism.[60] Much like the Flight of the Earls, these poets understood their plight within a providential and religious framework. Seán Ó Conaill's, "Tuireamh na hÉireann" (Ireland's lament) blamed Irish sins for their misfortunes under the Cromwellians and sought forgiveness, while the anonymous poem "An díbairt go Connachta" (The exodus to Connacht) imagined the journey of those transplanted from their homes to Connaught and finished with a version of a traditional Irish prayer normally spoken before undertaking a journey.[61] Familiar tropes were also employed to articulate the effect of the devastation and dislocation within Ireland. "Aiste Dáibhí Cúndún" (Dáibhí Cúndún's poem) claimed the Cromwellian transplantations deprived areas of their natural rulers and interrupted traditional aristocratic pursuits such as hunting and the study of the arts and languages.[62] Similarly the anonymous "Do chuala sceál do cléas gach ló mé" (I heard tidings that tormented me every day) explained that Ireland was oppressed and beaten, deprived of her faith, her true church, and her natural leaders.[63] All of this is reminiscent of the literary response to the Flight of the Earls and the Ulster Plantations. There is evidence, however, that some poets recognized the unparalleled nature and dire consequences of the Cromwellian conquest. Éamonn an Dúna's "Mo lá leóin go deó go n-éagad" (My day of sorrow until I die) is interrupted by a revealing clash between the Irish and English languages:

Le *execútion* bhíos súil an chéidfhir,
costas buinte 'na chuinne ag an ndéanach.
Transport, transplant, mo mheabhair ar Bhéarla.
Shoot him, kill him, strip him, tear him.
A Tory, hack him, hang him, rebel,
a rogue, a thief, a priest, a papist.[64]

Furthermore, the authors of both "Aiste Dáibhí Cúndún" and "Tuireamh na hÉireann" recognized that the wars and their consequences in the 1640s and 1650s were unprecedented. Reflecting on the impact of the Cromwellian conquest, transplantation, and transportation schemes, Seán Ó Conaill put it simply: "Ag so an coga do chríochnaig Éire" (This was the war that finished Ireland).[65] Thus, while some poets turned to well-known cultural constructions to explain the devastating consequences of these wars, others recognized that the crises of the mid-seventeenth century had a more traumatic impact than anything Ireland had previously witnessed.

What is remarkable about the 1660s and 1670s, when one looks at Irish-language intellectual outputs, is the paucity of activity. After the restoration of Charles II, the literary classes are silent and the press at Louvain is still. The careers of two notable poets provide further evidence for the silence of Ireland's trauma. Both men were born in the 1620s and produced poetry about political events in the 1640s and 1650s. Geoffrey O'Donoghue (d. 1678), from co. Kerry in the south of Ireland, even participated in the siege of Tralee castle. A poem he composed in c. 1658 had the pointed first line, "Ní fhuilngid Goill dúinn síothughadh in Éirinn seal" (The foreigners will not let us settle Ireland in peace), and asked God "go gcuireadh gan moil chugainn faoi chlú Gaedhil 'na gceart" (to restore without delay the Irish to their reputation and rights).[66] Despite experiencing firsthand the devastation and the effect of the wars in his locality, O'Donoghue's poetry no longer commented upon political events with one exception. "Is barra ar an gcleas" (This tops the trick) warned that the land settlement of 1662 was another reminder that those who upheld the Cromwellian administration in Ireland were still in control, despite Charles II's restoration.[67] Another poet, Dáibhí Ó Bruadair, also wrote "political" poems during the mid-seventeenth century wars. Ó Bruadair deployed a religious framework and believed Irish sinning contributed to their downfall.[68] Similar to the poetry that described the trauma of the Ulster Plantations, Ó Bruadair contrasted the honor of Irish aristocrats with the boorish nature of Cromwellian upstarts. Once again the devastation of Cromwellian policies and their effect on Ó Bruadair can only be measured by the silence of his political poetry. Except for a small number of wedding poems and elegies, little of Ó Bruadair's surviving poetry described political events in the 1660s and 1670s. It was not until the 1680s when Ó Bruadair began to write poems about political events once more, no doubt bolstered by the prospect of a Catholic king and the rise in fortunes of the Catholic Church in Ireland.[69]

The rich cultural response to Stuart colonization pre-1641 contrasts sharply with the silence of Irish culture after the Cromwellian regime, with a small number of exceptions. The prospect of a Catholic king after the conversion of James, Duke of York, prompted an outpouring of works. Roderick O'Flaherty's *Ogygia* (completed in 1665, but not published until 1685), provided a chronological history of Ireland in Latin. Meanwhile Ó Bruadair's pen composed a litany of political poems that chronicled the tumultuous events of the 1680s and 1690s. This gave way to a new generation of poets such as Aogán Ó Rathaille (c. 1670–1726), Cathal Buí Mac Giolla Ghunna (c. 1680–1756), and Peadar Ó Doirín (c. 1700–69), among others.[70] What makes the silent trauma of the c. 1650s–c. 1680s even more curious is that a similar silence can be witnessed in Ireland after the Great Famine (1845–49), where an estimated 20 to 25 percent of the population either died or emigrated as a result of the failure of the potato crop in Ireland. The generation that survived mass starvation and depopulation left a small imprint on the historical archive, what one scholar dubbed the "great silence."[71] A similar silence of trauma existed in Ireland after the Cromwellian conquest and colonization of Ireland.

Conclusion

This chapter began by evoking Ana Douglass's and James E. Young's advice that scholars of trauma consider, "*what happened* and *how it passed down to us* and *what are we doing with it now*." The consequences of the Nine Years' War paved the way for the Flight of the Earls and the Ulster Plantations, which in turn contributed to the outbreak of one of the most extreme episodes of violence in Irish history. These events were both a product of, and a catalyst for, deeply divided "publics" in Ireland that were polarized along ethnic and religious lines. The Flight of the Earls and the Ulster Plantations became key chapters in the formation of a new and distinct "Irish" identity in Ireland (and Europe), and one that transcended centuries-old ethnic divides by the creation of a new identity based on their shared faith and fatherland. Similarly, many reformed faiths pointed to the 1641 rebellion as an example of Catholic perfidy that further polarized sectarian divisions and later justified the passage of the penal laws in the late seventeenth and early eighteenth centuries. Interwoven with these competing historical and cultural narratives were stories of trauma that offered personal and local perspectives of the turmoil of the seventeenth century.

An investigation of the circulation of stories of trauma is difficult and any conclusions tentative. These stories of trauma were subjected to the complex interplay between the first person oral communication, manuscript production, performance, and print. Surviving evidence of individuals' responses to these stories is sparse, leaving historians to rely on educated guesswork when dealing with the nebulous world of early modern communication and reception. What is clear, however, is that much of the surviving evidence indicates that stories of trauma circulated widely among the major modes of early modern communication: namely, local gossip, storytelling, poems, sermons, and print. That these stories used the imagery of death and the language of grief to describe and explain what would now be considered the psychological impact of these traumatic events provides tantalizing clues as to how contemporaries both responded to and articulated their emotional responses. Such stories served didactic or providential purposes, which adds another important corollary: the ability of these cultural webs to shape an individual's perspective on trauma. Among Irish speaking communities, particularly on the Continent, stories of trauma underlined the extent to which they had been persecuted for their faith at the hands of English "heretics." This provided them with the necessary ammunition to lobby their European counterparts for aid (even military intervention) and a shared platform to shape a new Irish identity that transcended ethnic differences. Similarly, histories, stories, and sermons that spoke specifically of ghosts seeking vengeance for Catholic barbarity in 1641 helped in the process of "othering" Irish Catholics. Thus, our early modern counterparts readily used stories of trauma to shape collective identities, articulate individual perspectives on contemporary events, and mobilized others to support political initiatives such as the confederate wars of the 1640s or to justify the excesses of the Cromwellian army in Ireland.

Although the word "trauma" was not used to describe the deep psychological scars left by the turmoil of the seventeenth century, this chapter has indicated that contemporaries were aware of its impact on ordinary people. In the hotly contested debate over Ireland's sovereignty, commentators could turn to traumatic events to bolster their arguments, to invigorate their audiences, or to steer political participation. By focusing on violence, on key events, and on words spoken or written, however, early modern scholars can overlook another key aspect of trauma: silence. The acknowledgment of some poets that lived through the 1650s of the unprecedented nature of what was happening, coupled with the subdued nature of literary activity after the restoration of Charles II, contrasts sharply with the response of Irish literati after the Flight of the Earls and the Ulster Plantations. Thus, both the stories and the silences of trauma became stitched in the fabric of early modern Irish life and shaped both individuals' interpretations of events and their sense of belonging to broader collective identities.

NOTES

The author would like to thank Gearóidín de Butléir, Raymond Gillespie, and Nollaig Ó Muraíle for their insightful comments on an earlier draft.

1. Victor Treadwell, ed., *The Irish Commission of 1622* (Dublin: Irish Manuscripts Commission, 2006), 666.
2. Italics as in original. Ana Douglass, "Introduction," in *Witness and Memory: The Discourse of Trauma*, ed. Ana Douglass and Thomas A. Vogler, 1–54 (New York: Routledge, 2003); James E. Young, "Between History and Memory: The Voice of the Eyewitness," in Douglass and Vogler, *Witness and Memory*, 275–83.
3. Hannah Arendt, *The Human Condition* (Chicago: University of Chicago Press, 1958), 181–88; see also Maurice Halbwachs, *The Collective Memory* (New York: Harper and

Row, 1980); Michael Jackson, "West-African Warscapes: Storytelling Events, Violence, and the Appearance of the Past," *Anthropological Quarterly* 78, no. 2 (Spring 2005): 355–75; Dominick LaCapra, *Writing History, Writing Trauma* (Baltimore: Johns Hopkins University Press, 2014), ix; Christina D. Weber, *Social Memory and War Narratives: Transmitted Trauma among Children of Vietnam War Veterans* (New York: Palgrave Macmillan, 2015).

4. James C. Scott, *Domination and the Arts of Resistance: Hidden Transcripts* (New Haven: Yale University Press, 1990); Michael J. Braddick and John Walter, "Introduction, Grids of Power: Order, Hierarchy and Subordination in Early Modern Society," in *Negotiating Power in Early Modern Society: Order, Hierarchy and Subordination in Britain and Ireland*, ed. Michael Braddick and John Walter, 1–42 (Cambridge, UK: Cambridge University Press, 2001).
5. Eamon Darcy, "Political participation in early Stuart Ireland," *Journal of British Studies* 56, no. 4 (2017): 773–96; Laura A. M. Stewart, "Introduction: Publics and participation in Early Modern Britain," *Journal of British Studies* 56, no. 4 (2017): 709–30.
6. Maria Yellow Horse Brave Heart et al., "Historical Trauma Among Indigenous Peoples of the Americas: Concepts, Research, and Clinical Considerations," *Journal of Psychoactive Drugs* 43 (2011): 282–90; Aaron R. Denham, "Rethinking Historical Trauma: Narratives of Resilience," *Transcultural Psychiatry* 45, no. 3 (2008): 391–414.
7. Richard J. McNally, *Remembering Trauma* (London: Harvard University Press, 2003), 282–84.
8. Clifford Geertz, *The Interpretation of Cultures* (London: Perseus, 2000), 5.
9. Weber, *Social Memory*; Allan Young, *The Harmony of Illusions: Inventing Post-Traumatic Stress Disorder* (Princeton: Princeton University Press, 1995).
10. Barbara H. Rosenwein, "Problems and Methods in the History of Emotions," *Passions in Context* 1 (2010): 1–33; William M. Reddy, "Against Constructionism: The Historical Ethnography of Emotions," *Current Anthropology* 38, no. 3 (June 1997): 327–51; Clodagh Tait, "'Whereat his wife tooke great greef & died': Dying of sorrow and killing in anger in seventeenth-century Ireland," in *Popular Culture and Political Agency in Early Modern England and Ireland*, ed. Michael J. Braddick and Phil Withington, 267–284 (Woodbridge, UK: Boydell, 2017), 272; Michael E. Woods, *Emotional and Sectional Conflict in the Antebellum United States* (Cambridge, UK: Cambridge University Press, 2001).
11. Raymond Gillespie, *Seventeenth-Century Ireland: Making Ireland Modern* (Dublin: Gill and Macmillan, 2006).
12. Clodagh Tait, David Edwards, and Pádraig Lenihan, "Early Modern Ireland: A History of Violence," in *Age of Atrocity: Violence and Political Conflict in Early Modern*

Ireland, ed. David Edwards, Pádraig Lenihan, and Clodagh Tait, 9–32 (Dublin: Four Courts, 2007).

13. Erin Peters, "Trauma Narratives of the English Civil War," *Journal for Early Modern Cultural Studies* 16, no. 1 (2016): 79.

14. Orlando Patterson, *Slavery and Social Death: A Comparative Study* (Cambridge MA: Harvard University Press, 2018).

15. The exact number of followers is the subject of some debate. For the most comprehensive list of those in the earls' entourage see: Nollaig Ó Muraíle, *Turas na dTaoiseach nUltach as Éirinn: From Ráth Maoláin to Rome; Tadhg Ó Cianáin's contemporary narrative of the journey into exile of the Ulster chieftains and their followers, 1607–8 (the so called "flight of the earls")* (Rome: Pontifical Irish College, 2007), 409–35.

16. Micheline Kerney Walsh, *"Destruction by Peace": Hugh O'Neill after Kinsale* (Dublin: Cumann Seanchais Ard Mhacha, 1986).

17. Bernadette Cunningham, "The Louvain Achievement I: The Annals of the Four Masters," in *The Irish Franciscans, 1534–1990*, ed. Edel Bhreathnach, Joseph MacMahon, and John McCafferty, 177–88 (Dublin: Four Courts, 2009); Raymond Gillespie, "The Louvain Franciscans and the Culture of Print," in *Irish Europe, 1600–1650: Writing and Learning*, ed. Raymond Gillespie and Ruairí Ó hUiginn, 105–20 (Dublin: Four Courts, 2013); Mary Ann Lyons, "St Anthony's College, Louvain: Gaelic Texts and Articulating Irish Identity, 1607–1640," in Gillespie and Ó hUiginn, *Irish Europe, 1600–1650*, 21–43; Micheál MacCraith, "'Beathaíomh na Bráithre na Briathra': The Louvain Achievement," *Seanchas Ardmhaca: Journal of the Armagh Diocesan Historical Society* 21:2–22:1 (2007–8): 86–123; Thomas O'Connor, "Religious Change, 1550–1800," in *Oxford History of the Irish Book: The Irish Book in English, 1550–1800*, ed. Raymond Gillespie and Andrew Hadfield, 169–93 (Oxford, UK: Oxford University Press, 2005).

18. Ruairí Ó hUiginn, "Captain Somhairle and his books revisited," in *The Book of the O'Conor Don*, ed. Pádraig Ó Macháin, 88–102 (Dublin: Dublin Institute of Advanced Studies, 2010); Paul Walsh, "The books of Captain Sorley MacDonnell," *Irish Ecclesiastical Record* 30 (July–December 1927): 337–51, 561–68; Paul Walsh, "Captain Sorley MacDonnell and his books," *Irish Book Lover* 22 (1934): 81–88.

19. Katharine Simms, "The selection of the poems for inclusion in the *Book of the O'Conor Don*," in *The Book of the O'Conor Don*, 32–60, esp. 34.

20. Simms, "Selection of the poems."

21. Douglas Hyde, "The Book of the O'Conor Don," *Ériu* 8 (1916), 78–99; Ruairí Ó hUiginn, "Irish literature in Spanish Flanders," in *The Ulster Earls and Baroque Europe: Refashioning Irish Identities, 1600–1800*, ed. Thomas O'Connor and Mary Ann Lyons, 349–61 (Dublin: Four Courts, 2010); Hector McDonnell and Jane Ohlmeyer, "New

Light on the Marquis of Antrim and the 'Wars of the Three Kingdoms,'" *Analecta Hibernica* 41 (2009): 11, 13–66, 26–27.

22. eDIL s.v. acra. dil.ie/227, consulted October 5, 2018.
23. All quotations taken from William Gillies, "A poem on the downfall of the Gaoidhil," *Éigse* 13 (1969–70): 203–10.
24. Eleanor Knott, "The Flight of the Earls 1607," *Ériu* 8 (1916): 192–93.
25. Knott, 193.
26. Knott, 193.
27. Paul Walsh, *The Life of Aodh Ruadh O Domhnaill transcribed from the book of Lughaidh Ó Cléirigh* (Dublin: Irish Texts Society, 1957), vol. 2 of 2, 138–48; Paul Walsh, "The Book of O'Donnell's Daughter," *Irish Ecclesiastical Record* 33 (June 1929); Paul Walsh, "The Book of O'Donnell's Daughter," *Irish Ecclesiastical Record* 35 (January 1930).
28. Pádraig Ó Macháin, "'One glimpse of Ireland': The manuscript of Fr Nicolás (Fearghal Dubh) Ó Gadhra, OSA," in Gillespie and Ó hUiginn *Irish Europe*, 135–62, esp. 137.
29. Ó Macháin, 143–44.
30. Ó Macháin, 153.
31. Damian MacManus and Eoghan Ó Raghallaigh, *A Bardic Miscellany: Five Hundred Bardic Poems from Manuscripts in Irish and British Libraries* (Dundalk: Dundalgan, 2010), 65–67. The author would like to thank Gearóidín de Butléir for the translations.
32. Seán Ó Tuama and Thomas Kinsella, *An Duanaire 1600–1900: Poems of the Dispossessed* (Dublin: Foras na Gaeilge, 2002), 84–87.
33. Tom Dunne, "The Gaelic Response to Conquest and Colonization: The Evidence of the Poetry," *Studia Hibernica* 20 (1980): 7–30; Micheál Mac Craith, "Gaelic Ireland and the Renaissance," in *The Celts and the Renaissance: Tradition and Innovation*, ed. Glanmor Williams and Robert Owen Jones (Cardiff: University of Wales Press, 1999), 57–89; Michelle O'Riordan, *The Gaelic Mind and the Collapse of the Gaelic World* (Cork: Cork University Press, 1990).
34. Cathy Caruth, *Unclaimed Experience: Trauma, Narrative, and History* (Baltimore: Johns Hopkins University Press, 1996), 11; LaCapra, *Writing History*, 41; Weber, *Social Memory*, 7.
35. Bernadette Cunningham, *The World of Geoffrey Keating: History, Myth and Religion in Seventeenth-Century Ireland* (Dublin: Four Courts, 2004).
36. Toby Barnard, "'Parlour Entertainment in an Evening?' Histories of the 1640s," in *Kingdoms in Crisis: Ireland in the 1640s*, ed. Michael O'Siochru, 20–43 (Dublin: Four Courts, 2001); Eamon Darcy, *The Irish Rebellion of 1641 and the Wars of the Three Kingdoms* (Woodbridge, UK: Boydell and Brewer, 2013); John Gibney, *The Shadow of a Year: The 1641 Rebellion in Irish History and Memory* (Madison: University of Wisconsin Press, 2013).

37. Deposition of Elizabeth Price, Trinity College Dublin [hereafter T.C.D.], MS 836, f. 102.
38. Micheál Ó Siochrú, "Atrocity, Codes of Conduct, and the Irish in the British Civil Wars," *Past and Present* 195 (2007): 55–86.
39. Deposition of Elizabeth Price, T.C.D., MS 836, f. 102v.
40. Deposition of Elizabeth Price, f. 103.
41. Deposition of Katherin Cooke, T.C.D., MS 836, f. 92.
42. Deposition of James Shawe, T.C.D., MS 836, f. 112v; Deposition of Robert Maxwell, T.C.D., MS 809, f. 10v; Deposition of Joane Constable, T.C.D., MS 836, f. 89.
43. Deposition of Joane Constable, T.C.D., MS 836, f. 89.
44. Deposition of Robert Maxwell, T.C.D., MS 809, f. 10v; Deposition of Alice Gregg, T.C.D., MS 836, f. 95v; Deposition of Audrey Carrington, T.C.D., MS 833, f. 282v; Deposition of Anthony Stephens, T.C.D., MS 830, f. 430.
45. British Library, Harleian MS 5999, ff 33–34v.
46. Darcy, *The Irish Rebellion*, 132–67; Raymond Gillespie, "Temple's Fate: Reading *The Irish Rebellion* in Late Seventeenth-Century Ireland," in *British Interventions in Early Modern Ireland*, ed. Ciaran Brady and Jane Ohlmeyer (Cambridge, UK: Cambridge University Press, 2005), 315–33, 321–23; Kathleen Noonan, "'The Cruell Pressure of an Enraged, Barbarous People': Irish and English Identity in Seventeenth-Century Policy and Propaganda," *Historical Journal* 41, no. 1 (1998): 151–77.
47. John Temple, *The Irish Rebellion* (Dublin, 1646), 64; Ezekiel 25:17.
48. Temple, *Irish Rebellion*, 109.
49. Clarke, *General Martyrology* (London, 1652), 362–63.
50. Barnard, "Parlour Entertainment"; Toby Barnard, "The Uses of 23 October 1641 and Irish Protestant Celebrations," *English Historical Review* 106, no. 421 (October 1991): 889–920; Toby Barnard, "1641: A Bibliographical Essay," in *Ulster 1641: Aspects of the Rising*, ed. Brian Mac Cuarta, 173–86 (Belfast: Institute of Irish Studies, 1993); Gibney, *Shadow of a Year*.
51. *A Looking Glass for England* (London, 1667); *An Account of the Bloody Massacre in Ireland* (London, 1679); *An Abstract of the Unnatural Rebellion and Barbarous Massacre of . . . 1641* (London, 1689); *A Relation of the Bloody Massacre in Ireland* (London, 1689).
52. R.B., *History of the Kingdom of Ireland* (London, 1693), 51–52; Bernadette Cunningham, "Historical Writing, 1660–1750," in *The Oxford History of the Irish Book*: 264–81, 277–79.
53. Darcy, *The Irish Rebellion*, 77–101.
54. Royal Irish Academy, MS I IV 1, ff 52, 55, 58, 150, 157, 172, 192, 198; Gillespie, "Temple's Fate," 321–23.

55. William Lightburn, *A Thanksgiving sermon preached at Christchurch . . . upon 23 of October 1661* (Dublin, 1661), Sig A3v.
56. Bernadette Cunningham and Raymond Gillespie, "Lost Worlds: History and Religion in the Poetry of Dáibhí Ó Bruadair," in *Dáibhí Ó Bruadair: His Historical and Literary Context*, ed. Pádraigín Riggs, 18–45 (Dublin: Irish Texts Society, 2001); Weber, *Social Memory*, 41–42.
57. Micheál Ó Siochrú, *God's Executioner: Oliver Cromwell and the Conquest of Ireland* (London: Faber & Faber, 2008); James Scott Wheeler, *Cromwell in Ireland* (Dublin: Gill & Macmillan, 1999).
58. Charles Carlton, *Going to the Wars: The Experience of the British Civil Wars, 1638–51* (London: Routledge, 1994), 202–7.
59. For a short overview, see Michelle O'Riordan, "'Political' Poems in the Mid-Seventeenth Century Crisis," in *Ireland from Independence to Occupation 1641–1660*, ed. Jane Ohlmeyer, 112–27 (Cambridge: Cambridge University Press, 1995).
60. Padraigín Haicead, "Músgail do mhisneach, a Bhanbha," in *Filíocht Phádraigín Haiceád*, ed. Máire Ní Cheallacháin, 38–43 (Dublin: An Clóchomhar, 1962); "An Síogaí Rómhánach," in Cecile O'Rahilly, *Five Seventeenth-Century Political Poems*, 12–32 (Dublin: Institute for Advanced Studies, 1952); Seán Ó Conaill, "Tuireamh na hÉirean," in O'Rahilly, *Five Seventeenth-Century Political Poems*, 50–82.
61. Ó Tuama and Kinsella, *Poems of the Dispossessed*, 104–9.
62. "Aiste Dáibhí Cúndún," in O'Rahilly, *Five Seventeenth-Century Political Poems*, 33–49.
63. Pádraig de Brún, Breandán Ó Buachalla, and Tomás Ó Concheanainn, *Nua-dhuanaire—Vol I* (Dublin: Institute for Advanced Studies, 1971), 31–34, 109.
64. The first man's expectation is with execution / the last [man's is with] costs awarded against him / transport, transplant, [is] my understanding of English / etc etc; Éamonn an Dúna, "Mo lá leóin go deó go n-éagad," in O'Rahilly, *Five Seventeenth-Century Political Poems*, 83–100. Italics as in original.
65. Ó Conaill, "Tuireamh na hÉirean," 75.
66. John Minihane, *The Poems of Geoffrey O'Donoghue* (Cork: Aubane Historical Society, 2008), 20–21.
67. Minihane, 22–23.
68. Creacht do dháil mé, in John McErlean, *The Poems of David Ó Bruadair: Part 1 to 1666*, 26–51 (Dublin: Irish Texts Society, 1910).
69. Cunningham and Gillespie, "Lost Worlds," 39.
70. Vincent Morley, *The Popular Mind in Eighteenth-century Ireland* (Cork: Cork University Press, 2017).
71. Seán de Fréine, *The Great Silence: The Study of a Relationship between Language and Nationality* (Dublin: Mercier, 1965).

9

Trauma, Psychological Coercion, and Slaves Who Love Their Masters

The Case of William Okeley

ADAM R. BEACH

> I might be questioned in point of ingenuity: how I could be so unworthy to leave him who had loved me? Would not all that should hear of it condemn me of ill nature, to leave without taking leave one that had been a father to me, who might have used the right of a lord and used me as a child, who might have treated me as a slave?
>
> —William Okeley, *Ebenezer* (1675)

William Okeley's description of his loving relationship with his last slave master in Algiers remains one of the most troubling and misunderstood in the canon of British literature about slavery in the long eighteenth century.[1] It is troubling because it depicts a man who has come so far under the psychological control of his slave master that he has to argue with himself about whether or not it is ethical to escape his enslavement to him. This episode is unique among eighteenth-century slave narratives, and it demonstrates with shocking precision the ways that some slave masters were able to come very close to exercising absolute dominion over the minds of their slaves. It also shows us how slaves, like victims of all kinds of traumatizing violence, are highly susceptible to the strategies deployed by their oppressors to psychologically coerce them into obedient, and even loving, submission. Yet scholars have consistently misunderstood this moment in Okeley's text, and they have been more apt to read it as a sign of the master's kindness, goodness, and generosity than of his frightening domination. When we examine Okeley's narrative within a framework informed by studies of trauma, abuse, and psychological coercion, we can form a more accurate understanding of what is happening in this episode, and this reading strategy will help us analyze more carefully depictions of loving slaves in other eighteenth-century slave narratives like those of T.S., Joseph Pitts, and Olaudah Equiano.[2]

A number of scholars have examined Okeley's narrative, but their work does not engage the studies of psychological trauma and slavery that best illuminate the perverse dynamics evident in his text. Several of these scholars are generally more interested in the ideological resonances of the figure of the grateful or loving slave than in an exploration of the psychological traumas that help to explain its existence in texts like Okeley's. For example, George Boulukos briefly examines Okeley's effusions of gratitude toward his last master, as well as his eventual escape from him, to support his argument about the trope of "gratitude" and the way British authors used it to construct a sense of racial difference between Englishmen and West Africans.[3] In a similar way Joe Snader argues that depictions in English slave narratives of supposedly beneficent slave masters serve as a "textual disturbance" of what he sees as the authors' nationalist and imperialist agendas.[4] In the end both scholars are interested in Okeley's gratitude and loving posture as a kind of trope or textual effect, and neither is much invested in delineating the traumatic conditions that gave rise to his confusedly positive feelings for his master in the first place.

Another group of scholars take an especially problematic approach to Okeley's depiction of his last owner and to other English slaves in the Ottoman world who praise their masters. These scholars marshal English slave narratives to support their own arguments about the supposed relative benignity of some forms of slavery in North Africa or about the ways English slaves allegedly exaggerated the horrible circumstances of their enslavement in the Mediterranean. For example, historian Claire Norton pursues both these objectives in a recent essay in which she uses Okeley's experiences as evidence for her argument that English slaves in North Africa fictionally embellished their accounts of forced conversion to Islam. Part of her evidence comes from texts like Okeley's, which provide evidence, according to Norton, that slavery was not always all that bad in North Africa: "Some captives also testify to having a quite positive relationship with their captors or 'patroons,' which suggests that hostility and mistreatment of captives was not necessarily widespread.

Okeley was lent money by one master to set up in business, found 'love and friendship from [his] new patron,' enjoyed a considerable amount of freedom, and ended up as a successful trader in tobacco and wine, accruing a significant fortune."[5] Norton is not alone in making such an argument, and I have argued elsewhere against the views of scholars such as Linda Colley, Nabil Matar, and others on the basis that they promulgate a misapprehension of the basic workings of slavery.[6]

In my previous scholarship I take inspiration from the arguments of Claude Meillassoux and Orlando Patterson who, working from very different sets of data and methodologies, formulate similar theoretical models that delineate the fundamental structures inherent in systems of slavery.[7] Patterson's work, in particular, argues that there is an underlying structural similarity to all systems of slavery throughout human history. Some scholars of slavery in the Ottoman world have pushed back against Patterson, arguing that such an approach threatens to lose the historical and cultural specificity that structured the institution in particular times and places.[8] Patterson would acknowledge, of course, that there are differences between the way cultures created and maintained slave institutions in different epochs and locations. However, Patterson's main argument is that these differences constitute a variation on the same theme and do not fundamentally alter the underlying structure of slavery.

The problem that occurs in many studies of slavery in the Ottoman world is that scholars so want to distinguish the ways that Ottoman slave systems were different from those found in the Atlantic world that they begin to formulate ideas like those we see in Norton's essay, which posit the development of a form of slavery in which "hostility and mistreatment" are not necessarily constitutive. This is a position that is more aligned with the ameliorationist thinkers of the past that Boulukos examines throughout *The Grateful Slave* than with a critical antislavery scholarship. When our work is guided by rigorous theoretical models like those of Patterson and Meillassoux, we employ a critical perspective when reading the particular social, cultural, economic, religious, and political contexts from which any given slave narrative emerges. To my mind these theoretical models enhance our ability to delve into these contexts without getting lost in them. This is especially important when we face a culture that has developed very powerful ideologies that forward the idea that benevolence is not mutually exclusive with its practice of slavery, and even more so when we see a slave like Okeley giving voice to these ideologies in his own work.

In this chapter, I argue that we can move toward a fuller understanding of the troubling phenomena of slaves who profess to love their masters by examining more thoroughly the traumatic dynamics that help to explain their sometimes appreciative articulations about those who own them. While Meillassoux and Patterson point us in the right direction, neither scholar integrates work on trauma into their theoretical models. However, we are in a particularly good position today to develop an enhanced perspective about trauma and slavery because of the knowledge that is being acquired in our current moment due to the upsurge in slaveries around the world and the greater attention being paid to the victims of slavery among medical practitioners and psychologists in our own historical era. We are living in a unique time in the history of scholarship on slavery because mental health experts are currently treating and studying formerly enslaved people and learning a great deal about the traumas they have suffered.

This work is incredibly valuable in explaining how dynamics of psychological coercion and traumatic bonding are central to many forms of slavery. As we will see, many of these scholars of trauma move toward the universal, positing that these traumatic dynamics undergird many different kinds of abusive and coercive relationships. I argue in this chapter that these understandings can helpfully shed a light on the dynamics on display in a text like Okeley's, even as they show us that slaves like him who express affection for their masters are misunderstood in similar ways as victims of psychological coercion in our own historical moment, whose actions mystify many observers. In fact, the following contemporary mental health practitioners that I discuss are extremely concerned at the larger public's confusion about the effects of trauma and psychological coercion on victims of slavery and other forms of domination. Their scholarship represents a bracing call to form a much more sophisticated understanding of the damage done to today's slaves, and by attending to this work I believe that we can gain a greater appreciation of the psychological trauma that is evident in complicated and confusing seventeenth- and eighteenth-century slave narratives like Okeley's.

At the outset my desire to examine these theories about trauma and slavery, which have been derived from present-day clinical practices and psychological models, in relation to a seventeenth-century writer like Okeley raises some tricky methodological concerns and questions. One might question whether these modern understandings of trauma and slavery apply equally to present-day victims of human trafficking and to the experiences of an Englishman enslaved in seventeenth-century Algiers (not to mention slaves from other parts of the early modern world). I believe that we should be attentive to such questions and that they should push us to be as careful as we can to understand the unique contexts that structured the experience of Okeley and others like him. In the end, though, I believe the benefits of this approach far outweigh the risks. As I previously argued, we risk even more if we do not take up rigorous theoretical models with which to critically assess the experience of slavery: to put it simply, we run the risk of downplaying its horrors. Studies of slavery and trauma in our own time force us to read early modern slave narratives in a new way, one that is grounded in strident antislavery politics, that is sensitive to the varieties of psychological damage suffered by slaves, and that is hostile to the idea that some forms of slavery can offer genuinely loving relationships between masters and slaves. I now turn to an exploration of this recent work on slavery and trauma and the ways it can help to illuminate the troubling phenomenon of William Okeley's love for his last slave master.

Trauma, Psychological Coercion, and Understanding Victims of Slavery

In her now classic feminist study of trauma, medical doctor Judith Herman frequently discusses the ways in which outside observers have little sympathy for victims of trauma, including those who have been enslaved, and even come to make judgmental critiques of their behavior both during and after their traumatic experiences: "Most people have no knowledge or understanding of the psychological changes of captivity. Social judgment of chronically traumatized people therefore tends to be extremely harsh. Observers who have never experienced prolonged terror and who have no understanding of coercive methods of control presume that they would show greater courage and resistance than the victim in similar circumstances."[9] This extract encapsulates Herman's approach to the subject, and throughout her text she argues that we must study the dynamics of trauma and coercive control before we can comprehend the behaviors and motivations of victims. This is especially important for those in positions of power within the medical, juridical, and law enforcement establishments that come into contact with traumatized subjects, for these people have the ability to act ignorantly and revictimize those they are supposed to help.

Herman is not alone in framing her project as a plea for the understanding of victims. Consider, for example, the work of psychologist Elizabeth Hopper and medical doctor José Hidalgo, who work directly with contemporary victims of human trafficking and slavery. In their trenchant overview essay, Hopper and Hidalgo take on one of the key questions about slavery in our time: why these victims of slavery, who are often not physically restrained, do not resist and escape. They write that "It is easy to comprehend slavery created with chains. Physical forms of violence and control are understandable because of their visibility. . . . On the other hand, psychological abuse and coercion are easier to conceal and may be overlooked. Many people have difficulty understanding how psychological means can be used to manipulate other people."[10] As in Herman's work, Hopper and Hidalgo are concerned with the judgmental idea that many people hold about victims, as if they are somehow at fault for not showing more resistance to their abusive situations. Hopper and Hidalgo write that they hope their work will "increase empathy toward victims who are held in captivity through psychological means" and help medical practitioners and psychologists better prepare to identify and aid those who have been enslaved.[11]

This question of psychological coercion is a central issue in other areas of the scholarship on contemporary forms of slavery. In two widely cited articles, legal scholar Kathleen Kim reviews the definition of psychological coercion in the law and some of the difficulties faced by prosecutors when pursuing convictions of traffickers and enslavers who have not used direct physical violence against their victims.[12] In another study, Coral J. Dando, David Walsh, and Robin Brierley uncovered a widespread misunderstanding of psychological coercion in the general public, which they believe is hindering efforts to eliminate trafficking and slavery in Great Britain and to properly identify victims.[13] In their study of trafficked victims in the greater Los Angeles area, Susie B. Baldwin, Anne E. Fehrenbacher, and David P. Eisenman argue that: "Although the impact of psychological abuse on health has been analyzed in studies of domestic violence and torture, the psychological coercion that frames the experience of human trafficking has rarely been examined."[14] They go on to adapt models of psychological coercion first developed in studies of torture victims and brainwashed prisoners of war to help formulate a framework for identifying the kinds of coercion faced by contemporary victims of slavery and trafficking.[15]

One particular point that is emphasized by many of these writers is that masters inflict a set of interrelated cognitive, physical, psychological, and emotional damages upon traumatized victims of slavery. There is a distinctive biological and physiological element to trauma that these authors take pains to elucidate. Herman addresses this issue at every turn in her work, noting that, "Traumatic events produce profound and lasting changes in physiological arousal, emotion, cognition, and memory."[16] In her important chapter, "Captivity," she notes that the damage is even more pervasive in circumstances of enslavement and captivity because the victim is brought into "prolonged contact with the perpetrator, [which] creates a special type of relationship, one of coercive control."[17] She further outlines the strategies of perpetrators and their desire to damage the body and mind of their victims, to destroy their sense of autonomy and self, and to establish complete domination. The ill effects of physical torture and abuse, confinement, and lack of personal space, privacy, hygiene, adequate food, and medicine works in combination with, and reinforces, the slave master's attempts to dominate the slave psychologically and to keep the slave in a constant state of stress and fear. Slaves are less able to resist the master's psychological methods of control given their traumatized state and the continued stress under which they operate.

Other authors also elaborate on this frightening picture of enslavement. Baldwin and her colleagues discuss the "extreme stress" inflicted on victims through a combination of physical, sexual, and psychological violence: "Stress refers to the arousal of physiologic responses to environmental demands or pressures that exceed an individual's ability to adapt and absence of the means to obtain sought-after ends."[18] During the experience of enslavement, victims struggle with stress-induced changes to their physical and mental health and their cognitive abilities, all of which makes it more difficult for them to maintain a sense of autonomy and agency and to resist their oppressors.

Similarly, Hopper and Hidalgo explicitly build upon Herman's work with experiences from their own clinical practice, which is devoted to helping victims of trafficking. They include a long discussion of the biological and physiological damage done to those who live in a constant state of violence, stress, and threat. In an important discussion of the human body's response to traumatic environments, they state, "Remaining in continual readiness for confronting danger is a tremendous strain on the body. . . . Numbing and dissociative responses are common in the face of chronic trauma, and behavioral attempts at resistance may decline."[19] They argue that it is impossible to analyze the experiences of slaves without comprehending these dynamics of stress, trauma, and coercive control.[20] Everything the slave master attempts to accomplish involves the destruction of the slave's agentive self and "the creation of a sense of helplessness in victims."[21] In many cases slaves become so dominated that they barely have any biological or physiological resources left with which they can exercise control over their decisions or muster any kind of resistance to their masters. In this state they have become almost completely and totally enslaved.

Thus, we are living in a historical moment in which scholars, legal theorists, and medical practitioners are coming to terms with the continuation of slavery in our own time and laying out the proper frameworks for analyzing how enslavers come to so thoroughly dominate their victims. For the purposes of this chapter I would like to highlight one more important finding in this work, the importance of "good treatment" as a key tool for achieving domination over victims. All these studies posit that perpetrators often provide what looks like kindness or favors to abused victims as part of an overall strategy of control. They further argue that those held prisoner within an extremely stressful and toxic environment filled with threat, isolation, fear, and extreme degradation are susceptible to kind gestures, loving words, effusions of sympathy, and rewards for compliant behavior from their oppressors.

For example, in their study Baldwin and her colleagues found that the former slaves they interviewed in Los Angeles commented extensively on "occasional indulgences" as a key component of their enslavement: "By occasionally demonstrating compassion or kindness, traffickers countered their own abusive behavior and provided their victims positive motivation for compliance."[22] Thus, these scholars conclude that so-called good treatment or even gestures of familial belonging are not evidence of any sort of benignity on the part of the slave master. Rather, they demonstrate how slave masters deploy manipulations that play with the emotional and psychological equilibrium of their slaves. These findings are echoed by Herman and Hopper and Hidalgo.[23]

By torturing, abusing, and oppressing their slaves while also including them in these faux-familial emotional structures, slave masters assault their human chattel with an overwhelming and toxic array of psychological weapons to reduce them to socially dead and easily malleable creatures. Rather than being surprised, then, when slaves proclaim that they had strong attachments and loving feelings toward certain masters, we need to understand that such phenomena are intrinsic to the very structure of power that is operative in many forms of slavery. The works of both Herman and Hopper and Hidalgo argue that attachments of slaves to their masters are, in many cases, a normative and expected outcome, similar to the kinds of attachments that clinicians find in other exploitative relationships. For example, Herman asserts that victims who are held captive in many different scenarios, including domestic violence, hostage situations, and slavery, often become emotionally and psychologically dependent on their oppressors and form emotional relationships with them that are difficult for others to comprehend.[24] Hopper and Hidalgo take a similar line when they write about the perverse kinds of intimacy that can develop between perpetrators of slavery and its victims: "an *anxious attachment* is formed between the victim and perpetrator; because the victim is vulnerable and dependent on the trafficker, he or she may attempt to comply or to please the perpetrator to avoid outbursts of anger or sudden unexpected acts of violence. Because of the intense attunement needed for survival, a connection is often made with the perpetrator. Captives begin to identify with their captors initially as a defense mechanism, but over time a traumatic bonding occurs." [25] These are the very dynamics that we need to keep in mind when we turn our attention to examples of slaves who express love or affection for their masters in texts from the long eighteenth century.

I have found that the work of recent psychologists and medical practitioners like Hopper and Hidalgo and Herman reinforce the assertions on this subject made by previous scholars of slavery who examine it from a nonclinical perspective. Consider, for example, Orlando Patterson's emphasis on the importance of "fictive kinship" in slave cultures and "the practice of incorporating the slave as a fictive kinsman of his master," a situation that often includes relatively good treatment and the use of affectionate, familial terms between master and slave.[26] Yet Patterson warns us not to be fooled into thinking this type of slavery is somehow more benign that others, or that it morphs into a state that is different from slavery altogether: "It would be a great mistake, however, to confuse these fictive kin ties with the claims and obligations of real kinship or with those involving genuine adoption."[27] Instead, we need to be attuned to the ways masters deploy fictive kinship as a technique to control their slaves and to put a more benign face on their slavery practices. In some cases slaves participate in fictive kin relations with a "genuine expression of affection" for the master, which signals a degree of "psychological manipulation" of the slave.[28]

This point is further elaborated in Saidiya Hartman's brilliant study of slavery in Ghana, entitled *Lose Your Mother*. In her work Hartman includes a brief but powerful analysis of the Akan word for slave, *odonkor*, which etymologically derives from the words "love" and "don't go." Hartman continues to critique the ways "love" is used as a method of control in traditional Ghanian slave systems, which often proclaim to incorporate the slave as "kin" in a loving family: "Love encourages forgetting, which is intended to wash away the slave's past. Love makes a place for the stranger; it domesticates persons from 'outside the house' and not 'of the blood'; it assuages the slave's loss of family; it remakes slaveholders as mothers and fathers. Owning persons and claiming kin are one and the same; so love cannot be separated from dispossession or property in persons. Affection perhaps softens the sting of dishonor but does not erase it."[29] Here Hartman does not deny the place of "love" within slavery, but rather reveals it as a perverted, troubling double to the actual affection that may take place in a genuine family. The tenderness offered to slaves by their masters may seem like an authentic human emotion, but it really is a kind of trap that sucks the slave into an even more violated and emotionally abusive position. Love further deracinates slaves and acts like a kind of weapon that damages their emotional connections to their past lives and their real kin networks in their home communities.

If the medical and psychological literature I previously examined documents the ways that the stresses of slavery alter the mind, body, and emotional life of slaves, this, to my mind, illuminates some of the deep-seated realities of trauma and emotional abuse that lie at the heart of the phenomena investigated by Patterson, Hartman, and other scholars of slavery.[30] Of course we need to be careful in not assuming that traumatized victims of the past necessarily have the exact same reactions to the stresses of slavery as those who are enslaved in our own day. Yet Herman's chapter on captivity and slavery argues that there is something of a universal structure in systems of exploitation and domination: "The methods that enable one human being to enslave another are remarkably consistent. The accounts of hostages, political prisoners, and survivors of concentration camps from every corner of the globe have an uncanny sameness."[31] Of course Herman says nothing about the dynamics of abuse in early modern cultures or the applicability of her findings to people from different historical eras and cultures. At the same time, who would argue that seventeenth-century slaves did not experience the same biological, cognitive, and psychological consequences of traumatic stress as enslaved people in our own historical moment?

In the end I argue here that the models created by Herman and the others previously discussed have a powerful explanatory value when we start to examine early modern slave narratives. It is clear to me that many of these same dynamics are operative in the terrorizing methods of domination that structure many different seventeenth- and eighteenth-century slave cultures. Even still, we must be attuned to the cultural and historical contexts that inform the traumas inherent in any one particular form of slavery. For now I will make this case by turning to Okeley's slave narrative, which presents one of the most searing and thoughtful explorations written in the long eighteenth century of the psychology of slavery and of the ways that "love" can be used as a weapon to dominate slaves.

William Okeley and Traumatic Bonding

Thus far, scholars have paid very little attention to Okeley's poignant explorations of the state of slavery and the emotional and psychological challenges he faces during his time in Algiers. Until we delve deeper into the traumas of Okeley's experiences of bondage, we will not be in a good position to understand the powerful pull that his last, supposedly "kind," slave owner has on his emotions. Returning to Norton's discussion of Okeley's supposed good treatment in Algiers, we should note that she can only construct this picture of his enslavement by ignoring the signs of trauma that abound throughout the text. Reading the contemporary medical scholarship on slavery and trauma makes us more attuned to this aspect of his narrative. For example, she does not discuss the horrible surprise of deracination that takes place when Okeley's boat is stormed by the Algerians, that violent shocking experience of watching one's companions slaughtered—"six were slain and many wounded" (148)—and of being ripped from one's social context and life trajectory to be placed in a state of slavery, unknowingness, and complete lack of control: "Many weeks they kept us close prisoners at sea. We found many Englishmen in their ships, slaves like ourselves, from whom we had no other comfort but the condoling of each other's miseries" (149). Okeley has been transformed, almost in an instant, from a free Englishman into a socially dead slave who is sold like an animal in the marketplace of Algiers (150–52): these moments in his life represent a series of psychological blows from which he does not recover, no matter how his masters treat him in Algiers.

Many of the hallmarks of trauma that come from physical and psychological abuse are on display throughout the narrative. His first master's father beats him so badly that Okeley threatens to commit suicide in order to escape his violence (153), after which his master threatens to kill him with a knife. Later, Okeley's master forces him to violate his own conscience, a key strategy in breaking down the psychological resistance of victims, by making him serve on an Algerian ship that is setting out to capture more European slaves (154–55).[32] Okeley writes of the painful emotional and spiritual struggles that he encounters in this episode and of the submissive posture he is forced to take in response to the violent and domineering power of his master: "his commands were backed with compulsion, and whatever his authority was, he had more power than I had courage to deny or strength to resist, and go I did" (155). For a deeply religious and morally upright person like Okeley, who is always concerned about acting in accordance with God's desires and wishes, this is an extremely traumatic moment, one that reveals even more painfully to him the all-encompassing authority of the master, who can trample with impunity upon the ethical and moral beliefs of his slave.

The master also has complete power to change his mind on a whim, moving the slave from one condition and life experience to the next without any need to consult or explain himself. Upon returning to Algiers, Okeley finds that his master is under extreme financial duress because the ship he invested in brought back no rich prizes. He then basically abandons Okeley, casting him into the prison-like city to make an income and pay him two dollars per month in wages. Like most perpetrators of traumatic violence and psychological coercion, the master is free to make capricious demands and to bend his victims to his will. In this instance Okeley realizes that he is a disposable, usable creature, and he is bewildered as to how he is supposed to earn an income in a strange city with no friends or capital. He also understands that if he is unsuccessful in raising the money for his master each month, he will not "escape his lash" (155). Somehow Norton ignores all of the master's violence, compulsive power, and torturing depravity, stating that "Okeley was lent money by one master to set up in business," suggesting that he is doing this out of kindness or is attempting to mitigate Okeley's experience of slavery.[33] This idea is simply not correct. In giving Okeley a onetime peculium, which Patterson shows is very common in slave cultures throughout history, he has invested "a small modicum" (156), which we later find out that he considered a loan (166), and gets in return a variety of tangible benefits: in addition to the monthly income he will receive directly from Okeley's labors, he no longer has to outlay funds to feed, shelter, or clothe his slave (155–56), nor does he have to put up with the hassles of directly supervising him, as the state-paid spies do this work, which Okeley finds out firsthand later in the narrative (164–66).[34] Finally, the later episode where the master attempts to make Okeley work in a weaving shop, with disastrous results, makes it clear that he is at a loss as to how he can otherwise profitably employ his slave (166).

Thus, allowing Okeley to work as a merchant is a lucrative, stress-free way for the master to manage and profit from his slave.

Norton's idea that Okeley "enjoyed a considerable amount of freedom" is even more problematic.[35] She does not consider Okeley's own explorations of his traumatized psychological state during this time, one of mind-numbing passivity and utter defeat, one in which he reports no sense of liberty or enjoyment of any sort:

> It were tedious to trouble the reader how I wore out three or four irksome years in this way of trading. All this while there was no dawning of deliverance from our bondage. As one year left us, another found us and delivered us over captives to the next. Our condition was bad and in danger every day of being worse, as the mutable humors of our patrons determined upon us, for our shop and trade was no freehold. The truth is, in time we were so habituated to bondage that we almost forgot liberty and grew stupid and senseless of our slavery. . . . Long bondage breaks the spirits; it scatters hope off and discourages all attempts for freedom. And there were more evils attended our condition than the bodily torture which we were always liable to and sometimes endured. (157)

Okeley describes here a state of mind in which he is overwhelmed by the unending stresses inherent in the state of slavery, is cognitively and spiritually depressed, and is unable to muster any resources to resist. At this stage in his enslavement it is as if he cannot even imagine a scenario that involves struggle or escape, as if he has been stripped of any possibility of being an agent in his own life. For him time becomes a tedious march in intervals that are not clearly marked or remembered—"three or four irksome years." In a fascinating move he figures time itself as another kind of slave master who "delivered us over captives" from one year to the next. As Herman writes, "Traumatized people feel and act as though their nervous systems have been disconnected from the present."[36] Okeley certainly represents time in this manner: for him, to live in the state of slavery is to exist in a situation where time does not have the same meaning or rhythm as it does for free men. One cannot fully inhabit the present nor look forward to a future, as both are completely controlled by the "mutable humors" of the master. In Okeley's reckoning, to consider time is only to be reminded of the alternating horror and tedium of being a slave.

It is clear from this passage that Okeley's sense of the existential impasse of slavery is facilitated and heightened by the terrorizing environment of violence in which it takes place. He knows that he is "always liable to" be tortured at any time, ensuring that he lives in a constant state of threat, fear, and horror—this point alone undermines Norton's assertions. Okeley is quite sparse on the details of his own experience of the "bodily torture" that he "sometimes endured" at the hands of his master, and he shows a continual reluctance to discuss torture of slaves in depth, as if it forms part of an inassimilable aspect of his traumatic experience. This is an aspect of the text that the canonical work of Cathy Caruth on trauma and narrative should prepare us to see.[37]

One way that Okeley attempts to narrate what are otherwise unspeakable aspects of his traumatic sufferings is by turning to a third-person ethnographic description of Algerian practices instead of narrating a first-person account of his own experiences. His lengthy description of the ways slaves are sold in Algiers is a prime example, and it is followed by Okeley's matter-of-fact statement, in one concise utterance: "As for myself, I was sold the first market day to a Tagarene" (152). The ethnographic description of the indignities and horrors of the slave market, then, acts as a disassociating substitute for Okeley's own description of his thoughts, feelings, and experiences while being sold. Okeley deploys a similar strategy in his general discussion of Ottoman violence directed at the subjugated Moors in Algiers, a section in the text in which he highlights a series of spectacular executions and corporeal punishments that the Ottomans use to maintain public order and imperial control in the city. He then curiously says, "What cruelties they exercise upon poor slaves need not be mentioned," as if even the otherwise distancing mode of the ethnographic brings the details of torture and trauma too close to the surface (164). Needless to say, he does not discuss his own devastating experience of torture in any real detail, but rather provides in the next section a brief explanation of torture by bastinados to which his friend John Randal was subjected and which Okeley himself narrowly escaped after their arrest by the Algerian spy who accused them of trying to escape (165).

Only when we are alert to the state of slavery itself as a state of trauma and to these marks of the traumatic in Okeley's text are we adequately prepared to analyze his experiences with his last master. In his traumatized, depressed state Okeley is extremely susceptible to this insidious man who lavishes him with affection and indulgences in an attempt to gain a loving, ever-loyal, and perfectly obedient slave:

> And if I should be silent here, I should be the most ungrateful wretch living. I found not only pity and compassion but love and friendship from my new patron. Had I been his son, I could not have met with more respect nor been treated with more tenderness. I could not wish a friend a better condition than I was then in, except my bonds. If anything could be mingled with bondage to make it sweet, if anything could reconcile slavery to nature, if anything could beget an acquiescence in such a state, I did not, I could not, want it. (168)

This master is a kind of emotional parasite, playing with the mind of his traumatized slave, offering a fictive kinship that is meant to dissolve Okeley's desire to return home and to facilitate his submission as a loving slave. Okeley senses that his master is grooming him to take a management position at his farm in the country where he could have become "a petty lord and bashawed it over the rest of my fellow servants" (168). This, more than anything, reveals that the loving pose of this master is ultimately a stratagem meant to produce a slave who can be trusted to run his business. This man is certainly not a father to Okeley nor his friend.[38]

Okeley's text is particularly revealing on this point as it is precisely this promising situation and this loving master that compels him into action toward his desperate plan to escape. If he is removed outside the city to his master's farm and away from his community of fellow English slaves, he realizes that he will never escape Algiers (168). To succumb to the blandishments of the loving master and to take up submissively a more advantageous position in his system of power is to become, once and for all, completely enslaved. It seems that Okeley was severely tested by this master and this situation, as is evident by the paradoxes that he formulates to explain it: "indeed the freedom that I found in servitude, the liberty I enjoyed in my bonds was so great, that it took off much of the edge of my desire to obtain and almost blunted it from any vigorous attempt after liberty that carried hazard in its face" (168). Hartman's description of the dark magic of certain West African slave masters who use spells and rituals to seduce slaves into forgetting their past and forever "losing their mothers" finds its Algerian counterpart here.[39] Okeley is becoming pulled inside a sort of ideological dream factory that temporarily masks the true nature of his situation, but he eventually becomes "awakened" (168) enough to realize that his oxymoronic formulations make no sense: there is no freedom in servitude, no liberty in bonds, no matter how "mitigated" (143) his slave condition may seem. Any feeling that there might be such freedom within slavery is only a sign of a dangerous intensification of the slave's psychological subjection to his master and the dark illusions he is creating.

To that end Okeley decides to risk his life in a hair-raising attempt to make, launch, and row a canvas-covered boat across the Mediterranean. He ultimately prefers death to this supposedly benign form of slavery, which is anything but. This, above all, should remind us that what is at stake in slavery is the very soul and identity of a human being, the slave's desire for agency, true kinship, and human dignity, all of which Okeley values over his life and the loss of which cannot be compensated for by the favorable conditions he encounters with his last master. What fascinates me about Okeley's text, though, is that he ultimately cannot bring himself to critique this last master in an explicit way, and it is clear that this man still has an emotional hold on Okeley when he writes his narrative decades after he escaped from him. Nothing else shows the awful power of the loving slave master more than the fact that Okeley feels compelled to praise this "old gentleman," his belief that a failure to do so would mean that he is "the most ungrateful wretch living" (168), and the debate he records, which I quote in the epigraph to this chapter, as to whether or not it is ethical for him to escape from such a man.

Given the literature on the psychology of slavery, we should not be surprised that a slave master who wields affection and kind treatment as a weapon against his slave becomes successful, to some extent, in fostering in the slave a traumatic bond with himself. Thus, Okeley takes his place alongside countless other slaves and other victims of psychological coercion in many different times, places, and cultures who have been drawn into an affectionate relationship with their tormentors. While making this point has been the central thrust of this chapter, I also recognize that there are a host of cultural and historical contexts that provide a unique texture to the way this phenomenon is recorded in Okeley's narrative. I do not have space to adequately explore these contexts here, but in order to perform a fuller investigation, we would need to take up a number of issues in the text: the fact that Okeley believes that those who are born into slavery do not have the same right to resist the institution as those sold into slavery (171); his commonplace idea, which he draws from his reading of the Old Testament, that God uses slavery to punish the wayward (139); his notion, derived from the model of Joseph, that God enslaves certain people in situations where they can act out a part in God's plan of salvation (158–59); his sense that many of his readers will hold pro-slavery sentiments and condemn him for escaping, especially from a supposedly good master (144; 171); and the probable origins of such an idea in the "love-labor paradigm" that Roxann Wheeler has argued was widely disseminated via English patriarchal theories and that undergird many of the representations of grateful slaves in British literature and culture.[40] Such patriarchal theories have a profound hold on Okeley's thought, as evidenced by his insistence that his narrative should help different groups of English people to better appreciate their subordinate place in structures of power (140). In Okeley's case, then, we can see that his experiences and his narrative are informed by a particular mix of theological, political, and social ideologies that circulated in late seventeenth-century England and that, to my mind, make him even more susceptible to the kinds of self-blame, traumatic bonding, and psychological control to which many, if not most, slaves are subject.

In the end Okeley's strong religious and political beliefs were the primary means by which he was able to resist the dark magic of the good master. Describing his debate with himself about whether it was ethical to leave his slave master, Okeley writes that "one thought of England, and of its liberty and Gospel, confuted a thousand such objections and routed whole legions of these little scruples" (171). This passage can help us to marvel at Okeley's resilience and his heroic courage to escape, even as we simultaneously recoil from the effectiveness of the strategies of psychological control that are on display in his narrative. The fact that such a religiously motivated man could experience "whole legions" of doubts about the morality of escaping from his master should haunt all our discussions of slavery in the period. This moment, along with others that appear in the canon of slave narratives from the long eighteenth century, challenges our dominant paradigms, which stress, above all, slave resistance and agency. For every Okeley who was able to eventually withstand these psychological assaults, there were doubtless many, many more who became submissive and nonresistant, who fell under the spell of their masters, and who never escaped and, thus, were never able to write or publish their stories. Thus, Okeley's narrative, along with those of Joseph Pitts, Olaudah Equiano, and T.S., give us a glimpse into the lives of those who are psychologically coerced into relationships of traumatic bonding with their oppressors. They remind us to be ever vigilant in critiquing slavery and, especially, those supposedly kind masters that appear in these texts, and to never ignore the deep trauma and psychological coercion that ultimately account for the slaves who love them.

NOTES

1. William Okeley, *Ebenezer; or, A Small Monument of Great Mercy, Appearing in the Miraculous Deliverance of William Okeley*, in *Piracy, Slavery, and Redemption: Barbary Captivity Narratives from Early Modern England*, ed. Daniel J. Vitkus, [124–92] (New York: Columbia University Press, 2001), esp. 171. All subsequent citations will be found in the text.
2. For T.S.'s love for his master Reiz, see T.S., *The Adventures of (Mr T.S.) An English Merchant, Taken Prisoner by the Turks of Argiers* (London, 1670). For his love for his last master, who eventually freed him and offered him a filial relationship, see Pitts, "A True and Faithful Account of the Religion and Manners of the Mohammetans, with an Account of the Author's Being Taken Captive," in Vitkus, *Piracy, Slavery, and Redemption*, 218–340; and for his love for his master Pascal, see Olaudah Equiano, *The Interesting Narrative and Other Writings*, ed. Vincent Carretta (New York: Penguin, 1995), esp. 138.
3. George Boulukos, *The Grateful Slave: The Emergence of Race in Eighteenth-Century British and American Culture* (New York: Cambridge University Press, 2008), 29–32.
4. Joe Snader, *Caught Between Worlds: British Captivity Narratives in Fact and Fiction* (Lexington: University Press of Kentucky, 2000), 99–100.
5. Claire Norton, "Lust, Greed, Torture, and Identity: Narrations of Conversion and the Creation of the Early Modern Renegade," *Comparative Studies of South Asia, Africa and the Middle East* 29 (2009): 263.

6. See Adam Beach, "The Good Treatment Debate, Comparative Slave Studies, and the 'Adventures' of T.S.," in *Invoking Slavery in the Eighteenth-Century British Imagination*, 21–35 (Burlington VT: Ashgate, 2013).
7. See Claude Meillassoux, *The Anthropology of Slavery: The Womb of Iron and Gold*, trans. Alide Dasnois (Chicago: University of Chicago Press, 1991), esp. 99–115, and Orlando Patterson, *Slavery and Social Death: A Comparative Study* (Cambridge MA: Harvard University Press, 1982).
8. For one such critique of both Patterson's and Meillassoux's frameworks, see Ehud R. Toledano, *Slavery and Abolition in the Ottoman Middle East* (Seattle: University of Washington Press, 1998), esp. 22–24 and 158–65.
9. Judith Lewis Herman, *Trauma and Recovery* (New York: Basic, 1992), 115.
10. Elizabeth Hopper and José Hidalgo, "Invisible Chains: Psychological Coercion of Human Trafficking Victims," *Intercultural Human Rights Law Review* 1 (2006): 185.
11. Hopper and Hidalgo, 186.
12. See Kathleen Kim, "The Coercion of Trafficked Workers," *Iowa Law Review* 96 (2011): 409–74; and Kathleen Kim, "Psychological Coercion in the Context of Modern-Day Involuntary Labor: Revisiting United States v. Kozminksi and Understanding Human Trafficking," *University of Toledo Law Review* 38 (2007): 941–72.
13. Coral J. Dando, David Walsh, and Robin Brierley, "Perceptions of Psychological Coercion and Human Trafficking in the West Midlands of England: Beginning to Know the Unknown," *PLoS One* 11, no. 5 (May 5, 2016): 1–13, doi:10.1371/journal.pone.0153263.
14. Susie B. Baldwin, Anne E. Fehrenbacher, and David P. Eisenman, "Psychological Coercion in Human Trafficking: An Application of Biderman's Framework," *Qualitative Health Research* (November 2014): 1, doi:10.1177/1049732314557087.
15. For a similar methodology, see Cathy Zimmerman and Nicola Pocock, "Human Trafficking and Mental Health: 'My Wounds are Inside; They are Not Visible,'" *Brown Journal of World Affairs* 19, no. 2 (2013): 265–80.
16. Herman, *Trauma and Recovery*, 34.
17. Herman, 74.
18. Baldwin, Fehrenbacher, and Eisenman, "Psychological Coercion in Human Trafficking," 7.
19. Hopper and Hidalgo, "Invisible Chains," 205.
20. For a similar finding, see T. K. Logan, Robert Walker, and Gretchen Hunt, "Understanding Human Trafficking in the United States," *Trauma, Violence, & Abuse* 10 (2009): 3–30, esp. 16.
21. Hopper and Hidalgo, "Invisible Chains," 191.
22. Baldwin, Fehrenbacher, and Eisenman, "Psychological Coercion in Human Trafficking," 6.
23. See Hopper and Hidalgo, "Invisible Chains," 191, for the "alternating kindness and threats" used by perpetrators to control their victims. See Herman, *Trauma and Recovery*,

78, for a discussion of the use of "capricious granting of small indulgences" as part of a method of control.

24. Herman, *Trauma and Recovery*, 82.
25. Hopper and Hidalgo, "Invisible Chains," 198–99.
26. Patterson, *Slavery and Social Death*, 62.
27. Patterson, 63.
28. Patterson, 65.
29. Saidiya Hartman, *Lose Your Mother: A Journey Along the Atlantic Slave Route* (New York: Farrar, Straus & Giroux, 2007), 87.
30. See, for example, Srinivas Aravamudan's exploration of the idea of the slave-as-pet in his reading of Behn's *Oroonoko* in *Tropicopolitans: Colonialism and Agency* (Durham NC: Duke University Press, 1999), 29–70. For a similar critique of the slave master's sympathy and affection toward his slave, see Jonathan Lamb, "Modern Metamorphoses and Disgraceful Tales," in *Things*, ed. Bill Brown, 193–226 (Chicago: University of Chicago Press, 2004), and Marcus Wood, *Slavery, Empathy, and Pornography* (New York: Oxford University Press, 2002).
31. Herman, *Trauma and Recovery*, 76.
32. In "Invisible Chains," Hopper and Hidalgo note two key strategies of perpetrators of psychological coercion that are relevant in this case: "compulsory violation of taboos or religious beliefs" and "being forced to betray or harm others" (189).
33. Norton, "Lust, Greed, Torture, and Identity," 263.
34. See Patterson, *Slavery and Social Death*, 182–86, for an excellent discussion of the peculium in various slave cultures. See Robert C. Davis, *Christian Slaves, Muslim Masters: White Slavery in the Mediterranean, the Barbary Coast, and Italy, 1500–1800* (New York: Palgrave Macmillan, 2003), 90–93, for a discussion of slave practices in Algiers, which regularly required slaves to pay their masters a monthly tax for their maintenance.
35. Norton, "Lust, Greed, Torture, and Identity," 263.
36. Herman, *Trauma and Recovery*, 35.
37. See Cathy Caruth, *Unclaimed Experience: Trauma, Narrative, and History* (Baltimore: Johns Hopkins University Press, 1996), particularly 1–9.
38. For an important theoretical discussion of harm and injury that is relevant to Okeley's experience of slavery, see Sandra Macpherson, *Harm's Way: Tragic Responsibility and the Novel Form* (Baltimore: Johns Hopkins University Press, 2010).
39. Hartman, *Lose Your Mother*, 155–57.
40. Roxann Wheeler, "Powerful Affections: Slaves, Servants, and Labours of Love in Defoe's Writing," in *Defoe's Footprints: Essays in Honour of Maximillian E. Novak*, ed. Robert M. Maniquis and Carl Fisher, [126–52] (Toronto: University of Toronto Press, 2009), esp. 127.

10

Imperfect Enjoyments and Female Disappointments

Understanding Trauma in Aphra Behn's "The Disappointment" and *Oroonoko*

CYNTHIA RICHARDS

Aphra Behn's entry into the imperfect enjoyment genre, "The Disappointment" (1682), has frequently been compared to John Wilmot, the Earl of Rochester's, genre-defining poem "The Imperfect Enjoyment" (1680). In fact "The Disappointment" was long mistaken for his work, appearing in his posthumous 1680 collection *Poems Upon Several Occasions* and even assuming a new title, "The Insensible," in the Edmund Curll 1714 edition, while his "Imperfect Enjoyment" became "The Disappointment."[1] Contemporary recovery of the poem, however, has largely focused on a gendered differentiation between the two. Although the poem moves between male and female perspectives, its third-person narration provides space to register the woman's dismay, and unlike the more brutally misogynistic of the poems in this genre, including the French poem upon which it is based and Behn's poem, it does not place blame on the woman for the disruption of premature ejaculation. Some have even argued for the poem's more utopian tendencies, stating that it promotes a "reciprocal" vision of sexuality and does so radically in a form traditionally associated with unilateral male pleasure.[2] Rochester's poem, by contrast with the Ovidian amore upon which it is based, also treats its female figure more sympathetically, but still frames her body as a "cunt," an open wound that provokes the narrator's physical and emotional disintegration.[3]

Yet neither Rochester's nor Behn's poem promotes recovery, or in the case of Behn, even suggests closure. Reciprocity, moreover, if indeed suggested in Behn's poem, would at best require a repetition of another sexual episode with another uncertain and potentially traumatizing outcome, and what the narrator substitutes for such a promise is, in fact, an assurance that the loss is profound. That is true for both the male and female figures in the poem, both of whom remain damaged by their encounter at its conclusion and remain unable to envision for themselves a future outside of flight or figurative exile, or in Lysander's case, the more specific "hell of impotence."[4] Rochester's "Imperfect Enjoyment" also leaves his male narrator without hope of restoration while offering his female figure restitution of such magnitude—"10,000 abler pricks"—that it becomes difficult to imagine it as anything but hellish (l.17). By contrast Rochester offers in some of his female-voiced poems, namely, "The Platonic Lady" and "A Young Lady to her Ancient Lover," another response to bodily loss: he reframes the unrecovered male state as opportunity, and deliberately defers closure to increase female pleasure and shared satisfaction.[5]

This chapter argues that "The Disappointment," read in this context, becomes less an exposition of gendered difference, or utopian reciprocity, and more an example of psychological "acting out" or what Dominick LaCapra defines as the "arrested process" of "melancholia."[6] The poem ends abruptly and on a discordantly personal note. "The nymph's resentments," the final and only entirely original stanza reads, "none but I / Can well imagine or condole" (xiv: 1–2). In short, just as we expect Behn to name the woman's disappointment, that process is arrested—this is all we learn of her "resentments"—and the poem returns instead to enumerating his resentments and in language predictable for the form. Reading "The Disappointment" in this way does not diminish the poem's value or ignore its contribution to a gendering of sexuality. Rather, because we can read both the narrator and its female figure, Cloris, as "acting out," we can experience its female disappointment as a structural or constitutive loss, a psychological wounding that makes nameable a form of female trauma. Additionally, identifying female loss in the context of a genre associated with the cultural trauma of post–civil war England, a genre that has long shaped discussions of male vulnerability, links these gendered narratives rather than placing them in opposition to one another.

Applying a modern term such as "trauma" to an early modern text must always be done cautiously. This is particularly true for a term that emerges out of a historical moment, World War I, and in response to nineteenth-century industrial developments and a Victorian ideology that treated female desire as symptomatic rather than normative.[7] Moreover, the modern ideal of an integrated self, which the experience of psychological trauma purportedly disrupts, emerges in the late seventeenth century, and these poems can be read not as a failure to achieve that holistic sense of self but as a resistance or critique of that new, abstract ideal.[8] Yet acknowledging the similarities between these early explorations of unexpected, premature loss and the modern trauma narrative guards against equally problematic utopian recoveries, or modern "insistence[s]" that we are fundamentally "different from the people in the past," as historian Judith Pollmann has recently argued. As she points out, readers prior to the eighteenth century embraced the "virtues of anachronism" or what she calls "reading analogically," and, in fact, our "sense that the past is non repeatable" and exists apart from the present is itself a construct of the modern period.[9] Thus, not seeing resemblances can be as historically problematic as seeing them.

Both Rochester and Behn treat bodily and psychological loss as constitutive of human experience. If we chiefly celebrate, then, the recovery of a female voice in "The Disappointment" while emphasizing bodily injury in Rochester's poem, we lose sight of Behn's contribution to the genre, how she reshaped the classic image of the fleeing female as a signifier of female trauma rather than solely a reflection of male vulnerability, and how her poem resists mutually exclusive categories of gendered loss. Indeed, insisting on a history closed off to "the inevitability of displacement and substitution in acts of remembrance" creates competitive categories of loss, Michael Rothberg argues in *Multidirectional Memory*. "Multidirectional memory," by contrast, "draw[s] attention to the dynamic transfers that take place at diverse times and diverse places" and allows us "to work toward a rearticulation of historical relatedness beyond paradigms of uniqueness."[10] Behn's poem moves back and forth between the perspectives of her male and female characters while transferring the typically male expression of despair at a premature sexual climax to the premature departure of a distressed female. Moreover, she sharply abbreviates a poem that continues far longer in its original French version, an abrupt ending that allows female "disappointment" to carry the same resonance as male bodily wounding.

Yet arguably, it is the "dynamic transfer" suggested between this earlier poem and Behn's penultimate work, *Oroonoko*, that proves most revealing, and that this chapter will briefly relate.[11] If we take Behn at her word, she is remembering in *Oroonoko*, and remembering a story of extraordinary pain: the brutal execution and dismemberment of someone she knew and cared for. If it was a personal memory, those details would be hard to forget and reading a poetic account of a male body lifeless, cold, and dismembered—its figurative representation in the French original—would surely remind her of this traumatic event. When she returns at the end of her life to recount a story she had frequently retold but never put in writing, we can read this event as a narrative return to this loss. It allows for the possibility that she may be "working through"—coming to accept absence as absence—an experience that she psychologically "act[s] out" in "The Disappointment." Or to use Rothberg's terms, we can read these texts as operating multidirectionally, each substituting for and elucidating the other, and each speaking to the significance of their respective losses. This "multidirectionality" does not erase the radical power differential between the female narrator and the enslaved Oroonoko—or the narrator's shame in fleeing the scene of his death—but it does explain why the depiction of his suffering is neither "casual" nor "routine."[12] Understanding trauma can help account for "the vicarious suffering" that distinguishes this "melanchol[ic]" text, how *Oroonoko* renders its readers witnesses to a loss that is visceral rather than abstract.[13]

Trauma and the Imperfect Enjoyment Poem

The cluster of imperfect enjoyment poems that emerged in the 1670s and early 1680s in Restoration England marks both a repetition—a return to the impotency poem periodically practiced during times of cultural crisis and civil war since Ancient Rome—and the emergence of a distinctly new framing of that bodily loss and its corresponding psychological effects. George Etherege; John Wilmot, Earl of Rochester; Aphra Behn; and the anonymous poets of "Lost Opportunity Recovered" (1682) and "Against Fruition" (1684) all either strictly or loosely work from French poems to establish satiric narratives where male loss of physical control takes the form of premature ejaculation.[14] In Ancient Rome, and most notably in Ovid's *Amore* 3.7—generally accepted as the model for Rochester's "Imperfect Enjoyment"—male impotency arises from a temporary state of nonarousal and nods to a general decline in masculine virtue or bodily vigor, but the loss is neither sharp nor dramatic.[15] By contrast, in each of these Restoration poems the imperfection of the enjoyment lies in the abruptness of male climax. It leaves the male speaker momentarily disoriented in the face of a female pleasure that remains unaltered by the experience (disappointedly so) while his own body becomes visibly wounded.

In short, the structure of this cluster of imperfect enjoyment poems assumes a form akin to the modern trauma narrative. Cathy Caruth, whose definition of the form remains central, describes "trauma" as "an event"—a wounding—that is "experienced too soon, too unexpectedly, to be fully known and is therefore not available to consciousness until it imposes itself again, repeatedly, in the nightmares and repetitive actions of the survivor."[16] Similarly, an imperfect enjoyment poem, through its central conceit, describes an event that happens "too soon, too unexpectedly"—that is, premature ejaculation—and then typically chronicles the "survivor's" futile efforts to assimilate that event and often in language that imaginatively repeats, sometimes in nightmarish terms, the original unsettling. Moreover, as noted earlier, the loss of control associated with premature ejaculation takes the metaphoric form of wounding. The limp penis stands in for the body's literal death, and poets of the form rely heavily on such witty analogies to structure their protests. The seventeenth-century French poetic tradition of equating sexual climax, or *la petite mort*, with death further enforces how intractable this loss can prove. "These late Renaissance images of orgasm as a kind of death," Leo Braudy notes, "refer as well to the extinction of consciousness, the loss of control, the momentary oblivion of public identity."[17] Their satirical playfulness can be read, then, as masking the inevitability of physical dissolution and the presence of profound psychological pain.

Given these high stakes, not surprisingly, most of the English poems and all the French originals at least nominally foreground the wounded member's miraculous resurrection. As such they echo the Latin tradition of the impotency poem and the one previous English poem that employed this same structure—Thomas Nashe's "The Choise of Valentines" (1592)—by concluding with a coy or exaggerated recovery.[18] In the Restoration, however, that staged recovery proves so transparently compensatory that it appears to never fully eliminate the memory of the original loss. The sheer number of translations of Benech de Cantenac's "Lost Opportunity Recovered"—four of the five are translations of this poem—speaks to that dynamic. English poets keep repeating this French original, the repetition of that literary recovery suggesting that something remains unresolved or unassimilated in the telling.[19]

Moreover, temporality when reading this cluster of poems loses much of its meaning, as the inability to state definitively what poem was written first erases clear trajectories of progression. Roger Luckhurst refers to the "strange temporality of traumatic memory: an event can only be understood as traumatic *after* the fact."[20] The original circulation of these poems in manuscript form makes it difficult to determine the chronological order of their composition, and not being certain which poem comes first allows each to be read as, in effect, a belated response to the other. The uncertainty regarding attribution further compounds this effect. The titles of the poems prove interchangeable—both Etherege's and Wilmot's entries acquire the title of "Imperfect Enjoyment" and as noted earlier, for a while, so did Behn's. Indeed, as late as 1714 Behn's "The Disappointment" had yet to become unequivocally her own.[21]

Not surprisingly, then, the resurgence of the impotency poem in the late seventeenth century has generally been read as symptomatic of the political and cultural crisis occasioned through both the English Civil War and the Restoration of Charles II in 1660. In *The Impotency Poem from Ancient Latin to Restoration English Literature*, Hannah Lavery makes this connection most explicit. She reads this genre as having a long history of providing symbolic commentary during periods of civil rupture, but at no point more directly than in the Restoration. "The castrated nature of the Crown, following the literal removal of the royal figure-head in 1649, rent the image of divine, infallible monarchy," and the impotency poem with its images of masculine fallibility reemerge in force alongside the "return to the throne of a somewhat castrated symbol of monarchal authority."[22] The parallels, however, extend beyond this key image of fallibility and dismemberment. Recovery of masculine vigor as figured in most of these poems also mimics the tone of enforced, exaggerated celebration that occasioned the return of Charles II to the throne. That return also coincided with the 1660 Act of Free and General Pardon and Oblivion that legally mandated forgetting the Interregnum, or as Erin Peters describes it, "fixed erasure of the troubled past as the official policy." The reality, however, as Peters explains, was more complex as remembering "an older, prelapsarian state of being" simultaneously emerged as a popular motif in the political tracts of the period. "England in the early 1660s was thus characterized," she argues, "by a regime-inspired tension between acceptance of the unalterable traumatic impact of the recent past on national and individual identities and an attempt to reverse the effects of this trauma through the restorative re-enthronement of a Stuart king."[23] In this context Rochester's and Behn's departure from the others in this cluster of impotency poems becomes more politically charged, and psychologically resonant. Rochester's and Behn's narrators refuse to forget "the traumatic impact" of the premature ejaculation and instead choose to dwell on the effects of that loss while denying their speakers clear avenues for recovery. Both poets foreground attempts to name a loss that remains officially unspeakable within the Restoration.

Rochester and the Working Through of Loss

The traumatic undertones of Rochester's "Imperfect Enjoyment" are marked, pronounced even, among a cluster of poems that relish recitations of loss. He offers little to no hope for his narrator's resurrection. In fact his depiction of the absoluteness of the narrator's physical and emotional devastation can be read as so brutally certain as to not only deny his narrator recovery but also to expose how shallow and staged those boasts appear in other iterations of the genre. The poem does not conclude with the narrator's victorious restoration—his return to a kingly throne or the status of a Zeus "throw[ing] / The all-dissolving thunderbolt below" (ll.9–10). Rather his narrator becomes instead a "common fucking post," insensible to pleasure and doomed to repeat his original failure of sensibility in a state of unrelenting disassociation and nightmarish recovery (l.63) The imagery of the "post" itself points to how fixed the repetition of his insensibility will become, and how unlikely his return to psychic wholeness. Instead the speaker remains dismembered, disconnected from his offending organ and the emotional pain it has come to represent. At best he can anticipate further dissolution, trapped as he is by a recurring sense of suffering: "May'st thou to ravenous shankers be a prey / Or in consuming weepings waste away" (ll.66–7). Corinna's brief yet hopeful entreaty at the beginning of the poem, "Is there then no more?" only serves to reinforce his fate, and the constitutive nature of his loss (l.22). By the poem's end the answer to her question becomes clear: there is no more, of either the physical or spiritual variety, and the only outcome of this event yet another nightmarish and disassociative repetition—the promise to Corinna of "ten thousand abler pricks" "do[ing]" her "right" for him (l.72). This final repetition, however, is framed as hyperbole and not trauma, and the narrative of deferred recovery remains his.

Rochester's poem is most directly linked to Ovid's *Amore 3.7*, an impotency poem where the speaker recovers his masculine vigor, but too late to please his mistress who flees in shame. That poem speaks to a natural disintegration of the self, one that proves an inevitable part of life and that the speaker must philosophically prepare himself for: "What shall I do when I am old," the speaker asks, "supposing that I live so long, if I fail so lamentably now that I am young?" Lisa Starks-Estes connects this sense of constitutive loss—what she identifies as a "traumatic splitting of the self"—with the Ovidian form itself and demonstrates how Shakespeare employs that tradition to "expose the vulnerability that lurks just beneath the seemingly impenetrable wall of Roman *virtus*" or manliness.[24] Melinda Rabb argues that the "long eighteenth century" is replete with "male characters whose corporeality seems far more vulnerable and exposed" and links this phenomenon with the devastating consequences of the English Civil War.[25] Cynthia Marshall in *The Shattering of the Self* detects this tension emerging as early as the sixteenth century, connecting the Renaissance forays into the Ovidian form with a cultural resistance to emerging modern subjectivity. Its images of sadomasochistic textual violence reveal "the early modern impulse to undo or negate the emergent self." The sadomasochistic imagery of Rochester's revision of Ovid's *Amore 3.7* speaks to this continuing resistance. At this crucial moment in English history, the poem stages what, according to Marshall, was once a normative sense of the self—"the self as fluid, volatile, and vulnerable to outside influence"—as a moment of irrecoverable loss.[26] The self as "fluid," I would add, becomes a haunting, traumatizing memory, and the new reality of a more stable identity painfully emerges; as noted earlier our speaker becomes inexorably fixed, "a common fucking post."

By contrast with this representation of haunting male loss, the female figure as derived from the Ovidian form largely functions not as the one experiencing the loss but the one representing it. She mirrors back a painful image of the male speaker and his own wounded state. That is the case even when the female experience of pain is as profound as Ovid's Philomel, whose story becomes brutally reenacted in Shakespeare's *Titus Andronicus*. Starks-Estes describes, for example, Lavinia as a character "whose martyred body serves as a tableau of the traumatic effects of violence."[27] Linda Enterline also views Lavinia's "tongueless and handless" body as being presented not as a suffering subject in that play, but "as if she were an aesthetic object, a marred beauty best understood in terms of the dismembering rhetoric of the *blason*." Moreover flight from these "forma" cannot restore to Lavinia full subjectivity as "resistance and flight enhance beauty and nearly come to define it."[28] Ovid's *Amore 3.7* contains a glimpse of this dynamic. Ovid's Corinna flees the scene, splashing water on her body as she leaves to hide her shame. The male speaker's restored erection occurs nearly simultaneously.

The context of the imperfect enjoyment, then, points to the vulnerability of masculinity and a changing definition of the self in the late seventeenth century. It suggests an intensification of a sadomasochistic self just as the modern self takes hold. It does not, however, accommodate the experience of female trauma. In both the imperfect enjoyment genre and the Ovidian form, women serve as a silent or muted witness to the constitutive yet humanizing loss of the disintegrating male figure or as the very prototype of loss itself. She is wounding in her sensual impact because, ironically, she is herself already wounded symbolically through her female genitalia. Etherege's speaker, for example, does acknowledge the woman's body language: "she blushed and frowned," but reads these physical markers of distress as comments on his own experience: "perceiving we had done / The sports she thought we had yet begun."[29] The possibility of trauma experienced by the female figure proves irrelevant to the situation, and by analogy so does her humanity. Her capacity for pleasure only serves to reinforce his loss. Hence we have the faux promise delivered by Rochester's male narrator of a happy ending for Corinna—the "10,000 abler pricks"—that flagrantly fails to acknowledge the trauma of repetitive penetration or the legitimacy of her agency.

Rochester returns to this imagery in other poems, and particularly in two of his female-voiced ones, "The Platonick Lady" and "A Young Lady to Her

Ancient Lover." In these poems, however, female pleasure is linked with the inert or disabled male body. Its female speakers have no interest in fleeing the scene nor find their pleasure unaccommodated by male vulnerability. Nor is it their body that is preserved as an emblem of loss. "The Platonick Lady," as its title suggests, is quite explicit in its polemics. "I could love thee till I die," the female narrator begins, seemingly responding to a long Petrarchan tradition where the male speaker pleads for such enduring love (l.1). Yet, as in that tradition, the emotional and the physical are intertwined, and the female speaker reimagines that constant pleading as physical foreplay, and one that requires the male body to accept an inactive, deathlike status. The female speaker will happily defer her climax—her "dying"—and stay true to her lover—if the male addressee will only accept his limits and temporal nature: "Wouldst thou love me modestly," she says, "and ne'er press, whilst I live, / For more than willingly I would give" (ll.2–4). Here "press" suggests both the pressure of military enlistment and the pleasure of touch. In both readings accepting limits becomes key to its promise of reciprocity within a metaphorical battlefield of love. The connection to death becomes more explicit as the poem proceeds and reaches its most pronounced level of intimacy with this line: "I love a youth will give me leave / His body in my arms to wreathe / To press him gently and to kiss" (ll.13–15). The line is deceptive, seemingly full of action—her "leave" to "press him gently and to kiss" and the way "wreathe" near rhymes with "writhe." "Leave" can mean in the late seventeenth century to "raise an army" and the line indirectly gives him this power. But the metaphor, in fact, makes her body the sepulcher of his, her arms a wreath upon the tomb of his inactive physical frame, and her gentle pressing a form of memorial devotion. Metaphorically his body becomes "pressed" within the parchment of her desire. The language reverses the blazon of the Petrarchan tradition, making his body (not hers) the one itemized as her desire is deferred and pleasantly prolonged, and in the process her identity affirmed.

The reverse blazon is even more pronounced in "A Young Lady to Her Ancient Lover" as is its forgiving gaze on the vulnerable, temporal, and spent male body. Here the young lady seemingly hovers over the form of her ancient lover and lists in each stanza the physical features that inspire her enduring love. The middle stanza echoes the mid-poem climax of "Platonick Lady," in the process also feminizing his sexuality: "On thy withered Lips and dry, / Which like barren Furrows lie, / Brooding kisses I shall pour, / Shall thy youthful Heat restore" (ll.7–10). In this passage the ancient lover's body becomes the "cunt"; the female speaker gazes upon the "withered lips" and "barren furrows" of her ancient lover's wounding-because-wounded body. Yet in this poem the speaker reframes that imagery in the language of nature and its promise of renewing showers. That imagery does not eliminate loss, but rather draws attention to the limits nature imposes. Indeed, the first stanza anticipates the ancient lover's inevitable decline, describing him as "aching, shaking, Crazy, Cold" (l.3), and while the third stanza promises revival, it continues to document the effects of age and the temporality of life: "thy nobler part . . . by ages frozen grasp possest" (1.17).

Helen Wilcox has singled out this poem for its surprising provocativeness, its tendency to draw out disagreement among its readers because "the man is rendered secondary, dependent upon the 'lady' for his identity" and for "its intriguing reversal of the obsessive itemizing attention of the female body found in much Renaissance and 17th-century English love poetry." Noting the poem's "metaphors of the natural world" and its inclination to reverse gendered associations, with the "male lover" assuming the role of "the passive earth," she wonders whether "this materialist attentiveness" is "destructive or emboldening."[30] Trauma theory can provide a less divisive choice when reading these early modern expressions of inevitable loss. It can promote recognition that these female-voiced poems allow Rochester to express a different relationship, one that does not require kingly restoration to facilitate healing or demand female objectification to make significant the experience of male wounding. In short, we can read these female-voiced poems as early modern examples of "working through." According to LaCapra in *Writing History, Writing Trauma*, accepting absence as absence—in the case of these two poems, the physical inertness of the male figure "opens up empowering possibilities in the necessarily limited, nontotalizing, and nonredemptive elaboration of institutions and practices in the creation of a more desirable, perhaps significantly different—but not perfect or totally unified—life in the here and now. Absence is in this sense inherently ambivalent, both anxiety producing and possibly empowering, or even ecstatic."[31]

Rochester's female speaker in "Song" claims "the here and now" and a love neither "perfect nor totally unified." She reframes loss as possibility, and makes "art" a handmaiden to her own desire: "And for thy Pleasure shall improve, / All that Art can add to love" (ll.23–24). Yet the ambivalence of the poem's closing line—"yet still I Love thee without Art" (l.25)—makes the practice of that art "necessarily limited, nontotaling, and nonredemptive." In this regard it echoes the ambivalence found in the opening line of "Platonick Lady: I could love thee til I die," a statement that both affirms life—and indeed a life-giving activity—even as it announces the temporality of life and the limits of our bodies. The conditional "could" in the line emphasizes both the possibility of love and the anxiety such possibility inspires. Both poems accept the wounded body of the male speaker and make the fluid nature of female pleasure a mechanism for working through rather than acting out. These enjoyments are imperfect but no less ecstatic for being so.

As I have argued elsewhere Rochester's experience with traumatic loss was not only cultural but also profoundly personal. He lost unexpectedly and suddenly two comrades with a single cannonball at the Battle of Bergen in the Second Anglo Dutch War, a war that he was pressed to join by none other than Charles II. That event continued to shape him and his work throughout his lifetime, in his final months finally naming it "the great snare of his life." It would be an injustice to his art not to acknowledge how his revisions to the imperfect enjoyment genre speak to this loss: his comrades never returned from the dead to testify to a spiritual afterlife, as they promised to, and similarly Rochester anticipates no resurrection for his male narrator in "The Imperfect Enjoyment."[32] But in these two female-voiced poems, we also see Rochester working through other possibilities for addressing material and existential loss, and when we read Behn's "The Disappointment," the only female-authored poem in the English canon of impotency poems, we must keep these other possibilities in mind.

Behn's "The Disappointment" and Acting Out

Rochester's female-voiced poems speak significantly to the poem we want Behn's "The Disappointment" to be. Rochester's emphasis on shared satisfaction and the open avowal of female pleasure mark the kind of intervention in the imperfect enjoyment genre we retrospectively anticipate in a female writer of this period. Judith Keagan Gardiner finds such a moment mid-poem and notes that Behn alters her source material to emphasize "a union that is reciprocal, passionate, and simultaneously physical and emotional," evoking a prelapsarian "garden of earthly pleasures." But this reciprocity proves temporary at best, and there is no sustained "rosy" return "to the poetry written before the English Civil War," as Gardiner further argues. Rather, almost immediately the "pleasure turn'd to pain" (viii: 3) and the poem proceeds more conventionally with the narrator giving voice to the male's full-throated expressions of blame.[33] Rather when we read "The Disappointment" in the context of the imperfect enjoyment genre and in the context of Rochester's female-voiced poems, we realize just how fixed Behn's focus remains on the experience of bodily loss, and just how traumatic her rendering of that experience. In more concrete terms we notice just how much this poem focuses on the disintegrating male body and how that body is preserved as an emblem of loss.

In part Behn takes her cue from her source material—Cantenac's "Lost Opportunity Recovered"—which she loosely translates and deeply truncates. In the French poem Lysander's body moves from "limp" and "cold," to "groveling" and "useless," and for two full stanzas draws attention to the vulnerability of the masculine form. Behn's translation borrows from these descriptors but also adds a few others, and moreover aligns them in the opposite trajectory, moving from more subjective states of psychological disability to more starkly physical ones. In stanza 10 Lysander is described as "in despair," his "nobler part" having "no spark" (x: 3, 8), but by stanza 12, when Cloris surveys the damage, his debilitated body takes the more concrete form of being "disarmed" and "cold" (xii: 3–4). Lysander goes from being unanimated to being dismembered and dead. Most tellingly Behn eliminates the last twenty-seven stanzas of Cantenac's poem, where the French Lysander becomes resuscitated and restored. Hence we could say the French poem temporarily draws attention to the debilitated male body whereas Behn's poem dwells and insists on it.

Additionally, as in the Rochester poems, Behn's Cloris functions periodically as a witness to this event, as does the female narrator throughout. As noted, it is the poem's description of his body that proves most devastating. Moreover the female narrator is far from muted, even when Lysander's wounding becomes most explicit. The poem reads: "In vain he toils, in vain Commands / The insensible fell weeping in his hand" (ix: 9–10). This line makes use of the common analogy between the limp, spent penis and the wounded body of the male figure, but it only slightly less directly references Cloris's body, which is also "insensible," at this point having fallen into a trance, and done so while in his hands. The "weeping" thus becomes an expression of her psychological loss just as it conveys his physical one, linking the physical description of his wounded temporal state to her psychological one, and to the unsettled state of her deferred desire. This point is reinforced two stanzas later when Cloris's "blushes" move from her "hinder place" to "all her face" (xii: 6, 7). The poem briefly parallels the linkages that sustain Rochester's female-voiced poems—the promise of shared satisfaction and the force of female desire—although here that linkage reinforces a persistent damage both will experience.

In fact, rather than a "working through," an acceptance of absence as absence, this poem insists on "acting out." Cloris flees, exits the poem afraid and angry, and without having named her experience of loss. Behn substitutes for that direct expression her narrator's insistence that only she can "imagine or condole" this pain, and defers its naming by focusing instead on Lysander's debilitated state and abruptly ending the poem. Thus, any knowledge of Cloris's pain becomes "belated," and any grieving remains the province of our female narrator. Behn substitutes for a clear statement of the woman's pain its absence along with a final reminder that this unnamed pain will not soon go away. She abruptly ends the poem at an "impasse," in the way LaCapra describes the "arrested state of melancholia" or the psychological response of "acting out."

The poem's final refusal to describe the woman's emotional state also makes apparent earlier aborted attempts to name the nymph's experience; we realize this final statement repeats previously deferred expressions of loss. For example, soon after Cloris witnesses Lysander's spent body, the narrator asks: "Who can the nymph's confusion guess?" (xii: 5). The question establishes early on Cloris's emotional state as one she does not fully understand and cannot assimilate. The question also draws attention to the reader's gap in knowledge, and indirectly to a genre that has traditionally excluded women from the express experience of loss or the possibility of trauma. Behn reframes

Cloris's story of personal disappointment as "a crisis of representation, of history and truth" as Luckhurst describes the trauma narrative and even of "narrative time"—another of the crises the "belatedness" of naming provokes. The question becomes extratextual, referring to representations of male impotency and female silence that preceded this one, and those that will surely follow. Indeed, Behn's poem foregrounds a double mediation: Cloris's witnessing of Lysander's trauma and the female narrator's witnessing of Cloris's. Both mediations, however, draw attention to the woman's trauma, and substitute for Cloris's wounding because already wounded body—the traditional symbolic function of the female in the genre—his wounded, and newly re-imagined as symbolically wounding, body. Why else would Cloris need to "withdraw her hand" so quickly when she finds him "disarmed of all his powerful fires / And cold as flowers bathed in the morning dew" (xii: 3–4)? His body wounds, disrupts. The poem belatedly creates a space for naming female pleasure by granting Cloris the possibility of being rendered "insensible" and of wanting to distance herself from the direct knowledge of loss. As readers we experience the "lesser," and lesser only because not readily recognized, trauma of female impotence, or denied pleasure.

Interestingly, however, this reading of the poem most unambiguously locates trauma for the female when she encounters Lysander's disabled body and recoils from its touch and not when he "surprises" her with all his "vigor" at the beginning of the poem, a "surprise" that in the original French version clearly takes the form of sexual assault. The poem, then, reframes historical trauma—a loss that "can conceivably be avoided," or the very real trauma of assault—as a structural one, a constitutive loss that grants Cloris desire.[34] Cloris's trauma is that her desire is culturally unrecognized, and hence her consent irrelevant. In fact the poem initially presents naming that desire as the problem, the crisis in representation. Cloris "permits his force, yet gently strove" the narrator observes (iv: 4). Or a few lines later, she turns that confusion into an assertion: "She wants the power to say—Ah! what d'ye do?" (ii:10). Moreover, when Cloris's psychological state is finally referenced at the end of the poem, it takes a mythic form. Lysander's body becomes a proverbial "snake" hid among the "verdant" leaves (xi: 10). Thus, Cloris when she flees evokes both an Eve in exile and, through her flight, the "traumatized self" of many an Ovidian nymph before her. The difference here, however, is that Cloris flees the scene physically unscathed and thus unable to serve "as a tableau of the traumatic effects of violence." Nor does her flight reference her beauty, and unlike Ovid's *Amore 3.7*, no male erection accompanies the female's hurried departure. The abrupt conclusion makes inaccessible and irrecoverable the woman's experience; it becomes a gap, an aporia, in the text that paradoxically makes knowable or at least theoretically nameable Cloris's wounding.

It also means we, as readers, do not get the catharsis or "working through" we hope for at the beginning. Instead the poem concludes with what can look more like a "narcissistic identif[ication]with the lost object"—another marker of melancholia or "acting out."[35] It ends with a focus on *his* wounded body and leaves unspoken her unreciprocated desire. Yet it is this structural trauma as evinced through "acting out" that makes the female figure human, capable of disappointment in this poem, or as the narrator renames it in the final stanza, "resentments." Meaning "ill will caused by injury" or etymologically a "memory of injury," the reframing allows us to return to the narrator's previous questions and at least imagine an answer to questions of agency and consent, but only after establishing first the structural trauma of her desire. Only after framing her desire as a constitutive loss can we recognize the historical trauma of assault—can we name physical or sexual contact as unwanted. In all previous iterations of the genre, such a possibility is not considered, and sudden and unexpected loss can only trouble the male. Behn, like Rochester, reverses the blazon and makes central the female figure and her desire, but unlike him, defers voicing it and instead makes that delay the key point. Corinna's trauma, we can say, no longer functions as mere hyperbole, although Cloris's remains disappointingly unspecified.

Rather the poem ends with a fleeting acknowledgment of the woman's psychological pain and with the man's continuing physical debilitation. It refuses the narrative of recovery prescribed by the impotency poem and does so decisively. Lysander's body remains unrecovered, Cloris's psychological loss pointedly unnamed, and restoration, even during a period that celebrates a cultural Restoration, becomes simply unimaginable. Yet it becomes possible for a woman to "act out," to protest when her desire goes unacknowledged, and not simply reflect a wounding presumed only to be his. Suffering is shared, disappointments mutually traumatic.

Oroonoko *and Working through Historical Trauma*

Identifying trauma in "The Disappointment" can also expose trauma in *Oroonoko*, a narrative where a female narrator testifies to the horrific impact of the brutal execution of an enslaved African prince. For if we read this poem as an example of "acting out," it makes available *Oroonoko* as one of "working through." As Ramesh Mallipeddi describes it, "Documenting [Oroonoko's] tragedy becomes a form of deferred action."[36] Acknowledging the repetition in this work further reframes Behn's choices as neither theoretical nor aesthetic, but instead compulsory. By her own account Behn experienced Oroonoko's death as a personal, even visceral, loss. In the novella's opening paragraphs Behn's narrator makes firsthand knowledge of Oroonoko's story and a closeness with its protagonist key to the text's effect, claiming to learn directly from Oroonoko the parts of his story that she was not an "eye-witness to" herself (75). The biographical record gives this standard claim greater weight: Behn traveled to Surinam in the early 1660s, when it was an English and not a Dutch colony, and many of its personages and notable events correspond with factual accounts. Unquestionably, Behn wants her readers to treat the story of Oroonoko as an event her narrator experienced, and fellow playwright Thomas Southerne's comments suggest her contemporaries treated it as an event Behn herself experienced. He reports that Behn "always told [Oroonoko's] story more feelingly than she writ it" and speculates that she resisted writing it down because the actual experience proved so difficult to capture: "She thought either that no actor could represent him, or she could not bear him represented." Thus, it is only in her final year, while in declining health and writing with a lame hand, that Behn ultimately pens the narrative.[37] Such a delay indicates that recounting the story proved complicated—even "unbearable"—that its events may have been hard to assimilate and difficult to name.[38] The final circumstances of Oroonoko's death are depicted as abrupt and unexpected, and if true, Behn's memory of that event would have been likely wounding, even traumatic.

"The Disappointment" itself speaks to how powerful such a memory may have proved, and points to a possible "dynamic transfer" between this work and her later novella. Some twenty years after the death of a royal slave, Behn confronts images reminiscent of his physical dissolution in a French imperfect enjoyment poem. Translating that poem, she dramatically abbreviates it and instead abruptly ends her translation by pointing to a loss that only her narrator can imagine. And unlike the original poem, that adaptation does not conclude with the restoration of its male protagonist's virility, but rather with the persistent image of his debilitated, "lifeless" body and the unaccountable despair of a fleeing female. Some six years after the publication of this poem, *Oroonoko* will conclude with the memory of a dismembered, lifeless male form and just prior to that image a fleeing female who "journey[s] down the river" fearful of succumbing to a "fit" of "extraordinary melancholy" (139).[39] That same narrator, however, in what can be described as a final, disassociative shift in the text, witnesses via the reports of her mother and sister the devastating and premature death of its once princely hero, and indirectly attests to the significance of his individual loss. The language of her translation of the poem, in turn, emphasizes the brutality of that bodily loss and ends with the image of this divine-like figure "cold" and, most tellingly, "disarmed." In the poem the narrator and the female protagonist both directly witness the debilitated male form, and no consolation is offered. One text can read like the repetition of the other, each modifying, even correcting, the other's gaps.

Indeed, the similarities between *Oroonoko*'s ending and that of "The Disappointment" suggest that not just Cloris or the narrator in "The Disappointment" is acting out, but that Behn herself may be as well. In "The Disappointment" Behn remembers her traumatic loss as she translates a staged reenactment of bodily loss and psychological pain. She breaks off the poem abruptly in a belated yet not fully assimilated testimony to the effect of Oroonoko's unexpected death. She then returns to this same pattern in her final novel, when she retells, finally, that horrific story. Yet this time she does not appear to be "acting out" but rather "working through" that event. As Mallipeddi observes, Behn's narrator experiences a "vicarious suffering, made possible by her capacity for suffering." Witnessing his "tortured body" provokes her own "bodily suffering," and remembering Oroonoko becomes "a personal tragedy and, the writing of his history, an ethical responsibility."[40] Acknowledging the repetition between these two works underscores how scarring this tragedy is and how far from abstract Oroonoko's death. His physical loss becomes a concrete, temporal limit that narrative cannot erase or reframe as "redemptive." It becomes instead a wound that our narrator must acknowledge, and the reader "vicariously" experience.[41]

That the death proves hard to assimilate manifests in how frequently Oroonoko appears to die in this novel: it's not just the execution at the end or the whipping that follows from the initial rebellion but also a pre-execution attempt to end his own life, that have striking similarities to the imperfect enjoyment poem. We find Behn returning to old themes here, even reminding us of secondary female trauma, here no longer in the abstract. Not long after his capture, Oroonoko and Imoinda escape to "a wood" where they intend to "die" together rather than return to an enslaved state: first Oroonoko will kill Imoinda and then himself (135). "Die" is meant literally in this scene, but our narrator evokes as well its metaphorical association with sexual climax. She describes Oroonoko prior to Imoinda's death as "embracing her, with all the passion and languishment of a dying lover" (135). Imoinda, in turn, "lays herself down, before the sacrificer" (136) just as Cloris's body in "The Disappointment" becomes the "altar seized / Where gods of love do sacrifice" (v: 5–6). This repetition takes a scene that would otherwise only appear horrid—unspeakable in the suffering it describes—and reframes it as a familiar scene of intimacy. It even renders the hard-to-fathom motives of Imoinda to accept such a "death" knowable to the narrator: "for wives have a respect for their husbands equal to what any other people pay a deity; and when a man finds any occasion to quit his wife, if he loves her, she dies by his hand" (136). This line foregrounds the presence of Imoinda's desire. Behn wants her reader to see that Imoinda consents to this "death"—even experiences a form of satisfaction in its completion—and that her agency is manifest in a scene where we assume its negation. Thus, even as Behn acknowledges how abrupt and unexpected Imoinda's death is, she underscores Imoinda's humanity, much as she asserted Cloris's when she first addressed this question of consent in "The Disappointment."

By contrast Oroonoko proves unable to act, rendered figuratively impotent when confronted with the fact of Imoinda's death. Just as Lysander sees a Cloris "with no signs of life" and proves unable to "perform the sacrifice,"

Oroonoko sees Imoinda dead and cannot kill himself. He responds as one traumatized, and his reaction parallels that of Lysander: "his grief swelled up to rage; he tore, he raved, he roared" (136). He seems to act prematurely, and although he initially plans on revenge, before long, all he can do is acknowledge how deeply he feels her death and how limited the possibilities for restoration: "he had not power to stir from the sight of this dear object, now more beloved, and more adored than ever" (136). However, rather than recoiling from this scene, Behn, in this work, lingers here. Oroonoko's execution takes one paragraph; the description of Imoinda's death and Oroonoko's disabling response requires four. Moreover the tone of these extended paragraphs is more akin to Rochester's female-voiced poems of male impotence than Behn's "The Disappointment." As in Rochester's poems, the female narrator in this scene hovers lovingly over the figure of the vulnerable, spent male body, and advises her reader to view these events as deserving of compassion rather than blame. Her Oroonoko may no longer assume the form of a classic hero—a prototype to be mourned as representative of manliness or Roman *virtus*—but in exchange he also becomes profoundly human. In this tragic scene of "imperfect enjoyment" and aborted death, Behn seems to finally accept the physical limits and temporal nature of Oroonoko's body, his body serving as a literal blazon to his dissolution, as he tears from his flesh parts others would seek to claim.[42]

Accordingly, her novella ends with no kingly restoration: Oroonoko will not recover nor be returned to his royal status or to his native land. In this reenactment of loss Behn will instead "wreathe [Oroonoko's] body" in her narrative arms, much like Rochester's female narrator in "The Platonick Lady." She will reframe the death and loss of Oroonoko as possibility and remind the reader of the value of the limited, temporal body, of life in the here and now, and just how much is lost when even one body is abruptly taken. Revisiting her trauma and more significantly his, she will refuse yet again a cultural and literary expectation of miraculous recovery, but this time she will "work it through." She will use the "reputation of her pen" to speak the name of her loss and to make that "name survive all ages," along with that of "the brave, the beautiful, and the constant Imoinda" (140–41).

NOTES

1. For a discussion of the false attribution of this poem to Rochester, see Bruce Thomas Boehrer, "Behn's 'Disappointment,' and Nashe's 'Choise of Valentines': Pornographic Poetry and the Influence of Anxiety," *Essays in Literature* 16, no. 2 (Fall 1989): 172–89. Also see Jim McGhee, "Obscene Libel and 'The Imperfect Enjoyment,'" in *Reading Rochester*, ed. Edward Burns, [42–65] (New York: St. Martin's Press, 1995), esp. 59n.
2. Judith Gardiner, "Liberty, Equality, Fraternity: Utopian Longings in Behn's Lyric Poetry," in *Rereading Aphra Behn: History, Theory, and Criticism*, ed. Heidi Hutner [273–300] (Charlottesville: University of Virginia Press, 1993), esp. 33. For other readings emphasizing female recovery and liberation, see Lisa M. Zeitz and Peter Thomas, "Power, Gender, and Identity in Aphra Behn's 'The Disappointment,'" *Studies in English Literature* 37 (1997): 501–16, and Dorothy Mermin, "Women Becoming Poets: Katherine Phillipps, Aphra Behn, and Anne Finch," *ELH* 57, no. 2 (Summer 1990): 335–55. For a discussion of Rochester's misogyny see Stephan Clark, "'Something Genrous in Meer Lust'? Rochester and Misogyny," in Burns, *Reading Rochester*, 21–41.
3. John Wilmot, Earl of Rochester, "The Imperfect Enjoyment," l.18, in *Selected Poems*, ed. Paul Davis, [39–41] (Oxford, UK: Oxford University Press, 2013). All references are to this edition.
4. Aphra Behn, "The Disappointment," in *Oroonoko, The Rover, and Other Works*, ed. Janet Todd, [331–335] (London: Penguin, 1992), esp. xiii: 10. All references are to this edition.
5. John Wilmot, Earl of Rochester, "The Platonick Lady" and "Young Lady to her Ancient Lover," in Davis, *Selected Poems*. All references are to this edition. In "Something Genrous in Meer Lust," Stephan Clark places Rochester's "refusal of a culturally endorsed mastery" (39) within "the libertine ideal of mutually reciprocated desire" (23).
6. Dominick LaCapra, *Writing History, Writing Trauma* (Baltimore: Johns Hopkins University Press, 2001, 2014), 66.
7. See Roger Luckhurst, *The Trauma Question* (New York: Routledge, 2008), and Ruth Leys, *Trauma: A Genealogy* (Chicago: University of Chicago Press, 2000), for two genealogies of trauma that detail these various origins.
8. See Cynthia Marshall, *The Shattering of the Self: Violence, Subjectivity, and Early Modern Texts* (Baltimore: Johns Hopkins University Press, 2002), for an authoritative account of this emergence.
9. Judith Pollmann, *Memory in Early Modern Europe, 1500–1800* (Oxford, UK: Oxford University Press, 2018), 47, 48.
10. Michael Rothberg, *Multidirectional Memory: Remembering the Holocaust in the Age of Decolonization* (Stanford: Stanford University Press, 2009), 13.

11. Behn, "The Disappointment," in Todd, *Oroonoko, The Rover, and Other Works*. All references are to this edition.

12. In *Scenes of Subjection, Terror, Slavery, and Self-Making in Nineteenth-Century America* (Oxford, UK: Oxford University Press, 1997), Saidiya V. Hartman "call[s] attention to the ease with which such scenes are usually reiterated, the casualness with which they are circulated, and the consequences of this routine display of the slave's ravaged body" (3).

13. Ramesh Mallipeddi, *Spectacular Suffering: Witnessing Suffering in the Eighteenth-Century British Atlantic* (Charlottesville: University of Virginia Press, 2016), 45, 46.

14. George Etheredge, "Imperfect Enjoyment" (1672), in *The Poems of Sir George Etheredge*, ed. James Thorpe, [7–9] (Princeton: Princeton University Press, 1963); Anon., "The Lost Opportunity Recovered," in *Wit and Drollery* [1–16] (London, 1682); Anon., "Fruition was the Question in Debate," entitled "Imperfect Enjoyment," in *A New Collection of Poems and Songs*, [23-25] (London, 1664). See Richard Quaintance, "French Sources of the Restoration 'Imperfect' Poem," *Philological Quarterly* 42, no. 2 (Spring 1963): 190–99, for a discussion of the five French poems and the five English imperfect enjoyment poems that appeared between 1577–1682.

15. Ovid, *Amore 3.7*, in *The Love Books of Ovid*, trans. and ed. J. Lewis May (1930), accessed July 2020, http://www.sacred-texts.com/cla/ovid/lboo, book 3, elegy 7. This is a prose translation, with no line breaks. References are to this edition.

16. Cathy Caruth, *Unclaimed Experience: Trauma, Narrative, and History* (Baltimore: Johns Hopkins University Press, 1996), 4.

17. Leo Braudy, "Remembering Masculinity: Premature Ejaculation Poetry of the Seventeenth Century," *Michigan Quarterly Review* 33, no. 1 (Winter 1994): 181.

18. Thomas Nashe, "The Choise of Valentines" (1592), in *The Works of Thomas Nashe*, 5 vols., ed. R. B. McKerrow, [v. 3, 397-402] (London: A. H. Bullen, 1905).

19. Benech de Cantenac,. "L'Occasion Perdue Recoverte," in *Poesies Nouvelles et autres oeuvres galantes de monsieur de C.*, [1-12] (Paris: T. Girard, 1662).

20. Luckhurst, *The Trauma Question*, 5.

21. McGhee, "Obscene Libel," 59n. The information that I am citing is found in the note and not in the body of the essay. It is in the note that McGhee mentions that attribution of this poem remains unsettled n 1714.

22. Hannah Lavery, *The Impotency Poem from Ancient Latin to Restoration English Literature* (Burlington VT: Ashgate, 2014), 110–11.

23. Erin Peters, *Commemoration and Oblivion in Royalist Print Culture, 1658–1667* (New York: Palgrave Macmillan, 2017), 23.

24. Lisa Starks-Estes, *Violence, Trauma, and* Virtus *in Shakespeare's Roman Poems and Plays: Transforming Ovid* (New York: Palgrave MacMillan, 2014), 69.

25. Melinda Rabb, "Parting Shots: Eighteenth-Century Displacement of the Male Body at War," ELH 78, no. 1 (Spring 2011): 109.

26. Marshall, *The Shattering of the Self*, 5, 9.
27. Starks-Estes, *Violence, Trauma, and* Virtus, 83.
28. Linda Enterline, *The Rhetoric of the Body from Ovid to Shakespeare* (Cambridge, UK: Cambridge University Press, 2000), 8, 33. Marshall argues that Lavinia "serves as the site of others' emotion" and the "male characters" treat "uncannily her mutilation as their own" (108).
29. Etheredge, "Imperfect Enjoyment," in Thorpe, *The Poems of Sir George Etheredge*, ll.39–40.
30. Helen Wilcox, "Gender and Artfulness in Rochester's 'Song of a Young Lady to Her Ancient Lover,'" in *Reading Rochester*, ed. Edward Burns (New York: St. Martin's, 1990), esp.10.
31. LaCapra, *Writing History, Writing Trauma*, 58.
32. Cynthia Richards, "Wit at War: The Poetry of John Wilmot and the Trauma of War," *Eighteenth-Century Fiction* 27, no. 1 (Fall 2014): 25–54.
33. Gardiner, "Liberty, Equality, Fraternity," in Hutner, *Rereading Aphra Behn*, 279.
34. LaCapra, *Writing History, Writing Trauma*, 65. LaCapra distinguishes "historical losses" from "structural" ones. "Historical losses can conceivably be avoided, or when they occur, at least in part compensated for, worked through, or even to some extent overcome" (65). But contrast, "structural trauma (absence) is not an event but an anxiety-producing condition of possibility related to the potential for historical traumatization" (82).
35. LaCapra, 66.
36. Mallipeddi, *Spectacular Suffering*, 46.
37. See Janet Todd, *The Secret Life of Aphra Behn* (London: Pandora, 2000), 417–18. For a succinct recitation of what the biographical record reveals, see Mary O'Donnell, "Aphra Behn: The Documentary Record," in *The Cambridge Companion to Aphra Behn*, ed. D. Hughes and J. Todd, 1–11 (Cambridge, UK: Cambridge University Press, 2004), 1–11. O'Donnell notes that "there is independent documentation of the Surinam stay" (2).
38. Caruth describes trauma narratives as recording the "oscillation . . . between the story of the unbearable nature of the event and the unbearable nature of its survival" (7).
39. In *Oroonoko* the female narrator's flight bespeaks her privilege as a free woman and Oroonoko's dissolution operates as a sign of his enslavement, inverting the power differential in "The Disappointment."
40. Mallipeddi, *Spectacular Suffering*, 45, 46.
41. Mallipeddi, 46.
42. This reading of *Oroonoko* associates it with what Ian Baucom calls "melancholy realism," a "realism whose key unit is neither the type or the average but the sentimental, romantic, or melancholy case, scene or fact" (220), Ian Baucom, *Specters of the Atlantic: Finance Capital, Slavery, and the Philosophy of History* (Durham NC: Duke University Press, 2005).

11

Cultural Trauma, Exile, and the Birth of Jacobitism

ERIN PETERS

The Glorious Revolution, "one of the most unsettling events since the Reformation," prompted James II's move into French exile on December 23, 1688, and saw the birth of a popular movement that lasted well into the following century.[1] This important event, which has been largely overshadowed in terms of historical attention paid, by the mid-century civil wars and the later revolutions in France and America, had significant long-term consequences for the future of the British Isles. At the moment of its occurrence, however, the more immediate consequences were clear to all: the Glorious Revolution marked the second time during the seventeenth century that a Stuart monarch was deposed and the royal line of succession was interrupted. Although this "act of war against James II" certainly had the capacity to invoke comparisons with the regime change of the 1640s and the cultural trauma of the civil wars, the popular, and enduring, rhetoric of this event as a bloodless revolution seems to suggest an absence of collective suffering.[2] And yet the ousting of James in 1688–89 gave rise to a counter movement that lasted for over one hundred years and inspired two significant rebellions many decades after its birth: Jacobitism.

Described as an "enigmatic cult" by historian Paul Monod, James's followers could be found across the social spectrum—some enjoyed significant wealth while others suffered destitution—but these early Jacobites shared one overarching goal: the restoration of their king to the thrones of England, Scotland, and Ireland.[3] Moreover the most loyal Jacobites followed their king into exile: between 1689 and 1715 Europe saw a significant influx of exiles, individuals and whole families, Catholics and Protestants, who settled in France, Italy, and Spain. Daniel Szechi has described this mass exile as a diaspora deliberately to evoke a comparison with the expulsion of the Jews from the Holy Land, there to await a messiah to restore them. He explains that the Jacobites, too, "lost their homeland to infidels, and they too languished in exile awaiting a redeemer."[4] Exile and the cultural trauma associated with it were thus the precondition for the birth of Jacobitism, and the nature of the changes that took place in 1688–89—rapid, disruptive, and comprehensive—combined with cultural memories of recent past conflict and violence, is at the very core of early Jacobite identities and can be described as traumatogenic. This is because, rather than conceptualizing these changes as a "discourse of progress" or a "discourse of crisis," examining early Jacobite rhetoric reveals another applicable perspective: a "discourse of trauma," which suggests that certain types of change "may have adverse effects, bring shocks and wounds to the social and cultural tissue," and shifts the focus from critiquing the specific form of change to recognizing "the disturbing, destructive, shocking effects of change per se."[5]

Defining Jacobitism has been a source of discussion and controversy among historians since scholarly interest in this movement developed in the 1970s. Because of its treasonous nature, not much in the way of source material has survived, making it difficult to estimate how widespread sympathies for the exiled Stuarts and their supporters was. Furthermore, examining what evidence is available does not necessarily provide an accurate picture of a Jacobite, as there may have been those who were sympathetic without being active in the cause or perhaps those who could more accurately be defined as anti-William rather than pro-James.[6] Different ideas about how to identify and recognize a Jacobite combined with limited surviving evidence and evolving ideologies over the decades that followed the events of 1689 have led to discussions about the movement's significance. That said, it has been possible to detect a very wide range of commitment among a wide variety of supporters of the movement, and while "nobody lived every aspect of their lives as a Jacobite" and both those who remained in the British Isles and those who left it "were integrated into the social and economic milieu of their localities," Jacobites were both insiders and outsiders.[7] Whatever their level of commitment or coherence, their political outlook was risky and the "dissident and hazardous nature of Jacobitism should never be forgotten."[8] It challenged the newly emerging notion of a united national British identity and was, itself, an "enduring, dynamic community" preoccupied with resistance to the change in regime and subsequent change in cultural and national identity it inevitably engendered.[9]

While the nomenclature of "glorious" suggests an absence of violence and destruction, the experience of exile, extensive sociopolitical and cultural change, and memories of the recent civil wars influenced how those who supported the Stuart monarchy could conceptualize this event in the immediate period of its occurrence. If, as Judith Pollmann has argued, "memories of one atrocity could come to shape the narrating, memory, and perhaps even the experience of another," then the evidence presented in this chapter will serve to demonstrate that memories of past atrocities could also shape the ways in which the predicted consequences of current distressing events could be fashioned.[10] In what follows I shall explore specific examples of early Jacobite expressions of this experience, and ultimately I will suggest that these expressions can be read as evidence that the significant levels of wide-reaching change were culturally traumatic, tinged as they were with recourse to memories of past episodes of cultural trauma, and that this was a key component of early Jacobite identities. However, before exploring specific examples it is necessary to frame conceptually how we might understand and meaningfully analyze collective experiences of large-scale traumatogenic change in the period and how we can locate expressions of cultural trauma within these texts.

Major social change in post-conflict cultures often incurs critical social costs; however, it would be a considerable oversimplification to claim that social change induces trauma. Rather, for an apposite diagnosis of cultural trauma to be applicable, there are three broad and overlapping requirements: a specific type of sociocultural change, occurring at a particular moment in time, and manifesting in precise ways. Sociologist Piotr Sztompka, known for his research on contemporary cultures that have undergone vast social change, has provided a list of traits to identify a society that has endured the levels of change that can be perceived to be traumatogenic.[11] First, the change must be sudden and rapid, occurring within a relatively short span of time. The second trait has to do with the scope of change. It is wide and comprehensive. More specifically, "Revolution is a good example of traumatogenic social change because it usually embraces not only the political domain . . . it also affects the fate of many groups, if not all the population." The third trait of traumatogenic change is that it is radical, deep, and fundamental, for example, a transfer of political power or change in regime. The final trait is change that is unexpected or shocking. In his study of traumatogenic changes and the subsequent cultural trauma they induce, Sztompka specifically lists foreign conquest, breakdown of the political regime, and revolution as the examples of changes meeting the description.[12] That the events of 1688–89 were a period of unsettling change, and one that would certainly alter the direction of the future of the nation, was, of course, immediately recognized and anxiously acknowledged by contemporaries on all sides of the sociopolitical and religious divide. For example, an anonymous 1689 pamphlet titled *Reflections Upon our Late and Present Proceedings in England* worries, "What we do now, will transmit its good or ill effects to after-Ages; and our Children yet unborn, will, in all probability, be happy or miserable, as we shall behave our selves in this great Conjuncture."[13] Furthermore, as Tim Harris has noted, "when the seventeenth century English invoked the term 'revolution' in a political context . . . most typically they used the word to designate a sudden and dramatic change."[14] Thus, even as events were unfolding in 1689, contemporaries were publicly recognizing them as a pivotal moment. Applying Sztompka's definitions as an analytical lens through which to read early Jacobite texts reveals that, while they are often highly polemical in scope, the impulse at the foundation of what became the Jacobite movement was also a reaction to the scale of change.

Before turning to some textual examples, a final caveat is required. While historians debate the extent to which the Glorious Revolution can be considered a foreign conquest or a revolution, and what the criteria and definitions for identifying a Jacobite should or could be, a basic defining feature is simply a person who supported the Stuart claim, at whatever level.[15] While this support might not necessarily result from loyal devotion to the House of Stuart but, and perhaps more likely, from a sense of disillusionment with political developments over the previous few decades, or with the costs and consequences of the later Williamite wars, it is important to make this broad definition because it is one that contemporaries would have recognized. This contemporary recognition, even in such broad terms, is crucial because truly collective traumas "appear only when people start to be aware of the common plight, perceive the similarities of their situation with that of others, define it as shared. They start to talk about it, exchange observations and experiences, gossip and rumors, formulate diagnoses and myths, identify causes or villains, look for conspiracies, decide to do something about it, envisage coping mechanism."[16] Once this point is reached, and even if those definitions come from those who oppose the movement rather than those who adhere to it, the expression of cultural trauma can acquire more tangible forms (for example, "forming of groups, collective mobilization, creating social movements, associations") that can then be reproduced in narratives that give sense to the shared experience.[17] While what is potentially traumatizing on a cultural level certainly differs among various societies at various times, regardless of the culture or period in question the condition always requires some form of acknowledgment, framing, or defining. These interpretive efforts are drawn from a preexisting pool of available cultural references and meanings encoded in the shared culture of the society. Members of that society draw selectively from their shared culture to apply recognizable meaning to traumatic events.[18]

Thus, for the purposes of this chapter, whether James and his followers were forced into exile or fled in abdication is less important. Instead the focus is on how early Jacobites conceptualized and expressed their condition and the experience of change that can be described, according to Sztompka's identifying traits, as traumatogenic. In their own eyes they were exiles and suffered under that condition, both those who left their homeland and those who endured political and cultural marginalization under hostile domestic regimes.[19] This is because, in addition to physical dislocation, exile can also be "a state of mind not linked solely to migration."[20] While the Jacobite experience of exile is often associated with those "who fled to the Continent in 1688–9 and after were physically cut off from their roots and formed a visible community of exiles," Jacobitism was equally characterized by the ideological and emotional exclusion of "those who remained in the British Isles . . . and had to adapt themselves once more to living among people who neither knew nor cared for the cause."[21] In his broad survey of seventeenth-century experiences of exile, Christopher D'Addario identifies "interior" or "internal" exiles as a distinct group of sufferers.[22] As such, the experience of exile, whether as exclusion or expulsion, had the capacity to shape the political perceptions of the nation as a whole. Philip Major reminds us that exile also had a personal psychological impact, associated as it was with defeat, and points to evidence of the poignant "human responses to dislocation and dispossession."[23] Taking a slightly different approach, Giovanni Tarantino and Charles Zika underscore the emotional strategies used to cope with the trauma of exile "in the shadow of immense political and religious upheaval." Discussing the mental scars that seventeenth-century experiences of exile could inflict, Major points to Edward Said's description of exile: "It is the unhealable rift forced between a human being and a native place, between the self and its true home: its essential sadness can never be surmounted."[24] Major suggests that cautiously applying modern scholarship on the experience of exile, which has significantly enriched our current understanding of the psychological effects of displacement, to the experience of exile in the seventeenth century can "open up exciting possibilities for psychological and sociological comparative analysis."[25] Tarantino and Zika similarly suggest that adopting the methods and insights derived from the history of emotions can serve to integrate critical human dimensions into well-established stories from the early modern period. Doing so through a lens of cultural trauma analysis further opens the possibilities of reading the narrative of the Glorious Revolution and early Jacobite writings in a way that works to reveal a fuller landscape of its history.

The traumatic impact of exile—physical, ideological, or emotional—and, in this particular instance, its connection to recent events of the mid-century in the British Isles, was not lost on contemporary commentators: in 1705 the well-known propagandist and Dissenter Daniel Defoe offered the following conceptualization of the respective fates of Charles I and James II in response to High Church characterizations of religious nonconformity as a threat to church and state:

> To move the Gentlemen of the Church of England, to look back upon the Actions of these People [Dissenters], who they say, would pull down the Church. A Virulent and pretended Political Paper, I am Told has been Harping on the old String; that these People must be Dangerous to the

Church, because they Inherit the Old Principles of those, who once pull'd down the Church. . . .

If he means they are of the same Principle, in taking up Arms; &c. . . . The Balance, between 41 and 89 will appear to run against him and the difference between the dry Martyrdom of King James, by his Passive-Obedience, Church Subjects; and the wet Martyrdom of King Charles I by People that never made any such Pretence.[26]

Unable and unwilling to deny that the Dissenters' Puritan ancestors were responsible for the execution of Charles I, Defoe's counterargument pivots on a comparison of the severity of the royal father's and son's different treatments. His conclusion is perhaps surprising: James's suffering was greater than that inflicted on his father, because, unlike the Puritans, who were open and honest in their ideological and legal resistance to Charles, Anglican Churchmen had sworn unwavering allegiance to James as part of their doctrine of passive obedience, only then to betray him and inflict the "dry martyrdom" of foreign exile on him.[27] In Defoe's assessment the psychological dimension of the different fates comes to the fore: James had not only lost the crown due to Anglican subterfuge; he also had been forced to continue his earthly life in perpetual displacement and in the knowledge of his subject's underhand betrayal. From a wider perspective, the succession of William of Orange eventually moved the nation away from James II's isolationist, introspective stance and into a large-scale European war over the balance of power between major European dynasties. Indeed, the nation was at war for twenty-one of the twenty-five remaining years of Stuart rule. While the long-term result would be a transformation of the kingdom into a major world power, an immediate consequence was a prolonged period of political volatility that saw the revival of propaganda about the events of the 1640s in an effort to frame the view of the 1690s. With this in mind, to James and his supporters the awareness of his subjects' betrayal and his extended exile was regarded as more cruel and as causing more severe suffering than his father's violent end. In fact, the reaction to the trial and execution of Charles I in Europe had been "half-hearted irrelevance."[28] The conceptualization of the ousted king's "dry martyrdom" as severe psychological trauma, as an insufferable fate worse than physical execution, evidently struck a chord with those who had witnessed what has come to be termed the Glorious Revolution and its aftermath: Defoe's phrase even found a place in a House of Common's debate in 1710, further demonstrating the polemical uses of recalling past occurrences of cultural trauma to conceptualize and draw connections between a present situation and, more specifically, demonstrating the malleability of the past when it comes to fashioning a discourse of collective trauma. From this perspective, recognizing the events of the Glorious Revolution and its consequences as an extension of the post-conflict period after the civil wars, as well as a post-conflict period in its own right, is justified.[29]

Earlier publications were also drawing comparisons between the martyrdom of the father and that of his son. A 1699 publication by non-juror Bishop Thomas Ken, addressed to James, asserts that he was "the Heir not only of your Royal Father's Crown, but of his Afflictions and Sufferings; Exerting the like Constancy and Courage under them, as that Blessed Martyr did."[30] That James was now cast in the role of afflicted heir of his father, both "to his Suff'rings and his Throne," allowed his supporters to similarly be considered as victims of the heirs of "the same Disloyall Brood" who "did shed my Fathers sacred Blood."[31] Again what emerges here, in early Jacobite rhetoric and conceptualization of the removal of their king, is a direct paralleling of a well-known episode of inherited, or perhaps lingering, cultural shock and rupture that was deliberately superimposed upon a present situation in order to imbue it with the same value. This connection to the recent past was not only picked up by those who supported the newly displaced king. Writers who supported the revolution were also careful to draw comparisons and issue warnings about recognizing the similarity of experience between Charles I and James II, and to stress how the removal of the latter might easily be argued as the greater rebellion. For example, as early as 1689 political philosopher John Toland published a pamphlet in which he argued against the notion that Charles I was a martyr and argued for the removal of the observation of January 30 as a day of national atonement for the execution of the king because "the keeping of that day, furnisheth the *Jacobites* with a mighty Argument against the late happy and glorious revolution; for they argue thus. Since by Act of Parliament, the opposers of King *Charles* the First, who acted by authority of Parliament (mark that) are branded as Rebels, &c. how much more are they Rebels, that against their own Principles of *Passive Obedience* and *Non Resistance*, turned out their *Jure divino* King, the late Tyrant *James*."[32] As this warning highlights, in the early stages of fashioning a movement the loyal supporters of the Stuart cause were constructing an identity that positioned them as the heirs of the Royalists of '41, to suffer exile for a righteous cause along with their own martyr king. On the other hand, trauma appropriation appears to be precisely what the supporters of the revolution were concerned about when it came to depicting current events.

Just like Charles I and his Cavaliers, James II and his Jacobite supporters had suffered military and political defeat, and these defeats translated into a loss of freedom and a change of circumstance that was sudden and rapid. While Charles I had suffered loss of life, his son had lost all but his life. James himself, on the eve of his departure from Rochester on December 22, 1688, considered the fate that awaited both him and the nation he was leaving behind as a form of "slavery" and particularly "grievous especially to such as love their own country." James, of course, had suffered exile from his native lands before, and so his description of the slavery of exile is, to a certain extent, based on his previous experience. He highlights this fact by claiming that "the world cannot wonder at my withdrawing myself now this second time."[33] It is worth noting the congruence of the narrative framework of enslavement to describe the condition and experience of exile, and the rise of the transatlantic slave trade in England during the Restoration. In 1672 James himself had been influential in establishing the Royal African Company, which would control all English trading of enslaved Africans. Comparing the experience of exile with slavery can also be understood as a strategic redeployment of Whiggish arguments concerning the loss of liberties, as well as a reference to the culturally accepted connection between popery and slavery. With this in mind, the language being used to describe the experience combines historical, political, and biblical components.

Equating exile to a form of slavery, or captivity for those internal exiles, occurs in other early Jacobite publications as well, and demonstrates one way in which the experience of traumatogenic change in this early period of the movement was already being conceived. Thomas Ken's Jacobite pamphlet from

1699 explains that God "can soon put a Period to the Madness of the People, and bring us back from our Captivity."[34] Similarly, an anonymous poem makes the comparison between the suffering of exile and damage done to the body by appropriating James's voice to exclaim, "Where shall I go? Where shall I flye? . . . and of these wounds I cannot Dye."[35] Here again the lingering effects of the "dry martyrdom" outdoes that of the "wet martyrdom" of Charles I. Marginalized, Jacobites must endure the persistent pain of a nonmortal wounding, sometimes compared to the condition of slavery or captivity, as both involve living with constrained freedoms and without political autonomy. To mitigate this the exile of James and his followers was at times styled as a "palliated exile," one that was imposed in order to "palliate that Cruelty" of depriving the king of his right.[36] Evidently, early Jacobite writers were already undermining any attempt to disguise the seriousness of, as Francis Turner, Bishop of Ely, described, "a Prince whose Father was murther'd, and himself forced into banishment by his own Subjects! . . . while those who wish'd His Return, durst not whisper any thing tending to call the king back again."[37] And if the cultural trauma of the regicide of 1649, manufactured at the dawn of the Restoration and endorsed by annual January 30 commemorations, was superimposed onto how the exile of James was encouraged to be conceived, then these writings also worked to exhume memories of the trauma of national division from the mid-century wars.

As Christopher Highley has discussed, appropriating biblical tropes of exile and martyrdom in early modern Europe was "useful in order to make sense of personal and collective crises."[38] This allowed for the representation of exile to be equated with Christian notions of self-sacrifice and suffering. With the recent civil war past and the fate of James's father ever in the minds of the early Jacobites, the notion of the martyrdom of exile was a useful way of representing the present condition through recourse to collective memories of the recent past and political application of the Bible. Kevin Killeen has demonstrated that the Bible was much more than simply a resource for ecclesiastical or ethical doctrine. Rather, the scriptures were deployed to analyze seventeenth-century politics more broadly and particularly where it concerned biblical kings and the language used in contemporary political discussions. "At stake in this is a set of questions on the nature of political memory," Killeen explains, and seventeenth-century political thinkers had "a political heritage to which, in any crisis of statehood, political thought returned" to the Bible "not only to recalibrate as ever-shifting providential calculus, but for historical detail and didactic exemplarity."[39] As I have discussed elsewhere, the restored regime of Charles II was deeply preoccupied with molding the uses and representations of the nation's collective memories and trauma of its divisive civil war past, and this included culturally embedding authorized versions of commemorating Charles the Martyr.[40] If, as Kevin Sharpe has suggested, Charles I came to "symbolize the duty of allegiance" and the "sin of resistance" in post-Restoration Britain, then early Jacobite polemical writers could, and did, also make use of this familiar and preexisting form of prescribed biblical commemoration to construct an interpretive framework that allowed the manufactured cultural trauma of the regicide and experiments with non-monarchial government to inform the foundation for shaping their own experiences.[41] It should be remembered, however, that early Jacobite writings did not necessarily represent the "voice of the people" but rather "an imaginary reconstruction of that voice, a fantasy world of political extremism that was eagerly embraced."[42] Thus, early Jacobite writers, like ardent royalists during the first decade of the Restoration, revived the martyr king to legitimate his sons. The exilic writings demonstrate the struggle to claim cultural supremacy, and as such they include some of the same rhetoric that Philip Major identifies in the writings of exiles during the English Revolution and Restoration. That is, texts are "invested with kudos-giving authority," and use biblical references and comparisons, such as the Old Testament story of a chosen people cast into exile and stories of slavery, to attempt to encode conceptualizations of defeat and displacement with reference to the biblical promise of redemption and deliverance.[43] The Bible "was in full battle dress again" when applied to conceptualize James II's "dry martyrdom," and the language used to do so is particularly significant.[44]

While the January 30 sermons and fasts were still commemorated in the late 1680s, and many would have recognized the commemoration of the regicide as a moment of prescribed national shame that required annual atonement, it was the early Jacobite polemicists who made direct connections between the regicides and the Williamites. In her study of the memory of Oliver

Cromwell, Laura Lunger Knoppers points to a verse in a manuscript poem entitled *King James's Sufferings Describ'd by himself. A Pindarique* in which the author compares:

> Curst be the crue that would have done
> The same to Charles the Martyr's son
> But Curst of all their Race be those
> Who Basely did James depose
> Under Pretense to set us free
> They sold us into Slavery.[45]

Here not only is James's fate, imposed by a "race" of cursed rebels, depicted as being worse than that endured by his father, but the effects of James's banishment is the loss of freedom of the entire nation. All three kingdoms had been deprived of all except their life, and exilic Jacobites, both domestic and abroad, must now suffer this deep and radical change and endure the lingering effects of this loss. What is more, the division between slave-Jacobite and master-Williamite, is set up here to act as a reminder of the traumatic effects of the Cavalier-Roundhead divide of the 1640s. Finally, that the Jacobites were betrayed and "sold into slavery" by a cursed race of Williamites works to depict the Jacobite cause as a distinctly British one, while those who betray the British king for a foreign master consist of a different "race."

Popular print also upheld this notion. In 1692 Scottish politician and Jacobite plotter Sir James Montgomery continued to wonder at the use of the relatively benign term "abdicate" to characterize the exile of "a Prince, violently forced away by a surprizing Defection of his Children, Servants, Subjects, and Soldiers; and under the terror of dangers threatening his Life and Liberty."[46] He concludes "this strange and mysterious Word" is "to this day . . . not well understood."[47] Along with Montgomery, others were also suspicious of the term being used to describe the radical change that had produced the present situation. While Montgomery characterized the description of the king's exile as a desertion to be "fake news" (in his own words, an imposition of "Falsehoods for Truths"), a 1688 broadside ballad also questioned the use of the term "Abdicate" when it was not an option freely chosen.[48] The ballad begins with some examples to make the point (such as a man giving up his purse to armed robbers to avoid violence, "so 'tis Lawfully theirs by a Vote of our State / Because he did freely his Purse *Abdicate*," or a woman submitting to rape to avoid being further harmed, "And made a meer Whore by a vote of our State / 'Cause she freely her Maiden-head did *Abdicate*") and then comes to the real point:

> Now unless the Word *Abdicate* bears this strange sense
> New King and New Parliament are vanish'd hence;
> Coronation's a Foppery, our New Laws are gone,
> New Allegiance is Treason, New Officers none:
> Our Taxes are Robb'ry,
> We English Men slaves.[49]

The point being made in these examples of the use of the term "slavery" to describe the condition of external or internal exile is that the emphasis, rather than the loss of bodily autonomy, is on the ongoing sense of a loss of English rights and liberties. Thus, these Jacobite writers considered both internal and external exiles to have lost all rights as a consequence of the deep and radical changes the nation had undergone, and with the loss of "Religion, Liberty, and Law" there was also a loss of freedom of allegiance. As the poet, playwright, and onetime Whig Elkanah Settle explained in 1689, the choice was a stark one: to either live in "False Britain" who "wou'd her King Inslave" or face the consequences of banishment. Settle goes on to wonder at the state of affairs in which, "I for an Opinion, Fly / Or changing my Opinion, die."[50] Exile almost always involves the loss of rights, legal status, and access to land, and those who have lost the protection of their own government are forced to rely on the benevolence of a foreign one, with little to no legal protection, rights, or ownerships.[51] It is a change of national identity through the loss of national autonomy, and the danger, as Montgomery points out, is that "after we are become Slaves, we may quickly be made anything else."[52] Within this rationale, those who remained in the British Isles were now to be considered a "conquered people" who must endure the "present servitude which is the necessary consequence of Conquest."[53] The point is further developed in Montgomery's pamphlet as he discusses the radical change that will occur due to conquest. He explains, "The old musty Statute Books and Records of Westminster Hall and the Tower, may be committed to the Flames, as so much waste Paper . . . a Conquered people must aspire no higher, than to learn to obey submissively, and to eat the Bread of Tribulation and Affliction with Patience: The care and desire of Posterity will languish; being unwilling to beget Children, to become such Slaves, and as miserable as they are themselves."[54]

Besides the polemical rhetoric, what is clear in this description of the threat of a foreign ruler to the ancient rights and privileges of religion, liberty, and property, is a sense of change that affects the universal experience, whether private or public. It is depicted as a fundamental change to the very constitution of the ancient culture upon which the notions of collective or national identity were based. The author predicts that posterity will languish and eventually will face extinction under the "breach of so many sacred Tyes and Engagements, which we might have insured to ourselves and Posterity," but recent changes have "wreath[ed] a Yoke about our Necks."[55] Thus, the fundamental changes were being understood to have affected the core aspects of social life and cultural distinctiveness. Here, they are characterized as being radical enough to potentially pose a threat to the immediate life-world of every member of the society.[56]

That threat, and the experience of early modern exile, included a "profound sense of displacement, loss, and alienation."[57] Early Jacobites, both those who remained and those who fled the kingdoms of England, Scotland, and Ireland, explicitly discussed this loss, and the comprehensive change it induced, as the source of their distress. Thomas Ken clearly articulates "the Loss of what we formerly Enjoy'd, is that which makes us the most Uneasie, and gives us the greatest Disquiet."[58] While Ken goes on to relate this loss specifically to the king and court, lamenting, "When from the highest Pinacle of Glory, a Mighty King whom all the World obey'd, is turn'd a grazing with the very Beasts," behind the political rhetoric employed here, there is also evidently a sense that the loss experienced by those at the top of society might also affect others lower in the kingdoms.[59] Both Thomas Ken and James Montgomery are sure that "this abundantly confirms this Truth, That no Estate of Man on this side of Heaven is free from Mutability and Changes," and furthermore, "such bold Strokes against our most Fundamental Privileges and Laws" lead to questions of whether or not "there is any Right or Immunity, which we can call our own, or be assured of?"[60] As these concerns usefully illustrate, the loss and change sustained through the exile of James and his supporters was also suffered domestically. Supporters of James II depicted the king as the figurehead for ideals of collective identity, so that "there is no way to give us our Religion, Laws, Liberties, and Repose, but by recalling and fixing our King in his Lawful Throne. The Constitution of England being founded on Monarchy." While these sentiments echo those that circulated in late 1659 and early 1660, they serve to make the point that notions of a united collective identity were threatened by the exile of the king. In case the point was too subtly made here, the same pamphlet, by Elkanah Settle, goes on to warn that not supporting a Jacobite restoration would certainly "embroil the Nation in Eternal war . . . at a continual expense of English Blood."[61] The lawyer and Whiggish Jacobite Charlwood Lawton's 1693 pamphlet adds a providential element to the discussion, explaining:

> Nor can we hope God will work a Miracle to support so unjust a Quarrel. They may see all this War brought into our own Bowels, into this divided Kingdom; may see it make Havoc and Desolation upon this Island; in a word, may see Friends and Kindred killing and destroying one another, embruing their hands in each others Blood; and then our pretended Fears may become true, those Miseries overtake us, with the pretended Suspicions of which we have coloured over and countenanced our unrighteous Doings.[62]

While this extract presents a particularly agitated example, the sense that yet another removal of yet another Stuart monarch might lead to a repetition of past miseries is frequently noted. One pamphlet comments on "so great a Noise in this Divided State," while another comments, "three Kingdoms in Misery and Confusion . . . over the murther (or Dethroning) of Their King."[63] What is particularly interesting here is the author's description of the dethroning of the king as a murder, once again positioning the exile of James II as a culturally traumatic reenactment of the regicide of Charles I, with the prediction of similar consequences of ongoing national division and violence. This point also serves to highlight the culturally accepted notion of the unnaturalness of the forced removal of an anointed king, regardless of whether or not he was executed, for, as Montgomery warns, "dethroning of Kings, inverting the Nature of the Monarchy, and the interrupting of the Royal Line and Succession, Such Alterations have been accompanied in all Ages with such Confusions, Convulsions, Blood, Ruine, and Desolation."[64] This comprehensive change of regime, the removal of an anointed king in favor of a foreign one, allowed early Jacobite writers like Settle, Lawton, Turner, and Montgomery to ponder the nature of the structure of monarchy itself. That "we have turned our Hereditary Monarchy into an Elective. We have cut the Royal Line, interrupted the Succession, and destroyed the just Rights of innocent persons, upon a pretended Abdication" resonated in and against the areas of affirmed values and norms, patterns and rules, symbolic meaning and frames of discourse, all interrupted by recent, wide-spread, and unexpected change.[65]

The nature of unexpected or shocking cultural change has consequential bearings on notions of identity, and while Jacobite scholars have investigated both domestic and foreign networks and identities of those who supported the Stuart cause, with regard to remembering past collective trauma to frame the present political situation, publications that supported James II in the first decades after his exile did make this point. Although it was not likely that there would be very many people reading pamphlets in 1699 who would have personal memories of January 30, 1649, that did not prevent early Jacobite polemicists from making the claim. Thomas Ken, for example, was confident that "I need not question but there are many still alive, who can remember Charles the First, the Potent Monarch of Three Opulent and once Flourishing Kingdoms, O'ercome by His Rebellious Barbarous Subjects."[66] Ken, born in 1637 and age twelve at the time of Charles I's execution, was also quick to point out that the martyrdom of Charles I, like that of James II, was carried out under a "pretense of Justice, as if he had not been the Lord's Anointed! . . . My trembling Hand can hardly hold my Pen . . . for the Untimely Tragick Fall of this Illustrious Martyr."[67] That early Jacobites conceived of "the Setting up of a counterfeit Prince against a True One" as "unEnglish" is perhaps not surprising. If to be "English" and a member of the Church of England required loyalty, then after the exile of James II there was yet another cause to point to for an underlying sense of a crisis of collective identity. Francis Turner, the Bishop of Ely and one of James's closest Anglican associates, makes this point in a remonstrance from 1689 by explaining "there is no bearing true Faith and Allegiance to our King, when we do it not to our God; no being loyal Subjects to the One, while we are downright Traytors to the Other."[68] Indeed, religion and loyalty "Vertues," according to Elkanah Settle, "that used to go hand in hand among Good Christians and Men of Honor" and were traits of "all true English men" could no longer be claimed.[69] Charlwood Lawton makes a similar point in his pamphlet, explaining, "It is certainly the Nature of English-Men to delight in, and they have been used to a Limited, Explained, and Hereditary Monarchy," but now, echoing sentiments from the 1640s, he laments that "this Revolution has blotted out all our Original Contract, razed all our Statutes and Law-Books, turned our Monarchy topsy-turvy and scandalously prevaricated from all our Civil Compacts."[70] Thus, Britain was now once again "false" and "faithless," a point also made in *His Majestie's Royall Farewell to England, A Pindarique*, that appropriates James's voice to lament, "Adieu false Britains, False to your vows, Adieu!"[71] If James had been betrayed by his subjects, then his supporters might also conceptualize themselves as being betrayed by their fellow countrymen. Thus, the mental frame with which this event was encountered by supporters of the Stuart regime was depicted as one of surprise and disbelief. James Montgomery is baffled that "we have, with both our hands, been pulling Destruction upon our selves, and desperately risking our Religion and Civil Rights. . . . How strangely we are Altered."[72]

Beyond the sort of disbelief articulated here by Montgomery, the parallels drawn in early Jacobite print between the contemporary changes in regime and those of the 1640s haunted spectators. Charlwood Lawton once again highlights the national divisions that recent changes have caused, worrying that "I beseech God so to order things, that all Sects and sorts of English-men, may think it a National Good to restore our King." Lawton provides his reader with additional evidence that supports his claim to return the Jacobites from internal and external exile and incorporate them back into the national community. He explains, "I have read our Annals; I wish every Body had," and he points to the "Scars and Wounds, the Bloodsheds and Distresses, that the Violation of Hereditary Title" that "have cost the poor people of this Nation" and exist in the national memory as a collective trauma that has been evoked by this new period of change and now resurfaces as an aspect of the discourse of trauma evident in early Jacobite writing.[73] Montgomery also refers to "the Annals" to demonstrate the extraordinary levels of change and to form his opinion that, while "it is alleged, that we have the practice of our Predecessors to justify our present Measures, who have made much greater Breaches in the Lineal Succession, deposed Kings, and given the Crown to Persons remoter from the Royal Blood than the Prince of Orange," these "alterations have been accompanied in all Ages with such Confusions, Convulsions, Blood, Ruin, and Desolation."[74] In a similar manner Settle considers "how many Forms of Government" and "dangerous turns of State" have recently take place in the nation, and concludes not only that "restless Britain never is at ease" but that the current situation is "the worst of times; but, oh! Never so bad as these."[75]

It is worth noting that Lawton, Settle, and Montgomery all reference the nation's recent past as evidence to directly point to distressing change itself as an aspect of the present crisis. Montgomery describes the times in which he lives as a "Reforming Age," while Lawton, in "an Age big with Changes," hopes that people might "lay aside all Byasses of Factions and Friendships, and much more all enmities, that we may unanimously offer to the King right Notions, and thereby restore him to his Hereditary Kingdoms."[76] This contemporary recognition that certain experiences of change (those which, following Sztompka's criteria and evident in early Jacobite writings, are swift, comprehensive, radical, and unexpected) could be problematic is significant and further demonstrates that at least part of the foundation of the Jacobite movement in its infancy was a reaction to the scale of the sociopolitical and -cultural transformations under way. Lawton "would have a perfect Act of Oblivion" to restore national unity and undo the damage caused by recent changes.[77] To this end, he hopes it will become "a Crime as well as ill Manners, to revive any of our old Distinctions," and he calls for a "Healing Parliament" that "might not only end, but take away all occasions for, Strife and Change."[78] For his part, Montgomery hopes for "an Act which would bury in Oblivion" the recent transformations and national divisions in favor of a "Prince who is truly a Martyr."[79] These early calls for an act of oblivion are noteworthy because not only do they indicate awareness of the existence of national division that recent changes had induced, but that, importantly, these changes were being conceived of as threatening. With this in mind, publicly establishing a mnemonic connection between the restoration of a Stuart king in 1660 and the desire to restore another Stuart king in 1689 (and, in at least one of the previous examples, making connections between "martyred" Stuarts), these early calls for an act of oblivion reflect a desire to initiate a policy of national amnesia and amnesty in favor of erasing recent distressing changes to prevent against their potentially traumatic consequences. As early modern acts of oblivion were frequently called upon to end civil wars and revolutions, their purpose was to reestablish continuity in the wake of division and rupture. As such they could be considered a natural antidote to changes that can be conceived of as traumatogenic.

While historians debate the nature, causes, and realities of Jacobitism, and acknowledge its various and multifaceted forms, identifying a "discourse of trauma" surrounding the effects and the scale of change is, perhaps, one avenue of inquiry that serves to unite early Jacobitism in an area of common experience. Indeed, the dominant account of the events of 1688–89, frequently referred to as the Glorious Revolution and still popularly upheld today, pretends that little to no opposition occurred and that the nation was not deeply divided over loyalties, allegiances, and ethics. Rather, it produced considerable disagreement and confusion over where the boundaries of religious and civil law lay, and no little anxiety over what sort of nation and culture would emerge from the changes that were taking place. Jacobitism, as a movement, was in its infancy in the period discussed in this chapter and would go on to adopt different forms as it grew into a more mature and better organized undertaking further into the eighteenth century. However, the writings from the early decade of the Jacobite movement, disjointed as they were, reflect a desire for the return of the Stuarts in response to forms of recent change that can be perceived of as traumatogenic.

NOTES

I am grateful to Andreas Mueller, Christian O'Connell, and Edward Vallance for helpful comments on an earlier version of this chapter.

1. Gary S. De Krey, *Restoration and Revolution Britain* (Hampshire, UK: Palgrave Macmillan, 2007), 297.
2. De Krey, 252.
3. Paul Monod, *Jacobitism and the English People, 1688–1788* (Cambridge, UK: Cambridge University Press, 1989), 1.

4. Daniel Szechi, *The Jacobites: Britain and Europe, 1688–1788* (Manchester, UK: Manchester University Press, 1994), 126.
5. Piotr Sztompka, "The Trauma of Social Change: A Case of Postcommunist Societies," in *Cultural Trauma and Collective Identity*, ed. Jeffrey C. Alexander et al., 155–95 (Berkeley: University of California Press, 2004), esp. 156–57.
6. Tim Harris, *Politics under the Later Stuarts: Party Conflict in a Divided Society, 1660–1715* (London: Longman, 1993), 208–9, 217.
7. Paul Kleber Monod, Murray G. H. Pittock, and Daniel Szechi, "Introduction: Loyalty and Identity," in *Loyalty and Identity: Jacobites at Home and Abroad*, ed. Paul Kleber Monod et al., 1-8 (Hampshire, UK: Palgrave Macmillan, 2010), esp. 2–3.
8. Monod, Pittock, and Szechi, 4.
9. Monod, Pittock, and Szechi, 5.
10. Judith Pollmann, *Memory in Early Modern Europe, 1500–1800* (Oxford, UK: Oxford University Press, 2017), 162.
11. Sztompka, "The Trauma of Social Change," in Alexander et al., *Cultural Trauma.*
12. Sztompka, 158–60.
13. Anon., *Reflections upon our Late and Present Proceedings in England* (London, 1689), Harvard University Library R722 (Wing), 4.
14. Tim Harris, "Did the English Have a Script for Revolution in the Seventeenth Century?," in *Scripting Revolution: A Historical Approach to the Comparative Study of Revolution*, ed. Keith Michael Baker and Dan Edelstein (Palo Alto: Stanford University Press, 2015), 27.
15. Edward Vallance, "Introduction," in *Remembering Early Modern Revolutions: England, North America, France and Haiti*, ed. Edward Vallance, 1–10 (Oxford, UK: Routledge, 2019).
16. Sztompka, "The Trauma of Social Change," in Alexander et al., *Cultural Trauma*, 160.
17. Sztompka, 160.
18. Sztompka, 165.
19. Christopher Highley, "Exile and Religious Identity in Early Modern England," *Reformation* 15 (2010): 52.
20. Raymond Gillespie, "Contrasting Communities: A Comparative Approach to Irish Communities in Baroque Europe," in *The Ulster Earls and Baroque Europe*, ed. Thomas O'Connor and Mary Ann Lyons, 166-182[000–000] (Dublin: Four Courts, 2010), esp. 168.
21. Szechi, *The Jacobites*, 126.
22. Christopher D'Addario, *Exile and Journey in Seventeenth Century Literature* (Cambridge, UK: Cambridge University Press, 2007).

23. Philip Major, *Writings of Exile in the English Revolution and Restoration* (Surrey, UK: Ashgate, 2013), 3.
24. Edward Said, "Reflections on Exile," in *Reflections on Exile, and other Literary and Cultural Essays,* 173-86 (London: Granta, 2001), esp. 173. As quoted in Major, *Writings of Exile*, 4.
25. Major, *Writings of Exile*, 16.
26. Daniel Defoe, *A Review of the Affaires of France: With Observations on Transactions at Home* 2, no. 123 (December 18, 1705), 771.
27. This notion of underhand betrayal as being potentially worse than, or at least equal to, the martyrdom of Charles I is also picked up in other publications. For example, a pamphlet from 1699, discussing those who feign support for James II but in fact do nothing to help his cause, explains: "How many are there that pretend Love and Loyalty to our King, yet will show it no other way, but by Drinking his health. . . . It was these Fighters against Heaven that brought the Royal Martyr to the Block; and were more guilty of his Death than the Regicides that condemn'd him or the Villanous Executioner that sever'd his Royal Head from his Sacred Body: And it is such as these that have turn'd our Royal Master out of his Throne, and forc'd him to Abdicate (as some will have it)," Thomas Ken, *The Royal Sufferer: A Manual of Meditations and Devotions, Written for the Use of a Royal, though Afflicted, Family* (London, 1699), University of Cambridge Library K278 (Wing 2nd ed., 1994), 59–60.
28. Richard Bonney, "The European Reaction to the Trial and Execution of Charles I," in *The Regicides and the Execution of Charles I*, ed. Jason Peacey, 247–79 (Hampshire, UK: Palgrave Macmillan, 2001), esp. 270.
29. The comparison of the "wet martyrdom" of Charles I and the "dry martyrdom" of James II was brought up more than once during the trial of Henry Sacheverell (1710), *State Trials*, xv, 213, 324, 341. Also see Brian Cowan, "The Spin Doctor: Sacheverell's Trial Speech and Political Performance in the Divided Society," in *The Parliament History Yearbook Trust*, 2012, 39. https://doi.org/10.1111/j.1750-0206.2011.00283.x.
30. Ken, *The Royal Sufferer*, 1.
31. *A Collection of Loyal Poems Satyrs and Lampoons*, Beinecke Library, Osborn Shelves b. III, 10.
32. John Toland, *King Charles I, no such saint, martyr or good Protestant, as commonly reputed, but a favourer of Papists and a cruel and oppressive Tyrant all plainly proved from undeniable matters of fact . . .* (1689), Bodleian Library, J7 (Wing), 26. Italics in original.
33. James II, "Letter of King James II and VII, December 22, 1688," in Historical Manuscripts Commission, *The manuscripts of the House of Lords, 1689-1690 : presented to both Houses of Parliament by command of Her Majesty*, 12 report, part VI, (London:

Printed for H.M. Stationery Off., by Eyre and Spottiswoode, 1889), 19. https://archive.org/stream/hists52199538/hists52199538_djvu.txt.

34. Ken, *The Royal Sufferer*, 8.
35. *A Collection of Loyal Poems Satyrs and Lampoons*, Beinecke Library, Osborn Shelves b. III, 3.
36. John Northleigh, *Dr. Burnett's Reflections upon a Book, Entitled, Parliamentum Pacificum* (London, 1688), Harvard University Library N1298 (Wing), 11; Elkanah Settle, *A View of the Times with Britain's Address to the Prince of Orange* (London, 1689), Huntington Library V371 (Wing), 3.
37. Francis Turner, *The Remonstrance from the Reverend Father in God, Francis Lord Bishop of Ely, and several others, the most eminent divines of the Church of England, against the proceedings of the P: O. and the lords spiritual and temporal that invited him* (Dublin, 1689) Trinity College Library T3279 (Wing), 2nd ed., 16.
38. Highley, "Exile and Religious Identity," 53.
39. Kevin Killeen, *The Political Bible in Early Modern England* (Cambridge, UK: Cambridge University Press, 2017), 4–9.
40. Erin Peters, *Commemoration and Oblivion in Royalist Print Culture, 1658–1667* (Hampshire, UK: Palgrave Macmillan, 2017), 70–89.
41. Kevin Sharpe, "The Royal Image: An Afterword," in *The Royal Image: Representations of Charles I*, ed. Thomas N. Corns, 288-309 (Cambridge, UK: Cambridge University Press, 1999), esp. 305.
42. Paul Monod, *Jacobitism and the English People, 1688–1788* (Cambridge, UK: Cambridge University Press, 1988), 49.
43. Major, *Writings of Exile*, 171.
44. Killeen, *The Political Bible*, 154.
45. Laura Lunger Knoppers, "Reviving the Martyr King: Charles I as Jacobite Icon," in *The Royal Image: Representations of Charles I*, ed. Thomas N. Corns, 263-287 (Cambridge, UK: Cambridge University Press, 1999), esp. 268.
46. James Montgomery, *Great Britain's Just Complaint for her Late Measures, Present Sufferings, and the Future Miseries she is Exposed To* (Oxford, 1692), Harvard University Library, M2505 (Wing), 2.
47. Montgomery, 5.
48. Montgomery, 2.
49. "On the Word Abdicate" (1688), Beinecke Library Broadsides (BrSides By6 1688). Italics in original.
50. Settle, *A View of the Times*, 1–10.
51. Jennifer Hyndman and Wenona Giles, *Refugees in Extended Exile: Living on the Edge* (New York: Routledge, 2017), 7.
52. Montgomery, *Great Britain's Just Complaint*, 54.

53. Montgomery, 24–26.
54. Montgomery, 26.
55. Montgomery, 13.
56. Sztompka, "The Trauma of Social Change," in Alexander et al., *Cultural Trauma*, 159.
57. Greta Grace Kroeker, "Introduction," in *Religious Diaspora in Early Modern Europe: Strategies of Exile*, ed. Timothy G. Fehler et al., 1-8 (London: Pickering and Chatto, 2014), esp. 1.
58. Ken, *The Royal Sufferer*, 9.
59. Ken, 15.
60. Ken, *The Royal Sufferer*, 19; Montgomery, *Great Britain's Just Complaint*, 30.
61. Settle, *A View of the Times*, 6.
62. Charlwood Lawton, *The Jacobite Principles Vindicated: In Answer to a Letter Sent to the Author* (London, 1693), Lambeth Palace Library, l&39B (Wing, CD-Rom, 1996), 1–2.
63. Settle, *A View of the Times*, 11; Turner, *The Remonstrance*, 13.
64. Montgomery, *Great Britain's Just Complaint*, 12.
65. Montgomery, *Great Britain's Just Complaint*, 19; Sztompka, "The Trauma of Social Change," in Alexander et al., *Cultural Trauma*, 161.
66. Ken, *The Royal Sufferer*, 17.
67. Ken, 17–18.
68. Turner, *The Remonstrance*, 3.
69. Settle, *A View of the Times*, 2, 5.
70. Lawton, *Jacobite Principles Vindicated*, 3, 8.
71. Settle, *A View of the Times*, 8; "His Majestie's Royall Farewell to England, A Pindarique," *A Collection of Loyal Poems Satyrs and Lampoons*, Beinecke Library, Osborn Shelves, b. III, I.
72. Montgomery, *Great Britain's Just Complaint*, 18, 28.
73. Lawton, *Jacobite Principles Vindicated*, 29.
74. Montgomery, *Great Britain's Just Complaint*, 1, 12, 22.
75. Settle, *A View of the Times*, 6, 9.
76. Montgomery, *Great Britain's Just Complaint*, 50; Lawton, *Jacobite Principles Vindicated*, 10, 12.
77. Lawton, *Jacobite Principles Vindicated*, 18.
78. Lawton, 29.
79. Montgomery, *Great Britain's Just Complaint*, 61.

12

Tragic Trauma?

Remorse, Repetition, and the Orestes Myth

JOSEPH HARRIS

If the notion of "trauma" has any meaning, applicability, or validity beyond the resolutely modern world, then one figure who certainly deserves consideration is the Greek mythological hero Orestes. The elements of Orestes's life that concern us here are very straightforward: he is called upon by his sister Electra to kill their mother Clytemnestra and her new husband Aegisthus as revenge for the murder of their own father, the king Agamemnon, whose throne Aegisthus had usurped. Having killed his queenly mother (and thus committed the ghastly deeds of both matricide and regicide in a single blow), Orestes is hounded into madness by the snake-haired goddesses of vengeance known variously as the Erinnyes, the Eumenides, or—as early modern France knew them and as I shall call them here—the Furies.

The tale of Orestes has proved a compelling yet troubling one for dramatists across the ages, from Aeschylus to Sartre and beyond. Its recurrence across literary history might even suggest a cultural "repetition compulsion" in the attempt to constantly replay this disturbing tale and somehow set it to rest. On a narrative level too, the very structure of the Orestes myth is dominated by what one critic calls "an obsessive repetitive rhythm."[1] Iphigenia is sacrificed by her father Agamemnon; Agamemnon is murdered by Clytemnestra; Clytemnestra is killed by Orestes; Orestes, finally, is persecuted by the Furies. Theoretically, the vendetta could continue indefinitely; only the appeal to a supernatural agency—the monstrous Furies—draws the cycle of violence to a close. The primary focus of this article, however, is not the ancient Greek versions of the myth, but rather the ways in which the myth was understood, adopted, and developed in the late seventeenth and early eighteenth centuries. If each period adapts classical myth to suit and reflect its own concerns, then, as I hope to suggest, early modern Europe gives a particular psychological and even "traumatic" twist to the tale of Orestes. Drawing primarily on a handful of dramatic examples from the period, and especially the two *Electre* plays of Longepierre (1702) and Crébillon (1708), I will first gather the evidence in favor of a traumatized Orestes, before then exploring whether this conjuncture of traumatic tropes is any more than an intriguing coincidence.

Orestes's Wound and Remorse

There are various reasons why we might consider Orestes as "traumatized." Etymologically, of course, the word "trauma" means "wound," and it is striking how the image of the wound sporadically recurs in early modern discussions of Orestes long before his torments ever reached the stage. In the early seventeenth century the playwright Georges de Scudéry describes Orestes as suffering from a "wounded imagination"; similarly, the famous man of letters Guez de Balzac would suggest that it is only natural that Orestes, "having a wounded brain, and a troubled conscience, thinks that he can see what he does not" when he sees the Furies.[2] For seventeenth-century France, then, the wound provides a ready metaphor to evoke Orestes's troubled mental state; furthermore, it is surely significant that both these references to Orestes relate his metaphorical "wound" to his visions of the Furies. Rather than giving the Furies some ontological existence, both Scudéry and Balzac opt for more modern, psychological explanations. In this age of both Christianity and reason, the Furies can no longer be understood as real, infernal deities of vengeance; rather, they emerge as psychological symptoms of Orestes's wounded mind. Already, then, we have a general reversal of causality: in ancient Greece the Furies drove Orestes mad; in modern Europe it is Orestes's madness that causes him to see the Furies.

One factor that problematizes Orestes's claim to trauma is the fact that he is neither the victim nor an innocent onlooker of Clytemnestra's murder, but its perpetrator. Some commentators, such as Ruth Leys, have taken issue with the readiness of certain trauma theorists—notably Cathy Caruth—to extend the term "trauma" conceptually to cover perpetrators as well as victims. Perhaps significantly, Leys's debate with Caruth concerns another early modern text, one whose pertinence to trauma was first discussed by Sigmund Freud in *Beyond the Pleasure Principle*.[3] In Torquato Tasso's epic *Gerusalemme Liberata* (1581), Tancredi's unwitting killing of Clorinda is later replayed when he strikes a tree, which bleeds and cries out with his dead beloved's voice. As Leys objects, if "trauma" can be extended to affect perpetrators as well as victims, then "not only can Tancred be considered the victim of a trauma but [. . .] even the Nazis are not exempt from the same dispensation."[4] While Leys's objection has serious ethical ramifications, we might also want to take issue with her implicit suggestion that a perpetrator—and especially an unwitting perpetrator—cannot be traumatized. To acknowledge that wrongdoers might experience trauma does not necessarily mean absolving them of guilt or responsibility; nor does it necessarily mean conflating them with their victims. At the very least my perspective here is in tune with the ethos of the eighteenth century, whose theater often gravitated toward narratives in which wicked characters see the error of their ways and repent. Even the greatest of theatrical villains are sometimes surprised to find themselves prey to remorse. Perhaps most famously, Voltaire's Mahomet is aghast to find himself experiencing pangs of conscience, recognizing in surprise that "so remorse does exist!"[5] Especially as we move into the Enlightenment, remorse becomes an increasingly important moral term in both prose narrative and in the theater; indeed, all of the main characters of Longepierre's *Electre* speak of their own remorse for some past action. At the very least the term "re-morse"—etymologically "biting again"—contains elements of both wounding and repetition that surface throughout most modern theories of trauma.[6]

Given the early modern period's increasing valorization of remorse, it is unsurprising to see thinkers downplaying the Furies' original role as supernatural avengers. The eighteenth century, in particular, was quick to associate the Furies with remorse rather than vengeance. In an article on "contrition," for example, Diderot's *Encyclopédie* (1751–72) insists that the Furies "were nothing more than the secret reproaches and remorse of one's conscience."[7] Louis de Jaucourt's *Encyclopédie* article on the Furies themselves also stresses this interpretation: "Antiquity always regarded them as inexorable goddesses whose sole task was to punish crime, not only in Hades, but even in this life;

they tormented criminals, either through remorse that gave them no respite, or through terrible visions that often made them lose all sense."[8] This emphasis on remorse rather than vengeance will become all the more pronounced in post-Enlightenment representations of the myth; the nineteenth-century painter William-Adolphe Bouguereau entitled his painting of the Furies assailing Orestes *The Remorse of Orestes*, and the Furies famously appear in Sartre's play *Les Mouches* as "les déesses du remords" (the goddesses of remorse).[9] While this is not how the Greeks had understood the Furies, it does help illustrate how the early modern period was caught between two models—a classical pagan one, where the Furies represent an external avenging force, and a more modern secular one, where their role is essentially psychological.

Yet this general narrative of secularization and psychologization is not a clear-cut one. As the *Encyclopédie* reminds us, even some ancients recognized that the Furies were not literal agents of vengeance. Jaucourt quotes Cicero as saying, "Do not imagine that the wicked and impious are tormented by Furies that pursue them with their burning torches; the true Furies of which poets speak are the remorse that follows crime."[10] Indeed, even in their first extant dramatic incarnations—in Aeschylus's *Oresteia* cycle—the Furies are lent different degrees of "reality." Although the final play of the trilogy, *The Eumenides*, gives the Furies some ontological existence by having them performed onstage by actors, the preceding play, *The Libation Bearers*, has the terrified Orestes describe them as he sees them approach, unseen by the audience or by his companions onstage. We should not assume that the earlier play is necessarily more psychological, however, since mythological wisdom held that the Furies were invisible to all but their victim.[11] Likewise, we also find moderns such as Bouguereau and Sartre conferring some ontological existence onto the Furies by depicting them visually—whether on canvas or onstage. In early modern France, demands of what was called *vraisemblance* ("verisimilitude," a form of stylized "truth to life" or overall plausibility) prevented most dramatists from depicting the Furies physically onstage, although we do occasionally find them in Renaissance prologues such as Robert Garnier's *Porcie* (1568) or in court ballet; Louis XIV danced cross-dressed as a Fury in 1654, and we have eight Furies in the *intermède* of the collaborative tragedy-ballet *Psyché* (1671).

On the more traditional early modern tragic stage, however, the Furies are typically stripped of their empirical existence, internalized, and then—in a fit of hallucination—projected outward again, as a symptom of Orestes's disordered mind rather than as an empirical reality. So while they might therefore emerge to us, the audience, as agents of remorse, they are experienced by the traumatized (and superstitious) subject as agents of supernatural vengeance. The most famous example of this comes not in a direct adaption of the *Electra* plays but at the end of Racine's *Andromaque* (1667), a play that also features Orestes, albeit at a different stage in his life.[12] In this play Oreste, acting as ambassador of the Greeks, is called upon by his beloved Hermione to assassinate Pyrrhus, the king of Epirus. In fact, Pyrrhus ends up being butchered to death by Oreste's men, while Oreste himself does not get to strike a single blow. When Oreste announces Pyrrhus's death to Hermione, she is aghast, rejects him, and promptly commits suicide. It is when Oreste learns of her death that his madness takes hold. He sees all go black, and watches streams of blood gush out all around him. He then has still worse visions: of butchered ghosts and—perhaps most distressing of all—the deathly snake-headed Furies themselves. Powerful as it is, and influential as it would prove, this conclusion is not of course entirely Racine's invention, since it has precursors in Aeschylus' *Libation Bearers*. Yet Racine cleverly grafts this more famous episode of Orestes's life onto his own play in order to provide a powerfully dramatic conclusion.

Despite this "cut-and-paste" approach, Racine actually—as I have argued elsewhere—takes great care to smooth over the joins, motivating his Oreste's madness both causally and thematically within his own play.[13] Racine thus intertwines elements of the received myth with events from his own preceding plot. Oreste's various hallucinations pick up on certain motifs of Pyrrhus's botched assassination but redeploy them in new and troubling ways. Racine's main innovation at the end of *Andromaque* is to have his Oreste hallucinate not only the Furies—as audiences would expect—but also the ghosts of Pyrrhus and Hermione, whose deaths he has just inadvertently or reluctantly provoked. Indeed, Oreste's hallucinations replay elements of his botched murder of Pyrrhus in ways that suggest a strange repetition compulsion. He first sees Pyrrhus standing before him, apparently bloodied but still standing.

Curiously, rather than rejoice at Pyrrhus's apparent survival, Oreste attempts to prove himself—and to right the botched murder—by attacking him again, exclaiming, "Wait, wait, here is the blow that I have kept back for you."[14] Yet Pyrrhus now evades Oreste's blows for a second time, this time because the murdered Hermione suddenly reappears to whisk him to safety.

It is only after Hermione's appearance that the long-awaited Furies emerge, but even now Oreste defiantly rejects them, finally offering up his heart for Hermione to devour before collapsing into an unconscious heap. Racine thus taps into the awesome compelling mythological and dramatic power that the Furies hold, while nonetheless relegating them to a resolutely secondary position as products of Oreste's fevered psychology. Oreste's hallucinations here certainly resemble, in broad terms at least, what trauma theorist Cathy Caruth calls "the repetitive reenactments of people who have suffered painful events"—repetitions that "appear as the possession of some people by a sort of fate, a series of painful events to which they are subjected, and which seem to be entirely outside their wish or control."[15] And we should note in particular that in Racine's version, it is primarily through the ghosts of the freshly dead Hermione and Pyrrhus, rather than through the supernatural avengers the Furies, that this repetition compulsion becomes most apparent.

The Scandal of Matricide

Andromaque was Racine's first major box-office success, and, unsurprisingly, his powerful presentation of Oreste's madness soon established a clear intertextual template for both playwrights and audiences. Before Racine's play, earlier treatments of the Orestes myth had tended to follow Sophocles's *Electra* in stopping at the murder of Aegisthus rather than depicting Orestes's subsequent persecution by the Furies. In Lazare de Baïf's 1537 translation of *Electra*, for example, Oreste returns to the stage after killing his mother (whose dying screams we have just heard) to announce blithely that "everything is going very well for us."[16] After Racine, however, playwrights started to revisit the aftermath of Orestes's murder more fully. Racine's often-mocked rival Jacques (or Nicolas) Pradon produced an *Electre* in 1677–78, but since this tragedy has unfortunately not survived we do not know how, or even whether, it portrayed Orestes's psychological state after the matricide. The first surviving depiction of Orestes's madness after killing his mother is found in the classicist Hilaire-Bernard de Longepierre's *Electre* of 1702, a work shortly followed by Prosper Jolyot de Crébillon's *Electre* of 1708. Before turning to these two plays, however, it will be helpful to explore the ethical and narrative scandal that Orestes's matricide represented to early modern playwrights.

Since the Orestes myth already involves a seemingly compulsive cycle of crimes, it is important to consider why the murder of Clytemnestra should be so traumatic as to require supernatural punishment, in ways that the previous crimes had not been. Some clues are given by the dramatist Pierre Corneille, who discusses the myth at some length in his theoretical writings despite never tackling the Electra tale onstage himself. As Corneille points out, the ancients must have deemed Orestes's crime far worse than his mother's, since she was spared the Furies despite murdering her husband. Indeed, early modern culture as a whole deemed "parricide"—taken in its broadest sense of the murder of any blood relation, or of a king—as one of the most transgressive acts of all. Accordingly, Orestes's deed is presented in Crébillon's *Electre* as "the most horrible of crimes," and as "an act that makes nature shudder."[17]

Yet in addition to breaking one of culture's greatest moral taboos, Clytemnestra's murder also holds a peculiarly privileged yet problematic status in dramatic theory. In his *Poetics*, Aristotle had cited this specific murder as an example of the type of mythological plot that the dramatist has no right to change. A playwright, he says, "cannot interfere with the traditional stories, cannot, for instance, say that Clytaemnestra was not killed by Orestes."[18] Yet if Clytemnestra's murder is therefore "fixed" and unchangeable, it is also heavily problematic for early modern Europe. Corneille underlines but also complicates Aristotle's point by stressing that Orestes's murder, however nonnegotiable it is for dramatists, flagrantly defies *vraisemblance*, that criterion of an internally coherent dramatic plot: "it is not *vraisemblable* (plausible) that Clytemnestra assassinates her husband, that Orestes stabs his mother—but history tells it so, and representing these great crimes does not make spectators incredulous."[19]

What is at stake here, then, is not whether the myth is appropriate material for the stage—indeed, Corneille strongly suggests that it is—but rather about something far deeper. The conceptual scandal of Orestes's act is that, being *invraisemblable*, it marks the irruption of the brute facticity of history into a context where order and reason should dominate. The act cannot be incorporated into normal causality or rationality—it is a rationally unassimilable, unrepresentable event that, according to early modern French aesthetics at least, simply should not have happened, whether ethically or causally. And I would suggest that it is here, in its very incomprehensibility, that the murder's disruptive, traumatic power lies—both for dramatists working on the play and for the wretched Orestes himself. The murder cannot be logically processed: it is the case—history, or mythology, tells us so—and yet it does not make sense. In this respect, Orestes's subsequent madness might appear to displace onto a psychological level the inherent irrationality of his original act.

Yet although Aristotle claimed that Clytemnestra's murder was untouchable, various early modern thinkers and dramatists did feel compelled to reinterpret both the motivations behind—and even the nature of—the act itself in order to make it more acceptable to their audiences. Corneille, for example, professes to feeling a certain "delicacy" about Sophocles' depiction of Clytemnestra's death, and proposes rewriting the play in such a way that the ghastly event takes place by accident—or by some suicidal impulse on Clytemnestra's part—rather than by design:

> To correct this subject matter and make it suit our fashion, we would need Orestes to conspire only against Aegisthus and, feeling some residual respect and affection for his mother, defer to the gods for her punishment; insisting on protecting her adulterous lover, the queen would have to place herself between him and her son in such a way that she unfortunately receives the blow that the prince wanted to inflict on his father's killer. In this way, she would die by her son's hand, as Aristotle wants, but without Orestes's barbarous deed horrifying us as in Sophocles, or his action needing the avenging Furies to torment him, since he would remain innocent.[20]

In Corneille's imagined rewriting of the play, the ghastly event does take place, but by accident—or by some suicidal impulse on Clytemnestra's part—rather than by design. In this case, Corneille explains, the unnatural act would spare spectators the second-degree traumatic horror that it would cause were it premeditated, and spare the (now innocent) Orestes the need to be persecuted by the Furies.

Longepierre

Given the celebrity and status of his two predecessors, it is perhaps unsurprising that Longepierre's play is indebted both to Corneille's dramatic theory and to Racine's dramatic practice.[21] Like Corneille, Longepierre is evidently troubled by the idea that Oreste could murder his mother in cold blood; accordingly, following the earlier playwright's suggestion, he has Clytemnestre throw herself between her son and her husband and thus relieve Oreste of full responsibility for the bloody deed. Yet Longepierre goes even further than Corneille recommends, by making his Oreste entirely unaware of his actions at the crucial moment of murder. Before he rushes offstage to murder Egisthe in Act V, Longepierre's Oreste feels himself being fired up into a righteous trancelike passion and imagines that a god has possessed him.[22] When he returns to the stage, all he remembers is a haze of bloodshed and violence: "without knowing what I was doing, I ceased to be master of all my troubled senses; I know dimly that in my fit of passion I struck out, I dealt terror and death, I shed blood and spread carnage all around; and I think I saw, through a fog that the gods and my wrath had cast over my eyes, Apollo guiding my avenging blows."[23] Oreste's experience here—or rather his lack of it—thus curiously anticipates that "unclaimed" or "missed experience" that Caruth deems fundamental to trauma.[24] Longepierre introduces a temporal lag between the event itself (the murder) and the moment of its comprehension, and indeed milks this gap to full dramatic effect. Once he has recovered his wits after this first fit, Oreste's first thought is to console his mother, and to reassure her that his desire for vengeance does not extend to her. Horrified and uncomprehending, his companion Pamène exclaims that his mother is dead, and Oreste—again revealing his filial devotion—asks who could have committed such an "inhuman crime."[25] Pamène replies, perplexed: "What, my lord! Have you forgotten that the queen, seeing you about to strike the tyrant down, threw herself between you and received the blow in her chest?"[26]

This scene echoes the moment of revelation we have already seen in Racine's *Andromaque*, and produces a similar momentary confusion of life and death. In both plays, Oreste announces his desire to seek out a woman whom he believes alive; it then falls to his shocked and uncomprehending companion to clarify that she is in fact dead. The key difference, of course, is that Racine's Oreste, having been onstage during Hermione's offstage suicide, has good cause not to know this, while Longepierre's hero was already psychologically—or perhaps supernaturally—alienated enough from his actions not to realize what he was doing. What is justified spatially in Racine is thus displaced onto a psychological level in Longepierre.

As in Racine's play, Oreste's response to this horrific revelation in Longepierre is immediate and visceral; his blood freezes in horror, and he seeks only to hide himself away in shame. He wants to kill himself but is held back by a sudden cloud of darkness that he sees envelop him; he hears gruesome cries and threatening thunder. The only light he sees comes from hideous lightning bolts that reveal nothing but streams of blood.[27] Worse still, Clytemnestre now appears before him in a ghastly hallucination. He runs to embrace her, but she shows him her fatal wound, out of which gush torrents of blood. Electre tries to reassure him, but he mistakes her for one of the Furies—the "barbarous Eumenides."[28] He watches in horror as Clytemnestre exhorts them to punish him and feels himself physically torn open by her—"you are tearing open my side, you are ripping out my heart."[29] Oreste now begs the earth to swallow him up, before realizing that he will never escape his remorse or his tormentors even in the underworld.[30] At this point he faints; his companion Pylade exclaims, in a direct quotation of Racine's Pylade, "he has lost consciousness."[31]

As they had done in *Andromaque*, Oreste's irrational and uncontrollable hallucinations in Longepierre's play replay and yet recast certain aspects of the original murder. Like his victim Pyrrhus in Racine, Clytemnestre appears before Oreste not as she was before the murder but as she was afterward, bloodied and defiant. The hallucination, then, does not simply wind back the clock to before the murder, but rather juxtaposes elements of past and present. Clytemnestre offers herself up to her son again, but now that he consciously seeks reconciliation, what she offers him—her wound—is a stark, defiant reminder of his crime. Caruth speaks of the "oscillation," in trauma, "between a crisis of death and a correlative crisis of life: between the story of the unbearable nature of an event and the story of the unbearable nature of its survival."[32] We find a similar oscillation here between death and life; indeed, as we have seen, what finally unleashes Oreste's madness here, as in Racine, is the discovery that someone believed alive is actually already dead, and that he himself holds responsibility for this death. Yet the symbolic juxtaposition of life and death here is not just limited to the ghostly Clytemnestre; when she shortly lurches toward him, Oreste revealingly exclaims, "I am dead!"[33] This exclamation, no doubt wishful thinking on Oreste's part, symbolically inverts the original situation. The murder victim has now returned to life, visiting a form of symbolic death upon the murderer.

Crébillon

Given the passionate violence of the original myth and its later incarnations, it is unsurprising that Orestes held an interest for Crébillon, whose taste for brutality and horror is well known. In his 1708 version, Crébillon, like Longepierre, also follows Corneille's suggestion in having Clytemnestre throw herself between Oreste and her husband; he also echoes Longepierre in showing Oreste possessed by a frenzy or "fury" that blinds him to the full significance of his acts until later.[34] On returning to his senses, Oreste asks his governor Palamède what has happened to his mother; on learning that she is dead his first response is to vow vengeance on her killer. It is only now that Palamède breaks the further news that Oreste himself is the murderer: "Your mighty hand was about to end his life; in this fatal moment the queen seized it. You, without considering who might have been holding back a hand armed by the gods to punish him, you struck in a single blow that they were perhaps guiding, and shed all the blood from which they had had you born."[35] Interestingly, whereas Longepierre had presented some divine force as underlying Oreste's murderous trance, Crébillon downplays some of the supernatural overtones of Longepierre's version, cleverly interweaving divine and human motivations to suggest Oreste's at least partial responsibility for the murder. Although Palamède claims that Oreste's desire for vengeance on Egysthe is divinely mandated, his use of "perhaps" leaves some doubt about who is responsible for the deadly blow against Clytemnestre.[36]

After learning this terrible news, Crébillon's Oreste—much like his precursor in Longepierre—now sees the bloody figure of Clytemnestre appear before him. The difference is, however, that this Clytemnestre is real, and alive—if only just, as she is now fatally wounded by the blow that he has dealt her. It is only at this point that the dying Clytemnestre too realizes the identity of her murderer; she implores him to finish the deed, to spare her from the "tourment" of seeing who she has given birth to. When he refuses to and she staggers off, Oreste first implores the gods to take vengeance upon him, and then draws his sword to stab himself in the hope that his blood, remorse, and tears will placate the gods; Palamède swiftly disarms him. Now Oreste sees all go dark; he watches a passage to Hades open up before him, that he welcomes as somewhere to hide, but the ghostly shades are shocked by his appearance and seem to flee. He hears "groans" and "pained cries."[37] He now has a vision of Egysthe but is stopped from attacking it by a still worse vision: "Aegisthus! Ah! It is too much. In my rage I must . . . What do I see? In his hands, my mother's head!"[38] Oreste's hallucinations in Crébillon's play are strikingly different from those in his precursors, above all because they do not correspond in any direct way to their traumatic trigger; Clytemnestre, after all, was neither killed by Egysthe nor decapitated. And over the course of these few lines, the vision of Egysthe holding Clytemnestre's decapitated head seems to transform into a monstrous version of Clytemnestre herself—at least if Oreste's final appeal to her is anything to go by: "What a glare! Where shall I flee? Ah, furious monster, what spectacle do you dare present to my eyes? I am suffering only too much, stop, cruel monster, spare my terrified eyes this head. Ah, my mother, spare your wretched son . . ."[39]

Most strikingly, perhaps, Crébillon removes the Furies entirely from Oreste's final hallucinations, which concentrate solely on his descent into the underworld and the ghosts of Egysthe and his mother. If anything, Crébillon seems keen to present Oreste himself as the avenging Fury rather than as someone punished by them. When the fatally wounded Clytemnestre comes onstage to discover that her murderer is in fact her own son, she effectively disowns him, insisting that he is instead a "monster" engendered by "some Fury."[40] Yet this Oreste clearly has none of the remorselessness of the mythological Furies; indeed, as becomes clear in his final speeches, he suffers the mental anguish of the repentant perpetrator. To start with, he wishes to be punished for his crime, begging the gods to strike him down with a thunderbolt and denouncing their slackness: "Gods, you do not know how to punish a crime."[41] Realizing that the only way to expiate his crime is to commit suicide himself, he draws his sword against himself but is disarmed by Palamède. By this point he has come to see death as a release; when he watches the path to Hades open up in front of him, he attempts to flee down it, hoping to hide himself in its eternal darkness, but is then thwarted by a sudden return of light and the arrival of his ghostly victims. Unlike in Racine and Longepierre, Crébillon's Oreste remains conscious to the bitter end; he is not even granted their temporary reprieve of blacking out. In his despairing final lines, he exclaims in horror at the recognition that he is being punished excessively for a crime he did not voluntarily commit: "Gods! Are the worst criminals punished any more harshly?"[42] Having originally berated the gods for their lenience, Oreste has now learned over the course of this single scene that survival can bring such horrors that death seems like the lesser of two evils.

Conclusion: Classical Trauma?

We have seen, then, how the figure of Orestes is treated in some early modern French incarnations. But how appropriate is it to understand Orestes's affliction and hallucinations in terms of trauma? Intriguingly, the treatment of the Orestes myth in this period goes through broadly similar stages to the later development of "trauma" as a concept. In its rhetoric of Oreste's "wounded mind" or "wounded imagination," the early seventeenth century anticipates the nineteenth-century notion of trauma as a profound but metaphorical damage done to the psyche akin to bodily mutilation. In a second stage, Racine—like Freud—then amplifies and complicates this original model, figuring this psychological wound through hallucinations and compulsive yet distorted repetitions of the original experience. Finally, Longepierre's and Crébillon's reworkings of Racine's model anticipate Caruth's rereading of Freud, by casting the original traumatic event as one that the individual does not fully experience. Indeed, by 1708 Crébillon could comfortably abandon even the traditional narrative prop that the mythological Furies had provided, and thus concentrate his Oreste's torment solely on the hideous ghosts of his victims.

As these three stages imply, the early modern Oreste's claim to "trauma" rests on three main factors: the shocking, maddeningly horrific nature of his original experience; his compulsive and involuntary repetition of this experience through subsequent hallucinations; and, finally, his psychological absence from the original experience. The question we need to ask, therefore, is whether the early modern period understands these three factors as being interconnected—that is, as part of the same basic phenomenon—or whether their simultaneous occurrence in these plays by Longepierre and Crébillon is purely coincidental. Because we have already considered the logically and psychologically disruptive nature of the original murder, it is worthwhile focusing here on the other two factors—Oreste's hallucinations and his mental absence from the event itself—to see to what extent they are presented as being connected, within the poetic or the dramaturgical fabric of Longepierre's tragedy. Is it only our modern expectations that lead us to perceive a psychological connection between Oreste's moment of "unclaimed experience" and his subsequent hallucinations? As I shall propose, it in fact is almost impossible to establish Oreste's credentials as trauma victim with any certainty, because any argument in favor of one case seems to invoke counterarguments on another level.

Although Oreste's moment of mental absence during the brutal event seems to anticipate modern ideas on trauma, the early modern period clearly did not need a detour through modern theory in order to understand it. Rather, Oreste's mental absence makes sense to early modern dramatists as a practical solution to a technical, dramaturgical problem about how to make him an appropriate dramatic hero. As Corneille insists, audiences would simply be horrified by a plot in which someone knowingly kills their own mother. For the seventeenth century, then, Oreste's moment of unclaimed experience is better explained through an appeal to our own psychology as audiences—that is, to our own emotional response to the hero—than to his own fragile mental state. Importantly, too, for both Longepierre and Crébillon it is not the murder itself that triggers Oreste's descent into madness and his compulsive hallucinations; rather, what triggers this descent is the moment at which he is made conscious of his own past actions. If Oreste had been tormented by hallucinations *before* being confronted with the truth, it would certainly be easier for us to speak of his trauma. However, instead of Caruth's model—where the traumatic event remains subliminally recognized but essentially unprocessed—we have a more conventional tragic schema of "anagnorisis": the passage from ignorance to knowledge. What triggers Oreste's madness is not his moment of mental absence, but the point at which he realizes what he has done during this moment.[43] Longepierre therefore sunders the causal connection between "unclaimed experience" and hallucinatory repetition that modern trauma theory assumes. The "traumatic" event for his Oreste is not the original "unclaimed" act but rather the shock of anagnoritic discovery.

Yet, perhaps paradoxically, the sundering of these two elements might strengthen Oreste's case as trauma victim in another respect. This becomes clearer when we return to Corneille's reflections on the myth. Corneille insists that once a dramatist has removed Orestes's responsibility for the murder, Orestes no longer needs "the avenging Furies to torment him, because he would remain innocent."[44] From Corneille's perspective, it is precisely because Oreste is mentally absent from the murder that he is innocent, and therefore does not need to be punished. Longepierre, on the other hand, removes Oreste's culpability but nonetheless keeps the Furies—in order to inflict a punishment that, for Corneille at least, Oreste no longer deserves. And if there is now no longer an ethical or aesthetic reason to have the "innocent" Oreste persecuted by the Furies, then their appearance thus becomes essentially superfluous. Previously, Clytemnestra's murder had appeared as one of those brute givens of history that should not have happened but somehow did. Yet in Longepierre's subtle rewriting of the myth, Oreste's punishment becomes at least as horrific—as causally gratuitous, as scandalously unjustified—as the original murder. From this perspective, Oreste's hallucinations themselves become entirely independent of the deed itself—further evidence, perhaps, that we are not dealing with trauma in the strictest modern sense.

In this respect, it is thus—paradoxically—the very gratuitousness of Oreste's hallucinations that reaffirms his claims to trauma. After all, if his hallucinations are truly gratuitous, then Oreste, rather than being a being (just) a perpetrator, now becomes a true victim—both innocent of his original deed and undeservedly punished for it. We have, in a sense, a clash of theory and practice. According to early modern thought, the tragic narrative should preserve at least a semblance of poetic justice, and so the "unclaimed" nature of Oreste's experience is precisely what should spare him his hallucinations and compulsive repetitions. In dramatic practice, however, Oreste's unclaimed experience and his hallucinations can be juxtaposed and yoked together despite their theoretical incompatibility. In this clash of theory and practice, dramatic practice wins out. So although it may be impossible to offer a definitive answer to the simple question "is Orestes traumatized?" exploring his case opens up a range of fascinating further questions—not only about the interaction between modern and early modern theories of psychology but also about the nature of poetic justice, the awkward interplay of innocence and culpability in moments of mental absence, and the sometimes antagonistic relationship between dramatic theory and dramatic practice. Whether we regard Oreste as truly traumatized or as a mere part of the prehistory of trauma, Longepierre and Crébillon certainly move far closer in practice to modern notions of trauma than the theories of their period would apparently allow them to think.

NOTES

1. "Un ossessivo ritmo ripetitivo," Anna Barsotti, *Alfieri e la scena: Da fantasmi di personaggi a fantasmi di spettatori* (Rome: Bulzoni, 2001), 107.
2. "Imagination blessée," Georges de Scudéry, *Apologie du théâtre* (Paris: Courbé, 1639), 18. "Ayant le cerveau blessé, et la conscience troublée, [. . .] pense voir ce qu'il ne voit pas," Guez de Balzac, *Dissertations critiques* (Paris: Jolly, 1665), 544.
3. Sigmund Freud, *Beyond the Pleasure Principle*, in *The Standard Edition of the Complete Psychological Works of Sigmund Freud*, vol. 18 (1920–22): *Beyond the Pleasure Principle, Group Psychology and Other Works*, 1-283 (London: The Hogarth Press and the Institute of Psychoanalysis, 1955).
4. Ruth Leys, *Trauma: A Genealogy* (Chicago: University of Chicago Press, 2000), 297.
5. "Il est donc des remords!," Voltaire, *Mahomet*, in *Zaïre: Le Fanatisme ou Mahomet le prophète, Nanine ou l'Homme sans préjugé, Le Café ou l'Ecossaise*, ed. Jean Goldzink, 133–210 (Paris: Garnier-Flammarion, 2004), vol. 4, 1465.
6. For more on the repetition compulsion and its relationship to traumatic events, see Freud, *Beyond the Pleasure Principle*, 18:1–283.
7. "N'étoient autre chose que les reproches & les remords secrets de la conscience," *Encyclopédie, ou dictionnaire raisonné des sciences, des arts et des métiers*, ed. Denis Diderot et al., 28 vols. (Geneva: Briasson, 1754–72), vol. 4, 1073, s. v. "Contrition."
8. "L'antiquité les a toûjours regardées comme des déesses inexorables, dont l'unique occupation étoit de punir le crime, non-seulement dans les Enfers, mais même dès cette vie, poursuivant sans relâche les criminels, soit par des remords qui ne leur donnoient

aucun repos, soit par des visions terribles, qui leur faisoient souvent perdre le sens," *Encyclopédie*, vol. 7, 382.

9. "Les Remords d'Oreste." Jean-Paul Sartre, *"Huis clos" suivi de "Les Mouches"* (Paris: Gallimard, 1976), 2.2.8 [page 211].

10. "Ne vous imaginez pas [. . .] que les impies & les scélérats soient tourmentés par les *furies* qui les poursuivent avec leurs torches ardentes: les remords qui suivent le crime, sont les véritables *furies* dont parlent les poëtes," *Encyclopédie*, vol. 7, 382 (italics in original).

11. See Essam Safty, *La Mort baroque: Idéologie et mort dans la tragédie baroque en France* (Paris: L'Harmattan, 2005), 300.

12. Perhaps surprisingly, Racine does not make it clear whether the play takes place before or after Oreste's murder of Clytemnestra. Although the passage from Virgil's *Aeneid* that he quotes in his preface insists that Oreste is "driven on by the Furies for his crimes" [scelerus Furiis agitatus], the play itself tends to present Oreste as naturally melancholic rather than supernaturally persecuted. See Racine, *Œuvres complètes, I: Théâtre-poésie*, ed. Georges Forestier (Paris: Gallimard [Pléiade], 1999), 197. The issue is discussed by Peter France, "Oreste and Orestes," *French Studies* 23, no. 2 (1969): 131–37; France concludes that "Racine seems to me to succeed triumphantly in having it both ways" (136).

13. See "Racine's Spectral Stagecraft: *Andromaque* (1667)," in *Haunting Presences: Ghosts in French Literature, Film, Photography and Theory*, ed. David Evans and Kate Griffiths, 60–73 (Cardiff: University of Wales Press, 2009).

14. "Tiens, tiens, voilà le coup que je t'ai réservé," *Andromaque*, in Racine, *Œuvres complètes*, I. (5.5.1676). Further references to *Andromaque* will be to this edition. This edition gives the 1667 version of the play; in later versions this line will become l.1632.

15. Cathy Caruth, *Unclaimed Experience: Trauma, Narrative, and History* (Baltimore: Johns Hopkins University Press), 1, 2.

16. "Tout va tres bien pour nous," *Tragedie de Sophocles intitulée Electre*, trans. Lazare de Baïf (Paris: Roffet, 1537), F.ii.

17. "[Le] plus affreux des crimes," Prosper Jolyot de Crébillon, *Electre*, ed. John Dunkley (Exeter, UK: University of Exeter Press, 1980), 5.9.1650. All subsequent references to Crébillon's play will be to this edition. "Un coup dont frémit la nature" (5.7.1594).

18. Aristotle, *Poetics*, 1453b, in *Classical Literary Criticism*, ed. by D. A. Winterbottom, [51–90] (Oxford, UK: Oxford University Press, 1972), 68.

19. "Il n'est pas vraisemblable [. . .] que Clytemnestre assassine son mari, qu'Oreste poignarde sa mère; mais l'histoire le dit, et la représentation de ces grands crimes ne trouve point d'incrédules," Corneille, *Discours de la tragédie*, in *Œuvres complètes*, vol. 3, ed. Georges Couton, [142–73] (Paris: Gallimard [Pléiade], 1987), esp. 118.

20. “Délicatesse,.” Corneille, 118. “Pour rectifier ce sujet à notre mode, il faudrait qu'Oreste n'eût dessein que contre Egisthe, qu'un reste de tendresse respectueuse pour sa mère lui en fît remettre la punition aux Dieux, que cette reine s'opiniâtrât à la protection de son adultère, et qu'elle se mît entre son fils et lui si malheureusement, qu'elle reçût le coup que ce prince voudrait porter à cet assassin de son père. Ainsi elle mourrait de la main de son fils, comme le veut Aristote, sans que la barbarie d'Oreste nous fît horreur, comme dans Sophocle, ni que son action méritât des Furies vengeresses pour le tourmenter, puisqu'il demeurerait innocent,” Corneille, *Discours de la tragédie*, in Couton, *Œuvres complètes*, 161.
21. To make things more complicated, the ending to *Andromaque* was itself at least partly inspired by an episode from the end of Corneille's first comedy, *Mélite* (1629). For more on this, see Maurice Delcroix, “Eraste-Oreste,” *Cahiers de littérature du XVIIe siècle* 7 (1985): 141–59.
22. Hilaire-Bernard de Longepierre, *Electre*, ed. T. Tobari (Paris: Nizet, 1981), 5.2.1521–27.
23. “Sans plus me connaître, / De tous mes sens troublés j'ai cessé d'être maître; / Je sais confusément qu'en mon ardent transport, / J'ai frappé, j'ai porté l'épouvante et la mort, / J'ai fait couler le sang et régner le carnage ; / Et j'ai cru voir enfin à travers le nuage, / Qu'avaient mis sur mes yeux les dieux et mon courroux, / Apollon qui guidait ma vengeance et mes coups” (5.5.1617–24).
24. Caruth, *Unclaimed Experience*, 60.
25. “Forfait inhumain” (5.7.1672).
26. “Quoi, seigneur! avez-vous oublié que la reine, / Vous voyant au tyran porter un coup certain, / S'est jetée entre deux, l'a reçu dans son sein?” (5.7.1674–76).
27. See 5.7.1707–08.
28. “Barbares Euménides” (5.7.1721).
29. “Tu m'entrouves le flanc, tu m'arraches le cœur” (5.7.1735).
30. See 5.7.1739–40.
31. “Il perd le sentiment” (5.7.1741). See Racine, *Andromaque*, 5.5.1689.
32. Caruth, *Unclaimed Experience*, 7.
33. “Je suis mort!” (5.7.1732).
34. “Fureur” (Crébillon, *Electre*, 5.5.1537).
35. “Votre main redoutable alloit trancher sa [Egysthe's] vie : / Dans ce fatal instant la Reine l'a saisie. / Vous, sans considérer qui pouvoit retenir / Une main que les Dieux armoient pour le punir, / Vous avez d'un seul coup qu'ils conduisoient peut-être, / Fait couler tout le sang dont ils vous firent naître” (5.7.1601–6).
36. “Peut-être” (5.7.1605).
37. “Gémissemens” and “cris douloureux” (5.9.1659).
38. “Egysthe! ah! c'en est trop. Il faut qu'à ma colere . . . / Que vois-je? dans ses mains, la teste de ma mere!” (5.9.1661–62).

39. "Quels regards! où fuirai-je? ah, monstre furieux, / Quel spectacle oses-tu presenter à mes yeux ? / Je ne souffre que trop, monstre cruel, arrête, / A mes yeux effrayez dérobe cette tête. / Ah, ma mere, épargnez votre malheureux fils . . ." (5.9.1663).
40. "Monstre"; "quelque Furie" (5.8.1617).
41. "Dieux, vous ne sçavez point comme on punit un crime" (5.9.1634).
42. "Dieux! les plus criminels seroient-ils plus punis?" (5.8.1676).
43. That said, we might also note that the early modern example that both Freud and Caruth consider in their discussions of trauma—Tasso's *Gerusalemme liberata*—follows a similar pattern. Although neither Freud nor Caruth pick up on this fact, Tancredi is made aware of Clorinda's true identity shortly after killing her.
44. "Des Furies vengeresses pour le tourmenter, puisqu'il demeurerait innocent," Corneille, *Discours de la tragédie*, in Couton, *Œuvres complètes*, 163.

13

Trauma, Ritual, and the Temporality of War in George Farquhar's *The Recruiting Officer*

TAMAR LEROY

Silvia in breeches enters the stage of *The Recruiting Officer* (1706) near the close of the third act, and we quickly see that she serves as an echo of Captain Plume and a distillation of the idea of the soldier. As "Jack Wilful," wearing her recently deceased brother's suit of clothes, she sweepingly declares, "I live where I stand; I have neither home, house, nor habitation beyond this spot of ground."[1] Like Plume, Wilful has aristocratic airs yet nothing to prop herself up on in the world but a self-willed personal presence, as she replies with braggadocio when asked about her lineage, "I'm related to all the Wilfuls in Europe, and I'm head of the family at present" (3.2.146–47). Not yet enlisted, she displays a freedom of movement and backtalking to authority that far exceeds Plume, the protagonist of *The Recruiting Officer*, a captain just returned after the victorious Battle of Blenheim (August 13, 1704) to enlist new recruits for the ongoing War of Spanish Succession (1701–14).[2] Yet for Wilful/Silvia, as a man with apparently limited means and a penchant for trouble, enlistment and thus an end to this liberty is inevitable. Reveling in a loss of freedom by assuming a masculine position in which she is granted the means to point out these cultural ironies in the first place, she serves the role of the good joke-teller in Freudian terms, displaying "a kind of narcissistic carapace—triumphant and invulnerable to pain, yet fully cognisant of it."[3] The identity category of the soldier in the eighteenth century reflected an alternate valuation of worth based on skill rather than birth or fortune, but remained at the same time unmoored, even vagabond, a view connected to the exigencies of military life (long deployments; high mortality rate; poor physical health of soldiers and recruits) and cultivated by the British government.[4] The popularity of Silvia's breeches role in performance highlights an aspect of the play not often considered—the vulnerability of the soldier figure.[5] Lack of sustained consideration of the soldier's vulnerability in the play has left unexamined its management of the traumatic effects of prolonged military engagement, since the simultaneous inclusion and containment of the body's vulnerability in a time of war does not fit literary models of trauma that find closure and wholeness to be the goal of narration. The play, instead, serves as an often-repeated exercise in trauma-negotiating rather than healing, addressing insoluble cultural tensions.[6] The threat of violation that attends Silvia's breeches-role speaks to the way she is like the male soldier—a figure who is positioned, through enlistment, as imminently violable, already castrated. I propose that shifting the grounds of traumatic representation from the unrepresentable in experience to the irreconcilable in social practice helps account for the unpredictable ways *The Recruiting Officer* was taken up in performance—from patriotic and redemptive ends, to satire, subversion, or a placement of martial ethos above loyalty to the state.

Civilian life in *The Recruiting Officer* is suffused with military associations as the recruiters, Plume and Kite, intrude upon Shrewsbury and transform the rural locale into a quasi-martial space. This is highly appropriate, as the War of Spanish Succession was a "global war that witnessed pitched battles across Europe and at sea" and also enacted the intrusion of war abroad into everyday life in England to a degree not before seen.[7] The use of modern approaches to warfare (artillery and explosives, line-firing "between . . . closely packed troops," and innovations such as platoon firing) alongside older ones (cavalry, swords, siege tactics) made engagements in this period especially devastating; the Battle of Blenheim itself saw "over 30,000 casualties . . . out of the 108,000 combatants."[8] And while Blenheim was a much celebrated victory understood to be orchestrated by Marlborough's tactical innovations, the "limited victory" and massive casualties at Malplaquet (September 11, 1709) at a later date in the same war contributed to Marlborough's falling out of favor with much of the public and the further association of the war with the too-costly diversion of funds and lives entailed in maintaining a large-scale army.[9] It is significant that the play, in its frequent performances throughout the century, could be taken up in a variety of contexts; for instance, from celebrating Marlborough and the victory at Blenheim to satirizing Marlborough just a few years later.[10] While Farquhar's apparent participation in the militarization of English society is noted by critics of this play, I would like to reframe this intrusion of the modern soldier into the folkways of English country life differently: as a psychosocial problem of the soldier's homecoming.[11] The theater is one of the places, historically, that "combat veterans and . . . citizenry . . . meet together face to face in [the] daylight" of public life.[12] Plume and the other military figures' humor in the play, peppered with morbid, offhand references to battle, dismemberment, and the vulnerability of the body, subtly invites viewers to partake in the soldier's temporally distorted experience of the body, what Jonathan Shay describes in a twentieth-century context as the veteran's "cramped, eternal present, extending no further than the next C-rations, death, cigarette, or fire fight."[13] I suggest that by shifting the grounds of analysis from the play's "amiable" approach to the horrors of war and instead to the traumatic, ritual effect that humor in the face of extreme experiences often has, the morbid humor in *The Recruiting Officer* is revealed to function along an intersection of pain and public connection that evades the political uses that are often ascribed to the play's performances.[14] As an often-repeated performance that breaches traumatic content and evades clear ascriptions of ideological intent, the play is an expression of pain in the face of irreconcilable or increasingly entrenched social forces.

The undercurrent of traumatic or disrupted temporality in this comedy is carried via language and morbid joking that gives a sense of the closeness to death and injury that typifies enlistment; it is also carried via the eccentric army plot and the physical presence of soldier-figures that carry associations of vulnerability. The play begins with Captain Plume and Sergeant Kite, just returned from the War of Spanish Succession, prowling for fresh recruits in rural Shrewsbury. Their search intersects with Plume's courtship of Silvia, the daughter of Judge Balance, which is paralleled by the courtship of Melinda (Silvia's childhood friend) by Worthy, a local gentleman. Plume, realizing he cannot win Silvia to his bed before marriage, begins to concede his rakish ways and consider honorable marriage, and we find that Balance looks favorably upon Plume as a match for his daughter. This changes with the unexpected death of Silvia's older brother, which renders her heir to her father's fortune and propels her out of Plume's league (now that she is a more marketable catch, Balance forbids concourse between the two). Amid these developments Plume and Kite successfully recruit two Shrewsbury locals with rustic names, Costar Pearmain and Thomas Appletree. One is duped; the other enlists against his better judgment but out of affection for his more gullible friend. This sense of fellow-feeling in the army connects with the running joke in the play that the army is like marriage. This joke echoes a commonplace trope that looms large in the eighteenth century, the "metaphorical association between sexual aggression and war," as it is understood that Plume uses seduction tactics to gain recruits, and more darkly, that enlistment is like marriage in that it is often unto death.[15] In keeping with the morbid turn of the metaphor of enlistment as marriage, "the play refuses to sentimentalize the outcome for Pearmain and Appletree, making it clear that they are exchanging independence for a life of military slavery and probable death."[16] The army plot and the marriage plot fully intersect when Silvia cross-dresses as a young spark named "Jack Wilful" (and later named "Pinch") to observe Plume in his element, to see if he is sleeping with the country girl Rose, and to get recruited into the army by Plume (and, of course, to escape her father's attempt to send her away from Shrewsbury to keep her away from Plume).[17] Wilful is brought before her father, Balance the magistrate, for debauching Rose (unhappily for Rose, the two shared a bed but no debauchery occurred); after much hilarious hyper-masculine performance as a rake and ne'er-do-well, Jack Wilful eventually reveals that she is Silvia in disguise, and Plume and Silvia marry.

In *The Recruiting Officer*, humor potentially lays-bare deeply rooted cultural experiences of unease associated with war: trauma, uprootedness, precarity, injury. Humor in the play tends to be noted for its potential effect of naturalizing a rapidly technologized or changing experience of warfare, making ruthless warfare and its penetration into England and abroad the new normal and even attractively modern.[18] Yet how joking about vulnerability in this play fixates on and renegotiates the experience of pain and restriction brought on by modern warfare without resolving it suggests that humor has a more complicated function here. The comic performer or joke-teller in the context of trauma navigates painful subject matter, opening up the possibility of "collective-restorative intimacy" between performer and audience in a shared cultural situation of pain and unease.[19] This role is taken up by Plume and Kite, but most of all by Silvia for her unique position as a cross-dressing soldier who is at once both more and less vulnerable or physically constrained than the two recruiting officers. Her female embodiment makes her violability more apparent (as jokes and innuendo surrounding her cross-dressing role center around castration, impotence, and sexual violation). But as the female lead of high degree pursuing her lover within the framework of the comic plot, she is also able to back-talk to authority and flirt with enlistment without the risk of succumbing to the damage of the body that soldiers are subject to. Silvia takes on the ritual role of the comic performer who, as she is aware of pain associated with military service but also stands aloof of its silencing effects, "is able . . . to communicate, to figure, to embody risky, concrete-fantasy material (shock, profanity, unease)."[20] I call this negotiation because the comic performer serves the role of bringing forth, within the performative space of the "affective sociality of the group," aspects of social life or cultural contradiction "that everyone 'feels' but people often do *not* make explicit."[21] As some theorists of disability and trauma suggest, the acknowledgment of pain in art affirms an experience of collective existence that may not have previously had a language, forging a connection of life "lived in common," revealed through pain and vulnerability.[22] In this way, mediums such as public performance provide affective strategies for living with precarity.

Applying theories of disability and trauma that foreground the experience of bodily suffering—such as the concept of crip time—to the army plot of *The Recruiting Officer* helps to show how the play not only voices but ritually reenacts a nonnormative experience of temporality, one that is defined by its relation to disrupted life stages, non- or eccentric reproduction, and, most significantly, the foregrounding of death and physical debility in youth. *The Recruiting Officer* can be said to contain a bifurcated structure featuring a seemingly normative plotline (the marriage plot) that is simultaneous with what we might call a crip plot—the one of army life and recruiting.[23] To discuss this plotline as crip, I am using concepts of crip time that emphasize how illness, disability, or queerness, which create alternate or "strange temporalities," reveal the artificial structure of seemingly natural life stages rather than reaffirm their naturalness.[24] "Crip time" can be understood "as [a] resistant orientation" in the way that it eschews, or shows the impossibility of "engaging in particular behaviors at particular moments [that have] become reified as the natural, common-sense course of human development."[25] The bifurcation of the plot in Farquhar's play easily lends itself to cross-pollination between the two plotlines, with the marriage plot being cripped (or queered)—such as through Silvia's cross-dressing and the elements of the play that highlight discontinuity in life stages and vexed or eccentric reproduction.[26] The play ends on a note of eccentric and even morbid reproduction, with Plume declaring that by marrying, "with some regret I quit the active field, / Where glory full reward for life does yield; / But the recruiting trade with all its train / Of lasting plague, fatigue, and endless pain, / I gladly quit, with my fair spouse to stay, / And raise recruits the matrimonial way" (5.7.150–55). This remaining tension between the concluding marriage and the ongoing conflict is often noted about the play, for instance, that it "ends normatively with the 'taming' of Plume in the form of marriage to Silvia, but the captain's resolve to quit the 'recruiting trade'" and "'raise recruits the matrimonial way' accentuates rather than obscures the blurring of boundaries between military and civilian worlds in the play as a whole," yet the underlying effect of this continued tension remains to be explored.[27] That the two plots cross-pollinate and intersect, but are never fully reconciled, reflects the essential irreconcilability of large-scale modern military life in what are perceived as traditional or natural life-ways; the military is both at the heart of modern culture but always set apart (which is especially seen in the difficulty of reintegrating the returning soldier back into civilian life). The morbid military humor that becomes a cultural commonplace through plays like *The Recruiting Officer* continuously evokes this frisson of presence and displacement.[28]

As previously mentioned, *The Recruiting Officer* is suffused with darkly humorous references to the soldier's experience of temporality that break the soldier or veteran's world down to the details of survival and potential injury.[29] For instance, Plume asks early in the play, revealing a view of the world in which battlefield injury exists everywhere, "Suppose I married a woman that wanted a leg? Such a thing might be, unless I examined the goods beforehand" (1.1.231–32). When he agrees to join hands in matrimony with

Silvia and leave the martial life behind, he concedes, "Why then, I have saved my legs and arms, and lost my liberty; secure from wounds I'm prepared for the gout" (5.7.80–81), suggesting that the hazards of war differ in degree but not kind from the disabilities that await him in civilian life. References to disability are picked up by civilian characters; the civilian gentleman Worthy complains to Plume that his romantic progress with Melinda, Silvia's friend, goes "very slowly. Cupid had formerly wings, but I think in this age he goes upon crutches, or I fancy Venus has been dallying with her cripple Vulcan when my amour commenced, which has made it go on so lamely" (3.1.175–78). Metaphors, similes, and images that graphically reduce the body to blood and guts figure prominently in speech in the play. Kite's description of a ravelin ironically reveals the cruel effects of martial technology on the human body; Kite explains to the simpleminded rustic character Bullock, "Why 'tis like a modern minced pie, but the crust is confounded hard, and the plumbs are somewhat hard of digestion" (3.1.91–92). Captain Brazen (the army officer in competition with Worthy for Melinda's favors) crudely mangles the martial bravura that Plume displays more attractively (and Kite knowingly satirizes) in grotesque references to bodies dismembered in war, figuratively including his own. Brazen declares to Melinda: "My hand, heart's blood, and guts are at your service" (3.2.71–72); similarly, he bloviates before a duel, "Why then, fire and fury! I have eaten smoke from the mouth of a cannon. Sir, don't think I fear powder, for I live upon't" (5.6.13–14); and without catching how morbid the detail is, he fixates on the missed snack of "Poor Jack Laconic: he was killed at the battle of Landen! I remember that he had a blue riband in his hat that very day, and after he fell, we found a piece of neat's tongue in his pocket" (3.1.215–18). One has here the "cramped, eternal present" of the soldier according to Shay, in which the prosaic things on one's person—the blue ribbon, the "neat's tongue"—are attached, without distinction, to violence and sudden death, and are often voiced irreverently.[30] In *The Recruiting Officer*, strength and physical ability continuously fold back onto the capacity of a youthful, able body to be wounded and destroyed. The location of the moment of the militarization of the individual body to the moment of enlistment rather than on the battlefield demonstrates not only an understanding that military service thrusts the soldier (and by extension, the warring nation) into a temporality of injuring but also reflects an uneasiness with this insight.[31] In Farquhar's play the soldier carries wartime back with him, as it is understood to be enmeshed with his physical form, even if he has no visible wounds.

While *The Recruiting Officer* is a patriotic play that revels in the victory at Blenheim, it also has strongly satirical elements; recent analyses of the play have seen it as counterpoising pro-war and antiwar sentiment.[32] Another interpretive possibility would be that the play is, on some level, pre- or extra-ideological, embodying the trauma of war at the haptic level of experience, and that this has been the unarticulated source of the play's enduring appeal. "Haptic" techniques of identification, which are often found in performances and literature about the experience of war, encourage the viewer or reader to connect with characters at the level of the body.[33] Although "the non- or prelinguistic aspects of experience, perception, and affect" of haptic identification can be shored up in the service of an ideological message, they are also diffuse, unstable, and easily unfocused.[34] Trauma, as I will discuss, is deeply connected to ritual, and this play, especially for its obsessive re-performance throughout the eighteenth century, can definitely be considered ritualistic. Theatrical performance in general is very ritualistic—connected to the creation and continued remembrance of cultural material in an embodied, often-repeated structure. It is through performance, Joseph Roach suggests, that "culture reproduces and recreates itself," especially through "the process of surrogation [that] does not begin or end but continues as actual or perceived vacancies occur in the network of relations that constitute the social fabric."[35] It is for this reason that Marvin Carlson calls "the physical theater, as a site of the continuing reinforcement of memory by surrogation . . . not surprisingly among the most haunted of human cultural structures," carrying the burdens of cultural myths and substituted bodies that, as Roach states, stage the "doomed search for originals by continuously auditioning stand-ins."[36] *The Recruiting Officer*, Kevin Gardner notes, "performed at the beginning of each season" in London for most of the eighteenth century following its debut in 1706, also "inaugurat[ed]" the openings of many theaters in the colonies.[37] While the plot seems to come to a resolution (both on the level of marriage promised in comedy and of recruitment promised in the subject matter of the play), the language of Farquhar's comedy creates a dark undercurrent that gives a strong sense of the body's vulnerability and destruction in combat and, perhaps more significantly, foreshadowed in enlistment. This is heightened by the dual fragility and predation suggested in the characters of Plume and Kite, and which is made particularly visible in Silvia's cross-dressing role. While gender tends to be the focus in analyses of breeches roles on the Restoration and eighteenth-century stage, this is not usually considered in relation to the identity of the soldier, which should not be casually conflated with ideals of masculinity broadly as well as specific to the period.[38] As Silvia in breeches, Kite, and Plume display through their morbid humor and stage appeal, the soldier's body serves as a site where irreconcilable tensions of modernity—the toll of martial power on individual bodies, the molding of strong and "able" soldiers for disability and destruction—are publicly, ritually, contended with, contested, and explored.

The play can thus be said to be an often-repeated exercise in trauma negotiation rather than healing. Different cultural models of narrative lead to different ways of publicly addressing traumatic events or experiences.[39] For this reason Allan Young suggests that "trauma" in its contemporary usage as a label for addressing extreme suffering may be more usefully seen in the context of the ritual, cultural work of myth. The retelling and public acknowledgment of extreme events of suffering—such as the Holocaust, trauma connected to certain wars, or public movements that give voice to victims of sexual and childhood trauma—places the particular event or kind of suffering or extremity in the context of "trauma," which in turn defines how it is publicly addressed or even "sacraliz[ed]" via "the construction of collective mimetic rituals and sacred sites"; in this way, the extreme experience becomes a part of public recognition and collective mourning.[40] As Young suggests, an essential quality of the current concept of trauma is the public call to listen to the telling of the event, which elevates the traumatic event to the realm of "myth," understood to be "a narrative . . . [that] is shared by a group of people who believe that it . . . explains their collective identity . . . and illuminates their present condition."[41] Trauma is acknowledged publicly by an audience's attentiveness to the traumatic narrative and the memorialization of the event in public rituals; in this way, "the corresponding ritual attitude [to myth] is mimesis: a collective effort to enact the myth" by "efforts . . . aimed at imitating or identifying with people and tropes . . . from the past."[42] Young gives as a central example of this mythic-historicizing function of trauma the shift of the view of "the death camps" of Nazi Germany (which he suggests were originally not separated in public discourse from the general violence of the war) to the term "Holocaust" in the 1960s that memorialized the specific trauma of that event.[43] This is not to say that trauma does not exist; instead theorists such as Young shift trauma from the realm of the functioning of individual memory to the public arena of rituals of remembrance and collective mourning that are specific to certain time periods and cultural moments.[44]

While Farquhar's comedy does not give a narrative reconstruction of events, it ritually invites civilians and other soldiers into a sense of the temporal landscape of warfare—the certitude of injury or injuring the soldier is locked into at the moment of enlistment, and his morbid humor and other coping strategies to survive in this situation of heightened but constant, even banal, closeness to death. Wartime, as Elaine Scarry suggests, has its own temporality enmeshed with the physical and psychological experience of receiving and doling out pain. This sense of "anticipated injury," which pervades and defines not only combat but also the experience of enlistment and the development of battlefield strategy and tactics, refers specifically to "injury . . . judged to have the greatest effect if *foreseen*."[45] It is essentially a "temporal form of injuring" that begins far before the soldier sets foot on the battlefield and remains far beyond.[46] Language that draws attention to this nonnormative experience of temporality at the haptic level of bodily pain—in this play, language defined by the body's relation to injury, constraint, and imminent destruction—collectivizes rather than isolates the soldier's experience. It serves a different function than "victorious national fiction[s]" that purposefully set out to efface the primary purpose of war—injury and destruction.[47] In this way, the soldier in Farquhar's play is not exactly addressed as a mere pawn of the state machine that wages the war that potentially destroys his body, but is instead also a part of a community that has at least acknowledged, upon his return, this intimate and radical experience of suffering. This public evocation of how "anticipatory injury" is suffered brings it into the realm of what contemporary theorists call crip or trauma art, which gives primacy to the intimate ways in which time and place are defined by physical relations to constriction, pain, and relative ease of movement. Disability theorist Alison Kafer explicitly makes the connection between crip time and the modern understanding of trauma as post-traumatic stress disorder (PTSD), stating that the "'Strange temporalities' [of crip time] . . . include the experiences of those with PTSD . . . who live in a kind of anticipatory time, scanning their days for events or exposures that might trigger a response."[48] In the play the soldier's relation to his body through the destruction of it he anticipates on the battlefield merges with the evocation of emotional effects that last far beyond the war, the anticipatory time experienced by the traumatized individual who continuously recalls this sensation of anticipated injury. The public acknowledgment of this crip experience of time brings the play into the realm of "trauma art" and reveals its resistant potential.

Tobin Siebers defines "trauma art" in the context of disability aesthetics as a specifically "collective" form of expression through which "emotions . . . are created by allowing individual events, bodies, and objects to be overlaid with communal significance. This significance relates specifically to the power of trauma to invoke a vision of collective existence, which explains why . . . [such] work seems to 'contain' trauma, that is, both to expose and organize it, to witness it both as a threat to and symbol of [the social fabric]."[49] Often grim, irreverent, or disturbing, trauma art centrally fixates on the "traumatic bod[y]" that "may serve the collective representation of competing communities" and is thus expansive in the possible associations it may evoke.[50] As Siebers suggests, "Images of wounding, danger, disability, and disaster travel well for this reason," picked up by "competing communities" and to a variety of ends.[51] The play begins with the recruiting officers, Captain Plume and Sergeant Kite, positioned as outsiders, with Kite cajoling a "mob" of rustics and presenting them with the "cap of honour" to entice them to enlist (1.1.13). One of the mob's unidentified members retorts, "My mind misgives me plaguily," and announces that the cap "smells woundily of sweat and brimstone" (1.1.23–24). As Tiffany Stern observes, the smell of "sweat [on the cap] contains the essence of physical suffering within it."[52] It suggests not only the exertions of battle but also the pungent or putrid odors of blood, wounds, and gunpowder. The cap of honor, "smell[ing] woundily" and in this way inscribed with the extremity of its former wearer's experience, brings a piece of the foreign battlefields to an English audience. The cap, like the bodies of men returned from military conflict on the Continent and represented onstage as rakish war heroes, possesses a surplus of meaning connected both to symbolic status and to particular experiences.

The objects of war are at first positioned as grotesque and abject in the play. This subtly shifts when Captain Plume, also just returned from the successful Battle of Blenheim, replies to the local gentleman Worthy's exclamation, "Plume! My dear Captain, welcome. Safe and sound returned!" with: "I 'scaped safe from Germany, and sound, I hope, from London; you see I have lost neither leg, arm, nor nose. Then, for my inside, 'tis neither troubled with sympathies nor antipathies, and I have an excellent stomach for roast beef" (1.1.140–44). In this exchange, the objects indicative of war's destruction of the body are more clearly folded into their equivalents in civilian life. The conflation in *The Recruiting Officer* of injury anticipated and escaped in the battlefields abroad and the nightlife of London demonstrates how a sense of "anticipatory injury"—including its lasting effects on individual serviceman—is interwoven with the rakish, "devil-may-care" identity of the seasoned soldier Plume.[53] The alternate temporality of the battlefield is no longer placed in opposition to the normative time of the civilian world, which is more fully suggested to be beset by temporalities defined in nonnormative ways, such as by the presence of disease and death in youth via the sex work economy. The grotesque image of loss of an "arm, leg, [or] nose" conflates the dangers of the battlefield with the ravages of late-stage syphilis, and the recently outmoded reference to humoral balance of the body ("sympathies" and "antipathies") comically folds into a reference to fortitude and perhaps even a morbid sense of the almost certain fatality of intestinal wounds on the battlefield.[54] Analogy is invited between the temporality of the battlefield, defined by the certitude of injury or injuring, and the dangers to the body that pervade civilian life.

Ritual and the Body

Theatrical performance in the Restoration and eighteenth century—especially heroic drama—has a highly ritualistic function, as argued by Joseph Roach; in the performances he examines, this is connected to the symbolic displacement through performance of the "mysterious play of ethnic identity and difference" precipitated by the circum-Atlantic feedback loop of migration, commodification, and commerce.[55] Symbolic violence serves to ritually displace the real violence underlying the plentiful transactions across the Atlantic and the commodities they produced; at the same time, though, through the physicality of ritual performance—the necessary use of space, bodies, and objects—the traces of real violence carried in "circum-Atlantic memory remain visible, audible, and kinesthetically palpable to those who walk in the cities along its historic rim."[56] Like the "trauma art" discussed by Siebers, the damaged body serves as an unstable, but ritually powerful locus of emotion.

The character of Plume in *The Recruiting Officer* and the play's triumphal context—presented simultaneously as heroic and comic—subtly draws out the vulnerable side of martial victory or aptitude.[57] The ritual context of sacrifice that the plume carries on the stage in this period complicates the idea of Plume as an easy stand-in for a developing martial, masculine ideal; his association with an ideal of masculinity consistently flirts with satire. Furthermore, the plume, by the eighteenth century, is itself a vexed gender prop that "by 1620 . . . was fit neither for women nor for men. The feather" by the seventeenth century "came to inhabit a dangerous gray area, a no-man's land and a no-woman's land."[58] Catherine Howey suggests that the feather in English dress, once a purely masculine article of adornment, shifted in the early modern period with the adoption of this item into women's fashion. Women who wore the feather with other articles of male attire associated with outdoor activity would have seemed to be cross-dressing, or at least flirting with disrupted gender boundaries in dress starting in the sixteenth century. This, combined with the erotic visual association of fantastic feather headdress with unclothed inhabitants of the New World, leads Howey to suggest that "the feather best symbolizes the breakdown of visual labeling through dress" in the early modern period.[59] It comes to represent the uncertainty of symbols and visual markers, and is even unstable as a ritual accoutrement and gender prop. Yet in the subsequent centuries, rather than men dispensing with feathers because of these new associations with vanity and a New World exoticism that was also eroticized as feminine, "Men [wore] feathers well into the eighteenth century. . . . Just because feathers were being used in new ways did not mean that the old associations"—such as with martial prowess and masculinity—"were quickly discarded for new ones. Instead, new and contradictory associations of the feather existed simultaneously."[60] Thus, Captain Plume comes on the English stage in 1706 carrying a complex burden of disrupted gender norms, masculine vulnerability, and a sense of sullied heroism existing side by side with the feather as a prop associated with martial victory. One could say that Plume functions not so much as a new masculine ideal than as a ritual figure in which all these contradictory associations are publicly aired. The traditional military association of the feather folds into its vexed gendered connotations in much the same way that the elaborate or ostentatious image of the soldier in the eighteenth century simultaneously carried clashing associations, such as effeminacy, vanity, physical aptitude, bravery, and physical expendability, that could not be exorcised or resolved.[61]

The central function of Silvia's character in her cross-dressed role as Jack Wilful, who the recruiting officers in the play vie to enlist, is to underscore the body's vulnerability that is more subtly implied in Plume. She serves as a ghostly but more vibrant echo of Plume—free-talking, sprightly, but possessing a fragility and capacity for violation that may be easier for the audience to affectively access or conceptualize. Silvia's breeches role is usually explored in terms of what it potentially says of gender construction and fluidity, including the sublimation of masculine insecurities into calls for patriotic sacrifice.[62] Another view of the trope of the stage lothario who is actually a cross-dressed woman is the potential this scenario holds for satirizing "aggressive male behaviour."[63] Such humor often hinges on the superior seducing skills of the rake who is actually a woman (and thus does a male job better than men), but like any good joke, the implications are complex and often contradictory. The specter of rape and violation of both female and male bodies is not far behind in these comic tropes. In the courtroom, Silvia in breeches is "charged with rape";[64] Silvia retorts to the Constable: "Is it your wife or your daughter, booby? I ravished 'em both yesterday" (5.5.124). As Joel Schechter suggests, the context of this statement makes it especially multilayered, for "recited by an actress dressed as a man, these lines might have sounded comic to spectators, although the judges hearing her in the play take Silvia seriously," since her braggadocious statement plays upon real fears of the sexual violence of soldiers.[65] Another layer would be the implied threat of penetration that follows Silvia's character. Silvia in breeches must dodge male attempts to share a bed with her, a situation that might reveal that she is a woman under her male garb and, more sinisterly, may lead to her own rape or seduction. Thus, to deflect Plume's attempt to sleep in the same bed with her male alter ego Jack Wilful, Silvia doubles up for the night with Rose instead. The rustic maid expresses her disappointment the next day that she was not violated by the young man and "d[idn't] know whether [she] had a bedfellow or not" (5.1.6 and 5.7.131). While sleeping in bed with another woman preserves Silvia's chastity, her scheme ironically also threatens to reveal what hides beneath her breeches, her lack of the organ by which Rose desires penetration. Silvia distills the idea of the recruit (satirically and literally): she is actually willing to join, she is already a rake and a ne'er-do-well, and both like and unlike a male soldier, she serves as a symbol of castration and violability.[66] Silvia, as an emblem of the soldier in the play, is thus a figure who is already castrated, more recognizably subject to violation, yet one who is, as the cultural logic of the play demonstrates, more physically safe from the technologies of war than male soldiers and recruits (since her recruitment functions as a plot device rather than a real possibility of deployment). This shows us the way humor in the play is oriented—it flirts with the irreconcilable.

Thus, the most significant way that Silvia and Plume intersect in their capacity to attract fascination is through their doubled intersection of magnetic strength and vulnerability. Airy, "effervescent," yet in control, in her sharp words, overcompensating behavior, and even uniform of white and silver (which offers a ghostly yet elegant echo of the male uniform), it is not difficult to see Silvia condensing the unstated but implied vulnerability of Plume, hinted at in the symbolism and semiotics of plumage.[67] Focusing on this image of Silvia as the center of the play speaks to what has been missed in examinations of the play's appeal—the social functioning of humor. This is especially important in the context of how humor mediates individual and collective trauma, which the play's subject matter and grim undercurrents tap into. Comic performance evokes tensions that cannot be resolved or even directly addressed.[68] This consideration is especially necessary to the play's malleability, the way it can move through so many performative contexts so as to seem incoherent, ideologically. Rather than humor necessarily being a vehicle for an underlying and coherent message—subversion and satire or a shoring up of loyalty to the state—humor can be seen, more fundamentally, as a medium for testing deeply rooted social contradictions and tensions.

Joking in the structure of trauma, according to Iddo Tavory and Iain MacRury, essentially involves displacement of "traumata," but this displacement comes to function as one of the ways to access collective sympathy and commiseration, in daily life, for what is too painful, awkward, or confounding to address outright.[69] Two other key points are that this sort of humor functions as a strategy for coping in situations of daily extremity or psychological distress, and that for the joke to make sense in a collective context it must reveal a shared sense of fellow-feeling, with the audience, at the haptic level of the body. The joke must strike a chord in this way, either by forging a way to publicly address a shared but private experience of vulnerability, or by making intelligible the joke-teller's experience of distress by picking up on the wavelength of a broader cultural experience. Jokes surrounding Silvia's adept performance as a male soldier that also suggest nervousness about castration reoccur in the play with significant implications for Silvia's function as an echo of Plume and other soldiers. As Melinda Rabb argues, "The long eighteenth century" abounds with "male characters whose corporeality seems far more vulnerable and exposed than the" widely used "theory of the [male] gaze would suggest."[70] Rather than the safely "intact body of the male subject, on one hand, [and] eroticized female parts as objects of desire and fear, on the other," the period proliferates with literary and stage depictions of damaged male bodies, castration, and vulnerably exposed phalluses, from the obsession with castration in *Tristram Shandy*, to Lemuel Gulliver's awkwardly exposed or pruriently viewed body in *Gulliver's Travels*, to the dismembered human remains that haunt *Robinson Crusoe*, to name just a few examples.[71] Rabb suggests of this obsession throughout the period: "We might say that if the concealed male organ is the [cultural] norm, then its exposure to the gaze is a kind of displacement, a dislocation of a body part from a position of secure concealment to a position of threatened detachment, misplacement, or devaluation."[72] Rabb traces this trend back to the traumatically disruptive and destructive English Civil War, connecting this literary fascination with exposing the phallus to view (and possible destruction) to the memory of the dehumanizing capacity of modern warfare, enacted all too close to home.[73] If we are to see Silvia's breeches-role identity, Jack Wilful, as a displacement of contradictory ideas about the physical state, identity, and masculinity of the soldier, jokes that touch upon fears, insecurities, and humorous situations involving castration or sexual inadequacy are significant.

The implied sexual prowess or powers of seduction of the woman in disguise as a man serves as a comic trope in *The Recruiting Officer*.[74] This resonates on many levels, including as a jab at the clumsy seduction techniques of men and the danger of the cross-dresser being exposed and rendered sexually or socially vulnerable. This trope is especially carried from Act 4 to the conclusion of the play, initiated by Silvia's shift to sleep with Rose to evade doubling up with Plume or any other male soldier for the night. When Silvia in disguise as Wilful deflects Plume's attempt to share a bed with her for the night (he cannot tell she is a woman, but feels an attraction to her), she reiterates that she has agreed on another companion: "No, no, Captain, you forget Rose; she's to be my bedfellow you know" (4.1.163–64). Plume replies: "I had forgot; pray be kind to her" (165). Even here, the trope plays on a contrast between sexual vulnerability and sexual prowess, while also playing upon the capacity for these two opposites to fold into each other. Occurring right after Plume's speech that he is "not that rake that the world imagines" (4.1.157), it quickly becomes entangled with questions about disjunctions between the world's perception of the soldier's life and his lived experiences. Silvia's shift to sleep with Rose is necessitated by her secretly vulnerable position, the female body beneath her hypermasculine performance; this is echoed in Plume's perception of Rose as vulnerable in his injunction to Wilful: "pray be kind to her."

This dynamic is inverted by Rose's own reaction to the lack of penetration she experiences during her night with Wilful. The morning after:

> SILVIA: I have rested but indifferently, and I believe my bedfellow was as little pleased. Poor Rose! Here she comes. . . . Good morrow, my dear, how d'ye this morning?
>
> ROSE: Just as I was last night, neither better nor worse for you.
>
> SILVIA: What's the matter? Did you not like your bedfellow?

ROSE: I don't know whether I had a bedfellow or not.

SILVIA: Did I not lie with you?

ROSE: No. I wonder you could have the conscience to ruin a poor girl for nothing.

SILVIA: I have saved thee from ruin, child. Don't be melancholy; I can give you as many fine things as the captain can.

ROSE: But you can't I'm sure. (5.1.1–12)

Although this brief scene only occurs in the Q1 version of the play, part of the joke here ("I don't know whether I had a bedfellow or not") occurs word for word near the end of the play, further highlighting Rose's dissatisfaction and Silvia's loss or displacement of signifiers of male embodiment.[75]

A further point is that the threat of the lack of the phallus extends from Silvia, who embodies this lack and the vulnerability it suggests, to Plume, who does not seem to lack it, but who, as a soldier uniquely subject to the body's vulnerabilities, is continuously threatened by its loss. In the following exchange all these elements come together—with Silvia and Plume both standing in for plenitude and lack. Balance, Silvia's father, knows that Wilful (the "young gentleman soldier") is his own daughter Silvia, but Plume does not yet:

BALANCE: Pray, Captain, what have you done with your young gentleman soldier?

PLUME: He's at my quarters, I suppose, with the rest of my men.

BALANCE: Does he keep company with the common soldiers?

PLUME: No, he's generally with me.

BALANCE: He lies with you, I presume.

PLUME: No, faith. I offered him part of my bed, but the young rogue fell in love with Rose, and has lain with her, I think, since he came to town.

BALANCE: So that between you both, Rose has been finely managed.

PLUME: Upon my honour, sir, she had no harm from me.

BALANCE: [*Aside*] All's safe, I find. (5.7.21–32)

This exchange affirms that Silvia has not been violated; again, the joke that Rose desires the opposite returns and is played upon, absurdly twisting Silvia's real fear of rape but also underscoring the plenitude entailed in the phallus and the loss entailed in its absence. In the exchange, Silvia does not keep "company with the common soldiers," but Rose keeps company with two young gentleman soldiers (Wilful and Plume). Rose, like Silvia, is the repeated subject of sexual innuendo in these comic exchanges and, like Silvia, remains unviolated ("between you both, Rose has been finely managed"). Furthermore, in the double entendre "finely managed," Silvia's lack of the phallus, connected to her vulnerability and capacity to be violated, subtly folds into Plume's. Rose has "had no harm" from either Silvia or Plume; the two officers are both part of the implied sexual lack in the construction of these comic exchanges.

Vulnerable yet adept in the role of a soldier, the female soldier who dresses as a man in performance opens up a public space for reflecting on the intimate ways in which martial masculinity itself is an artificial imposition, revealing the connection between the transformation wrought on the body by military training and the cruelty inherent in this transformation, as it locks the body in the certitude of injury and injuring.[76] Silvia's cross-dressing role serves as an experiential bridge, where the more familiar or culturally legible vulnerabilities and threats of violation to the female body function to give partial access to the experience of soldiering in a rapidly technologized (and increasingly violent and large-scale) military and configuration of warfare. Looking for expressions of trauma in unexpected performative or narrative spaces—such as the subtle wavelength of shared experience that makes a joke about living with pain, fear, or vulnerability strike a chord with an audience at large—opens up new ways of understanding how trauma was negotiated in everyday life in the eighteenth century.

NOTES

1. George Farquhar, *The Recruiting Officer*, ed. Tiffany Stern (London: New Mermaids, 2010), 3.2.149–50. All parenthetical references are to this edition.
2. Denys Van Renen, "'The Air We Breathe': Warfare in Farquhar's *The Recruiting Officer*," *College English* 43, no. 2 (2016): 397–426, esp. 397.
3. Iain MacRury, "Humour as 'social dreaming': Stand-up comedy as therapeutic performance," *Psychoanalysis, Culture & Society* 17, no. 2 (2012): 185–203, esp. 189.
4. Hurl-Eamon suggests, for instance, that the British army's discouragement of marriage via policy and army culture is connected to the convenience of having unmoored

men in the military. Jennine Hurl-Eamon, *Marriage and the British Army in the Long Eighteenth Century: "The Girl I Left Behind Me"* (Oxford, UK: Oxford University Press, 2014).

5. Elizabeth Heard, *Experimentation on the English Stage, 1695–1708: The Career of George Farquhar* (London: Pickering and Chatto, 2008), 87.
6. As Iddo Tavory suggests in examining the function of morbid joking in social situations of extremity, "*Humor does not resolve tensions, but sustains them*," giving access to ironic connections that may be otherwise unspeakable (or inaccessible). Iddo Tavory, "The Situations of Culture: Humor and the Limits of Measurability," *Theory and Society: Renewal and Critique in Social Theory* 43, nos. 3–4 (2014): 277; italics in text.
7. As Van Renen continues, "the daily newspaper appeared for the first time during this period," giving English civilians frequent information on military engagements in far-flung places in this war, Van Renen, "The Air We Breathe," 397.
8. Jeremy Black, *European Warfare: 1660–1815* (New Haven: Yale University Press, 1994), 111, 112.
9. Black, *European Warfare*, 111; quote in Bruce Lenman, *Britain's Colonial Wars, 1688–1783* (Harlow, UK: Pearson, 2001), 37. On Marlborough's falling out of public favor, see Richard Holmes, *Marlborough: England's Fragile Genius*. (London: Harper, 2008), 441, 460–61. For platoon firing and Farquhar's play, see Kevin J. Gardner, "George Farquhar's *The Recruiting Officer*: Warfare, Conscription, and the Disarming of Anxiety," *Eighteenth Century Life* 25 (2001): 51.
10. *The London Stage* includes a contemporary account of a 1710 performance of *The Recruiting Officer* in which a raucous song was performed by soldiers, satirizing Marlborough's "avarice" (p. 227). *The London Stage, 1660–1800: Vol. 1, Part 2; 1700–1729*, ed. Emmett L. Avery (Carbondale: Southern Illinois University Press, 1965).
11. Shay, in *Achilles in Vietnam*, argues that how the returning soldier is received back into the civilian world has profound effects on the mental health of veterans. Jonathan Shay, *Achilles in Vietnam: Combat Trauma and the Undoing of Character* (New York: Atheneum, 1994). In terms of the militarization of English culture in the eighteenth century, Gardner and Van Renen see *The Recruiting Officer* as a successful attempt to condition the nation for ongoing military conflict and violent colonial venture. As Gardner suggests, this is also connected to attempts to shift public perception of soldiers away from distrust, since soldiers returned from conflict could be volatile members of the playhouse audience. Gardner, "Theatrum Belli: Late Restoration Comedy and the Rise of the Standing Army" *Theater Survey* 36, no. 1 (1995): 37–54.
12. Shay, *Achilles in Vietnam*, 194.
13. Shay, *Achilles in Vietnam*, 190. Gardner notices a similarity between *The Recruiting Officer* and war humor deployed in the wake of twentieth-century armed conflicts, which "continues even today to make war appear amusing, for it defuses potential

anxiety over" the way war is enmeshed with the structures of modern life. Gardner, "George Farquhar's *The Recruiting Officer*," 57. Stern views humor in the play more ambiguously, noting that "hardly surprisingly, the recruiters have bad memories; their jokes and hard drinking may relate to this" in Stern, "Introduction," xiii.

14. On the humor in the play as "amiable satire," see Gardner, "George Farquhar's *The Recruiting Officer*," 43.
15. Gillian Russell, "The eighteenth century and the romantics on war," in *The Cambridge Companion to War Writing*, ed. Kate McLoughlin, 112–25 (New York: Cambridge University Press, 2009), 113.
16. Russell, 117.
17. Silvia takes the name "Pinch" in court (5.2.62–64).
18. See Gardner, "George Farquhar's *The Recruiting Officer*," and Van Renen, "The Air We Breathe."
19. MacRury, "Humour as 'social dreaming,'" 201.
20. MacRury, 193.
21. MacRury, "Humour as 'social dreaming,'" 202; Tavory, "The Situations of Culture," 286; italics in text.
22. Tobin Siebers, *Disability Aesthetics* (Ann Arbor: University of Michigan Press, 2010), 100–120, esp. 111.
23. The play is often noted as having two plots, but the subversive content of the army plot has not been linked to crip temporalities.
24. Alison Kafer, *Feminist, Queer, Crip* (Bloomington: Indiana University Press, 2013), 38.
25. Kafer, 35, 40.
26. Kafer explicitly draws out overlaps between crip time and queer temporalities in order to emphasize the resistant potential of affirming crip modes of life. Contrary to this, Silvia's breeches role is instead often seen as largely affirming the marriage plot, since like the stereotypical cross-dressing "woman warrior" of eighteenth-century performance and narrative, she puts on a male identity in the heterosexual context of seeking out her male love interest. For a reading of Silvia in an American performative context as the patriotic "woman warrior," see Jason Shaffer, "The 'Female Martinet': Mrs. Harper, Gender, and Civic Virtue on the Early Republican Stage," *Comparative Drama* 40, no. 4 (2006): 411–32, esp. 423. Also see Beth H. Friedman-Romell, "Breaking the Code: Toward a Reception Theory of Theatrical Cross-Dressing in Eighteenth-Century London," *Theatre Journal* 47, no. 4 (1995): 459–79, on this common structure in cross-dressing performances.
27. Russell, "The eighteenth century," in McLoughlin, *The Cambridge Companion to War Writing*, 118.
28. As Russell suggests, "Shrewsbury in the play stands for 'Fortress Middle England,' a stable and secure social community able to distance itself from the wars fought in

its name. But even here, war is able to penetrate in the form of Captain Plume and his agent, the wily and ruthless Serjeant Kite. . . . The space of the stage, in standing for both Shrewsbury and Plume's larger freewheeling domain, signifies the extent to which these two 'theaters of war' are inextricable." Russell, 117.

29. As Stern suggests, "youthful fatality" plays a prominent role in the plot, and "death overshadows the drama, as is predictable in an army play." Stern, "Introduction," xiv.
30. Shay, *Achilles in Vietnam*, 190.
31. See Elaine Scarry on how the structure of warfare locks the soldier (and warring nation) in a "temporal form of injuring," in *The Body in Pain: The Making and Unmaking of the World* (New York: Oxford University Press), 79.
32. Especially see Gardner, "George Farquhar's *The Recruiting Officer*," and Van Renen, *The Other Exchange: Women, Servants, and the Urban Underclass in Early Modern English Literature* (Lincoln: University of Nebraska Press, 2017), for how this balance can be shored up to normalize the war effort.
33. For an analysis of sympathetic techniques in early war films, see Jaimey Fisher, "The Haptic Horrors of War: Towards a Phenomenology of Affect and Emotion in the War Genre in Germany, 1910s to 1950s," *Seminar: A Journal of Germanic Studies* 50, no. 1 (2014): 51–68. According to Fisher, war necessitates certain approaches to representation focused on the sensations of the body. On techniques of identification between character and viewer in horror and war films, Fisher states that "horror has consistently posed a problem" for critics of film "because it so clearly plays on negative affects and emotions that complicate any facile identificatory" structure (54).
34. Fisher, 52.
35. Joseph Roach, *Cities of the Dead: Circum-Atlantic Performance* (New York: Columbia University Press, 1996), 2.
36. Marvin Carlson, *The Haunted Stage: The Theatre as Memory Machine* (Ann Arbor: University of Michigan Press, 2002), 2; Roach, *Cities of the Dead*, 3.
37. Gardner, "George Farquhar's *The Recruiting Officer*," 1, 3, 58.
38. On ways the soldier diverged from masculine ideals, see Louise Carter, "Scarlet Fever: Female Enthusiasm for Men in Uniform, 1780–1815," in *Britain's Soldiers: Rethinking War and Society, 1715–1815*, ed. Kevin Linch and Matthew McCormack, 155–80 (Liverpool: Liverpool University Press, 2014), and Hurl-Eamon, *Marriage and the British Army*.
39. On this, see Michelle Balaev, *The Nature of Trauma in American Novels* (Evanston IL: Northwestern University Press, 2012).
40. Allan Young, "Bruno and the Holy Fool: Myth, Mimesis, and the Transmission of Traumatic Memories," in *Understanding Trauma: Integrating Biological, Clinical, and Cultural Perspectives*, ed. Laurence J. Kirmayer, Robert Lemelson, and Mark Barad, 339–62 (New York: Cambridge University Press, 2007), esp. 352.

41. Young, 339.
42. Young, 339, 347.
43. Young, 351.
44. As Balaev argues, the traumatic event does not necessarily disrupt a previous wholeness in the protagonist's consciousness, but instead often serves as the disruptive event that precipitates the individual's reevaluation of their positioning to outside forces and social structures. Balaev, *The Nature of Trauma*, 40.
45. Italics in text. Scarry, *The Body in Pain*, 79.
46. Scarry, 79.
47. Scarry, 136.
48. Kafer, *Feminist, Queer, Crip*, 38.
49. Siebers, *Disability Aesthetics*, 109, 110.
50. Seibers, 118.
51. Seibers, 118.
52. Stern, "Introduction," xiii.
53. Scarry, 79. Myers, William, introduction to *The Constant Couple; The Twin Rivals; The Recruiting Officer; The Beaux' Stratagem*, by George Farquhar, ed. by William Myers (New York: Oxford University Press, 1995), xxi.
54. Geoffrey L. Hudson finds that theories of the humors heavily inflected wounded veterans' views of their own bodies in the early modern period. "Disabled Veterans and the State in Early Modern England," in *Disabled Veterans in History*, ed. David A. Gerber, 117–44 (Ann Arbor: University of Michigan Press, 2012), esp. 130–32. Plume appears to carry over this older framework of humoral balance in his view of the emotions in Farquhar, *The Recruiting Officer*, 16n143.
55. Joseph Roach, *Cities of the Dead: Circum-Atlantic Performance* (New York: Columbia University Press, 1996), 153.
56. Roach, 30.
57. For a discussion of plumes in the context of ritual sacrifice, heroic drama, and transatlantic trade, see Roach, *Cities of the Dead*.
58. Catherine Howey, "The Vain, Erotic, Exotic Feather: Dress, Gender, and Power in Sixteenth- and Seventeenth-Century English," in *Religion, Gender, and Culture in the Pre-Modern World*, ed. Alexandra Cuffel and Brian M. Britt, 211–40 (New York: Palgrave Macmillan, 2007), esp. 234. For gender props, see Jarred Wiehe, "Propping Up and Stripping Down: Stage Properties as Technologies of Gender in Edward Ravenscroft's *The Careless Lovers* and *The London Cuckolds*," *Restoration: Studies in English Literary Culture, 1660–1700* 40, no. 2 (2016): 20.
59. Howey, "The Vain, Erotic, Exotic Feather," 233.
60. Howey, 233.

61. On these complicated and contradictory associations with military masculinity in the period, especially see Hurl-Eamon, *Marriage and the British Army*, and Louise Carter, "Scarlet Fever," in Linch and McCormack, *Britain's Soldiers*.
62. For instance, actresses playing Silvia in breeches could deploy specific recruiting elements in the performance, such as by performing the manual exercises, as Shaffer discusses in "The 'Female Martinet.'" Schaffer also discusses the patriotic uses of the "woman warrior" trope on the stage.
63. Joel Schechter, *Eighteenth-Century Brechtians: Theatrical Satire in the Age of Walpole* (Exeter, UK: University of Exeter Press, 2016), 21.
64. Schechter, 21.
65. Schechter, 21.
66. On the prevalence of images of martial male vulnerability and castration in the eighteenth century, see Melinda Rabb, "Parting Shots: Eighteenth-Century Displacements of the Male Body at War," *ELH* 78, no. 1 (2001): 103–35.
67. J. Loftis et al., *The Revels History*, quoted in Heard, *Experimentation on the English Stage*, 87.
68. As Tavory points out, deeply entrenched cultural, social, or experiential tension is central to the way humor functions: "jokes" are legible as such "because unresolved tensions and condensations of meaning always exist in social life." Tavory, "The Situations of Culture," 278.
69. MacRury, "Humour as 'social dreaming,'" 193.
70. Rabb, "Parting Shots," 109.
71. Rabb, 108–9.
72. Rabb, 109.
73. Rabb, 109–10.
74. As Wiehe says of the 1673 play *The Careless Lovers* by Edward Ravenscroft, "A young woman convincingly cross-dresses as a sexually viable gallant. Dressed as a man, she carries her masculinity so well that two experienced London whores fight for her attention." Wiehe, "Propping Up," 5.
75. As noted by Stern, the line is repeated by Rose at 5.7.131.
76. Beyond presenting "military masculinity's status" as an artificial imposition or "theatrical performance," I am suggesting the female soldier on the eighteenth-century stage shows how this imposition goes deeper, beyond gender props and braggadocio, to the profound changes wrought on the body via military training and deployment. Shaffer, "The Female Martinet," 423.

14

For Those Who Did Not See It

Transgenerational Trauma and Postmemory in Defoe's *A Journal of the Plague Year*

ANDREAS K. E. MUELLER

In 1720 the news of an outbreak of the bubonic plague in the French city of Marseille caused "an unprecedented panic" in London.[1] Occasional apprehensions about the plague had not been uncommon among Londoners since the Great Plague of 1665, the last outbreak of the disease in England, but between 1720 and 1722 it was widely assumed that London was almost certainly going to be visited by the deadly disease again. The anxiety caused by the specter of plague was at least partly anchored in a circumstance that differentiated the 1720s scare from those of the previous century: very few people had personal experience of a pestilential visitation. With the average life expectancy at around sixty years, the 1665 visitation barely fell within a statistically normal lifespan in 1720, which meant that the vast majority of London's inhabitants were simply too young to know what it meant to confront—and what could be done to survive—the plague.[2] The plague's long-term absence from English shores not only contributed to a "decreasing significance of epidemic disease" within popular culture but had also stunted the advancement of medical knowledge: "between the pestilence of 1665 and the threat of 1720, the plague had received little attention" with regard to new treatment methods.[3] This demographic context and the correlated absence of direct plague knowledge are neatly illustrated by the prominent physician Dr. Richard Mead, who in the 1720s advised the government and the public on methods to contain the disease. Born in 1673 Dr. Mead had never personally witnessed a case of plague and he therefore had to acquire his knowledge of the disease by studying official documents about and reports of previous visitations in England and around Europe.[4] Importantly, Dr. Mead was no exception: "English writers," as Paul Slack has pointed out, "had no direct acquaintance with plague themselves, despite their appeals to experience."[5]

The general lack of plague knowledge undoubtedly fueled the vigorous response of London's print market to the anticipated arrival of a pestilential epidemic. Old medical tracts were reissued alongside newly composed ones, some of which, such as Dr. Mead's *A Short Discourse Concerning Pestilential Contagion* (1720), were commissioned by the government; several pamphlets purported to offer medicinal recipes for the effective treatment of plague; and descriptive accounts of plague outbreaks, mostly of the Marseille epidemic or the Great Plague of 1665, sought to give Londoners an idea of plague pathology. Clergymen seized on the scare to deliver sermons, many of which were published, that framed plague as divine punishment, exhorting the nation to repent its sins and embrace a godly life.[6] Several publications combined some or all of these elements. The thirst for plague knowledge was considerable: between mid-1720 and 1722, when the Marseille-induced panic in London faded away, dozens of pamphlets and books concerned with plague were published, many going to several editions. This wave of plague tracts included one of the most famous English accounts of an early modern pestilential epidemic, Daniel Defoe's *A Journal of the Plague Year* (1722). The exceptional status of Defoe's disaster narrative is now a critical commonplace: for example, David Roberts considers the *Journal* to be "the most ingenious, dramatic, and eclectic work to have been prompted by the Marseilles plague."[7] Paul Slack, in his important study of early modern plagues in England, asserts that Defoe's "eagerness to describe the issues [of an official response to plague] in human terms gave his writing flashes of insight which none of his contemporaries or predecessors could match."[8]

Placing the general absence of firsthand plague knowledge in 1720s London in relation to Defoe's "flashes of insight" into the experience of a devastating pestilential visitation, the present chapter will read Defoe's *Journal* as, first and foremost, a narrative of transgenerational trauma. To be sure, the *Journal*'s exploration of the mind in extreme distress has been widely noted, but while Defoe's lively depictions of horrific plague suffering have figured centrally in several critical assessments, the book has rarely been read within a conceptual framework that privileges the transmission of a substantive collective trauma experience to readers who had not themselves lived through a plague epidemic.[9] Even when the concept of trauma has been explicitly invoked with regard to the text's generic features and narrative techniques, as, for example, by Katherine Ellison and Nicola Parsons, the analyses, for all their important insights, only fleetingly treat the *Journal* as an immersive trauma narrative.[10] In what follows I will make a case for reading Defoe's plague narrative as a performative text that sought to re-create, for a readership generally unfamiliar with plague, the psychological experience of a devastating pestilential visitation. I will do so by situating Defoe's narrative within the framework provided by what Marianne Hirsch has conceptualized as "postmemory" in relation to the transmission of Holocaust trauma memories to later generations.[11] Harnessing Hirsch's key observation that "postmemory's connection to the past" is not "mediated by recall but by imaginative investment, projection, and creation," I will ultimately argue that Defoe's exceptionally vivid depictions of plague trauma were intended to have a psycho-prophylactic purpose; that is, to offer a type of "mind training" that other plague publications lacked.[12]

The exceptional status of the *Journal* has predominantly been anchored in the text's perceived historical verisimilitude in representing the devastating effects of plague. As Robert Mayer has pointed out, Defoe's *Journal* successfully convinced eighteenth-century readers that they were encountering a genuine eyewitness account of the Great Plague of 1665: "the prevailing view was that the *Journal* was an authentic piece of historical writing" and, in contrast to later centuries, it was "first read as a genuine memoir" of the devastating visitation suffered by Londoners over half a century earlier.[13] Modern critics have generally agreed with the book's first readers that the vivid depiction of authentic experiences is the most salient attribute of Defoe's *Journal*: Maximillian Novak, for example, has asserted that few readers "would argue with the notion that the most compelling aspect of the book involved the terrible scenes of pain and death."[14] Indeed, the book's sustained engagement of the reader's visual and auditory imaginative powers is arguably the narrative feature that has excited the most critical commentary: for example, while Raymond Stephanson stresses that "Defoe's preoccupation with the eye and the ear—with sights and sounds—is everywhere evident in the *Journal*," Frank Lay finds the *Journal*'s descriptions of the plague environment to be "extremely physical and immediate."[15] The psychological authenticity typically associated with literary realism has thus been particularly prominent in commentary on Defoe's plague narrative: the *Journal* "moved historical fiction closer to the psychological bent of the mainstream English novel and to the desire to convey the fullness of individual experience," explains Paula Backscheider, contending that the book "expanded the reality fiction can convey."[16] The *Journal*'s modern reputation as a masterpiece of historical fiction is thus to a significant extent anchored in twentieth-century theories of the emergence of psychologically verisimilar realist prose fiction in the eighteenth century, and it is this particular aspect that has earned the *Journal* its elevated position among early modern plague narratives.[17]

In common with the vast majority of Londoners in the 1720s, Defoe had no direct experience of the Great Plague.[18] Consequently, Defoe too had to construct the scenes he depicts in the *Journal* from oral and existing printed accounts of the 1665 and even older plague visitations.[19] In other words, Defoe's vivid account of the Great Plague of 1665 may plausibly be described as an exercise in postmemory. Marianne Hirsch defines postmemory as "a *structure* of inter- and transgenerational return of traumatic knowledge and embodied experience" that describes "the relationship that the generation after those who witnessed cultural or collective trauma bears to the experience of those who came before." Since later generations lack the direct experience of the traumatic event, "postmemory's connection to the past," Hirsch emphasizes, is not anchored primarily in recall but in acts of "imaginative investment, projection, and creation"—it is thus "a *consequence* of traumatic recall . . . at a generational remove."[20] Drawing on the memories of eyewitnesses in its reimagination of the traumatic event, postmemorial work "strives to *reactivate* and *re-embody* more distant political and cultural memorial structures by reinvesting them with resonant individual and familial forms of mediation and aesthetic expression." It is important to acknowledge that Hirsch's concept of postmemory is predicated on a specific medium of transmission: the photographic image. Photos, claims Hirsch, are the most effective, indeed, the most affectively powerful medium for the "embodied and affective experience in the process of transmission" of the trauma of others.[21] In its privileging of modern technology, Hirsch's conceptualization of postmemory betrays a bias that is characteristic of the field of memory and trauma studies, but Hirsch's suggestion that the combination of the visual with the familial and the individual represents the central structure of postmemory can nevertheless be harnessed for a productive reading of the postmemorial work that Defoe's *Journal* performs.[22]

To fully appreciate the postmemorial work that the *Journal* performs in an early modern context, it is important to explore Defoe's thoughts concerning the medium of transmission available to him: the written word. The possibility of authentically preserving individual life experiences for posterity held some fascination for Defoe. In a tract written only four years after the *Journal*, *An Essay upon Literature* (1726), Defoe traces the history of writing, which he celebrates as a divine gift bestowed on humankind in the form of the tablets of stone given to Moses. In contrast to literate societies, oral cultures, asserts Defoe, had been unable to build the knowledge base and understanding of the world necessary for sophisticated insights, because they lacked a "Method to convey the Mind, without speaking." With the arrival of letters, writing became "the preserver of Knowledge," and of a "truer History" than oral accounts could provide.[23] Defoe's insistence that a system of physical characters is able faithfully to convey the contents of an author's mind is important: unlike oral cultures in which the individual's thoughts and feelings could be imparted to others only via the audible voice of the living, a literate society had a medium that made it possible for the dead to speak. Defoe dwells on the mechanism for this diachronic transmission of the mind: writing is "to make a piece of Paper speak, and to stamp a Voice and Words, which were neither more nor less than meer Sounds, to stamp them on a Paper, and empower other People to speak over again."[24] Reading a written text is thus essentially an act of ventriloquism to Defoe, a mental reenactment of the original thoughts and emotions of the author. Not only can writing allow the reader to gain an intimate insight into the author's mind, but a chronologically distant moment could be reexperienced: through letters "the Sense of Things was convey'd from Man to Man, and from Age to Age."[25] According to Defoe, a written text had the power to revive the voices and experiences of the dead.

Defoe's thoughts about the divine art of writing should not be taken to suggest that he considered all types of writing equally successful in the faithful transmission of past experiences. His comments in the preface to his historical novel *Memoirs of a Cavalier*, published two years before the *Journal*, are particularly revealing in this respect. *Memoirs* narrates the soldierly life of an English royalist during the Thirty Years' War and the English Civil Wars, but Defoe is keen to stress that his book is different from conventional histories and memoirs. Seeking to establish a qualitative difference between traditional historical accounts of dates and deeds and his book, he asks rhetorically: "But do those relations give any of the beautiful ideas of things formed in this account? Have they one half of the circumstances and incidents of the actions themselves that this man's eyes were witness to, and which his memory has thus preserved? He that has read the best Accounts of those Battles, will be surprised to see the Particulars of the Story thus preserved."[26] Even seemingly well-known histories and historical personages, adds Defoe, "receive a Lustre from this Man's Relations, which the World was never made sensible of before." Borne out of the "circumstance and incidents of the actions themselves," the narrative iridescence of his account is located in the detail of individualized historical experience, or, to use Defoe's phrase, the text's ability to make the reader "sensible" to the observations, thoughts, and feelings experienced a lifetime ago by this particular cavalier. Defoe's ideas concerning "experiential" historical writing are akin to Hirsch's definition of the function of postmemory, which is "to reactivate and reembody" cultural memories and "plain facts" of historical accounts "by reinvesting them with resonant individual and familial forms of mediation and aesthetic expression."[27] This conceptualization of historical narratives frames Defoe's *Journal* both chronologically and conceptually, and shapes the postmemorial work that it performs.

Defoe's championing of historical accounts that move beyond facts and figures to transmit the lived experience of past events through a process of "imaginative investment, projection, and creation," to use Hirsch's phrase, spoke directly to London's eroded "plague knowledge-scape," particularly to what Defoe considered to be an utter psychological unpreparedness for a visitation. In his first long plague tract published only a month before the *Journal*, *Due Preparations for the Plague* (February 1722), Defoe presents his reader with an extended conversation, set during the early days of the 1665 visitation, between a mother who had directly witnessed both the 1625 and 1636 plagues and her three adult children about her advice that "everyone prepare themselves for Death."[28] The plague-experienced mother's steadfast insistence that death will inescapably embrace the entire city soon has the desired effect on her children, as her son laments, "You make ones Blood run chill in the Veins to hear you talk so . . . this is enough to make one die with the fear of it." This, Defoe has the mother point out, is the best preparation for her family and London's inhabitants to face the plague: "I wish I cou'd see them so out of their Wits," she asserts, because she "should expect that then some Miracle of Deliverance would follow," reiterating a few pages later that "to prepare themselves for the worst, is to frighten them." The notion that imagining the horrors of plague death and thereby affectively to engage with the anticipated trauma event affords the most effective preparation for the epidemic's arrival is finally internalized by the daughter: "I dare not say I am prepar'd, unless it be to die at the very Thought of it." Pointing to the purpose of the "mind training" that she recommends, the mother explains that "a serious perswading Men to Repent and Prepare, is perswading them to put themselves into such a Posture, as they may not be frightened or surpriz'd or alarm'd, for to be prepared, is to be past being frighted."[29] After a lengthy debate in which the merchant son argues against "alarming the People" because it "injures Trade" and "sinks Credit," the mother is granted the concluding speech that pivots on the key message of the passage: "A Mind suitably prepar'd, is a Mind fortify'd and made bold to meet the Worst."[30] The austere religious didacticism of this story is, it should be noted, exclusively—and quite conventionally—aimed at encouraging the moral reformation of London's citizens in the face of the divine judgment that is the plague, but the most effective mechanism of preparation advocated by the plague-experienced mother in *Due Preparations*, a mental playing-through of an anticipated traumatic situation, gestures toward one of the fundamental functions of the *Journal*.

The advice rendered by the mother that "every Body prepare for the Plague, by preparing for Death" may productively be read in a more literal way, beyond a purely spiritual application.[31] If *Due Preparations* positions an intense fear of death resulting from a failure to repent one's sins as debilitating during the distressing event, the *Journal* secularizes this fear by transposing it to the paralyzing effects plague trauma has on the individual's ability to act rationally. Defoe spends much time in the early sections of the *Journal* on describing a range of examples of psychological breakdown caused by the traumatic effects of the disease on minds unprepared for the gruesome sights of plague death. The *Journal* repeatedly directs the reader's attention toward the emotional and psychological impact of plague suffering:

> The Face of Things, I say, was much alter'd; Sorrow and Sadness sat upon every Face . . . London might well be said to be all in Tears . . . the Voice of Mourning was truly heard in the Streets; the shriecks of Women and Children at the Windows, and Doors of their Houses, where their dearest Relations were, perhaps dying, or just dead, were so frequent to be heard, as we passed the Streets, that it was enough to pierce the stoutest Heart in the World, to hear them. Tears and Lamentations were seen almost in every House. (15–16)

An early concern expressed by the narrator, H.F., is thus the impact of the widespread distress caused by the epidemic on the mental well-being of Londoners. The "almost universal melancholy Apprehensions" that had descended on the city quickly led to an explosion of "Prophesies, and Astrological Conjurations, Dreams, and old Wives Tales," which further "terrified the People to the last Degree" and "agitated the minds" (19–21, 28). Having "a more than ordinary Influence upon the Minds" of Londoners, ghost stories and "strange Relations" had given "the People the Vapours in abundance, and sent them away trembling, and frighted" (20, 21, 24). Across several pages H.F. describes the unmitigated psychological impact of the plague, exacerbated by the activities of "Fortune-tellers, Cunning-men, and Astrologers" (26), as a serious public problem: "Those Terrors and Apprehensions of the People, led them into a Thousand weak, foolish, and wicked Things" (24). At its most extreme the psychologically destabilizing effect of plague suffering led distracted individuals to harm themselves and others, occasionally even causing death without a pestilential infection:

> It is scarcely credible what dreadful Cases happened in particular Families every Day; People in the Rage of the Distemper, or in the Torment of their Swellings, which was indeed intollerable, running out of their own Government, raving and distracted, and oftentimes laying violent Hands upon themselves, throwing themselves out at their Windows, shooting themselves, etc. Mothers murthering their own Children, in their Lunacy, some dying of meer Grief, as a Passion, some of meer Fright and Surprize, without any Infection at all; others frighted into Idiotism, and foolish Distractions, some into despair and Lunacy; others into mellancholy Madness. (81)

This evident concern with the lack of psychological resilience among Londoners is, we should note, maintained throughout the book: "A Plague is a formidable Enemy," exclaims H.F. deep into the narrative, "and is arm'd with Terrors that every Man is not sufficiently fortified to resist, or prepar'd to stand the Shock against" (202). While Defoe's *Journal* could not alleviate the physical torment of the infected, it could work toward addressing one aspect of "the unprovided Condition, that the whole Body of People were in at the first coming of this Calamity," namely, London's general lack of psychological readiness for the horrors of a plague epidemic (105). It is to this end that postmemory, in a manner that anticipates Hirsch's conceptualization, is employed in the *Journal*.

Defoe's prophylactic aim in the *Journal* of offering a highly visual emotive reading experience is readily evident in his "penchant for stark detail, and a desire to make those details congeal into a portrait of grim destruction."[32] The perhaps most effective narrative technique Defoe employs in the book is a series of what may be called textual *tableaux vivants* that represent various scenes of plague suffering in vivid and evocative detail. Emerging as a popular form of entertainment in the eighteenth century, the *tableau vivant* (living picture), in its consciously artistic arrangement of a group of silent and motionless people to represent a scene or incident, shares many of the functions of photographs, in particular staged ones or those deliberately taken for documentary purposes.[33] Defoe's tableaux are often generic in their outlines but specific with regard to the horror they depict. An illustrative example of this central narrative technique in the *Journal* is the scene depicting "one of the most deplorable Cases, in all the present Calamity" (116), birthing mothers and their babies: "where the Mother had the Distemper, there no Body would come near them, and both [mother and child] sometimes perish'd: Sometimes the Mother has died of the Plague; and the Infant, it may be half born, or born but not parted from the Mother. . . . I could tell here dismal Stories of living Infants being found sucking the Breasts of their Mothers, or Nurses, after they have been dead of the Plague" (100, 103).

Since the plague indiscriminately kills all human beings, the individuality of the plague victims in this tableau is of little consequence, but this anonymity is counterbalanced by the familial context of the scene—familial in the perhaps most profound sense of the very moment of family generation, the birth of offspring. In what is characteristic for the *Journal* as a whole, the affective work of the scene is performed by its memorable graphic details: with two short phrases, Defoe creates the traumatic images of deceased babies half emerged from the dead maternal body and babies newly born but still tethered to their dead mother by the umbilical cord. The function of the *Journal*'s tableaux, which are frequently located around the threshold of life and death, is to generate, through relentlessly unswerving visualizations, the mental experience of the horrors of a plague visitation.[34] H.F. is resolved, as John Richetti has rightly pointed out, "to see it in all of its horrifying fullness," but this fullness is not so much located in the amount of detail offered as in the scenes' emotional purchase: Defoe's many tableaux become memorable by virtue of a single inescapable horrifying aspect that emblematically represents and thereby shares the traumatic experience of an earlier generation with those who never witnessed or experienced it themselves.[35] The *Journal*'s reading experience, that is, its production of postmemories, is predicated as much on quantity as on unforgettable details: the book's episodic structure subjects the reader to repeated confrontations with images of plague trauma. If the mother in *Due Preparations* insists that "a Mind suitably prepar'd, is a Mind fortify'd and made bold to meet the Worst," it is the *Journal* that provides the training ground for this preparation.[36] John Richetti has suggested that the *Journal*'s "original purpose . . . was intensely practical rather than imaginative"—I would suggest that, if read as a postmemorial trauma narrative, it becomes apparent that, in fact, the book merges the practical and the imaginative.[37]

The *Journal*'s many tableaux are supplemented by several longer episodes that provide greater detail and that, importantly, give the reader an insight into H.F.'s own emotional and psychological responses to the trauma he observes. One of the most frequently discussed stories is that of husband and wife, Robert and Rachel, and their children. Once again focusing on a familial scene, H.F. has a direct encounter with Robert, a waterman, on one of his excursions and the two strike up a lengthy conversation. H.F. learns that Robert has been earning money by shipping goods up and down the river to maintain his family. The reader finds out that one child has already succumbed to the plague, and that Rachel and a second child have also contracted the disease. To avoid infecting himself and consequently being unable to provide for his family, Robert has been residing alone on his barge, leaving money and food for his family on a stone near their small house on a daily basis. Unsurprisingly, these events have a profoundly distressing effect on the waterman, but, importantly, Robert's story also directly affects H.F.'s emotional state. In a direct address to the reader, H.F. asserts, "I saw the Tears run very plentifully down his Face; and so they did down mine too, I assure you" (92). Repeatedly, the reader is told that, overcome by his emotions during the telling of his story, Robert "stopt, and wept very much," and that H.F. "could no more refrain from Tears than he" (94). The episode has been used, plausibly enough, to illustrate that "the main impulse behind *A Journal of The Plague Year* was a demonstration of human pity and fellowship in the worst of disasters."[38] However, if we read the episode as shaped by Defoe's desire to produce a narrative that could psychologically prepare Londoners for a new plague visitation, another purpose emerges into view. While Robert is in the midst of experiencing a series of traumatic familial events and exhibits deep emotional distress as a result, his actions remain unfailingly rational. Defoe duly ascribes Robert's continued ability to function as a provider to his "Courage resting on God," but he is also quick to stress that "he used all possible Caution for his Safety" (108). Faith alone does not save lives—psychological resilience and rational conduct are the other crucial components for survival.

After many examples of terrified and distressed Londoners who become psychologically unstable and commit "a Thousand weak, foolish, and wicked Things," the waterman episode offers the reader an example of an individual who, despite experiencing significant trauma, copes emotionally and psychologically with the suffering and death of loved ones (24). Deeply affected by the plague trauma his family has already suffered, Robert is nevertheless able to continue to provide for his wife and children because he is able to regulate his emotions and responses. It is this psychological resilience in the face of severe trauma that impresses H.F., who himself has, of course, already witnessed many traumatic scenes around London by this stage of the visitation. Indeed, H.F., psychologically prepared by his many observations of plague trauma, mirrors the waterman's conduct. Although becoming emotionally affected by the waterman's story, Defoe's narrator remains in control of his actions and avoids direct contact with the family as well as initially with Robert. This is not to say that H.F. has become hardened to suffering: his ability to empathize is not compromised by what he has witnessed, and he ultimately supports the family by offering some money, but his conduct remains rationally cautious throughout. The story of the waterman and his family is a key passage in the *Journal* because neither Robert nor H.F. become psychologically incapacitated by the trauma that they experience and witness. If the shorter trauma tableaux are aimed at an imaginative conditioning of the reader, this longer episode offers a postmemory of resilience and ideal conduct in the face of severe trauma and emotional distress. Moreover, Defoe's individualizing of the family members in this story reminds us of a key feature of the structure of postmemory: "the language of family can literally reactivate and re-embody an archival image whose subjects are, to most viewers, anonymous."[39]

There is much in Defoe's plague books to suggest that he was particularly concerned about the damaging psychological impact of plague trauma and that his publications, unlike the raft of other plague books, were designed to address this specific issue. However, while making the reader of the *Journal* "sensible" to the traumatic experience of pestilence is repeatedly signaled as a central goal of the *Journal*, Defoe himself, as has been noted, seems to question the efficacy of his narrative with regard to the representation of trauma at certain points in the text.[40] H.F.'s compulsive recording of all he sees and hears in pestilential London is on a number of occasions accompanied by a disavowal of the power of language adequately to convey the horrors he witnesses. Thus, Defoe has his narrator assert that it is "impossible to describe" a particular scene or, focusing on emotional responses, that the "discontents can hardly be described" (173, 141). Occasionally, H.F. even appears to capitulate in the face of seemingly unrepresentable extreme suffering, as, for example, when, after reporting that some delirious plague sufferers threw themselves into a burial pit to expire there, he remarks that "this may serve a little to describe the dreadful condition of that day, though it is impossible to say anything that is able to give a true idea of it to those who did not see it, other than this, that it was indeed very, very, very dreadful, and such as no tongue can express" (53). While the compulsion to represent "the dreadful condition of that day" is evident throughout the book, it is qualified by the awareness that plague causes sights and sounds potentially too overwhelming for words: "were it possible to represent those Times exactly to those that did not see them, and give the Reader due Ideas of the Horror that everywhere presented itself, it must make just Impressions upon their Minds and fill them with surprise" (15). Defoe's notion that the most effective historical narratives offer minutely rendered, individualized scenes that allow readers imaginatively to relive past experiences is thus gestured toward in these statements, but as concerns plague trauma, it is positioned, at least initially, as linguistically out of reach.

And yet the repeated acknowledgments of the unspeakability of pestilence-induced physical and psychological suffering, most of which appear early in the book, sit uneasily—even paradoxically—among the many carefully rendered tableaux and longer episodes that pay detailed attention to how the experience of plague looked, sounded, and felt to those who lived through it. Indeed, as I have already noted, the evocative realism of Defoe's book has long been considered one of its most noteworthy features, which rather belies the narrator's initial exclamations concerning the limits of his narrative efforts. Importantly, it is H.F. who eventually overturns his earlier doubts by asserting the efficacy of his narrative's transmission of plague trauma to those who did not see it: presenting the reader with the story of a bed-bound man who set fire to himself to escape his "insufferable torment," H.F. confidently asks, "What can be said to represent the misery of these times more lively to the reader, or to give him a more perfect idea of a complicated distress?" (152). As the *Journal*'s tableaux and illustrative episodes accumulate, H.F. moves from a position of doubt to one of confidence in his text's ability to make the reader genuinely sensible of the experience of plague trauma. Moreover, it is important to read H.F.'s early disavowals of the representability of the suffering experienced by Londoners in 1665 in the context of an established generic convention: identifying inexpressibility as a common trope in the plague publications of the 1720s, Daniel Gordon makes the important observation that "the insistence on unspeakability does not undermine, but rather adds to, description," in that the described scene or experience becomes closely associated with the metaphysical realm of the incomprehensible divine absolute.[41] While the *Journal*'s documentary purpose is not predominantly anchored in the spiritual realm, H.F.'s early comments concerning the representative failure of language do similarly serve the rhetorical purpose of concentrating the reader's attention on the extreme nature of the traumatic experience; that is, on emphasising the "complicated distress" that Defoe's narrator asserts his narrative conveys, ultimately successfully, to the minds of readers who did not witness it.

Echoing Slack's assertion that Defoe's book offers "flashes of insight which none of his contemporaries or predecessors could match," Alan Rosen has noted that the "length and breadth of [Defoe's] description of the plague" far surpasses those of the sources he used for his account.[42] While one might be tempted to cite commercial reasons for Defoe's production of the arguably most vivid account of the 1665 plague, the book's relative belatedness in the context of the Marseille scare seems to speak against this motivation.[43] A more likely explanation is that Defoe believed that none of the plague tracts published in response to the scare, for all the attention they paid to the pathology of the plague, preventative practical measures against and potential remedies for the disease, and the spiritual meaning of the visitation, sufficiently addressed what he considered a crucial aspect of preparations for the arrival of the plague: the necessary psychological readiness for pestilential horrors. If we read the *Journal* as an example of postmemorial work that has a practical purpose at its heart, Slack's comments that Defoe included "imagined incidents" with little "obvious relevance" and that he "saw too much" to develop a coherent argument in his plague tracts rather miss the point of the book: it is the very act of seeing too much close up that represents the central narrative technique that gives the *Journal* its psycho-prophylactic properties.[44] Margaret Healy's description of Defoe's *Journal* as "dynamic history" is felicitous, although her related comment that the text harnesses "the past in order to confront the anxieties and mediate and shape the debates of the author's own time" is properly applicable only if we read the book purely as a politico-religious response to the threat of plague.[45] If we read the *Journal* first and foremost as a text of transgenerational memory, as an exercise in postmemory that seeks to reactivate and reembody historical and, in 1720, culturally distant plague trauma, the dynamism of Defoe's history and the manner in which it connects the present with the past is thrown into much clearer relief.

While one should exercise caution in transposing patterns evident in modern trauma narratives and attendant analytical theories and concepts to early modern texts and contexts, I would like to conclude by drawing a parallel between Walter Benn Michael's commentary on the use of history in Tony Morrison's 1987 novel *Beloved*, which attempts to give a narrative frame to the trauma of mid-nineteenth-century slavery, and the postmemorial work performed by Defoe's *Journal*. Michaels makes the important distinction between simply knowing historical facts and developing a sense of remembrance of the actual experience of the historical event:

> Without the idea of a history that is remembered or forgotten (not merely learned or unlearned), the events of the past can have only a limited relevance to the present, providing us at most with causal accounts of how things have come to be the way they are, at least with objects of antiquarian interest. It is only when it's reimagined as the fabric of our own experience that the past can become the key to our own identity. A history that is learned can be learned by anyone (and can belong to anyone who learns it); a history that is remembered can only be remembered by those who first experienced it and it must belong to them. So if history were learned not remembered, then no history could be more truly ours than any other.... It is only when the events of the past can be imagined not only to have consequences for the present but to live on in the present that they can become part of our experience and can testify to who we are.[46]

It seems to me that Defoe's distinction between conventional histories and his own immersive historical narratives is akin to Michael's distinction between merely learned and reimagined or remembered history. In other words, a list of dates and a plain description of deeds insufficiently represents the historical event, according to Defoe; it is an imaginative investment in the rendering of personal experience that makes a historical event come to life and that allows the reader to understand the event more fully. In the *Journal* Defoe ultimately depicts the 1665 identity of the city of London and its inhabitants as plague survivors. To assume this identity once again in the 1720s, Londoners had to access and utilize the lived experience of those who had survived a major pestilential visitation before, an experience that went beyond storing provisions or the implementation of effective quarantine laws. "A Mind suitably prepar'd, is a Mind fortify'd and made bold to meet the Worst," Defoe asserted in *Due Preparations*, and a month later the *Journal of the Plague Year* provided the necessary mental training ground to fortify London minds.[47] Unlike the other plague tracts that responded to the Marseilles scare, Defoe's book attempted to help Londoners develop the psychological strength necessary to triumph once more over the perhaps most powerful adversary their city could face.

NOTES

1. Paul Slack, *The Impact of Plague in Tudor and Stuart England* (Oxford, UK: Clarendon, 1985; 1990), 326.
2. Given that humans do not retain memories of at least the first three years of their life, one needed to be a minimum of fifty-eight years old in 1720 to have personal memories of the 1665 plague, but several years beyond sixty for clear memories. Average life expectancy across the seventeenth century and into the eighteenth century remained relatively consistent. It should be acknowledged that the average figure is potentially misleading, since it varied significantly depending on context: the infant mortality rate was relatively high during the period, but if an individual lived until the age of thirty, the chances of living up to and beyond the average of sixty years increased significantly. It is below sixty if all deaths are included in the statistics. Location mattered too: the death rate for all ages was significantly higher in London than in rural areas and higher among the poor. While not entirely unthinkable, Frank Bastian's suggestion that, in the early 1720s, Defoe "may well have visited some alms-house for the aged poor" ("Defoe's *Journal of the Plague Year* Reconsidered," *The Review of English Studies* 16, no. 62 [May 1965]: 165) to gather 1665 plague anecdotes seems an unlikely scenario in the context of the below-average life expectancy for the London poor. For the

demographic context see E. A. Wrigley and R. S. Schofield, *The Population History of England 1541–1871* (Cambridge, UK: Cambridge University Press, 1981), 250; and R. A. Houston, *The Population History of Britain and Ireland 1500–1750* (Cambridge, UK: Cambridge University Press, 1995), 40.

3. William H. McNeill, *Plagues and Peoples* (New York: Doubleday, 1976), 227; Charles F. Mullett, "The English Plague Scare of 1720–23," *Osiris* 2 (1936): 494.
4. Anita Guerrini, "Mead, Richard (1673–1754)," *Oxford Dictionary of National Biography* (Oxford, UK: Oxford University Press, 2004); online edn, https://doi.org/10.1093/ref:odnb/18467. January 2008; Slack, *Impact of Plague*, 327.
5. Slack, *Impact of Plague*, 330.
6. On the request of the secretary of state, James Craggs, Dr. Mead published *A Short Discourse Concerning Pestilential Contagion and the Methods to Be Used to Prevent It* in 1720. The publication went to seven editions within a year and appeared in an expanded eighth edition in 1722. A good overview of the range of publications elicited by the news of the Marseille plague may be found in Charles F. Mullett, "The English Plague Scare of 1720–23," *Osiris* 2 (1936): 484–516.
7. David Roberts, "Introduction," in Daniel Defoe, *A Journal of the Plague Year*, ed. Louis Landa (Oxford, UK: Oxford University Press, 2010), xv. All subsequent parenthetical references are to this edition.
8. Slack, *Impact of Plague*, 335. It should be noted that, alongside the *Journal*, Slack includes Defoe's journalism and the earlier *Due Preparations for the Plague, as Well for Soul as Body* (London, 1722) in his observation.
9. For example, Raymond Stephanson, "'Tis a speaking Sight': Imagery as Narrative Technique in Defoe's *A Journal of the Plague Year*," *Dalhousie Review* 62, no. 4 (1982): 680–92, and Frank Lay, "The Exploitation of Subjectivity: Daniel Defoe's *Journal of the Plague Year*," in *Marginal Voices, Marginal Forms: Diaries in European Literature and History*, ed. Rachel Langford and Russel West-Pavlov, 35–49 (Amsterdam: Rodopi, 1999), explore the sensory dimension of Defoe's representations of plague suffering and death.
10. Referencing the fragmented and incomplete nature of twentieth-century trauma narratives associated with the Holocaust, Katherine Ellison makes the important observations that, in contrast, Defoe created a narrator who "will not malfunction when he witnesses mass death" and that the *Journal* "brings together multiple individual stories to form a total portrait of the plague as traumatic experience." See *Fatal News: Reading and Information Overload in Early Eighteenth-Century Literature* (New York & London: Routledge, 2005), 95, 106. Nicola Parsons points out that the "temporal order [of the *Journal*] is dislocated by the trauma of the plague and the linear narrative is thrown into disarray." The text thus "displays many of the features that contemporary theorists associate with attempts to narrate the traumatic past."

See "Reading and Remembering History in *A Journal of the Plague Year*," in *Reading Historical Fiction: The Revenant and Remembered Past*, ed. Kate Mitchell and Nicola Parsons, 119–35 (Basingstoke: Palgrave Macmillan, 2013), esp. 129–30.

11. Importantly, Hirsch notes that, while she draws on the Holocaust as her historical frame of refence, her analysis "is relevant to numerous other contexts of traumatic transfer that can be understood as postmemory." See "The Generation of Postmemory," *Poetics Today* 29, no. 1 (Spring 2008): 108.
12. Marianne Hirsch, *The Generation of Postmemory. Writing and Visual Culture After the Holocaust* (New York: Columbia University Press, 2012), 5.
13. Robert Mayer, "The Reception of a *Journal of the Plague Year* and the Nexus of Fiction and History in the Novel," *ELH* 57, no. 3 (Autumn 1990): 533.
14. Maximillian E. Novak, "Defoe and the Disordered City," *PMLA* 92, no. 2 (March 1977): 241.
15. Raymond Stephanson, "'Tis a speaking Sight," 682; Frank Lay, "The Exploitation of Subjectivity," in Langford and West-Pavlov, *Marginal Voices, Marginal Forms*, 38.
16. Paula R. Backscheider, *Daniel Defoe: Ambition & Innovation* (Lexington: University Press of Kentucky, 1986), 136.
17. Novak concludes that H.F. is a new type of narrator in the context of early modern realist prose fiction and that he "set a pattern for fictional narrators that has been central to the development of the novel." See "Defoe and the Disordered City," 250.
18. Paula Backscheider, *Daniel Defoe: His Life* (Baltimore & London: Johns Hopkins University Press, 1989), 7.
19. In spite of its publication date, Watson Nicholson's *The Historical Sources of Defoe's Journal of the Plague Year: Illustrated by Extracts from the Original Documents in the Burney Collection and Manuscript Room in the British Museum* (Boston: Stratford Co., 1919) remains a useful overview of some of the sources used by Defoe. For a later exploration of Defoe's sources (and a discussion of Nicholson's conclusion that the *Journal* represents authentic history), see Bastian, "Defoe's *Journal of the Plague Year* Reconsidered," 151–73.
20. Hirsch, *The Generation of Postmemory*, 5–6.
21. Hirsch, *The Generation of Postmemory*, 33.
22. Hirsch's contention that "more than oral or written narratives, photographic images . . . function as ghostly revenants from an irretrievably lost past world" is not actually supported by concrete evidence that demonstrates the assumed superiority of photographs in the process of the re-embodying and re-individualizing of cultural/archival memory. Photographic images are not purely indexical but are also iconic, explains Hirsch, which allows them to "assume symbolic status" (*The Generation of Postmemory*, 36–37). The notion that images generated in written narratives cannot achieve the same effect is problematic: one only needs to think of *Robinson Crusoe*'s iconic image

of the single footprint on the beach (which, as a signifier of a deadly human threat on his island, severely distresses the novel's protagonist) to realize that written texts do indeed have the power to create images that assume widely recognized symbolic status. A similar sense of modern technological exceptionalism in the formation of cultural or public memory is evident in Alison Landsberg's related conceptualization of "prosthetic memory," which privileges the medium of film. See *Prosthetic Memory: The Transformation of American Remembrance in the Age of Mass Culture* (Cambridge MA: Harvard University Press, 2004).

23. Daniel Defoe, *An Essay Upon Literature* (London, 1726), 10, 18.
24. Defoe, 16.
25. Defoe, *An Essay Upon Literature*, 17. We might note here that Samuel Johnson privileges sensory impression in his definition of "sense": the first signification assigned to "sense" in his *Dictionary* is "Faculty or power by which external objects are perceived; the sight; touch; hearing; smell; taste," followed by the second entry, "Perception by the senses; sensation." In contrast, "Opinion; notion; judgment" and "Meaning; import" are, respectively, the seventh and tenth meanings identified by Johnson. See *A Dictionary of the English Language* vol. 2 (London, 1755), 1787–88.
26. Daniel Defoe, *Memoirs of a Cavalier*, ed. James T. Boulton (Oxford, UK: Oxford University Press, 1978), 2.
27. Hirsch, *The Generation of Postmemory*, 111.
28. Daniel Defoe, *Due Preparations for the Plague*, 146, 148.
29. Defoe, 148–54, 159.
30. Defoe, 157, 160.
31. Defoe, 150.
32. Alan Rosen, "Plague, Fire, and Typology in Defoe's *A Journal of the Plague Year*," *Connotations* 1, no. 3 (1991): 260.
33. One might note here that in one of the two photographs Hirsch discusses, the individuals depicted, mother and son, consciously pose for the camera.
34. Also see Stephanson's discussion of Defoe's use of imagery in the *Journal*. Stephanson's central contention is that, in line with *Due Preparations*, the book's overarching goal was to "affect the reader's imagination in an immediate and graphic manner (despite the limitations of any written account) in order to prompt our religious obligation to repent." See "'Tis a speaking Sight," 687.
35. John Richetti, *The Life of Daniel Defoe: A Critical Biography* (Oxford, UK: Wiley-Blackwell, 2005), 319.
36. Defoe, *Due Preparations*, 157, 160.
37. Richetti, *Life of Daniel Defoe*, 302.
38. Novak, "Defoe and the Disordered City," 248.
39. Hirsch, *The Generation of Postmemory*, 35.

40. For example, falling in line with Defoe's exclamations Nicola Parsons contends that "recording information yielded by his observing eye does not allow H.F. to construct a narrative that either effectively conveys or appropriately commemorates the traumatic experience of life in the infected city." See "Reading and Remembering History," 123. As should be readily apparent by now, I disagree with Parson's reading of this aspect of the *Journal*.
41. Daniel Gordon, "The City and the Plague in the Age of Enlightenment," *Yale French Studies* 92 (1997): 87.
42. Slack, *The Impact of* Plague, 335; Rosen, "Plague, Fire, and Typology," 260. It should be noted that, alongside the *Journal*, Slack includes Defoe's journalism and the earlier *Due Preparations for the Plague* in his observation. A further example of Defoe's *Journal* representing an end point to the English plague writing tradition is Ernest B. Gilman's *Plague Writing in Early Modern England* (Chicago: University of Chicago Press, 2009), which also concludes with a discussion of Defoe's book.
43. David Roberts has rightly drawn attention to the *Journal*'s belated appearance in the plague print market of the early 1720s: "Plague books started to dry up in 1722 as the Marseilles scare abated, and Defoe's was the last substantial title to make it to the marketplace, probably a few months too late." See "Introduction," in Defoe, *A Journal of the Plague Year*, xv.
44. Slack, *Impact of Plague*, 335.
45. Margaret Healy, "Defoe's *Journal* and the English Plague Writing Tradition," *Literature and Medicine* 22, no. 1 (Spring 2003): 26.
46. Walter Benn Michaels, "'You Who Never Was There': Slavery and the New Historicism, Deconstruction and the Holocaust," *Narrative* 4, no. 1 (1996): "'You Who Never Was There': Slavery and the New Historicism, Deconstruction and the Holocaust," 7.
47. Defoe, *Due Preparations*, 160.

Afterword

Early Modern Trauma and the Generation of Satire

MELINDA RABB

Seen through the complex lens of contemporary trauma theories, the early modern world discloses its vulnerabilities, its catastrophes, and its strategies for representing experiences that defy representation. Each of the preceding chapters focuses on historical realities that occurred between the late sixteenth and early eighteenth centuries, experiences that inflicted wounds—individual and collective—on minds, bodies, and the natural world: colonialism, slavery, technology, disease, religious dissent, political faction, rebellion, genocide, and war. Each chapter judiciously connects recent concepts about trauma to past occurrences of profound loss and to the texts that have preserved them. The effect is to make us, as Raymond Williams says in *The Long Revolution*, see in new ways.[1] The present chapter aims to close the collection by opening some further possibilities. What might be a next step that carries this volume's insights forward? The foregoing analyses draw on many kinds of writing: diaries, essays, letters, plays, poetry, journals, prophecy, history, cryptography, legal documents, medical records, memoir, translation, and fiction. Each chapter captures an instance in which the sense of loss is disorienting, in which the world looks different, and therefore new and diverse ways of coping are required. The cumulative effect of this diversity not only tests the historical validity and the limits of theory in specific cases but also builds a general momentum for additional scholarship. Among these new insights is a revised understanding of the relationship between trauma and a mode of discourse mentioned only briefly on the preceding pages but certainly one of the period's crucial legacies and achievements: satire.

By reframing and recognizing early modern trauma, the authors encourage us to rethink our assumptions about how modes of expression evolve and then in retrospect seem to define an era. The powerful emotions analyzed by the contributors—remorse, melancholy, disappointment, sympathy, loss, doubt, frustration, and desperate need—have an urgency that can transition at times into the distancing and mitigating effects of irony in works, for example, by Shakespeare, Donne, and Rochester. The shift away from direct confrontation with suffering, a move from the earnest toward the sardonic, presages the creative deployment of anger among the other strong emotions provoked by the world's ills. The impulse to wound, cited frequently as the motivation for satire, is also retaliation for being wounded. Trauma's infliction of pain should factor into assumptions about satire's vitriolic militancy and into rationales for its status as a distinguishing achievement of the eighteenth century. Understood as an adaptive discourse rather than a genre governed by strict conventions, satire can inhabit many forms and combine them. Its shape-shifting versatility adjusts to poetry, prose, essay, and drama, and transforms existing forms like epic, pastoral, epistle, fable, tragedy, and song. Its protean capacity is responsive to the demands of traumatic history, in keeping with Thomas Anderson's observation that "significant cultural loss alters normative modes of expression and representation."[2]

Extraordinary intellectual energy invigorated such altered discourse within the same historical parameters, and in response to the same devastating culture-shifting events that give rise to the material assessed in this volume. If the parents have eaten a sour grape, as the prophet Jeremiah foretold, the children's teeth will be set on edge (Jer. 31:29). Satire responds to, depicts, and processes sources of personal and collective trauma. And conversely, trauma, as concept and remembered experience, instigates much of the innovative outpouring of satire, epitomized by the literary careers of Jonathan Swift and others, including John Dryden, Samuel Butler, John Wilmot, Earl of Rochester, Aphra Behn, Delarivier Manley, Alexander Pope, John Gay, Tobias Smollett, and Laurence Sterne. Further, trauma theory offers frameworks for understanding how satire's crucial vehicle of irony (frequently motivated by suppressed feelings of aggression and anger) could enhance language's power to cope with pain and to assign culpability to its perpetrators. As a means of distancing emotion and destabilizing literal meaning, irony becomes a pervasive mode of discourse for a world remembering, incurring, and committing wrongs. Theories of trauma and of irony coincide in their dependence on ideas like displacement, obscurity, dissociation, masking, and emotional distancing. Ultimately this discussion will examine in some detail the implication of these converging ideas in an example from Swift, the ultimate satirist in the English language, in order to demonstrate how the insights in this volume can be applied more broadly to other texts, including the most canonical ones. Swift, not alone among his peers in representing situations of profound damage to body and mind, offers a critical paradigm with far-reaching implications.

Early Modern Trauma: *Europe and the Atlantic World* charts a trajectory of experiences in which many kinds of wounds—the "rape" of a French river by industrial pollution, the spiritual agony of a woman prophet, the slaughter of the Irish, the mistreatment of an African slave, or the heaving of plague victims into the Great Pit—leave scars that never completely disappear. Whether incurred through war or natural disaster, through religious suffering or colonial abuses, through solitary exile or group oppression, trauma permanently marks the course of history and influences the formation of the individual and communal self. As editors Erin Peters and Cynthia Richards claim, extreme events "fragment the notion of identity and community" and are "irrecoverable and irreversible." This critical position offers a perspective that differs importantly from other views of the early modern period and of the development of the European and Atlantic worlds of the later eighteenth century.

Peters and Richards point out that many of the chapters in the collection refer to experiences between 1640 and 1720, that is, to the violent upheavals of the English Civil Wars and their later reverberations throughout the Three Kingdoms, Europe, and the Atlantic world. These same events have been invoked elsewhere to support a very different interpretation of the past and of what we can learn from it. Instead of images of trauma's enduring scars and lingering memories, some have invoked images of healing and rebirth. A seminal passage from Jean Jacques Rousseau's *Social Contract*, for example, has encouraged a more sanguine depiction of the decades leading to the American and French Revolutions. In 1762 still some years before shots were fired in Lexington and Concord and before the storming of the Bastille, Rousseau contemplated the unprecedented seventeenth-century English civil conflict and regicide not only as a bodily bloodbath of soldiers, civilians, and king but also as a psychological trauma with personal and collective ramifications: "certain afflictions unhinge men's minds and banish their memory of the past, so there are certain violent epochs and revolutions in states which have the same effects on peoples." Distanced by time and geography, however, Rousseau imagines that the horrifying memories of this violent epoch can be (and have been) subsumed into a process of miraculous rebirth: "Instead of forgetting the past, they look back on it in horror, and then the state after being consumed by civil war, is born again, so to speak, from its own ashes, and leaps from the arms of death to regain the vigour of youth." The success story across the channel, so it would seem, is one of full recovery from all losses.[3]

Early Modern Trauma constructs a narrative not of rebirth but of a legacy of modification through which "normative modes of expression and representation" must permanently change in response to historically specific crises. The phoenix, pace Rousseau, does not rise good as new from its own pyre. Its singed wings always must alter the quality of its future flights. In the chapters by Susan Broomhall, Amelia Zurcher, Katherine Ellison, Ismini Pells, Peter Walmsley, and Melissa Antonucci, full recovery is not an option despite different "structures of restoration": a poem about defiled nature cannot cleanse a polluted river; cryptology estranges language in the process of communicating distress; the petitions of a maimed soldier can perform his suffering but cannot recuperate his lost limb; a medical observer may keep meticulous records of a slave's anger and depression without understanding or redressing her misery; a biracial protagonist suffers the trauma of cultural exile and colonialization, for which religious conversion is palliative, but not fully compensatory. Similarly, studies by Eamon Darcy, Adam Beach, Cynthia Richards, Erin Peters, Joseph Harris, Tamar LeRoy, and Andreas Mueller offer new ways to read difficult texts that were generated by early modern circumstances of extreme suffering and loss through slavery, rebellion, war, and disease.

My purpose is not to reiterate the arguments of the former chapters but rather to show how the process of identifying historical sources of trauma and viewing them through the insights of contemporary theory helps to forge links between traumatic loss, subsequent alterations in normative modes of representation and belief, and the production of satire. Many writers with firsthand knowledge of England's troubles turned satirist by the end of the seventeenth century. Samuel Butler (*Hudibras*, 1663–78) and the Earl of Rochester (*A Satyr Against Reason and Mankind*, 1674) were both battle veterans. John Dryden began his prolific career as the author of odes, plays, panegyrics, translations, fables, and criticism, but increasingly became, and identified himself as, a satirist (*Absalom and Achitophel*, 1681; *Mac Flecknoe*, 1682; *To the Memory of Mr. Oldham*, 1684). Andrew Marvell (*Last Instructions to a Painter*, 1667) had direct dealings with Parliamentarian leader Oliver Cromwell, his general Lord Fairfax, and King Charles II. But arguably the role of attuning trauma to satire largely fell to the next generations, beginning with works like Daniel Defoe's *The True-Born Englishman* (1701) and *The Shortest Way with the Dissenters* (1702), and with Swift's *Battel of the Books* and *A Tale of a Tub* (1704). Fittingly, the word "catastrophe" occurs first in the satirical *Gargantua and Pantagruel* by Francois Rabelais, whom Swift, the *ne plus ultra* of ironists, cited as an intellectual and artistic mentor.

The possible points of connection between early modern trauma, theories of trauma, and the production of satire are many, although this discussion will follow the lead of the group of chapters in this collection that take the violent seventeenth century as a focal point. Satire allowed writers to process the most disturbing failures of human endeavor. If satire can be understood, as Edward Rosenheim proposes, as an attack by means of a manifest fiction upon recognizable historical particulars, then the choice of fictions by eighteenth-century practitioners is telling.[4] Many satirists were deeply influenced by "historical particulars" not as firsthand experience but as what Marianne Hirsch calls postmemory.[5] These writers process the burden of a traumatic inheritance displaced from preceding generations, giving new meaning to John Milton's remark that "Satire . . . was born out of Tragedy."[6] Paul Fussell describes how "war detaches itself from its normal location in chronology" to become an "essential condition of consciousness" for those "too young to have experienced it directly": "these writers have derived their myth . . . not from their predecessors but from their predecessors' predecessors . . . [in] a general tendency . . . to return to some of the standards of the modal grandfather."[7] In 1750 Samuel Johnson had anticipated this phenomenon. "The heart burnings of the civil war are not yet extinguished," insists Euphelia in *Rambler #46* "the same families inhabit the same houses from age to age, they transmit and recount the faults of a whole succession . . . the malignity is continued without end, and it is common for old maids to fall out about some election, in which their grandfathers were competitors" (*Works of Samuel Johnson*, iii, 250–51).[8]

Grandparents cast long shadows. Henry Raczymow points out regarding twentieth-century conflicts that "trauma . . . is defined in part by its belated effects . . . not just an individual matter . . . it may under certain circumstances, be transmitted to generations born after the war."[9] Eighteenth-century writers endorse this claim of generational deferral from the prior century. In Swift's autobiographical fragment, the most vivid episode is not actually about Swift but about the violent adventures of his Royalist grandfather Thomas against Roundhead enemies.[10] In Laurence Sterne's *Tristram Shandy*, Uncle Toby makes model armaments using leather from boots his grandfather wore in the Battle of Marston Moor—and this same transformed remnant of bloody defeat also is complicit in the wound dealt to great-grandson Tristram when he is nine years old.[11] When Oliver Goldsmith's foolish Vicar of Wakefield sends his son to the army, he charges him to "remember thy brave grandfather" who served Charles I and Lord Falkland. The first was beheaded, and the second died in despair (the fictional grandfather supposedly with him) at the Battle of Newbury in 1643.[12] These generation-skipping stories, artifacts, and scenes imply that coming to terms with displaced historical trauma can be crucial to coming to terms with one's own life, of seeking self-knowledge and finding one's "identical spot," as Sterne puns when describing Uncle Toby's relentless search for the origin of his wound.[13]

Of course, eighteenth-century satirists lacked terms like "shell shock" or "post-traumatic stress disorder" or "survivor guilt" to give names to complex experiences that press against the limits of representation. But they did not lack the need to, or the means of, negotiating between memory and oblivion. "Belatedness," as Cathy Caruth argues, reveals a "peculiar paradox: that in trauma the greatest confrontation with reality may also occur as an absolute numbing to it."[14] What grandparents avoid touching, the grandchildren may handle again and again. Hirsch writes that "individuals may be haunted by events that they never experienced, but which have been passed down, often in attenuated or even 'unconscious' forms, by parents and grandparents."[15] When eighteenth-century satirists invoke Juvenal's famous line—"*Difficile est saturum non scribere*" (It is difficult not to write satire), we may recontextualize it within Hirsch's theory of postmemory: "those removed from the immediacy of traumatic events can nonetheless still suffer from the effects of those moments because they may 'feel compelled to re-member, to re-build, to re-incarnate, to replace, and to repair.'"[16]

Satire and irony are important means of satisfying this compulsive urge toward reparation during the eighteenth century. Dominick LaCapra in *Writing History, Writing Trauma*, discusses a debate over the adequacy of literal versus figurative language; that is, between "modes that merely reproduce or mimic trauma versus those that work through it."[17] Satiric fictions enable a powerful "working through" of traumatic loss by reimagining and redeploying it in scenes of apocalypse, chaos, dismemberment, and genocide. Pope's *Dunciad* ends with the complete destruction of civilization and a return to primal chaos; Gay's *The Beggar's Opera* replaces God with the death-dispensing leader of a criminal underworld; in Sterne's *Tristram Shandy*, wounds to the groin cause sexual disfunction that guarantees the termination of the family line. In Manley's *The New Atalantis* Virtue has fled the earth so that political leaders can be dismembered by a mob and women are left to be raped and dangle from gibbets. Swift's works are especially rich in ironic fantasies of extreme loss and destruction: in *A Modest Proposal* infants are sold for food by suffering parents who themselves long for suicide; in *The Drapier's Letters* Irish citizens swallow explosive fireballs and become ambulatory bombs; in *The Battle of the Books* men are skewered like a brace of roasted woodcocks. *Gulliver's Travels* is a compendium of traumatic scenes. Shipwreck, cowardice, piracy, and mutiny leave Gulliver stranded and vulnerable. His four voyages include political treachery (the plot to blind, murder, and dismember him in Lilliput), disease (the giant cancerous breast in Brobdingnag), environmental disaster (the ruined landscape of Balnibarbi), colonization (the oppression of Lagado), and unrelieved bodily degradation (the Struldbruggs' travesty of immortality). The miseries of war are represented to the king of Brobdingnag and again, more horrifyingly, to the Houyhnhnm-Master: "dying Groans, Limbs flying in the Air: Smoak, Noise, Confusion, trampling to Death under Horses' Feet: Flight, Pursuit, Victory; Fields strewed with Carcases left for Food to Dogs, and Wolves, and Birds of Prey; Plundering, Stripping, Ravishing, Burning and Destroying."[18] Last but not least is the revelation that a partial genocide of the enslaved Yahoos (humans) has already occurred, while yet another is being contemplated. Back in England, traumatized Gulliver lives as an exile from Houyhnhnmland and suffers from melancholia and madness. According to traditional humoral theory of the spleen, satire is the result of an excess black bile leading to states of depressive melancholia and irrationality. Readers of eighteenth-century satire will recognize the recurrent madness theme in Swift and others.

Additional characteristics of eighteenth-century satire are consonant with the transgenerational representation of trauma. Characters are not psychologically complex, autonomous, or round; they are shifting persona with fractured, circumstantial identities. Endings resist closure. *The Beggar's Opera* rejects both the poetic justice of tragedy and the comic resolution of marriage by simply offering its final scene for sale. The "uncreating words" of the last lines of *The Dunciad* bury everything in universal darkness yet also dazzle readers with brilliant verse. The narrative thread of *A Tale of a Tub* is ruptured by ellipses and becomes tangled in digressions. Conflicting interpretations of the fourth book of *Gulliver's Travels* and the last chapter of *Tristram Shandy* have elicited endless critical debate. Satire aims to vex readers with irony, paradox, ambiguity, contradiction, and with equally unsatisfactory choices between fools and knaves, between beggars and criminals, between outsides of worthless tinsel and insides of guts and excrement, between prurience and tears, between blustering spiders and itinerant bees, between Yahoos and Houyhnhnms. It does so because of a fundamental doubt about the realistic possibility of resolution or redress.

In its skillful control of tone, satire can enunciate horrors with seeming detachment. But its displacement of overt emotion is inseparable from the depth of its underlying feelings. The financial calculations and instructions for the sale and cooking of children in *A Modest Proposal* are coolly delivered, but no one calmly forgets the white-hot protest against colonial exploitation.

Sometimes satire represents suffering as the consequence of a single episode (like flaying a woman), but sometimes intense suffering is the unrelenting condition of every day (like the poverty of the Irish, or life among the Yahoos, or the nightly risk of betrayal and hanging among London's thieves, or the infantilization of the Dunces). Satiric fictions insist on the woundable, grotesque, mortal body in order to shock the senses and to arouse discomfort. Dunces dive into human waste while verbal swords slash the buttocks of fools and miscreants. Like cryptography, satire delights in cyphers to convey dangerous information and to protect itself from libel; its "keys" decode hidden meanings. The three brothers in *A Tale of a Tub* ingeniously pick out letters to deduce subversive subtexts in their Father's Will.[19] Pope wrote a facetious *Key to the Lock. Or, a Treatise Proving . . . the Dangerous Tendency of a Late Poem, Entituled, The Rape of the Lock, To Government and Religion* that identifies the innocent heroine Belinda as the Whore of Babylon.[20]

But even more pervasively, satire relies on irony to destabilize the way that language functions. Satiric irony gives voice to a traumatized world in which confidence in clear and enduring meaning has been lost. Unthinkable catastrophes elude adequate expression, although the need to articulate them is powerful. Irony allows the writer to surpass the limits of literal expression by replacing what cannot be precisely conveyed with what continues to reverberate with possibility. Satiric irony also enables a key strategy for coping with trauma (according to theorists like Judith Herman) in its ability to establish a comprehending group, an inner circle that "gets it," that recognizes and understands that something valuable has been lost: "Traumatic events destroy the sustaining bonds between individual and community. . . . The solidarity of the group provides the strongest protection against . . . despair, and the strongest antidote to traumatic experience."[21]

But most importantly, eighteenth-century satire documents the kind of permanent shift in belief systems—that irreversible fragmentation of the notion of identity and community—that *Early Modern Trauma* proposes as the most fundamental consequence or measure of catastrophic loss. The new normal, so to speak, assumes a world lacerated beyond healing by religious and political factions (Anglicans, Catholics, Dissenters; Whigs and Tories; civil and foreign wars) and yields the integrity of human and natural life to profit-seeking ventures at home and abroad (manufacture, stock companies, colonialism, the slave trade), to the dissipation of art and trivialization of intellectual pursuit, and to the loss of peace-giving governance. Satire registers the consequences of disaster as loss of earlier systems of meaning. The new normal, in its satiric representations, can accommodate madmen as authorities, criminals as the ruling class, fornicators as spiritual leaders, and numskulls as the guardians of learning.

Early Modern Trauma acknowledges that in prior centuries, "the notion that spiritual growth was to be had from a terrible experience was widely available as a cultural model." The irrecoverable losses of the emerging modern world begin to weaken this notion. Sectarianism and religion-based political conflict exert pressure on the supposed benefits of earthly suffering to be compensated in heaven by a providential deity. The Judaeo-Christian foundation of Western culture traced its essential codes of conduct back to the Old Testament. The fundamental biblical program of reward and punishment as given in Deuteronomy seems straightforward. Obey divine laws and in due season, the sun will shine, rain will fall, crops will grow, children will be born, prosperity and contentment will follow. Disobey divine law, and not only will this basic happiness disappear but people will be driven to such anguish and hopelessness, that they will consume their own sons and daughters.[22]

Swift was both satirist and clergyman. In both roles he was obsessed with traumatic memories and consequences of the English Civil Wars. His work provides a useful measure of declining confidence in religion's traditional moral guide. *Sentiments of a Church of England Man* and "On the Testimony of Conscience" acknowledge the ancient system of benefits and penalties both in life and the hereafter, but they do so in mundane pragmatic terms: "Human nature is so constituted that we can never pursue any thing heartily but upon hopes of a reward. If we run a race, it is in expectation of a prize, and the greater the prize the faster we run."[23] Swift, given his fantasies of cannibalizing the young, seems keenly aware of Deuteronomy's promises and threats. Michael Deporte points out that Swift "sought to demonstrate . . . particularly the doctrine of eternal rewards and punishments, [as] the only sure foundation of a moral life . . . but it is by no means clear how much real efficacy he thought the doctrine had."[24] We know of few personal religious practices that he strictly followed. But the one we are sure he regularly performed is highly relevant to the present discussion: on each of his birthdays he read that supremely traumatic text, the third chapter of the book of Job in which the suffering protagonist rails against God and curses the day he was born. Why should the supreme satirist in the English language compulsively return to the book of Job? The answer, I believe, lies in the dark and disturbing irony of the third book, which interrogates and challenges the traditional system of benefits and penalties in light of extreme human trauma.

In the beginning of the story, Job epitomizes goodness: "perfect and upright . . . one that feared God and eschewed evil."[25] His extensive family, lands, wealth, and influence are balanced by his personal righteousness, social responsibility, and good deeds. The payoff is utter contentment: a continual round of feasting and sanctifying. Suddenly, every source of happiness—emotional and material—is stripped away. Despite death of loved ones, complete impoverishment, and extreme physical and mental anguish, Job remains sinless and accepting of his undeserved suffering and loss—until excruciating pain from festering boils makes him wish for death. In book 3 he curses God and his own existence. Of Swift's attraction to Job's bitter and despairing outcry for self-annihilation, Deporte wrote: "It is easy to imagine him asking Job's question, 'Wherefore do the wicked live, / Become old, yea, wax mighty in power?'—and hearing in return something like the inscrutable power that comes out of the whirlwind: 'Where wast thou when I laid down the foundations of the earth?'" It is true that the voice from the whirlwind asserts vast divine power—to make the morning stars sing together, to shut up the gates of the sea, to separate dark and light—and humbles the presumption of the puny human who dares to curse life. Job eventually concedes: "therefore have I uttered that I understood not; things too wonderful for me" (42:3, 6).

At first, the lesson seems to be that weak mortals simply must submit to their share of joy or misery. But that is not what is Swiftian about this text as a narrative of trauma. Readers of the book of Job know something that Job never knows, something that the voice in the whirlwind never acknowledges. The dramatic irony that underpins the entire narrative is that Job has *not* suffered for inscrutable reasons. Readers (including Swift apparently) know exactly why he has been stripped of every source of happiness: because in book 1, God made a wager with his adversary Satan. Being perfect and upright was not enough to keep Job safe from the rivalry of forces beyond his ken. The Bible's carefully articulated system of reward and punishment seems irrelevant, and the value of human goodness, ineffectual. Of course, the book of Job ends with a spectacular restoration: a set of replacement children (seven new sons and three more beautiful daughters); twice the property as formerly (fourteen thousand sheep, six thousand camels, and a thousand each of oxen and asses); and longevity (he lives for 140 years). Is this happy ending comparable to the mythical phoenix rising from its ashes to reinvigorated life, to which Rousseau alludes?

We must ask with Swift what has happened to the traumatic memory of the earlier disasters: the dead family, the poverty, the disease? Can restoration ever fully patch up the failure of a flawed system of recompense and retribution? Job's life would seem to have both personal and political meaning for Swift, especially as it overlaps with his abiding interest in the events and aftermath of the Civil War. In his sermon "On the Martyrdom of King Charles I," he writes, "But, as a house thrown down by a storm is seldom rebuilt, without some change in the foundation, so it hath happened, that, since the late Revolution, men have sate much looser in the true fundamentals both of religion and government, and factions have been more violent, treacherous, and malicious than ever."[26] Surviving generations need a modified system of coping with traumatic loss in an age "rebuilt" with a "change in the foundation" of "both religion and government" and with the inherited memory of a latent threat that is "violent, treacherous, and malicious." Full restoration of a prior order is not possible because the traumatic losses of the past are always carried forward, making (trauma theorists argue) "the generations after . . . [the] guardians of a problematic, unique, and volatile legacy," a "missed encounter with death" can lead to a "reformulating of life," an "imperative to live that still remains not fully understood."[27]

Swift's annual return to Job, its disturbing irony, and its challenge to inherited systems of belief is symptomatic of the affinity between satire and trauma. Satire participates in the process of protesting the necessity of living in a world in which the irremediable griefs of the past are a persistent legacy, and an always already impaired futurity mitigates against the notion that chances and conditions will improve. The energy and creativity that distinguishes eighteenth-century satire are generated in reaction to the kinds of losses enumerated in *Early Modern Trauma*. In this sense, it carries forward the implications of many of the chapters in this collection. Questioning belief in a just system that reliably protects good behavior and exacts vengeance for misdeeds, represented here by Swift, contributes generally to the outraged idealism that gives rise to works like *Gulliver's Travels*, *The Dunciad*, and *The Beggar's Opera*. Attacks on various topical targets are channeled through fictions of disasters with enduring multigenerational consequences: crime replaces honesty; darkness obscures light; uncreation undoes creation; infant death negates new life; impotence prevents succession; exile banishes home; captivity and incarceration (physical and mental) prevent liberty; madness overcomes reason. Satirists are willing to attack evils that prior generations confronted. Their aggressive fictions displace strong emotion and channel it through an artistic medium capable of humor, metaphor, obscenity, frustration, laughter, anger, and absurdity. Cathy Caruth argues that questions about crisis "can never be asked in a straightforward way, but must . . . be spoken in a language that is always somehow literary: a language that defies, even as it claims our understanding."[28] Irony is such a language, and satire is such a literature.

NOTES

1. Raymond Williams, *The Long Revolution* (London: Chatto & Windus, 1961), 18.
2. Thomas P. Anderson, *Performing Early Modern Trauma from Shakespeare to Milton* (London: Routledge, 2006), 3–4.
3. Jean Jacques Rousseau, *The Social Contract*, trans. Maurice Cranston (New York: Penguin, 1977), 89.
4. Edward W. Rosenheim Jr., *Swift and the Satirist's Art* (Chicago: University of Chicago Press, 1963), 25.
5. Marianne Hirsch, "The Generation of Postmemory," *Poetics Today* 29 (2008): 103–8.
6. John Milton, *An Apology against a pamphlet call'd A modest confutation of the animadversions upon the remonstrant against Smectymnuus* (London: John Rothwell, 1642), 33.
7. Fussell began his career as an eighteenth-century scholar, although here he refers to World War I. Paul Fussell, *The Great War and Modern Memory* (Oxford, UK: Oxford University Press, 1975, 2000), 321.

8. Samuel Johnson, *The Rambler*, vol. 3, ed. Walter Jackson Bate and Albrecht B. Strauss, *The Yale Edition of the Works of Samuel Johnson* (New Have: Yale University Press, 1969), 250–51.
9. Henry Raczymow, "Memory Shot Through with Holes," in *The Holocaust: Theoretical Readings*, ed. Nel Levi and Michael Rothberg, in *Poetics Today* 29:1 (2008), 103–28 (New Brunswick NJ: Rutgers University Press, 2003), 407.
10. "The Family of Swift," in *The Prose Writings of Jonathan Swift*, vol. 5, *Miscellaneous and Autobiographical Pieces, Fragments, and Marginalia*, ed. Herbert Davis (Oxford, UK: Blackwell, 1962).
11. Laurence Sterne, *The Life and Opinions of Tristram Shandy, Gentleman*, ed. Melvyn and Joan New (Gainesville: University of Florida Press, 1978), i, 96. Uncle Toby, while building his model battlefield, combines leather from his grandfather's boot with a piece of the window mechanism that allows the sash to fall and crush Tristram's penis.
12. Oliver Goldsmith, *The Vicar of Wakefield*, ed. Arthur Friedman (Oxford, UK: Oxford University Press, 1981), 118.
13. Sterne, *The Life and Opinions of Tristram Shandy, Gentleman*, 96.
14. Cathy Caruth, "Trauma and Experience" in Neil Levi and Michael Rothberg, *The Holocaust: Theoretical Readings*, 192–98, esp. 195.
15. Studies of the aftereffects of twentieth-century trauma, such as the Holocaust, also demonstrate the important role of the grandchildren's generation: "the grandchildren were the ones who opened the windows into . . . the burden of the past," Hadas Wiseman and Jacques P. Barber, eds., *Echoes of the Trauma* (Cambridge: Cambridge University Press, 2008), xii.
16. Laura Murphy, "The Curse of Constant Remembrance: The Belated Trauma of the Slave Trade in Ayi Kwei Armah's *Fragments*," *Studies in the Novel* 40 (Spring and Summer 2008): 53.
17. Dominick LaCapra, *Writing History, Writing Trauma*, 2nd ed. (Baltimore: Johns Hopkins University Press, 2014).
18. Jonathan Swift, *Gulliver's Travels*, ed. David Womersley (Cambridge: Cambridge University Press, 2012), 366.
19. Jonathan Swift, *A Tale of a Tub and Other Works*, ed. Marcus Walsh (Cambridge: Cambridge University Press, 2010), 54–59.
20. Alexander Pope, *A Key to the Lock, Or, a Treatise Proving . . . the Dangerous Tendency of a Late Poem Entituled, The Rape of the Lock, to Government and Religion*, in *The Prose Works of Alexander Pope*, vol. 1, ed. Norman Ault (Oxford, UK: Blackwell, 1936); vol. 2, ed. Rosemary Cowler (Hamden: Archon Books, 1986).
21. Judith Lewis Herman, *Trauma and Recovery* (New York: Basic Books, 1992), 214.
22. Robert Alter, *The Five Books of Moses: A Translation with Commentary* (New York: W. W. Norton, 2004), 897–1037. The laws are set out in Deuteronomy 4 through 30.

The warnings about disobedience in 28.60 include the dire "you shall eat your own issue, the flesh of your sons and daughters." The passage is considered so traumatic that Jewish custom is to recite it at top speed and in a whisper during the annual reading of the Torah.

23. Jonathan Swift, *Irish Tracts 1720–1723 and Sermons*, ed. Herbert Davis and Louis Landa (Oxford, UK: Basil Blackwell, 1963), 150–58; *The Prose Works of Jonathan Swift*, ed. Herbert Davis (Oxford, UK: Basil Blackwell, 1939–74), 9:244.
24. Michael Deporte, "Swift, God, and Power," in *Walking Naboth's Vineyard: New Studies on Jonathan Swift*, ed. Christopher Fox and Brenda Tooley, 73–97 (Notre Dame: University of Notre Dame Press, 1994), 81.
25. Job in *Tanakh: The Holy Scriptures* (Philadelphia: Jewish Publication Society, 1985), 1339–1403.
26. Swift, *Irish Tracts*, 224.
27. Alan L. Berger and Naomi Berger, eds, *Second Generation Voices: Reflections by Children of Holocaust Survivors and Perpetrators* (Syracuse NY: Syracuse University Press, 2001), 3.
28. Cathy Caruth, *Unclaimed Experience* (Baltimore: Johns Hopkins University Press, 1996), 5. Katherine Ellison also cites this passage in her contribution to this collection.

CONTRIBUTORS

MELISSA ANTONUCCI, an assistant teaching professor at the University of Oklahoma, completed her dissertation "Reluctant Adventurers: The Risky Business of Female Travel in Stories by Anglophone Women, 1767–1830" in 2015 at the University of Tulsa. Her research concerns women's transnational mobility within the early Atlantic world and offers a new context for thinking about the ways in which texts centered on female mobility participate in reorienting women as adventurers in their own right. Her piece in this collection marks the beginning of a new research trajectory that explores the interconnectedness between trauma that results from exile, embedded social and cultural values of geographical environments, and the reconstitution of home as they merge within imagined early British Atlantic landscapes.

ADAM R. BEACH is professor of English at Ball State University. His most recent work, which investigates British depictions of slavery in Morocco and the Ottoman Empire, has appeared in *Eighteenth-Century Studies*, *Eighteenth-Century Fiction*, *Studies in Eighteenth-Century Culture*, and *The Eighteenth-Century: Theory and Interpretation*. He has also coedited with Srividhya Swaminathan the collection of essays *Invoking Slavery in the Eighteenth-Century British Imagination* (Ashgate, 2013).

SUSAN BROOMHALL is director of the Gender and Women's History Research Centre at the Australian Catholic University. Her research explores women and gender; emotions; science and knowledge practices; material culture; cultural contact and global encounters; and the heritage of the early modern world. She is currently completing *Gender and the Dutch East India Company* for Amsterdam University Press and *The Identities of Catherine de' Medici* for Brill. Her next projects include *Gender and Agency in Jesuit circulations across East Asia, 1580–1650* for ARC Humanities Press and a monograph, with Carolyn James and Lisa Mansfield, entitled *Gendering the Italian Wars*.

EAMON DARCY is a historian of early modern Ireland and a member of the Arts Humanities Institute in Maynooth University. Since the publication of *The Irish Rebellion of 1641 and the Wars of the Three Kingdoms* (Boydell and Brewer, 2013), Dr. Darcy's research focuses on two interconnected areas: political participation and early modern communications. Current projects include: memory and memorization techniques c. 1400–1700, and oral and literate cultures in the early modern Irish world. Dr. Darcy is also deeply interested in teaching and learning in higher education and has coauthored articles on information literacy and undergraduates' academic writing.

KATHERINE ELLISON is professor of English at Illinois State University. She has published *A Material History of Medieval and Early Modern Ciphers* (Routledge, 2017, coedited with Susan Kim), *A Cultural History of Early Modern British Cryptography Manuals* (Routledge, 2016), *Fatal News: Reading and Information Overload in Early Eighteenth-Century Literature* (Routledge, 2006), and numerous articles on early intelligence, cryptography, and information. She coedited *Topographies of the Imagination: New Approaches to Defoe* (AMS Press, 2014) and served as coeditor of *Digital Defoe: Studies in Defoe & His Contemporaries*. She is working on three projects: a collection on John Matthews Manly and Edith Rickert, a scholarly edition of seventeenth-century cryptography manuals, and a monograph on the Restoration fop as intelligencer.

JOSEPH HARRIS is professor of early modern French and comparative literature at Royal Holloway, University of London, and specializes in early modern French literature, especially theater. He is author of *Hidden Agendas: Cross-Dressing in Seventeenth-Century France* (Narr, 2005) and *Inventing the Spectator: Subjectivity and the Theatrical Experience in Early Modern France* (Oxford University Press, 2014). He has published widely on such topics as cross-dressing, spectatorship, laughter, and death in early modern France; and is currently working on two monograph projects: one on death in the writings of Pierre Corneille, and one on misanthropy in European literature from Shakespeare until the early nineteenth century. His critical edition *"Le Misanthrope corrigé": Two Eighteenth-Century Sequels to Molière's "Le Misanthrope"* (Modern Humanities Research Association) appeared in 2019.

TAMAR LEROY IS a doctoral candidate in English literature at the University of Maryland, College Park. She is currently completing her dissertation, "Embodied Performance: Soldiers, War Trauma, and Disability on the Restoration and Eighteenth-Century Stage," in which she examines the often surprising ways the disorienting effects of contemporary warfare resonated in plays of the period, including comedy (as with the chapter in this collection), sentimental tragedy, and revisions and re-performances of Shakespeare's drama. She has served as an associate editor for *Restoration: Studies in Literary Culture 1660–1700*, for which she also writes theater reviews.

ZACKARIAH LONG is an associate professor of English at Ohio Wesleyan University. He has published essays on early modern memory, trauma, and theater in journals such as *English Literary Renaissance* and *Journal of Literature and Trauma*, as well as in edited volumes, including *The Routledge Handbook of Shakespeare and Memory*, *Staging Pain, 1580–1800: Violence and Trauma in British Theatre*, and *Forgetting in Early Modern English Literature and Culture: Lethe's Legacies*. He is currently at work on a book about *Hamlet* and Renaissance memory theater.

ANDREAS K. E. MUELLER is professor of English at the University of Northern Colorado. He has published extensively on Daniel Defoe's verse and nonfictional prose and has recently coedited a three-hundred-year anniversary collection of essays on *Robinson Crusoe*. He has also worked on the literary criticism of Richard Hurd and late eighteenth-century cultural nationalism.

ISMINI PELLS is currently a postdoctoral research fellow at the University of Leicester, where she is project manager of a large research project investigating pensions awarded to maimed soldiers and war widows from the seventeenth-century British Civil Wars. She previously worked as a research associate at the University of Exeter on a project examining early modern medical practitioners, during which she researched the careers of practitioners in civil war armies. Ismini studied for her PhD at the University of Cambridge, where her thesis explored the career of Philip Skippon, commander of the infantry in parliament's New Model Army. Her publications concentrate on early modern military history and the impact of warfare on medical developments in this period.

ERIN PETERS is an early modern historian at the University of Gloucestershire, with specialist interests in seventeenth-century Britain. Combining historical research with an interdisciplinary background in memory studies, her research focuses on early modern print culture, trauma and nostalgia, and early modern forms of memory in post-conflict cultures. Recently, she is the author of *Commemoration and Oblivion in Royalist Print Culture, 1658–1667* (Palgrave, 2017), as well as several publications that concentrate on post-conflict collective memory and cultural trauma.

MELINDA RABB is professor of English at Brown University. She is the author of *Satire and Secrecy in English Literature 1650–1750* (Palgrave, 2007) and *Miniature and the English Imagination: Literature, Cognition, and Small-Scale Culture 1650–1765* (Cambridge University Press, 2019), as well as numerous chapters and articles on satire, women's writing, fiction, war, and on authors including Swift, Pope, Defoe, Johnson, Fielding, Sterne, Manley, Collier, Scott, and Godwin. She has been the recipient of grants, fellowships, and awards from the National Endowment for the Humanities, the Lilly Foundation, the Ford Foundation, the Cogut Institute for the Humanities, the American Society for Eighteenth-Century Studies, and the Winterthur Museum. Her current book project, *Parting Shots*, focuses on displacements of seventeenth-century civil war trauma in eighteenth-century literature.

CYNTHIA RICHARDS is professor of English at Wittenberg University. Her most recent work on the body and the representation of trauma in the long eighteenth century has been published in *Eighteenth-Century Fiction*, *English Literary History*, and *The Future of Feminist Eighteenth-Century Scholarship: Beyond Recovery* (Routledge, 2017). She is coeditor along with Mary Ann O'Donnell of *Approaches to Teaching Behn's* Oroonoko (Modern Language Association, 2013) and is currently working on a monograph, *The Body, Trauma, and War, 1667–1798.*

PETER WALMSLEY teaches English and cultural studies at McMaster University and is the author of *The Rhetoric of Berkeley's Philosophy* and *Locke's Essay and the Rhetoric of Science.* His current project, *Manufacturing Subjects: The Cultural Politics of Labour in Britain, 1690–1750*, investigates the revaluation of skilled work and personal industry in genres as diverse as sermons, trade handbooks, novels, and scientific texts.

AMELIA ZURCHER is associate professor of English and director of the University Honors Program at Marquette University. She is the author of *Seventeenth-Century English Romance: Allegory, Ethics, and Politics* (Palgrave, 2007), editor of Judith Man's *An Epitome of the Historie of Argenis and Poliarchus* (Ashgate, 2003), and has published several essays on sixteenth- and seventeenth-century British literature. She is currently working on a book about gender and the construction of civility in seventeenth-century Britain and another on the seventeenth-century Irish-English Boyle siblings.

INDEX

Page numbers in italics indicate illustrations.

IIN THE EARLY MODERN CULTURAL STUDIES SERIES:

Courage and Grief: Women and Sweden's Thirty Years' War
By Mary Elizabeth Ailes

Travel and Travail: Early Modern Women, English Drama, and the Wider World
Edited and with an introduction by Patricia Akhimie and Bernadette Andrea

At the First Table: Food and Social Identity in Early Modern Spain
By Jodi Campbell

Separation Scenes: Domestic Drama in Early Modern England
By Ann C. Christensen

A Warning for Fair Women
Edited by Ann C. Christensen

Misanthropoetics: Social Flight and Literary Form in Early Modern England
By Robert Darcy

Portrait of an Island: The Architecture and Material Culture of Gorée, Sénégal, 1758–1837
By Mark Hinchman

Deza and Its Moriscos: Religion and Community in Early Modern Spain
By Patrick J. O'Banion

Early Modern Trauma: Europe and the Atlantic World
Edited by Erin Peters and Cynthia Richards

Producing Early Modern London: A Comedy of Urban Space, 1598–1616
By Kelly J. Stage

Words Like Daggers: Violent Female Speech in Early Modern England
By Kirilka Stavreva

Sacred Seeds: New World Plants in Early Modern English Literature
By Edward McLean Test

My First Booke of My Life
By Alice Thornton
Edited and with an introduction by Raymond A. Anselment

Age in Love: Shakespeare at the Elizabethan Court
By Jacqueline Vanhoutte

The Other Exchange: Women, Servants, and the Urban Underclass in Early Modern English Literature
By Denys Van Renen

To order or obtain more information on these or other University of Nebraska Press titles, visit nebraskapress.unl.edu.

CPSIA information can be obtained
at www.ICGtesting.com
Printed in the USA
LVHW091354020821
694313LV00001B/19

9 781496 208910